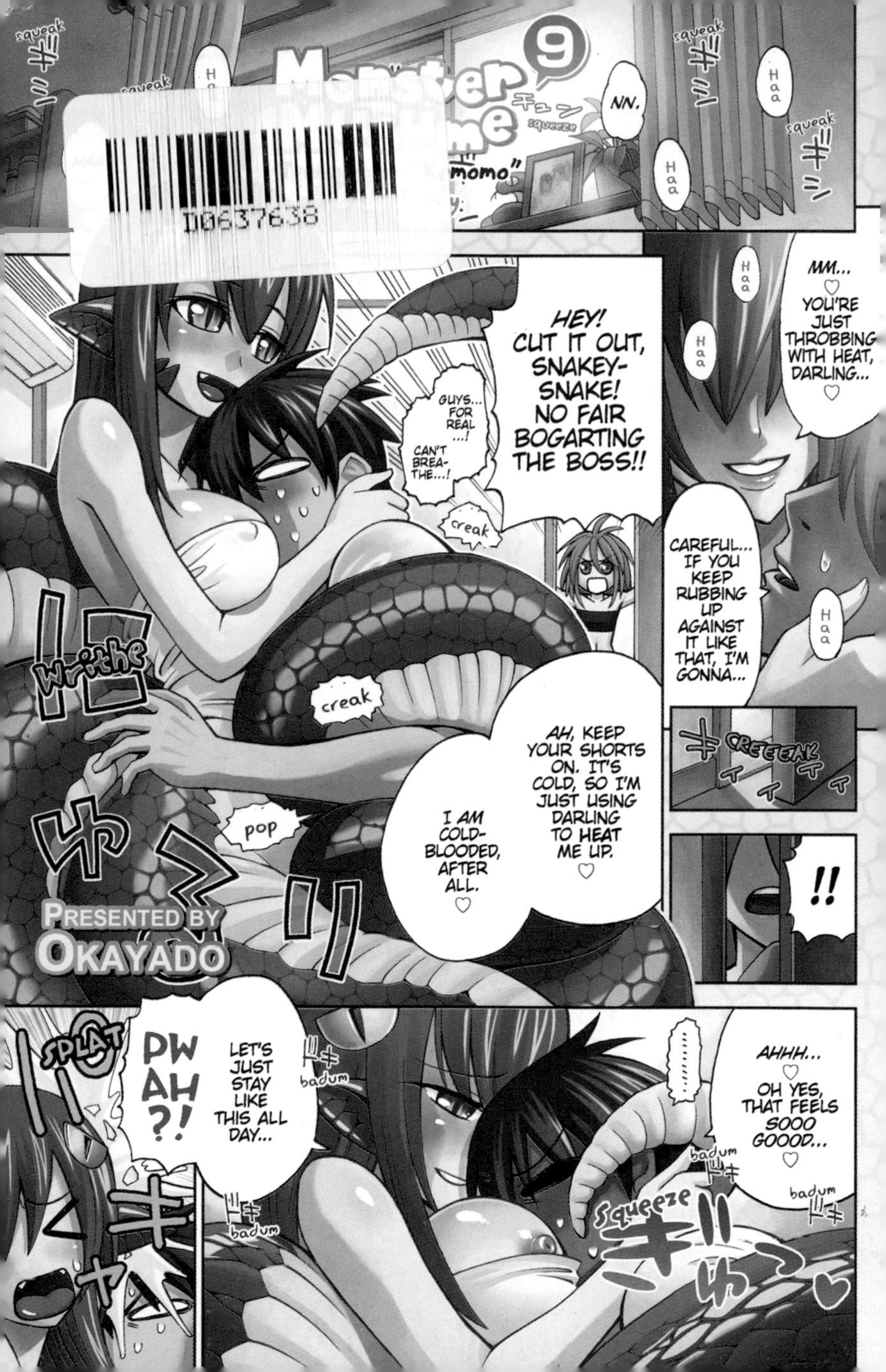

squeak
Haa
NN.
squeeze
Haa
squeak
9
squeak
squeak
Haa
Haa
MM... ♡ YOU'RE JUST THROBBING WITH HEAT, DARLING... ♡
Haa
CAREFUL... IF YOU KEEP RUBBING UP AGAINST IT LIKE THAT, I'M GONNA...
Haa
CREEEEAK
!!
HEY! CUT IT OUT, SNAKEY-SNAKE! NO FAIR BOGARTING THE BOSS!!
GUYS... FOR REAL...! CAN'T BREA-THE...!
creak
AH, KEEP YOUR SHORTS ON. IT'S COLD, SO I'M JUST USING DARLING TO HEAT ME UP. ♡
I AM COLD-BLOODED, AFTER ALL. ♡
creak
writhe
pop
PRESENTED BY OKAYADO
AHHH... ♡ OH YES, THAT FEELS SOOO GOOOD... ♡
......
badum
badum
squeeze
LET'S JUST STAY LIKE THIS ALL DAY...
badum
badum
PWAH?!
SPLAT

O K A Y A D O

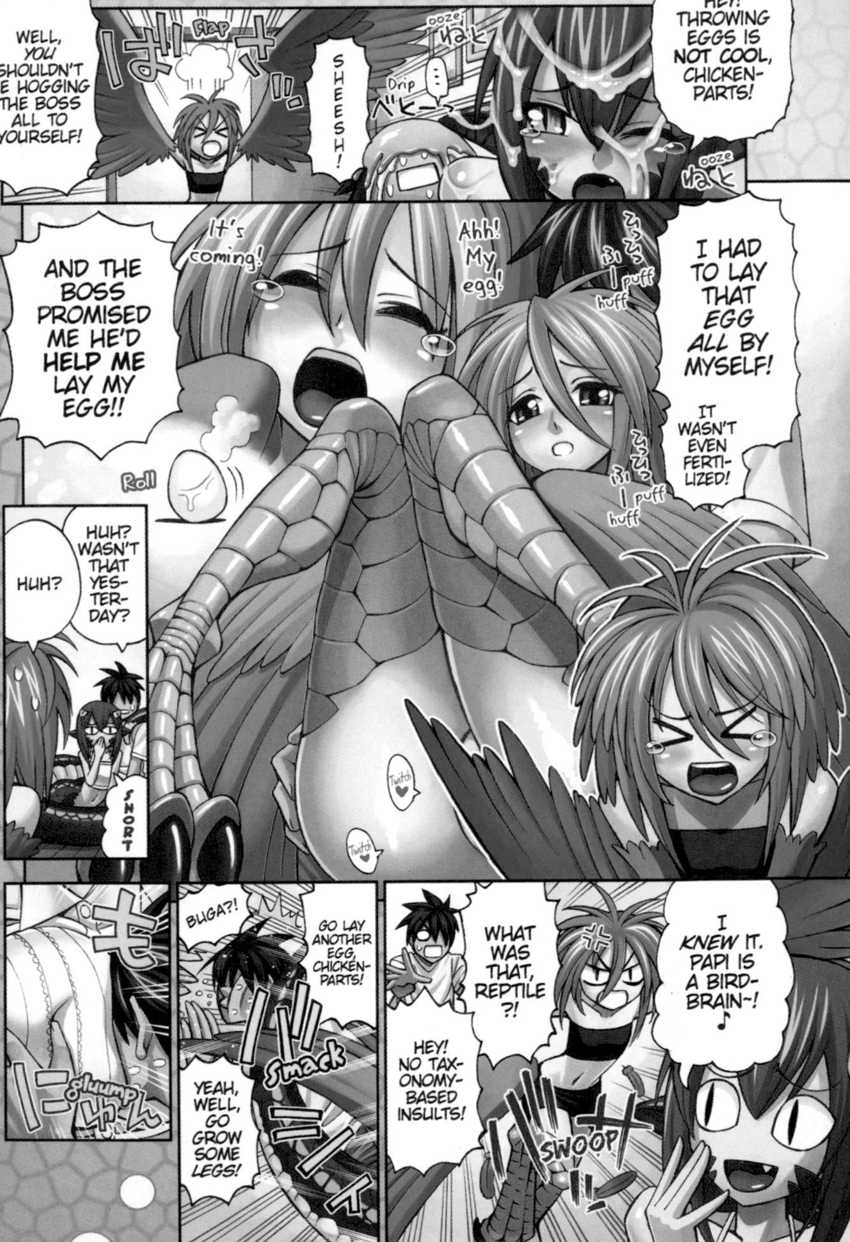
HEY! THROWING EGGS IS NOT COOL, CHICKEN-PARTS!
ooze ぬと
ooze ぬと
Drip べとー
...
SHEESH!
Flap
WELL, YOU SHOULDN'T BE HOGGING THE BOSS ALL TO YOURSELF!
I HAD TO LAY THAT EGG ALL BY MYSELF!
puff huff
IT WASN'T EVEN FERTILIZED!
puff huff
Ahh! My egg!
It's coming!
AND THE BOSS PROMISED ME HE'D HELP ME LAY MY EGG!!
Roll
Twitch
Twitch
HUH? WASN'T THAT YESTERDAY?
HUH?
SNORT
I KNEW IT. PAPI IS A BIRD-BRAIN~! ♪
WHAT WAS THAT, REPTILE?!
HEY! NO TAXONOMY-BASED INSULTS!
SWOOP
GO LAY ANOTHER EGG, CHICKEN-PARTS!
BUGA?!
Smack
YEAH, WELL, GO GROW SOME LEGS!
も
gluump にゅん

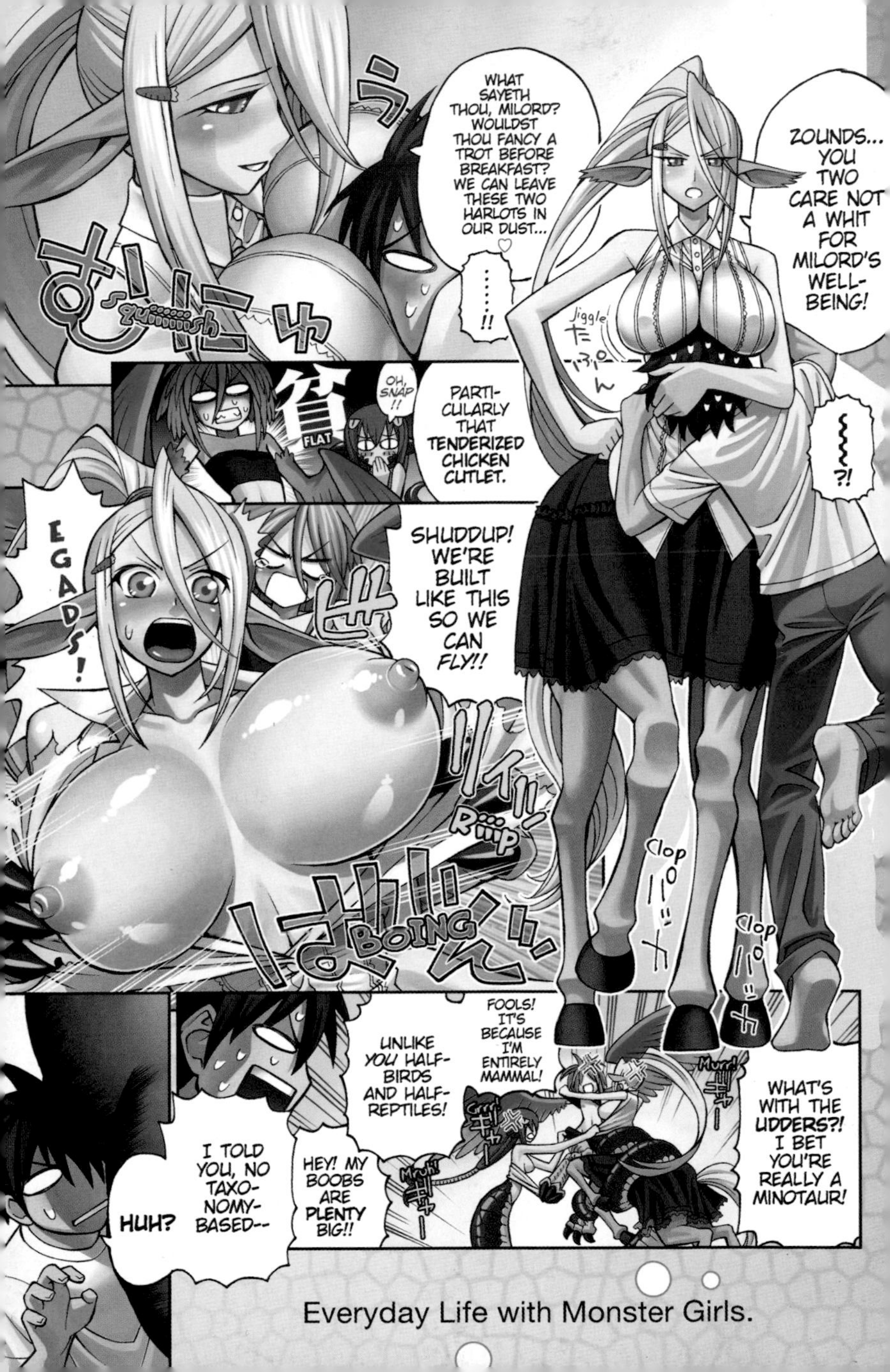
ZOUNDS... YOU TWO CARE NOT A WHIT FOR MILORD'S WELL-BEING!
Jiggle
Clop
Clop
......?!
WHAT SAYETH THOU, MILORD? WOULDST THOU FANCY A TROT BEFORE BREAKFAST? WE CAN LEAVE THESE TWO HARLOTS IN OUR DUST...
......!!
squish
PARTI-CULARLY THAT TENDERIZED CHICKEN CUTLET.
OH, SNAP!!
FLAT
SHUDDUP! WE'RE BUILT LIKE THIS SO WE CAN FLY!!
EGADS!
RiiiP
BOING
WHAT'S WITH THE UDDERS?! I BET YOU'RE REALLY A MINOTAUR!
Murr!
FOOLS! IT'S BECAUSE I'M ENTIRELY MAMMAL!
UNLIKE YOU HALF-BIRDS AND HALF-REPTILES!
Grrr!
HEY! MY BOOBS ARE PLENTY BIG!!
Mrrh!
I TOLD YOU, NO TAXO-NOMY-BASED--
HUH?
Everyday Life with Monster Girls.

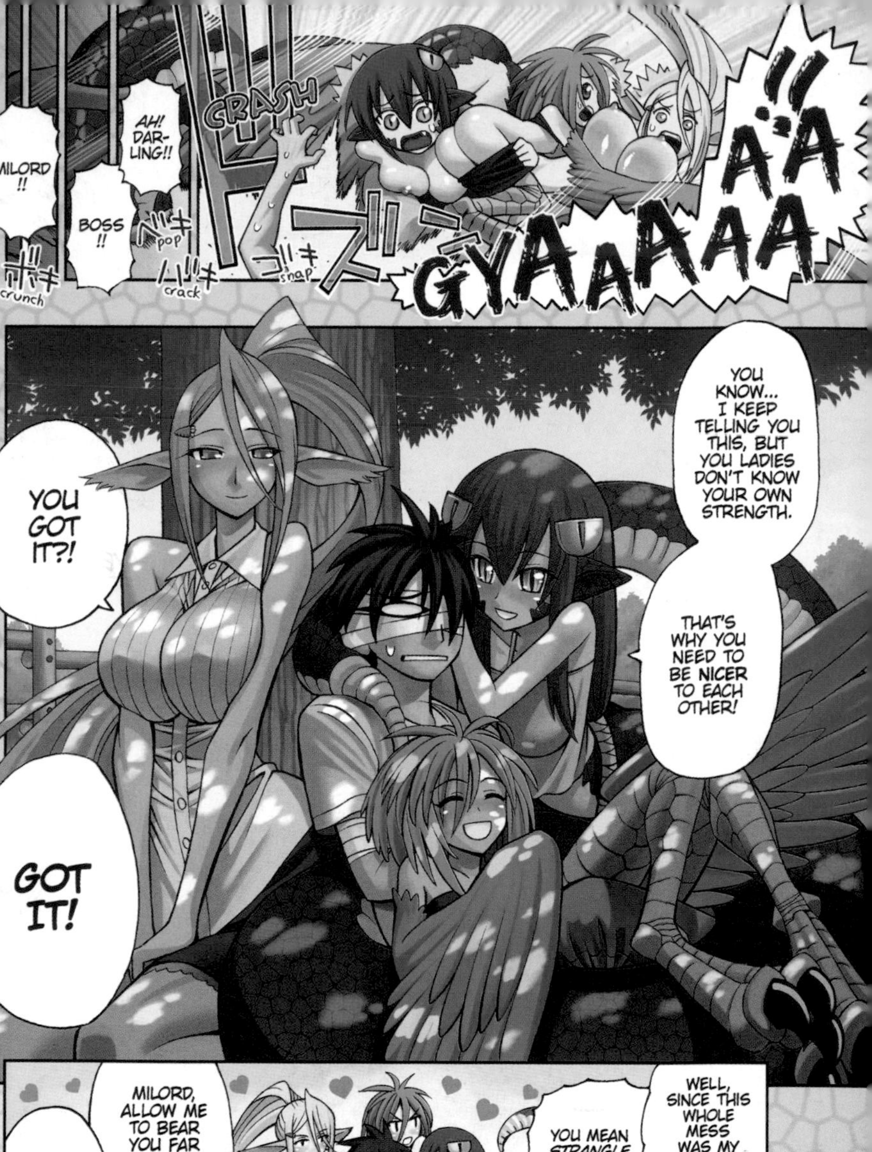
GYAAAAAAAA!!
CRASH
AH! DARLING!!
BOSS!!
MILORD!!
pop
snap
crack
crunch
YOU KNOW... I KEEP TELLING YOU THIS, BUT YOU LADIES DON'T KNOW YOUR OWN STRENGTH.
THAT'S WHY YOU NEED TO BE NICER TO EACH OTHER!
YOU GOT IT?!
GOT IT!
WELL, SINCE THIS WHOLE MESS WAS MY FAULT, I'LL NURSE DARLING BACK TO HEALTH.
YOU MEAN *STRANGLE* HIM AGAIN?! MY FEATHERS'LL DO THE TRICK BETTER!
MILORD, ALLOW ME TO BEAR YOU FAR FROM THESE TWO BARBARIANS.
"GOT IT." YEAH, RIGHT...

Technicolor "Kemomo" Side Story: **END**

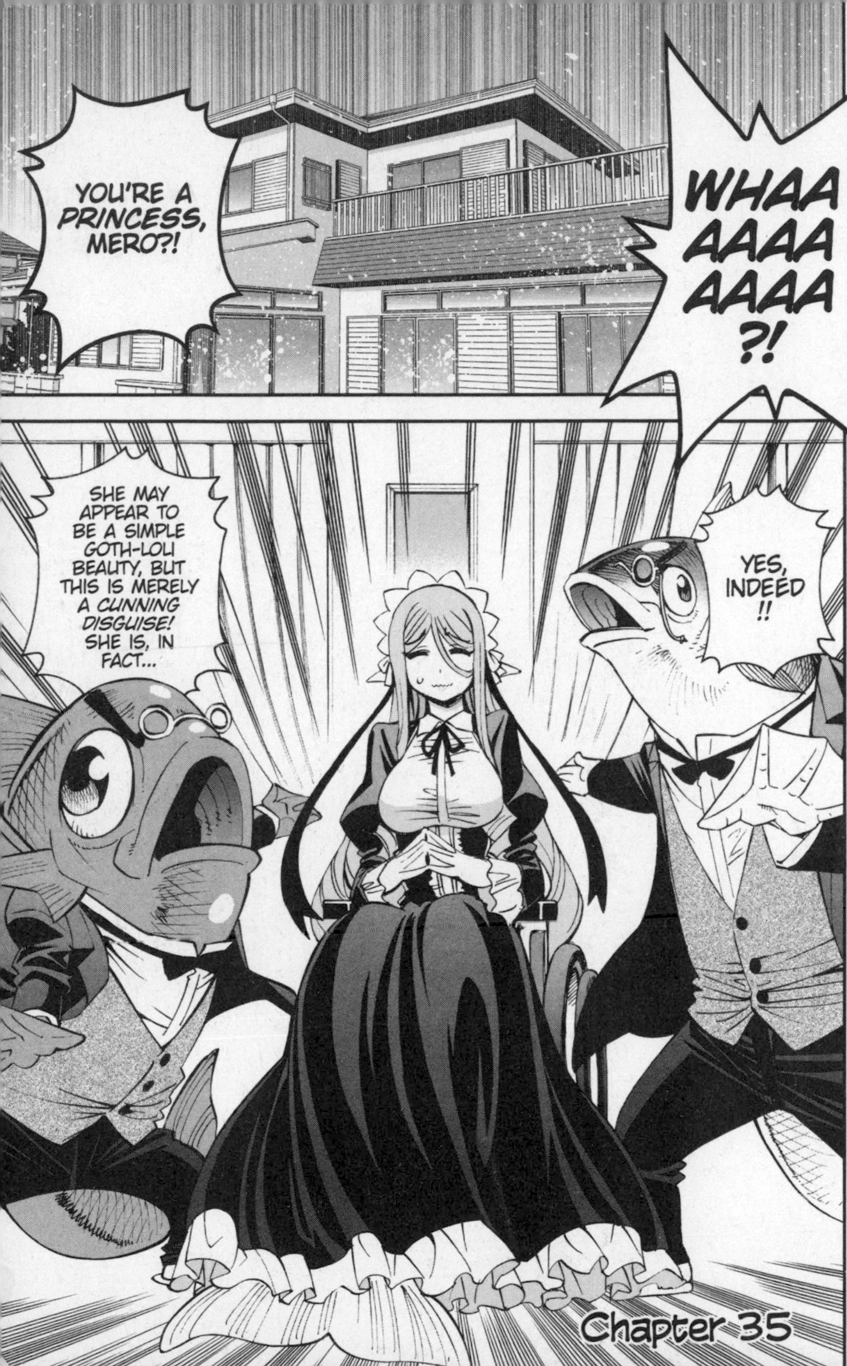
WHAA AAAA AAAA ?!
YOU'RE A PRINCESS, MERO?!
SHE MAY APPEAR TO BE A SIMPLE GOTH-LOLI BEAUTY, BUT THIS IS MERELY A *CUNNING* DISGUISE! SHE IS, IN FACT...
YES, INDEED !!
Chapter 35

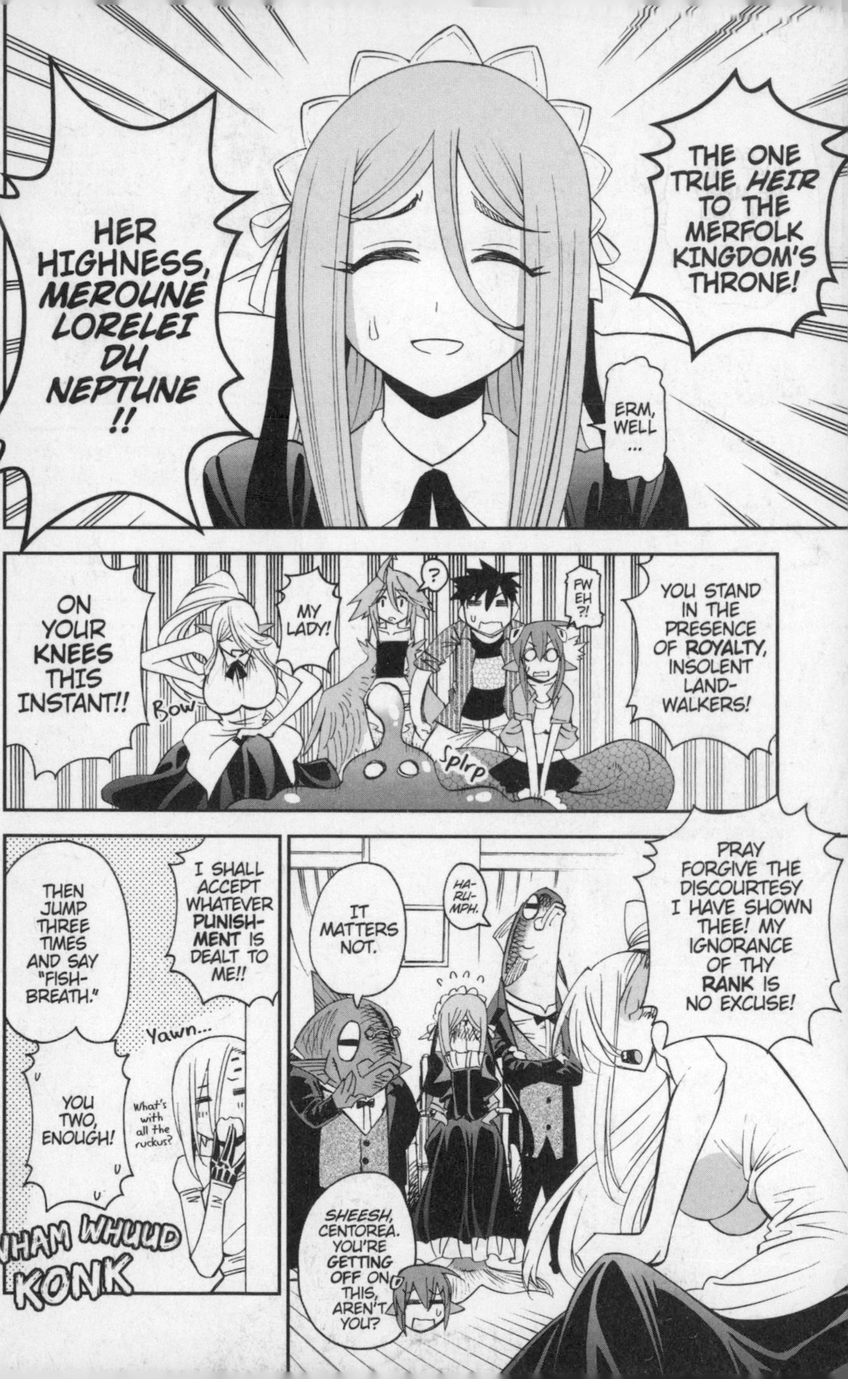
THE ONE TRUE HEIR TO THE MERFOLK KINGDOM'S THRONE!
HER HIGHNESS, MEROUNE LORELEI DU NEPTUNE!!
ERM, WELL...
YOU STAND IN THE PRESENCE OF ROYALTY, INSOLENT LAND-WALKERS!
FWEH?!
?
MY LADY!
ON YOUR KNEES THIS INSTANT!!
Bow
Splrp
PRAY FORGIVE THE DISCOURTESY I HAVE SHOWN THEE! MY IGNORANCE OF THY RANK IS NO EXCUSE!
HA-RUMPH.
IT MATTERS NOT.
SHEESH, CENTOREA. YOU'RE GETTING OFF ON THIS, AREN'T YOU?
I SHALL ACCEPT WHATEVER PUNISHMENT IS DEALT TO ME!!
THEN JUMP THREE TIMES AND SAY "FISH-BREATH."
Yawn...
What's with all the ruckus?
YOU TWO, ENOUGH!
WHAM WHUUD KONK

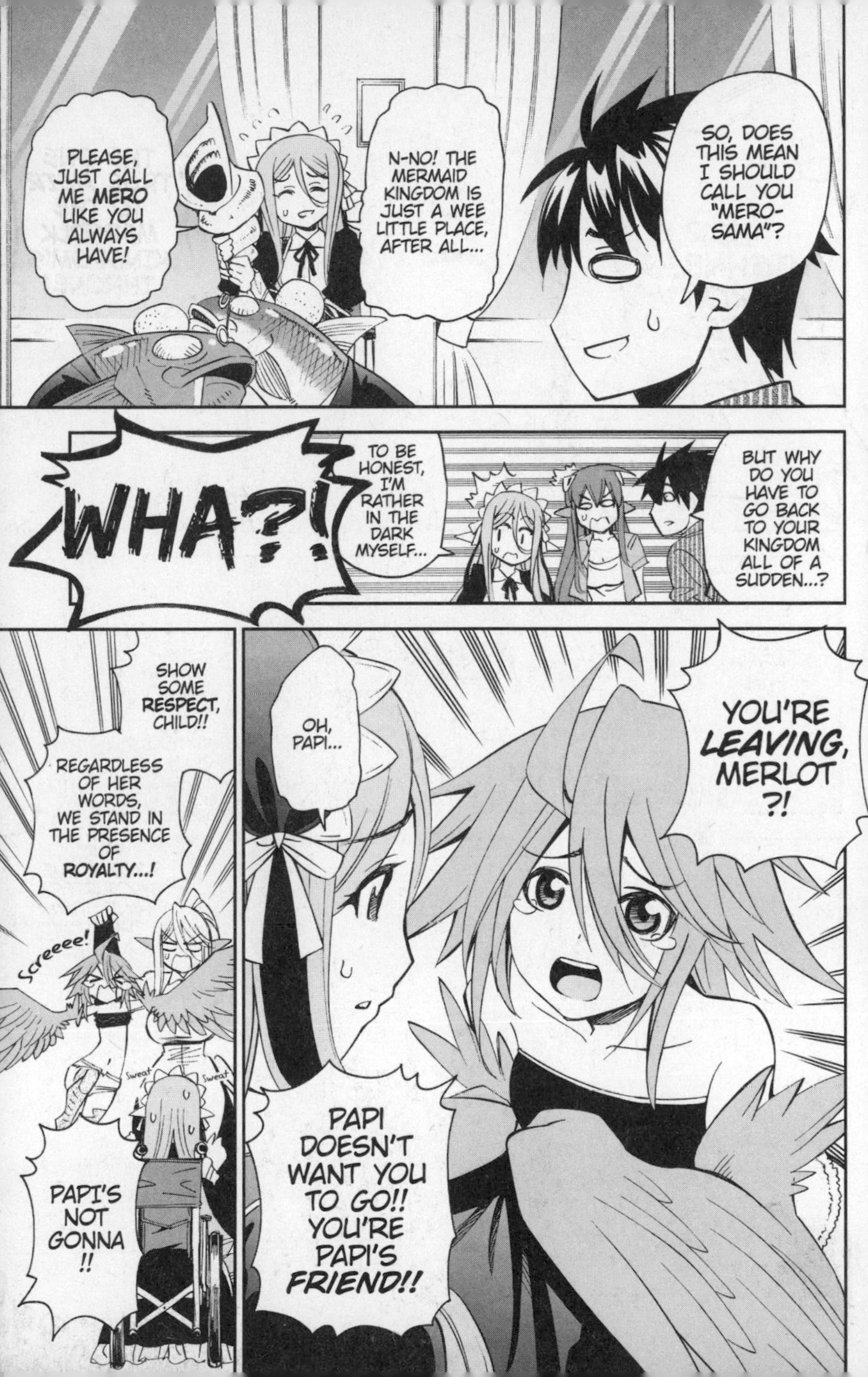
SO, DOES THIS MEAN I SHOULD CALL YOU "MERO-SAMA"?
N-NO! THE MERMAID KINGDOM IS JUST A WEE LITTLE PLACE, AFTER ALL...
PLEASE, JUST CALL ME MERO LIKE YOU ALWAYS HAVE!
BUT WHY DO YOU HAVE TO GO BACK TO YOUR KINGDOM ALL OF A SUDDEN...?
TO BE HONEST, I'M RATHER IN THE DARK MYSELF...
WHA?!
YOU'RE LEAVING, MERLOT?!
OH, PAPI...
PAPI DOESN'T WANT YOU TO GO!! YOU'RE PAPI'S FRIEND!!
SHOW SOME RESPECT, CHILD!!
REGARDLESS OF HER WORDS, WE STAND IN THE PRESENCE OF ROYALTY...!
Screeeee!
Sweat
Sweat
PAPI'S NOT GONNA!!

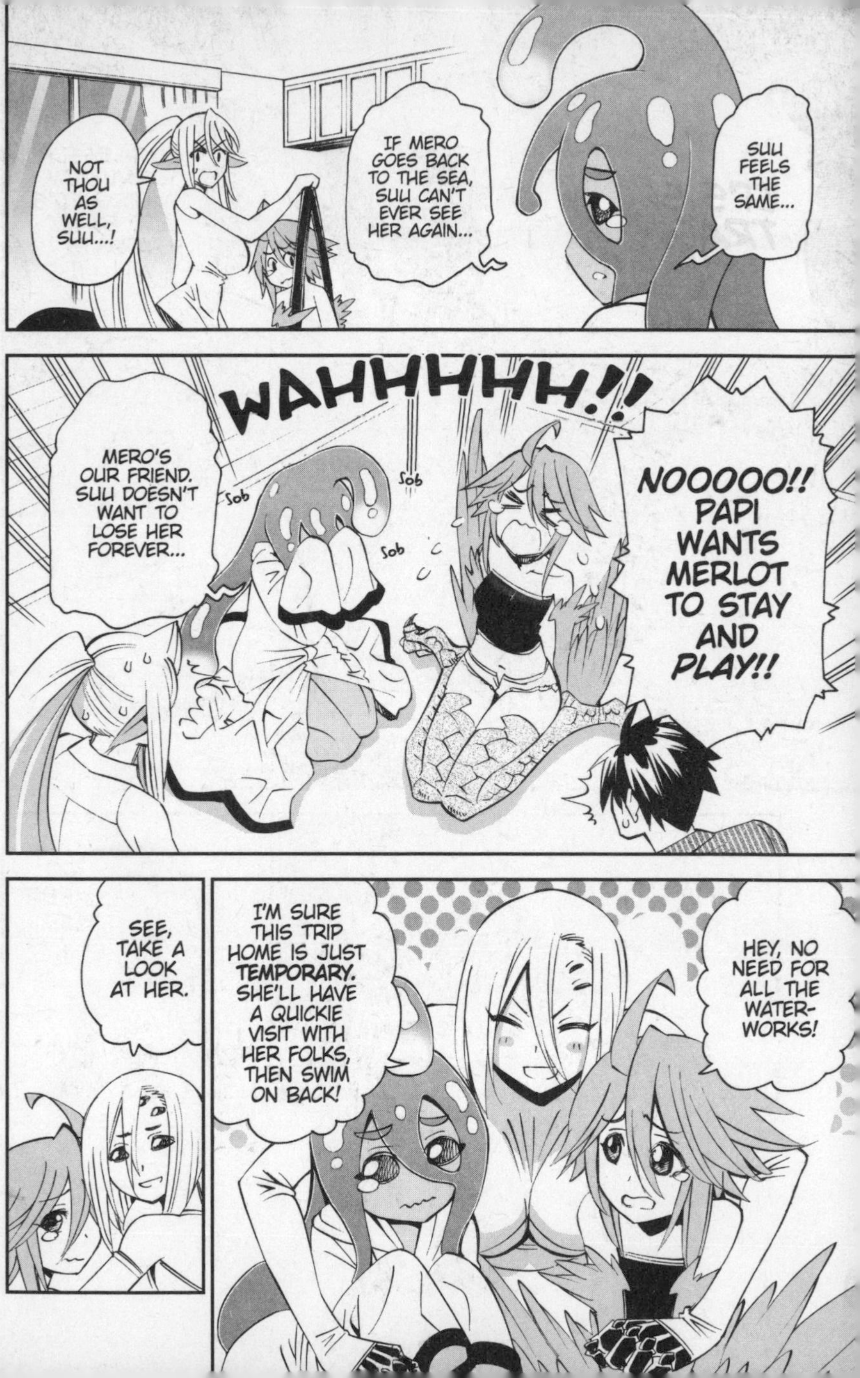
SUU FEELS THE SAME...
IF MERO GOES BACK TO THE SEA, SUU CAN'T EVER SEE HER AGAIN...
NOT THOU AS WELL, SUU...!
WAHHHHH!!
NOOOOO!! PAPI WANTS MERLOT TO STAY AND PLAY!!
Sob
Sob
Sob
MERO'S OUR FRIEND. SUU DOESN'T WANT TO LOSE HER FOREVER...
HEY, NO NEED FOR ALL THE WATER-WORKS!
I'M SURE THIS TRIP HOME IS JUST TEMPORARY. SHE'LL HAVE A QUICKIE VISIT WITH HER FOLKS, THEN SWIM ON BACK!
SEE, TAKE A LOOK AT HER.

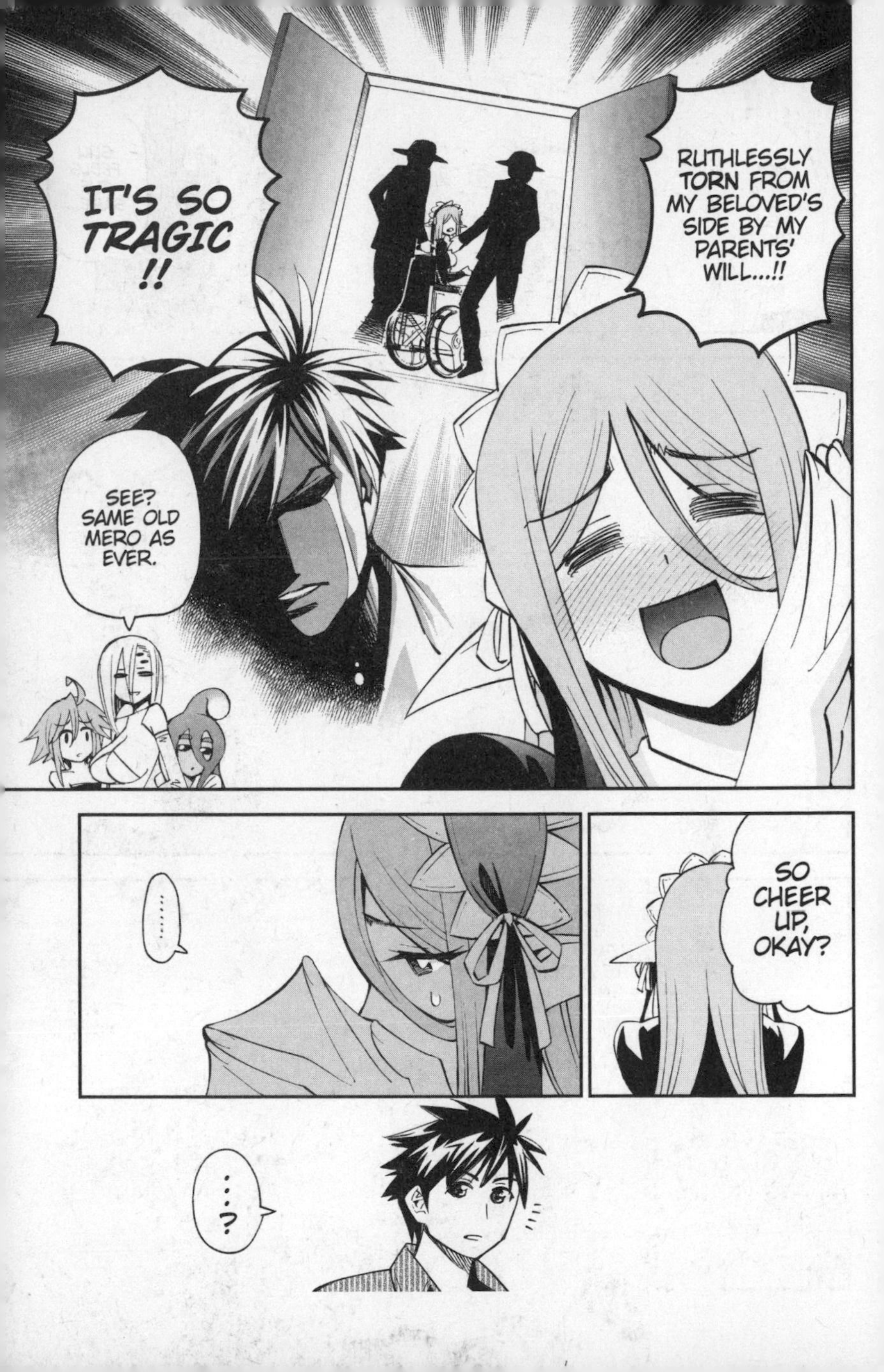
RUTHLESSLY TORN FROM MY BELOVED'S SIDE BY MY PARENTS' WILL...!!
IT'S SO *TRAGIC* !!
SEE? SAME OLD MERO AS EVER.
SO CHEER UP, OKAY?
......
...?

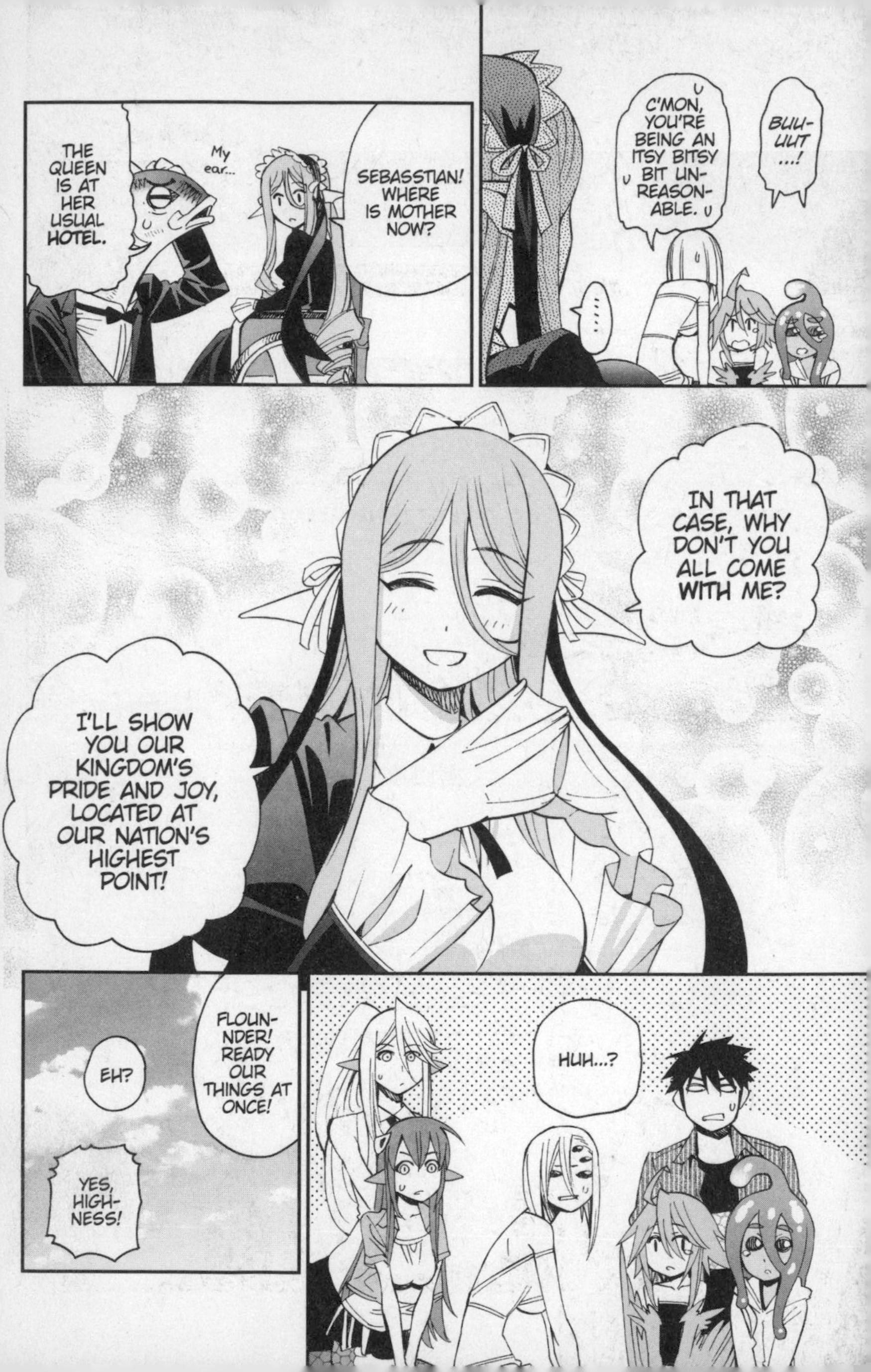
BUU-UUT ...!
C'MON, YOU'RE BEING AN ITSY BITSY BIT UN-REASON-ABLE.
...
SEBASSTIAN! WHERE IS MOTHER NOW?
My ear...
THE QUEEN IS AT HER USUAL HOTEL.
IN THAT CASE, WHY DON'T YOU ALL COME WITH ME?
I'LL SHOW YOU OUR KINGDOM'S PRIDE AND JOY, LOCATED AT OUR NATION'S HIGHEST POINT!
HUH...?
FLOUN-NDER! READY OUR THINGS AT ONCE!
EH?
YES, HIGH-NESS!

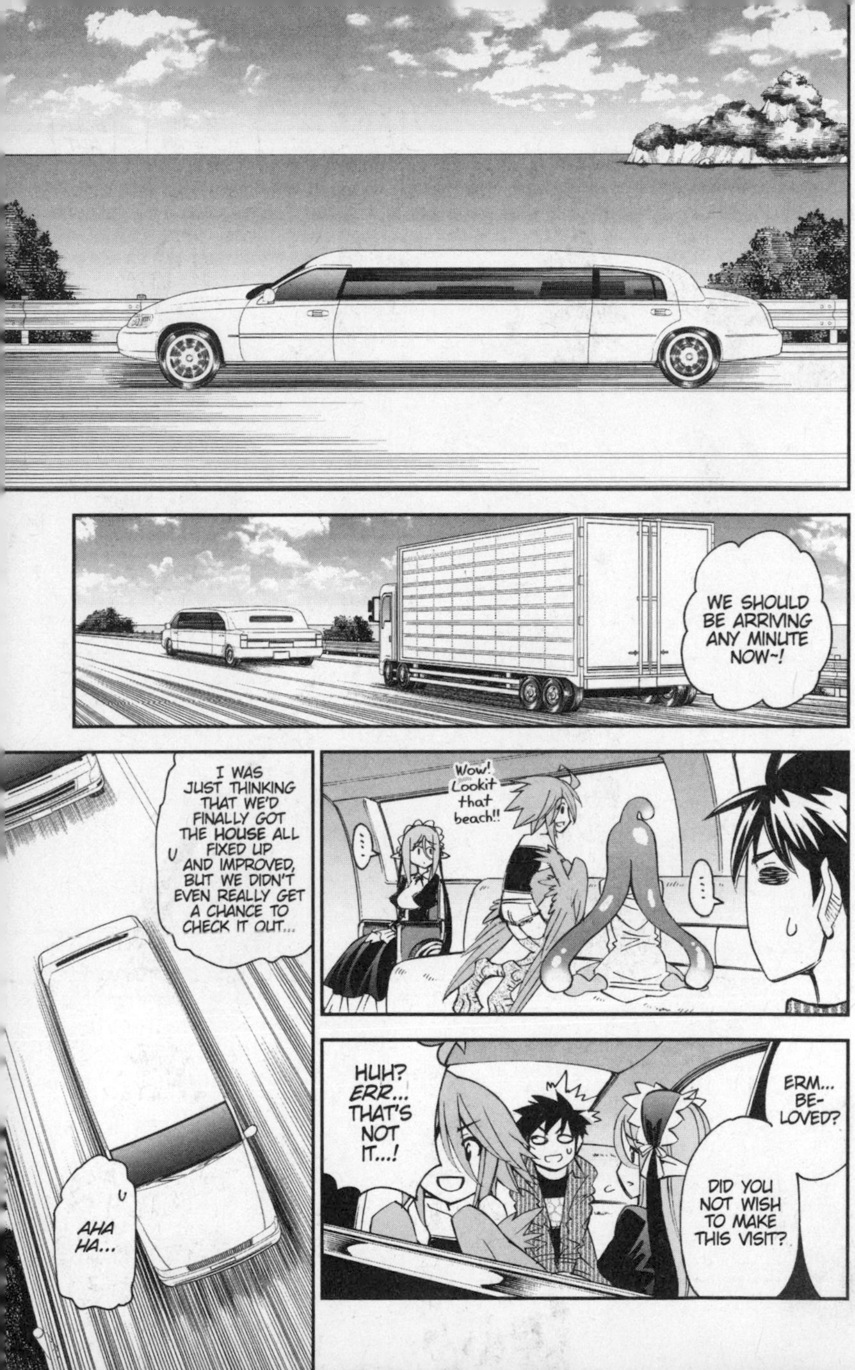
WE SHOULD BE ARRIVING ANY MINUTE NOW~!
...
Wow! Lookit that beach!!
...
ERM... BE-LOVED?
DID YOU NOT WISH TO MAKE THIS VISIT?
HUH? ERR... THAT'S NOT IT...!
I WAS JUST THINKING THAT WE'D FINALLY GOT THE HOUSE ALL FIXED UP AND IMPROVED, BUT WE DIDN'T EVEN REALLY GET A CHANCE TO CHECK IT OUT...
AHA HA...

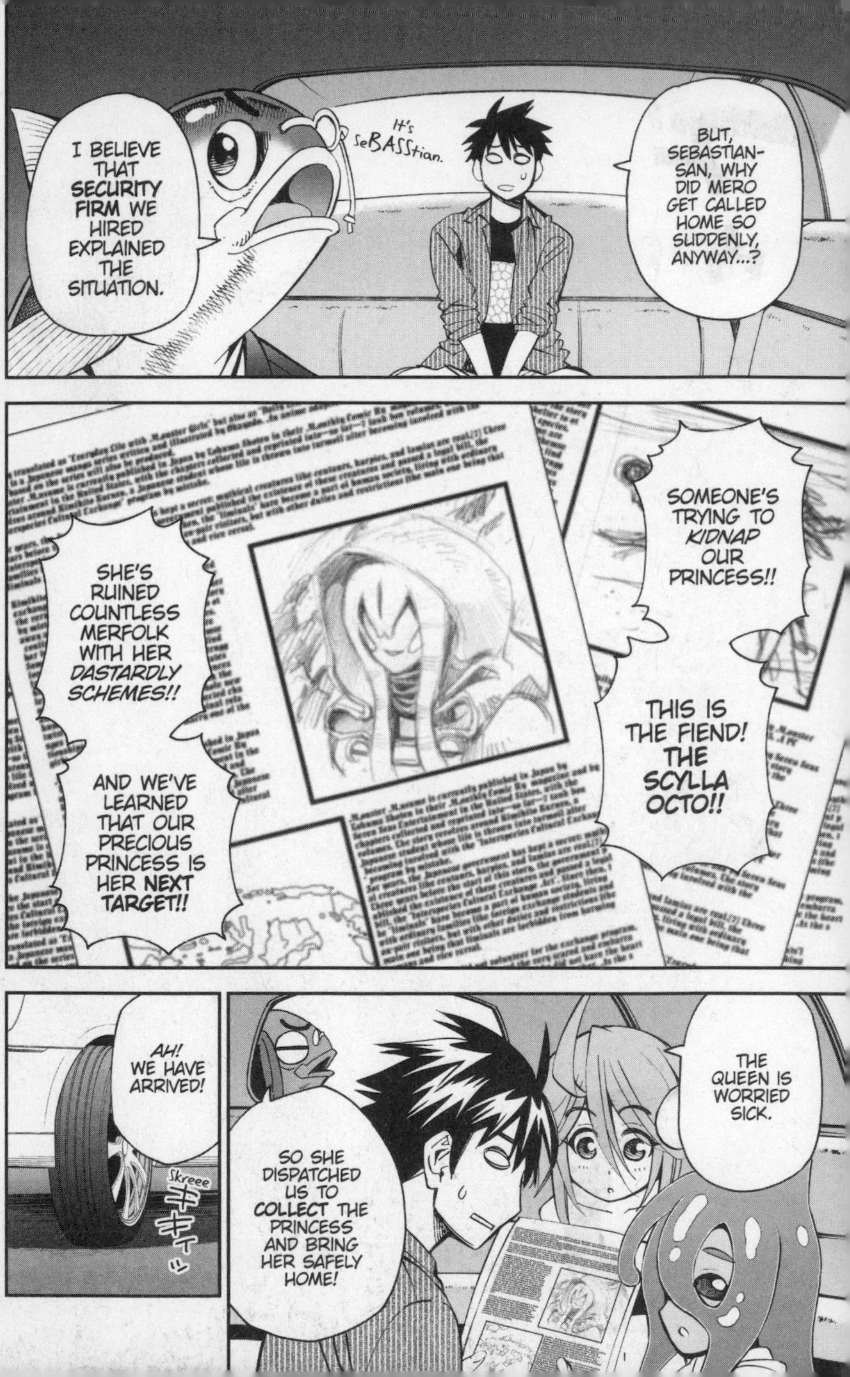
BUT, SEBASTIAN-SAN, WHY DID MERO GET CALLED HOME SO SUDDENLY, ANYWAY...?
It's SeBASStian.
I BELIEVE THAT SECURITY FIRM WE HIRED EXPLAINED THE SITUATION.
SOMEONE'S TRYING TO KIDNAP OUR PRINCESS!!
THIS IS THE FIEND! THE SCYLLA OCTO!!
SHE'S RUINED COUNTLESS MERFOLK WITH HER DASTARDLY SCHEMES!!
AND WE'VE LEARNED THAT OUR PRECIOUS PRINCESS IS HER NEXT TARGET!!
THE QUEEN IS WORRIED SICK.
SO SHE DISPATCHED US TO COLLECT THE PRINCESS AND BRING HER SAFELY HOME!
AH! WE HAVE ARRIVED!
Skreee
キキィッ

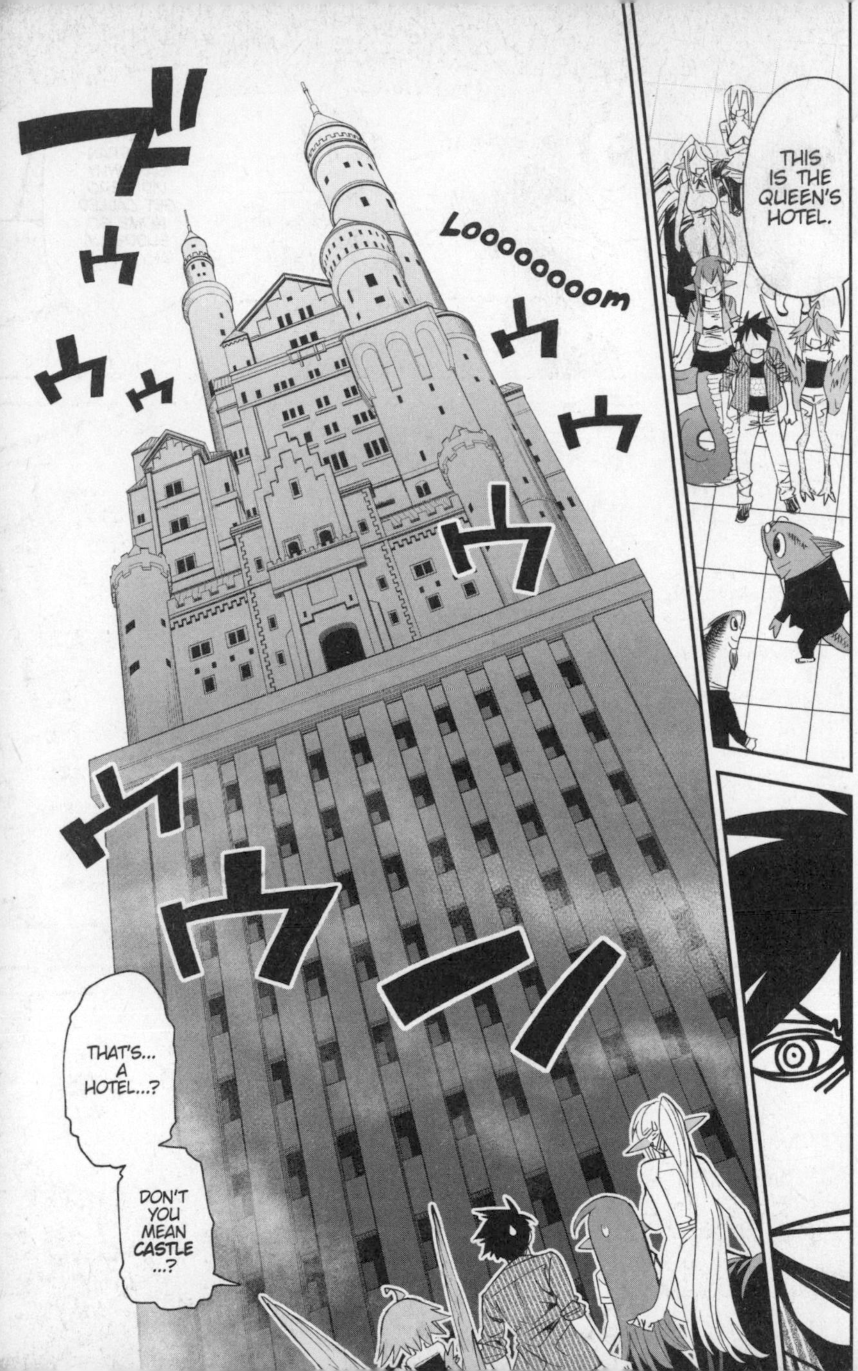
THIS IS THE QUEEN'S HOTEL.
Looooooooom
THAT'S... A HOTEL...?
DON'T YOU MEAN CASTLE ...?

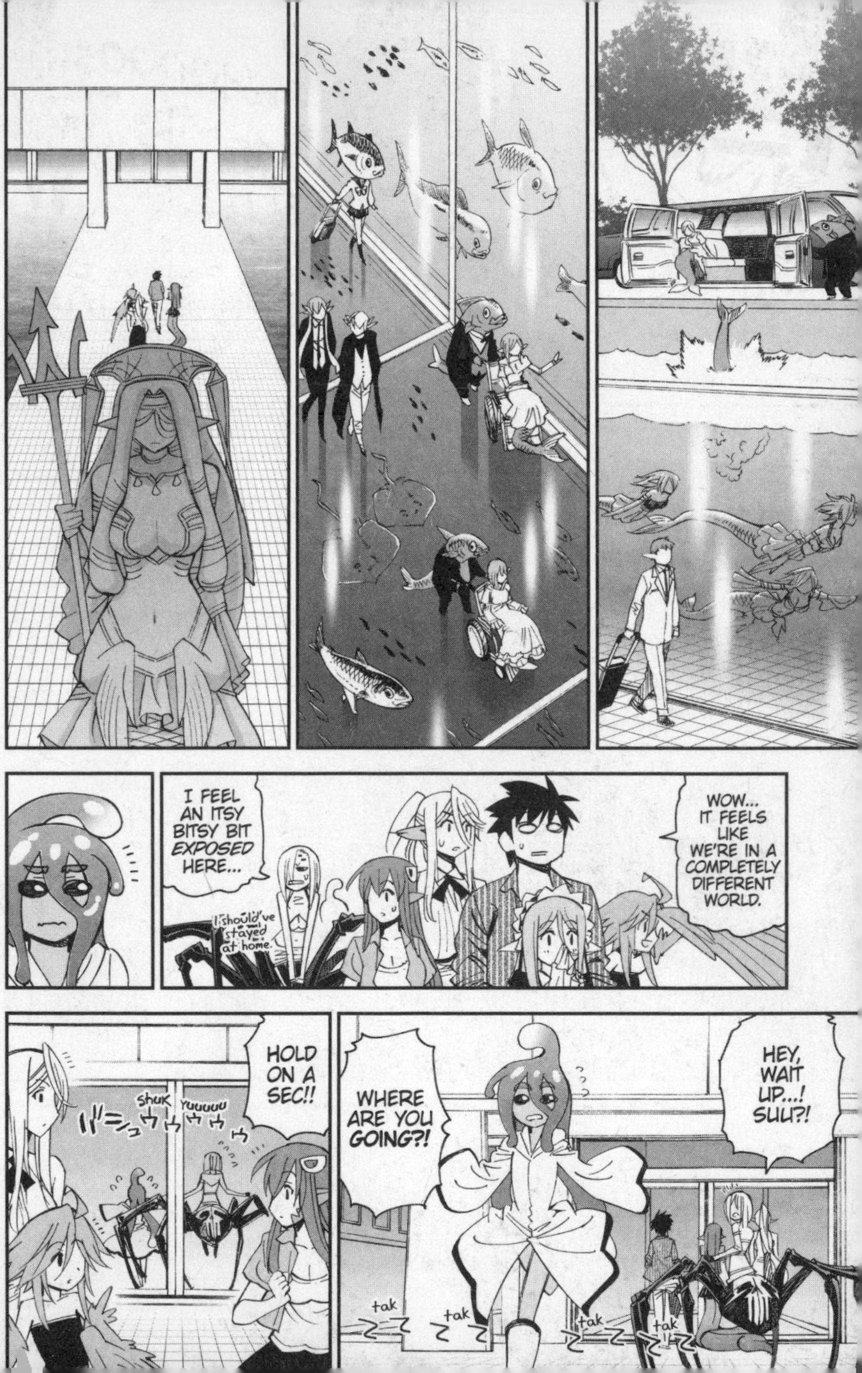
WOW... IT FEELS LIKE WE'RE IN A COMPLETELY DIFFERENT WORLD.
I FEEL AN ITSY BITSY BIT EXPOSED HERE...
I should've stayed at home.
HEY, WAIT UP...! SUU?!
WHERE ARE YOU GOING?!
tak
tak
tak
tak
HOLD ON A SEC!!
shuk Yuuuuuu

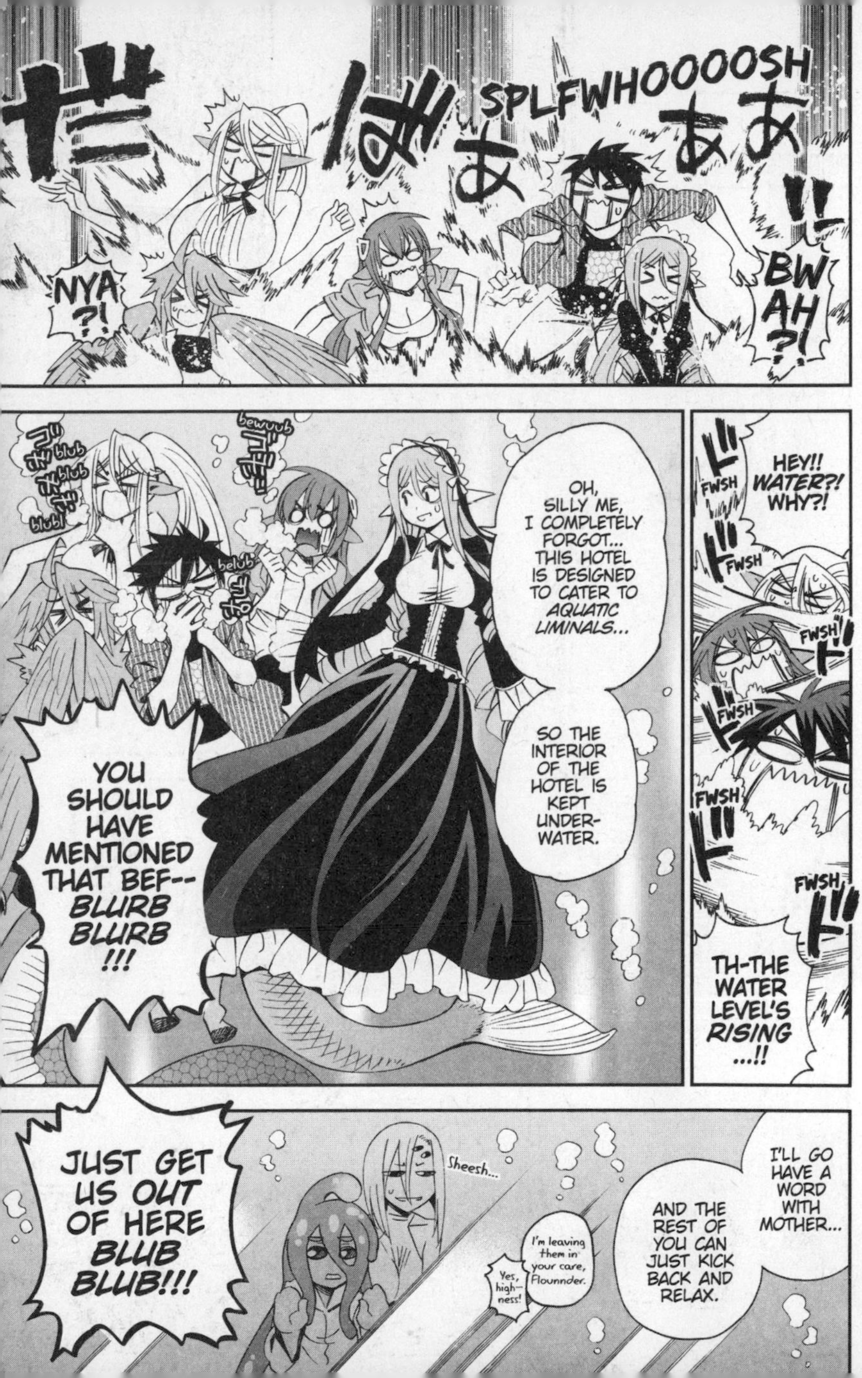
SPLFWHOOOOSH
BWAH?!
NYA?!
HEY!! WATER?! WHY?!
FWSH
FWSH
FWSH
FWSH
FWSH
FWSH
TH-THE WATER LEVEL'S RISING...!!
OH, SILLY ME, I COMPLETELY FORGOT... THIS HOTEL IS DESIGNED TO CATER TO AQUATIC LIMINALS...
SO THE INTERIOR OF THE HOTEL IS KEPT UNDER-WATER.
bewuub
blub blub blub!
belub
YOU SHOULD HAVE MENTIONED THAT BEF-- BLURB BLURB !!!
I'LL GO HAVE A WORD WITH MOTHER...
AND THE REST OF YOU CAN JUST KICK BACK AND RELAX.
Sheesh...
I'm leaving them in your care, Flounnder.
Yes, high-ness!
JUST GET US OUT OF HERE BLUB BLUB!!!

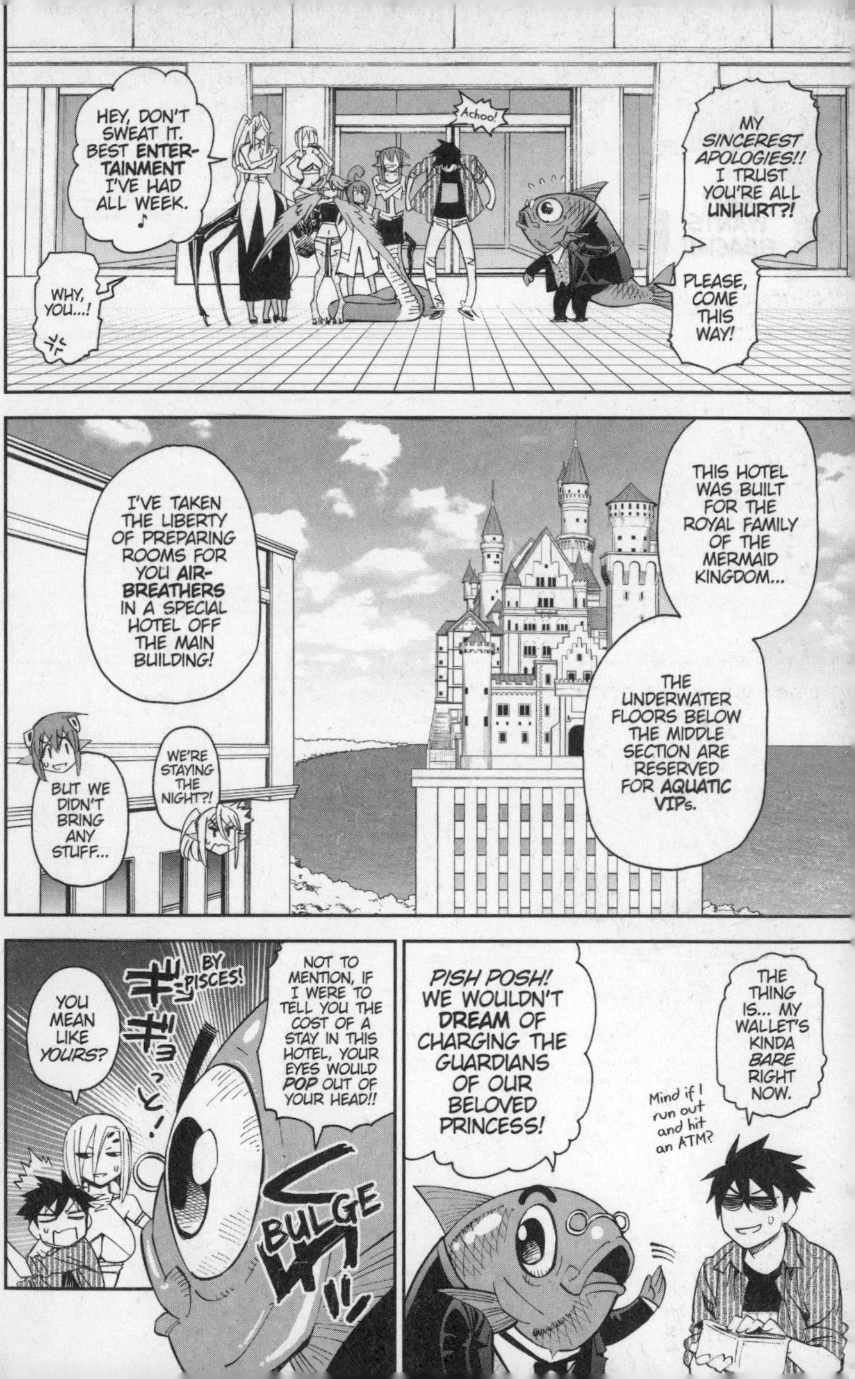
MY SINCEREST APOLOGIES!! I TRUST YOU'RE ALL UNHURT?!
PLEASE, COME THIS WAY!
Achoo!
HEY, DON'T SWEAT IT. BEST ENTERTAINMENT I'VE HAD ALL WEEK. ♪
WHY, YOU...!
THIS HOTEL WAS BUILT FOR THE ROYAL FAMILY OF THE MERMAID KINGDOM...
THE UNDERWATER FLOORS BELOW THE MIDDLE SECTION ARE RESERVED FOR AQUATIC VIPs.
I'VE TAKEN THE LIBERTY OF PREPARING ROOMS FOR YOU AIR-BREATHERS IN A SPECIAL HOTEL OFF THE MAIN BUILDING!
WE'RE STAYING THE NIGHT?!
BUT WE DIDN'T BRING ANY STUFF...
THE THING IS... MY WALLET'S KINDA BARE RIGHT NOW.
Mind if I run out and hit an ATM?
PISH POSH! WE WOULDN'T DREAM OF CHARGING THE GUARDIANS OF OUR BELOVED PRINCESS!
NOT TO MENTION, IF I WERE TO TELL YOU THE COST OF A STAY IN THIS HOTEL, YOUR EYES WOULD POP OUT OF YOUR HEAD!!
BY PISCES!
YOU MEAN LIKE YOURS?
BULGE

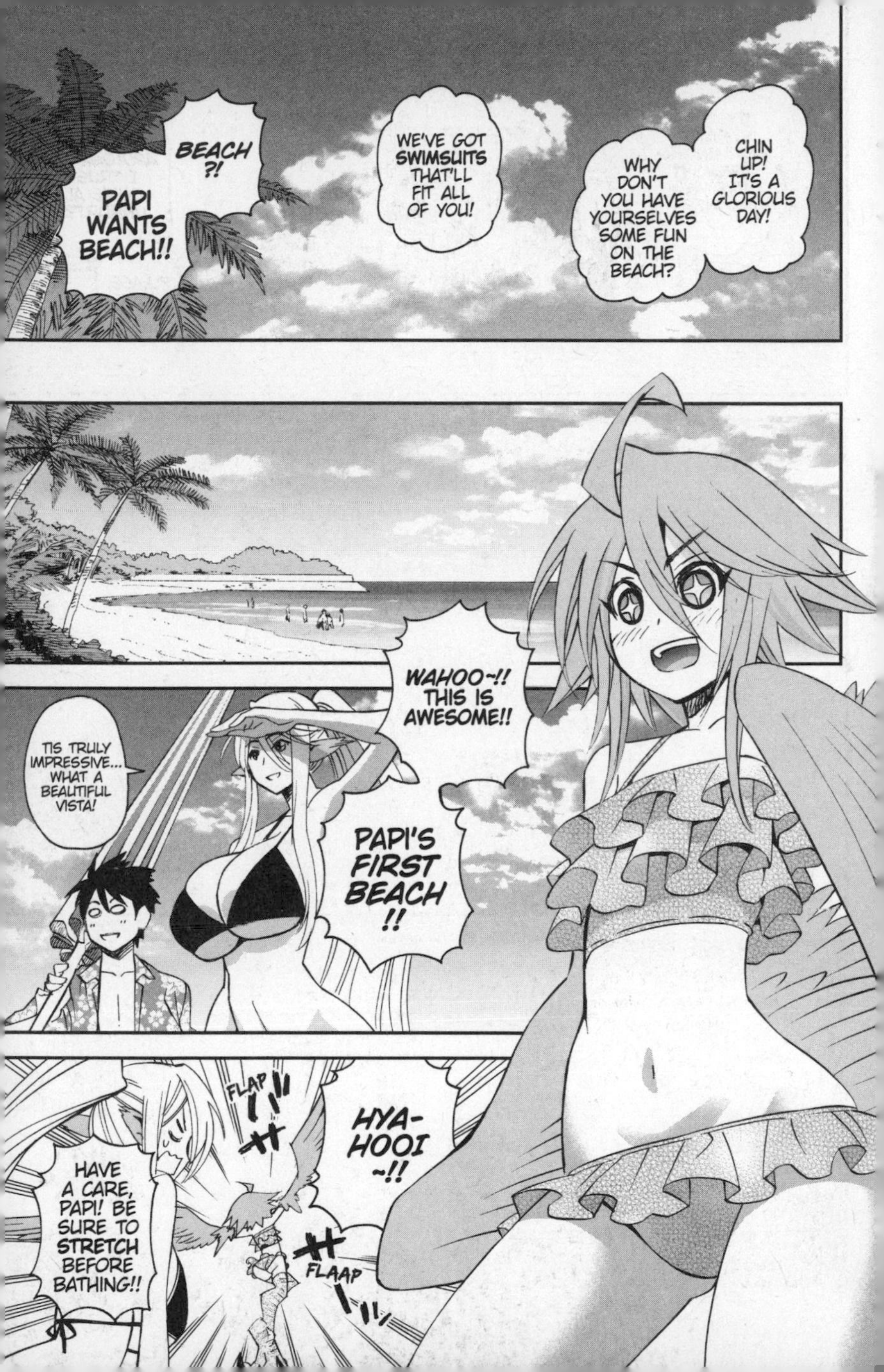
CHIN UP! IT'S A GLORIOUS DAY!
WHY DON'T YOU HAVE YOURSELVES SOME FUN ON THE BEACH?
WE'VE GOT SWIMSUITS THAT'LL FIT ALL OF YOU!
BEACH?!
PAPI WANTS BEACH!!
WAHOO~!! THIS IS AWESOME!!
PAPI'S FIRST BEACH!!
TIS TRULY IMPRESSIVE... WHAT A BEAUTIFUL VISTA!
HYA-HOOI~!!
FLAP
FLAAP
HAVE A CARE, PAPI! BE SURE TO STRETCH BEFORE BATHING!!

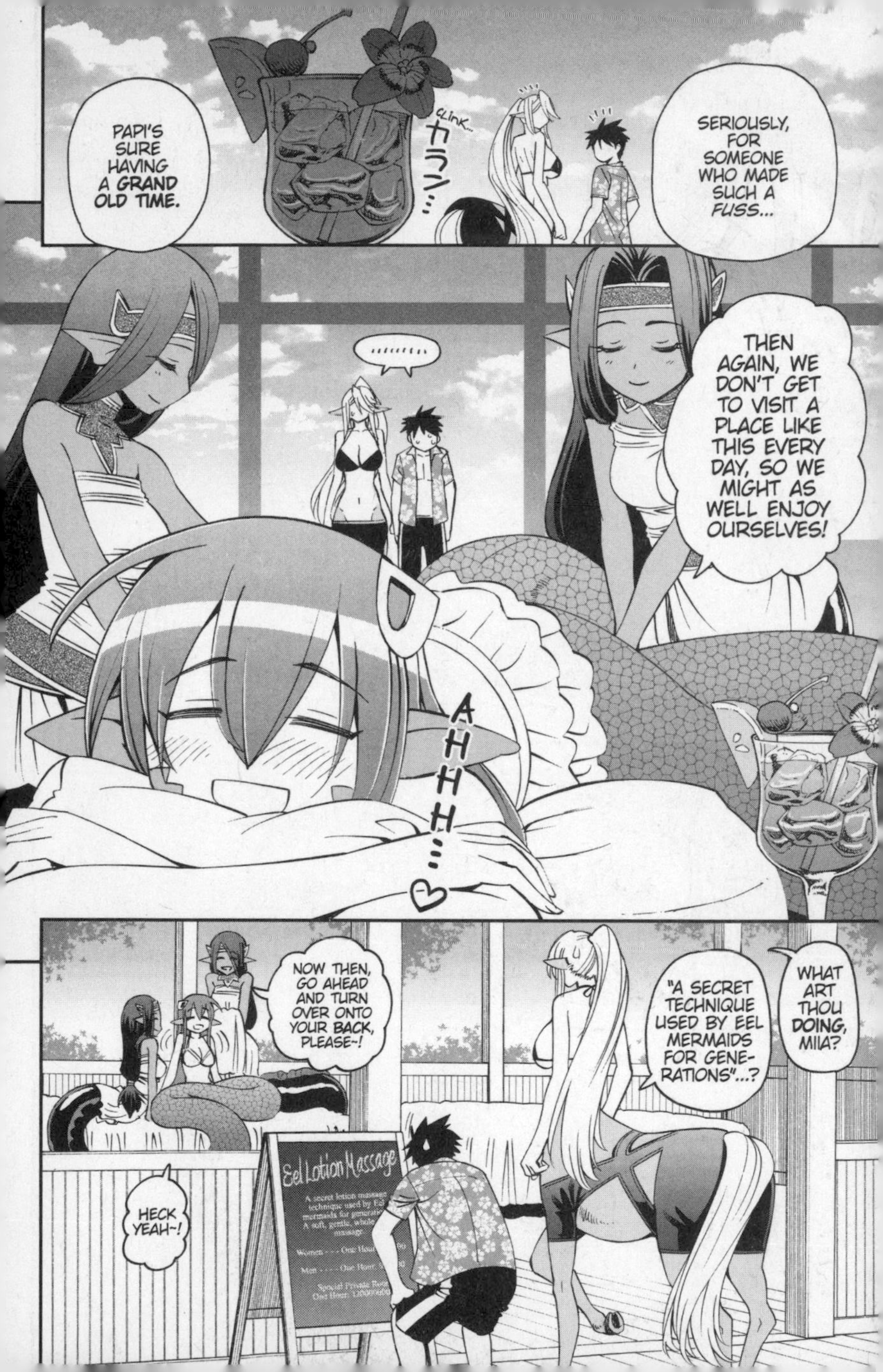
SERIOUSLY, FOR SOMEONE WHO MADE SUCH A FUSS...
CLINK...
カラン...
PAPI'S SURE HAVING A GRAND OLD TIME.
THEN AGAIN, WE DON'T GET TO VISIT A PLACE LIKE THIS EVERY DAY, SO WE MIGHT AS WELL ENJOY OURSELVES!
......
AHHHH...♥
WHAT ART THOU DOING, MIIA?
"A SECRET TECHNIQUE USED BY EEL MERMAIDS FOR GENERATIONS"...?
NOW THEN, GO AHEAD AND TURN OVER ONTO YOUR BACK, PLEASE~!
HECK YEAH~!
Eel Lotion Massage

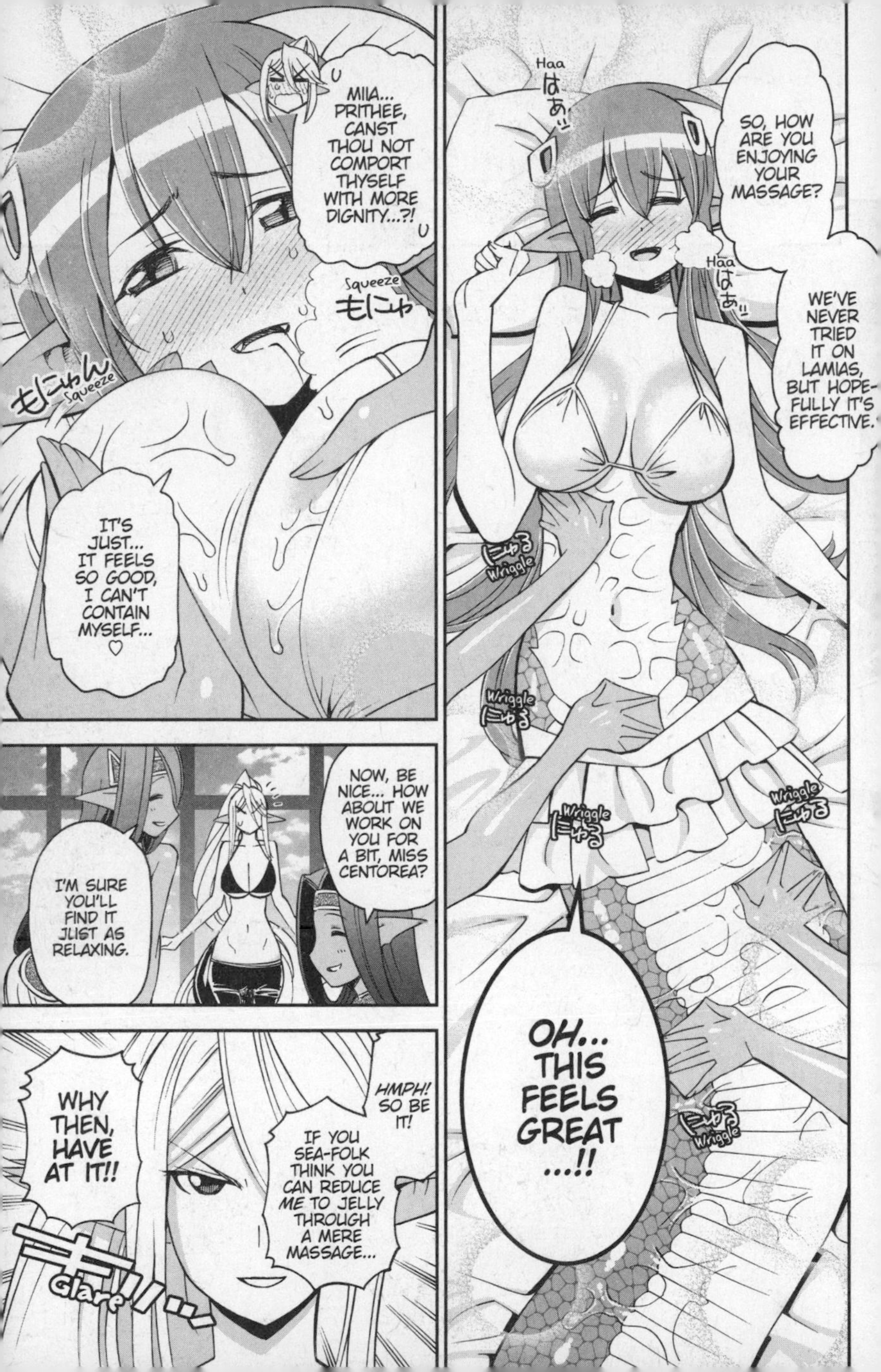
Haa
はあっ
SO, HOW ARE YOU ENJOYING YOUR MASSAGE?
Haa
はあっ
WE'VE NEVER TRIED IT ON LAMIAS, BUT HOPE-FULLY IT'S EFFECTIVE.
にゅる Wriggle
Wriggle にゅる
Wriggle にゅる
Wriggle にゅる
OH... THIS FEELS GREAT ...!!
にゅる Wriggle
MIIA... PRITHEE, CANST THOU NOT COMPORT THYSELF WITH MORE DIGNITY...?!
Squeeze
もにゃ
もにゅん Squeeze
IT'S JUST... IT FEELS SO GOOD, I CAN'T CONTAIN MYSELF... ♡
NOW, BE NICE... HOW ABOUT WE WORK ON YOU FOR A BIT, MISS CENTOREA?
I'M SURE YOU'LL FIND IT JUST AS RELAXING.
HMPH! SO BE IT!
IF YOU SEA-FOLK THINK YOU CAN REDUCE ME TO JELLY THROUGH A MERE MASSAGE...
WHY THEN, HAVE AT IT!!
Glare

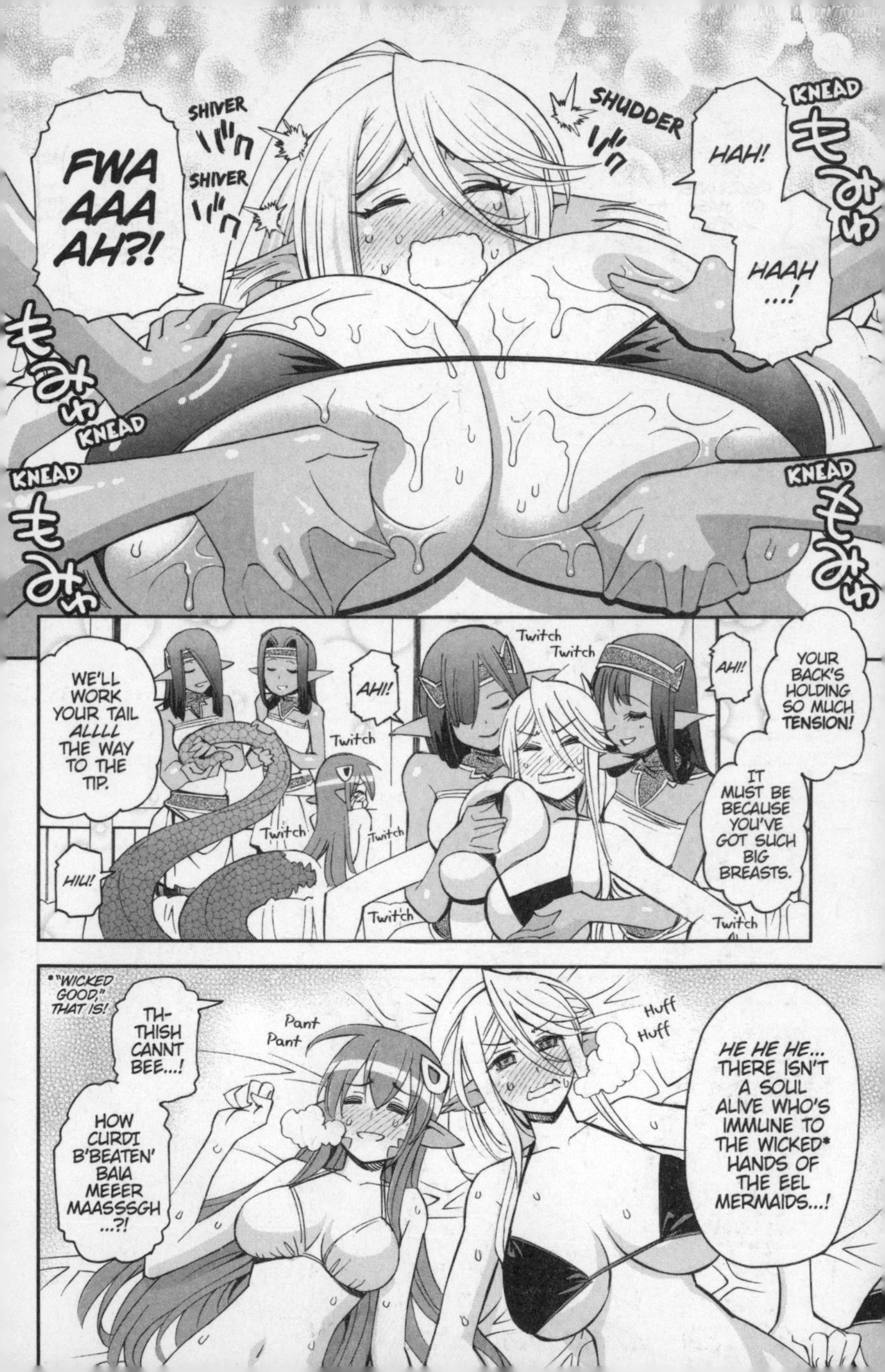
KNEAD
もみゅ
HAH!
HAAH ...!
SHUDDER
SHIVER
SHIVER
FWA AAA AH?!
KNEAD
もみゅ
もみゅ
KNEAD
KNEAD
もみゅ
YOUR BACK'S HOLDING SO MUCH TENSION!
AH!
IT MUST BE BECAUSE YOU'VE GOT SUCH BIG BREASTS.
Twitch
Twitch
AH!
Twitch
Twitch
WE'LL WORK YOUR TAIL ALLLL THE WAY TO THE TIP.
Twitch
Twitch
HIU!
Twitch
HE HE HE... THERE ISN'T A SOUL ALIVE WHO'S IMMUNE TO THE WICKED* HANDS OF THE EEL MERMAIDS...!
Huff
Huff
Pant
Pant
TH-THISH CANNT BEE...!
HOW CURDI B'BEATEN' BAIA MEEER MAASSSGH ...?!
*"WICKED GOOD," THAT IS!

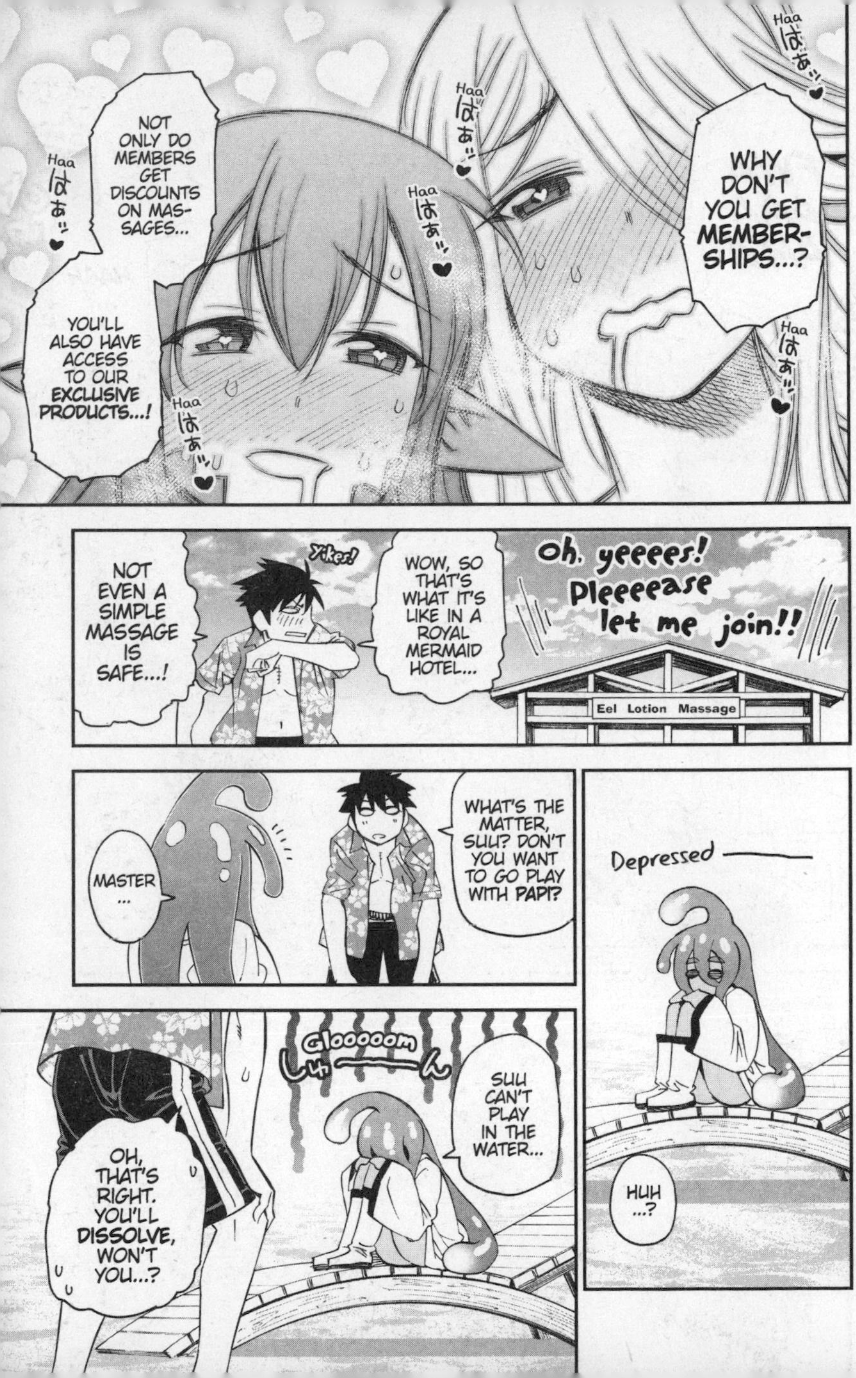
Haa
はぁッ
Haa
はぁッ
WHY DON'T YOU GET MEMBERSHIPS...?
Haa
はぁッ
Haa
はぁッ
NOT ONLY DO MEMBERS GET DISCOUNTS ON MASSAGES...
Haa
はぁッ
YOU'LL ALSO HAVE ACCESS TO OUR EXCLUSIVE PRODUCTS...!
Haa
はぁッ
Oh, yeeees! Pleeeease let me join!!
Eel Lotion Massage
WOW, SO THAT'S WHAT IT'S LIKE IN A ROYAL MERMAID HOTEL...
Yikes!
NOT EVEN A SIMPLE MASSAGE IS SAFE...!
Depressed ———
HUH ...?
WHAT'S THE MATTER, SUU? DON'T YOU WANT TO GO PLAY WITH PAPI?
MASTER ...
Gloooom
しゅ———ん
SUU CAN'T PLAY IN THE WATER...
OH, THAT'S RIGHT. YOU'LL DISSOLVE, WON'T YOU...?

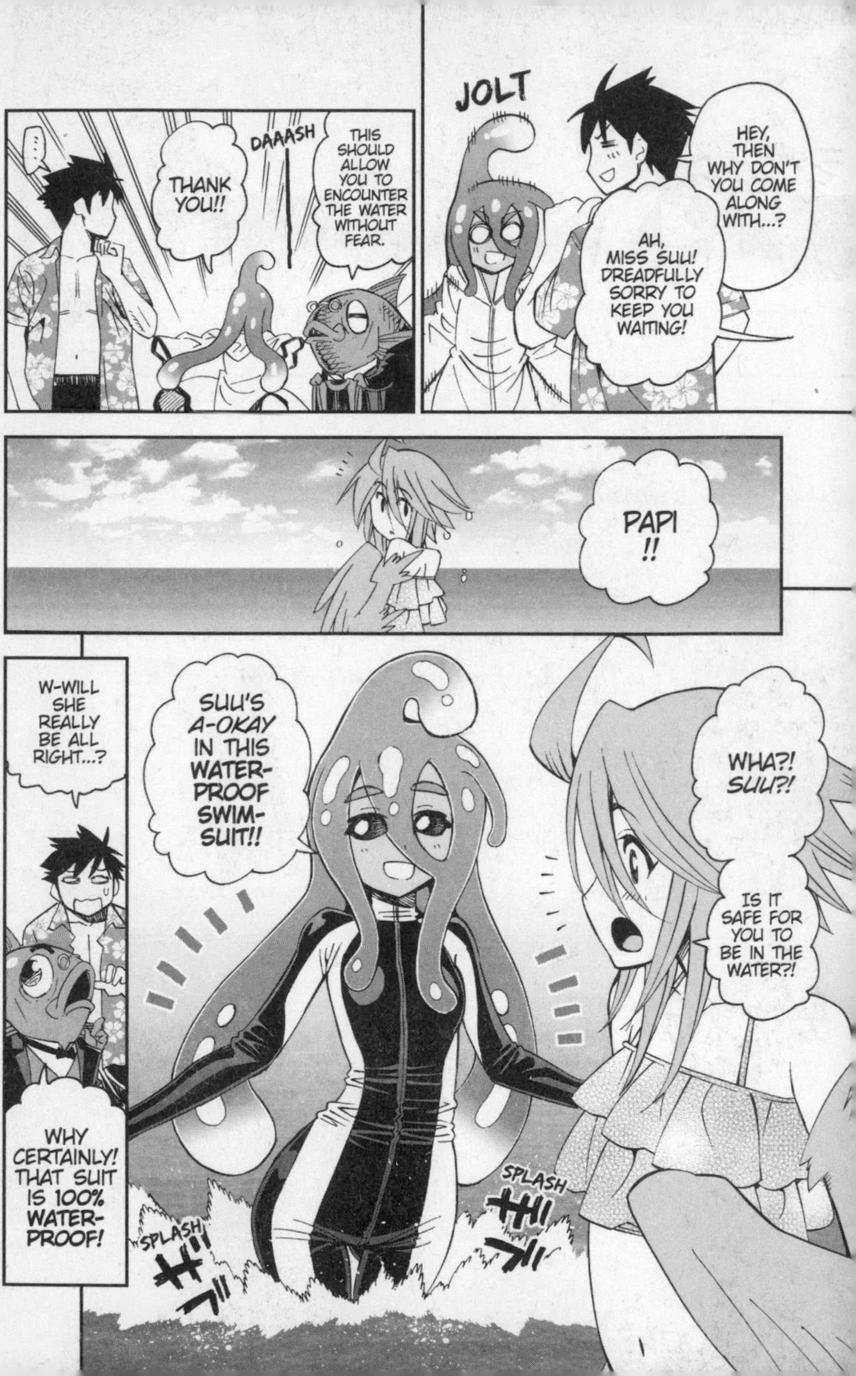
JOLT
HEY, THEN WHY DON'T YOU COME ALONG WITH...?
AH, MISS SUU! DREADFULLY SORRY TO KEEP YOU WAITING!
THIS SHOULD ALLOW YOU TO ENCOUNTER THE WATER WITHOUT FEAR.
DAAASH
THANK YOU!!
...
PAPI !!
WHA?! SUU?!
IS IT SAFE FOR YOU TO BE IN THE WATER?!
SUU'S A-OKAY IN THIS WATER-PROOF SWIM-SUIT!!
SPLASH
SPLASH
W-WILL SHE REALLY BE ALL RIGHT...?
WHY CERTAINLY! THAT SUIT IS 100% WATER-PROOF!

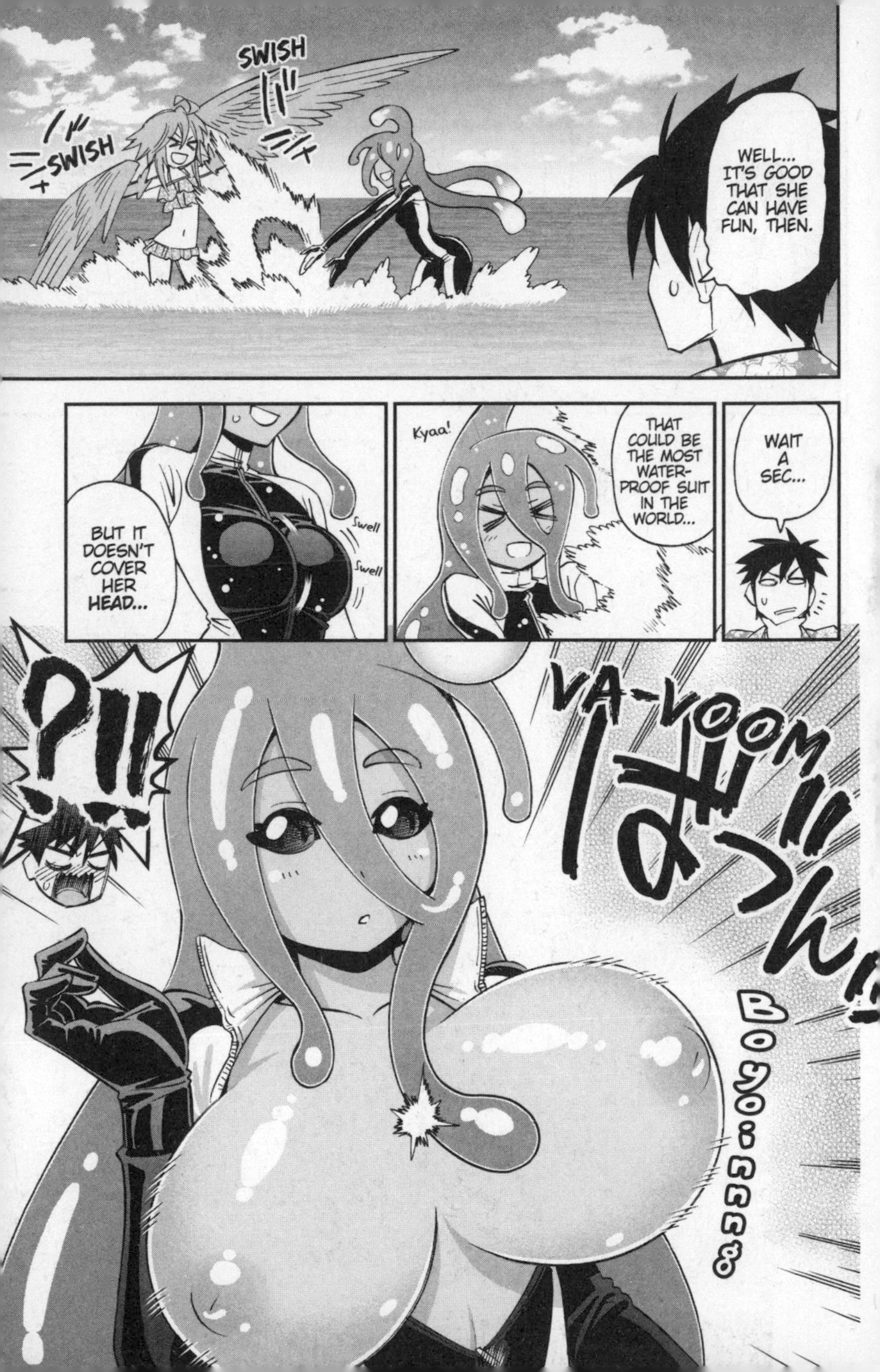
WELL... IT'S GOOD THAT SHE CAN HAVE FUN, THEN.
SWISH
SWISH
WAIT A SEC...
THAT COULD BE THE MOST WATER-PROOF SUIT IN THE WORLD...
Kyaa!
Swell
Swell
BUT IT DOESN'T COVER HER HEAD...
VA-VOOM
Boyoinnn
?!!

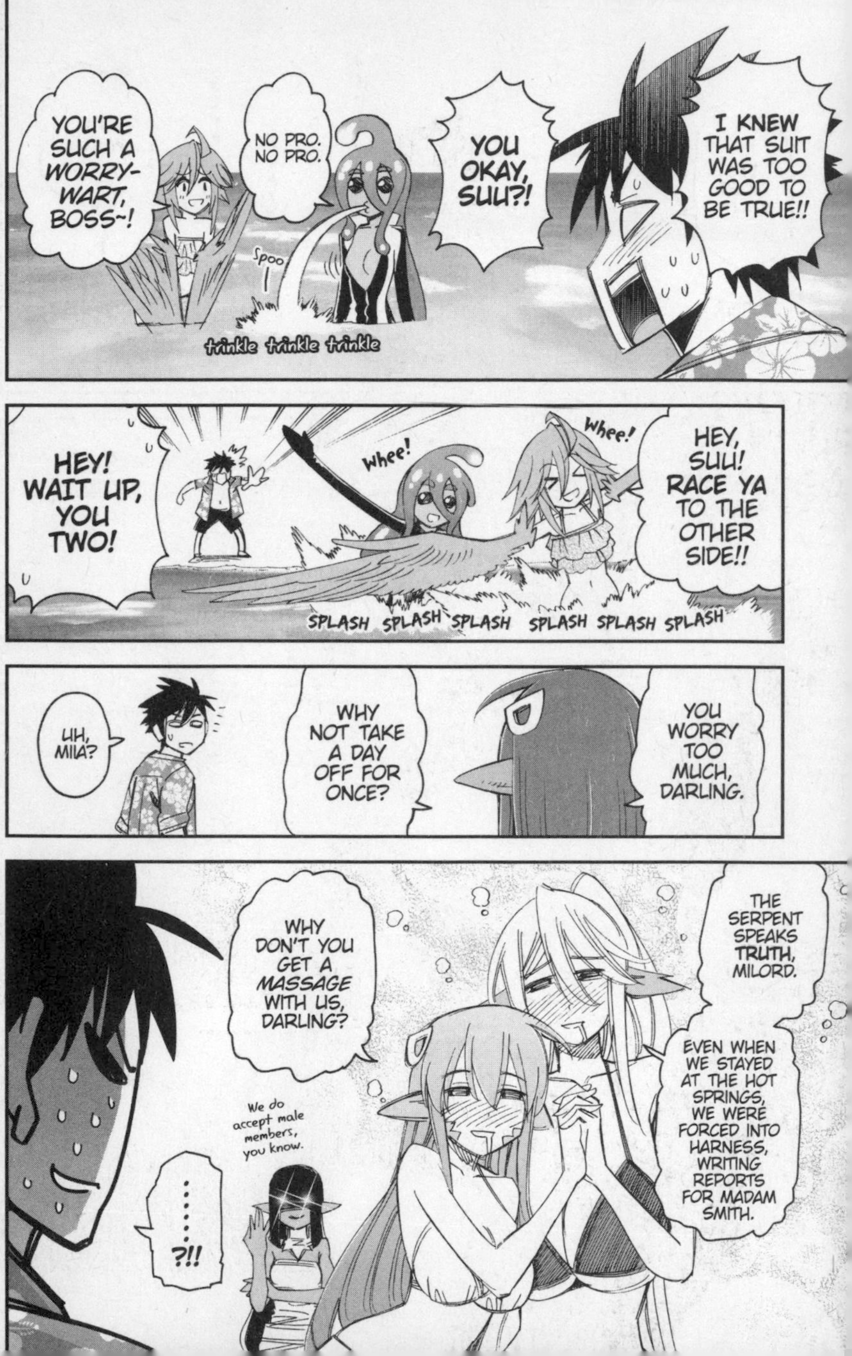

I KNEW THAT SUIT WAS TOO GOOD TO BE TRUE!!
YOU OKAY, SUU?!
NO PRO. NO PRO.
YOU'RE SUCH A WORRY-WART, BOSS~!
Spoo
trinkle trinkle trinkle
HEY, SUU! RACE YA TO THE OTHER SIDE!!
Whee!
Whee!
HEY! WAIT UP, YOU TWO!
SPLASH SPLASH SPLASH SPLASH SPLASH SPLASH
YOU WORRY TOO MUCH, DARLING.
WHY NOT TAKE A DAY OFF FOR ONCE?
UH, MIIA?
THE SERPENT SPEAKS TRUTH, MILORD.
EVEN WHEN WE STAYED AT THE HOT SPRINGS, WE WERE FORCED INTO HARNESS, WRITING REPORTS FOR MADAM SMITH.
WHY DON'T YOU GET A MASSAGE WITH US, DARLING?
We do accept male members, you know.
......?!!

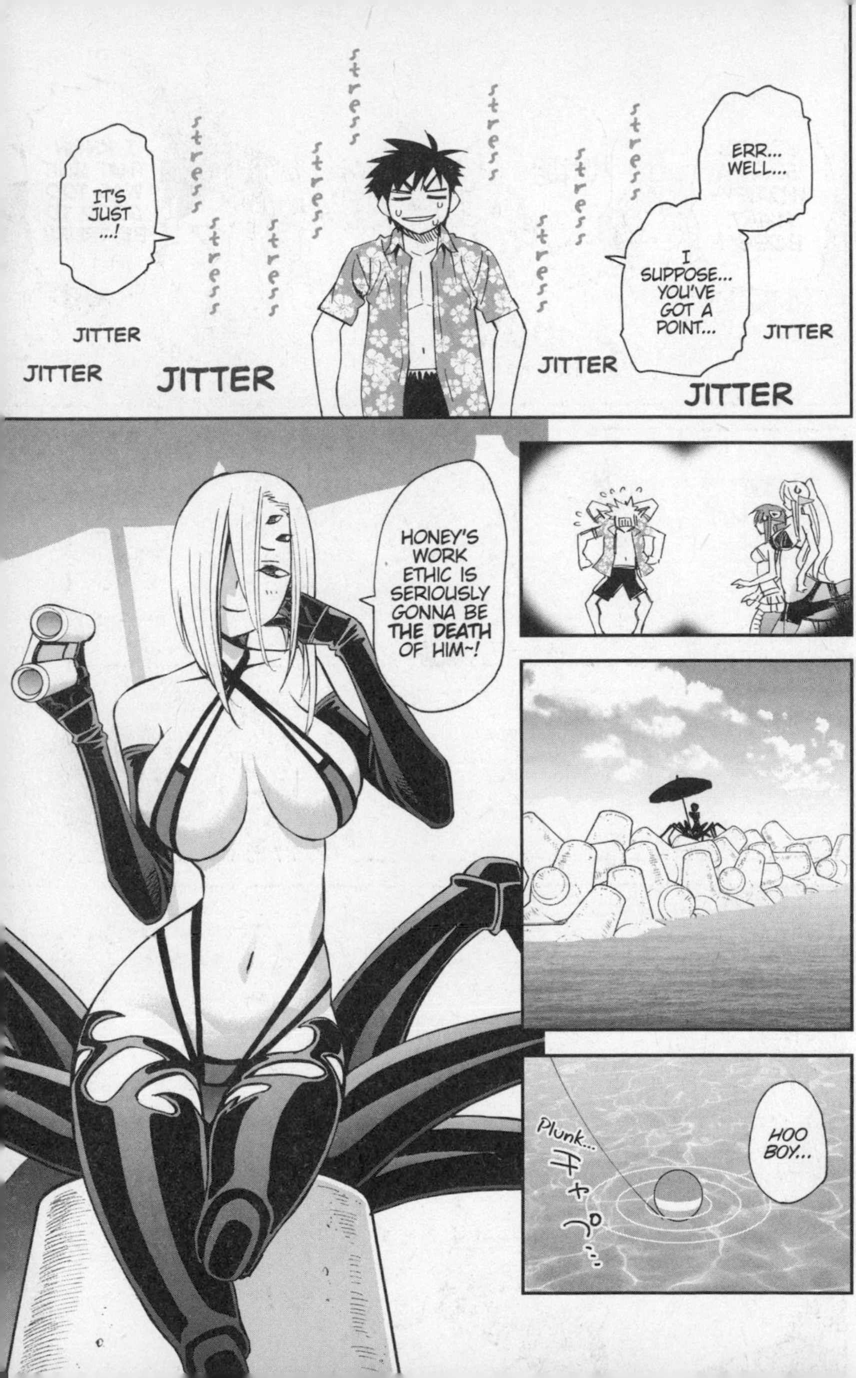
ERR... WELL...
I SUPPOSE... YOU'VE GOT A POINT...
stress
stress
stress
stress
stress
stress
stress
stress
JITTER
JITTER
JITTER
IT'S JUST ...!
JITTER
JITTER
JITTER
Plunk...
チャプ...
HOO BOY...
HONEY'S WORK ETHIC IS SERIOUSLY GONNA BE THE DEATH OF HIM~!

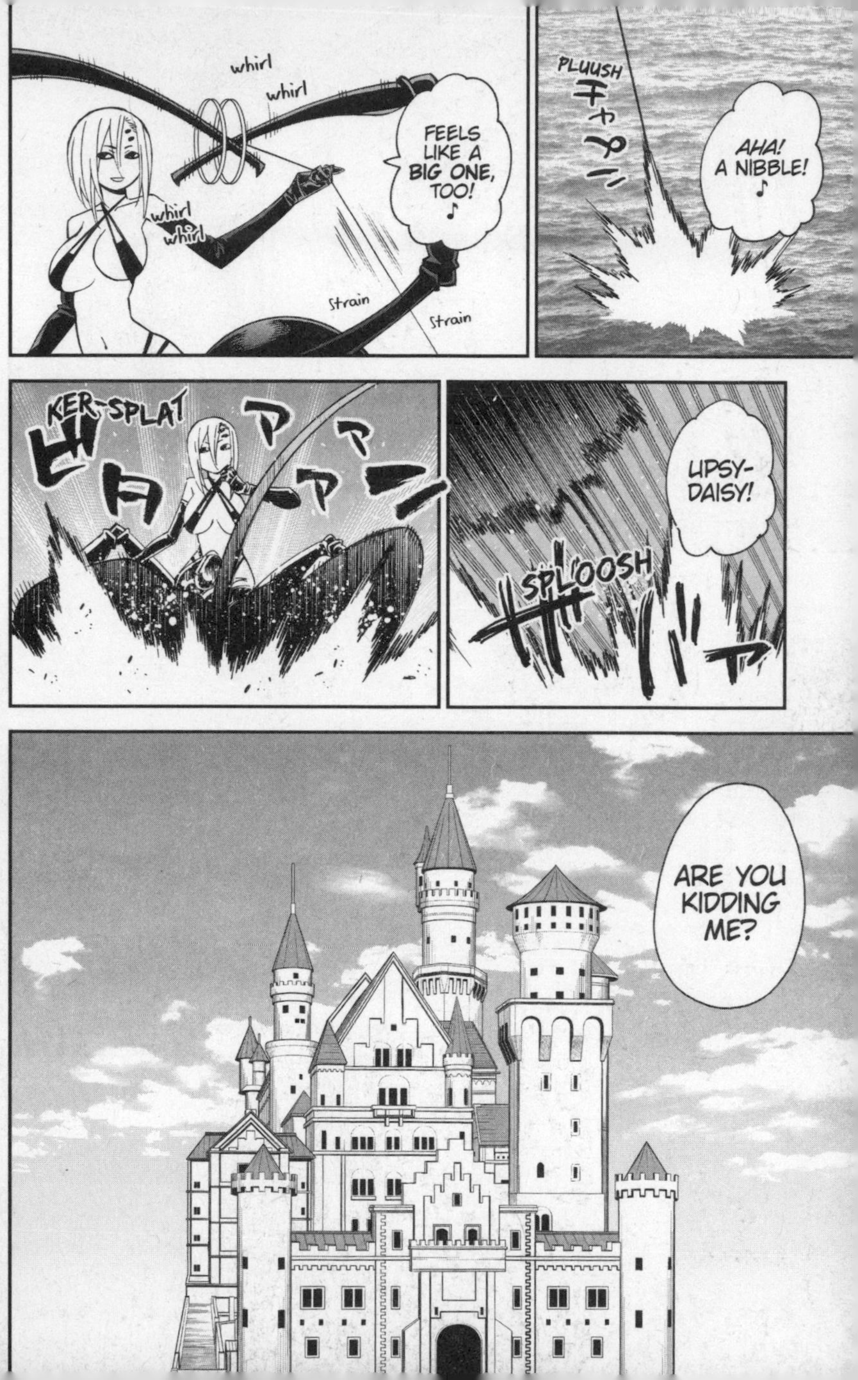
PLUUSH
AHA! A NIBBLE! ♪
whirl
whirl
FEELS LIKE A BIG ONE, TOO! ♪
whirl
whirl
Strain
Strain
UPSY-DAISY!
SPLOOSH
KER-SPLAT
ARE YOU KIDDING ME?

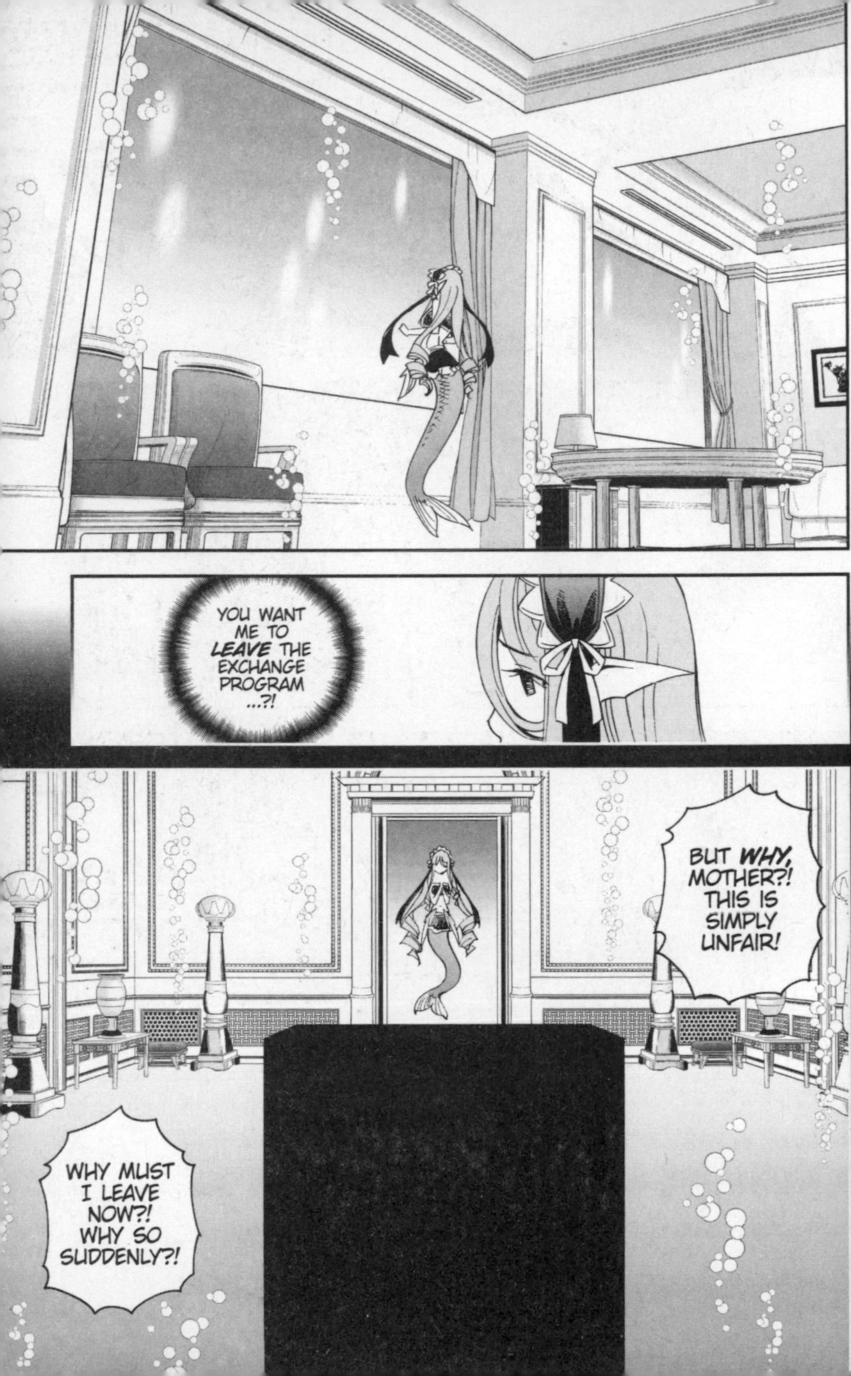
YOU WANT ME TO LEAVE THE EXCHANGE PROGRAM ...?!
BUT WHY, MOTHER?! THIS IS SIMPLY UNFAIR!
WHY MUST I LEAVE NOW?! WHY SO SUDDENLY?!

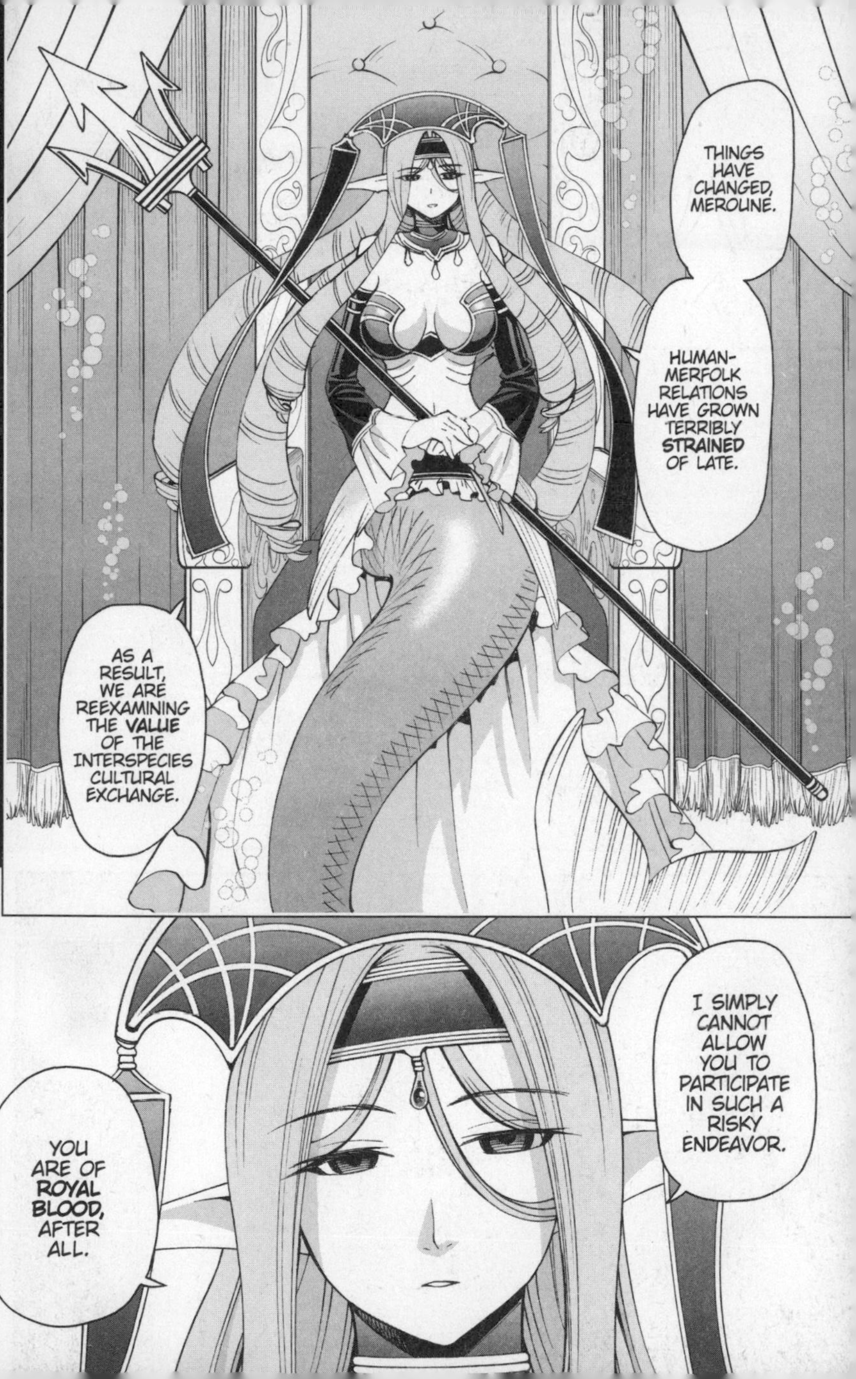
THINGS HAVE CHANGED, MEROUNE.
HUMAN-MERFOLK RELATIONS HAVE GROWN TERRIBLY STRAINED OF LATE.
AS A RESULT, WE ARE REEXAMINING THE VALUE OF THE INTERSPECIES CULTURAL EXCHANGE.
I SIMPLY CANNOT ALLOW YOU TO PARTICIPATE IN SUCH A RISKY ENDEAVOR.
YOU ARE OF ROYAL BLOOD, AFTER ALL.

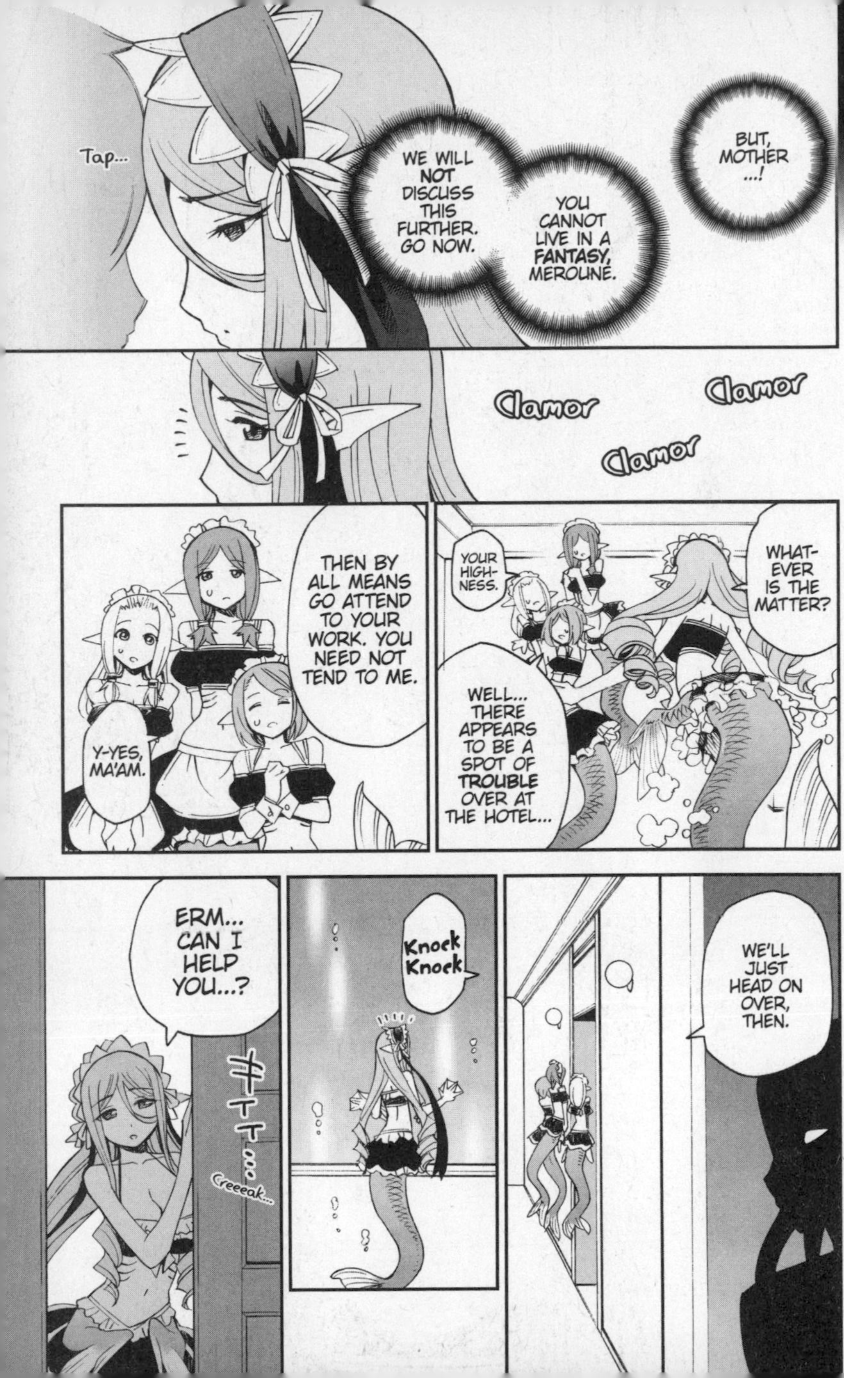
BUT, MOTHER ...!
YOU CANNOT LIVE IN A FANTASY, MEROUNE.
WE WILL NOT DISCUSS THIS FURTHER. GO NOW.
Tap...
Clamor
Clamor
Clamor
WHAT-EVER IS THE MATTER?
YOUR HIGH-NESS.
WELL... THERE APPEARS TO BE A SPOT OF TROUBLE OVER AT THE HOTEL...
THEN BY ALL MEANS GO ATTEND TO YOUR WORK. YOU NEED NOT TEND TO ME.
Y-YES, MA'AM.
WE'LL JUST HEAD ON OVER, THEN.
Knock Knock
ERM... CAN I HELP YOU...?
Creeeak...

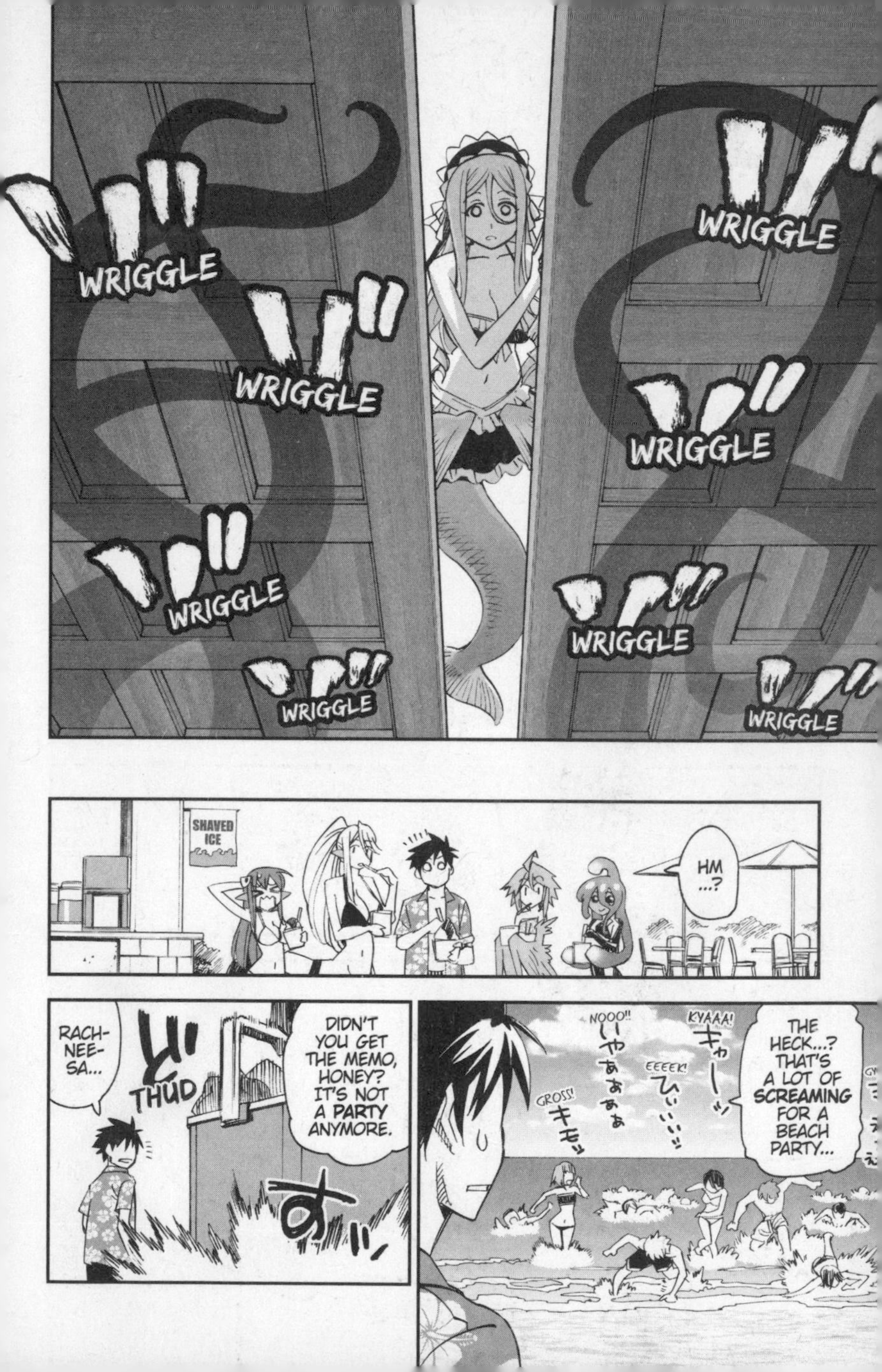
WRIGGLE
WRIGGLE
WRIGGLE
WRIGGLE
WRIGGLE
WRIGGLE
WRIGGLE
WRIGGLE
WRIGGLE
WRIGGLE
SHAVED ICE
HM ...?
THE HECK...? THAT'S A LOT OF SCREAMING FOR A BEACH PARTY...
KYAAA! キャーッ
NOOO!! いやあぁぁぁ
EEEEK! ひぃぃぃ
GROSS! キモッ
DIDN'T YOU GET THE MEMO, HONEY? IT'S NOT A PARTY ANYMORE.
THUD
RACH-NEE-SA...

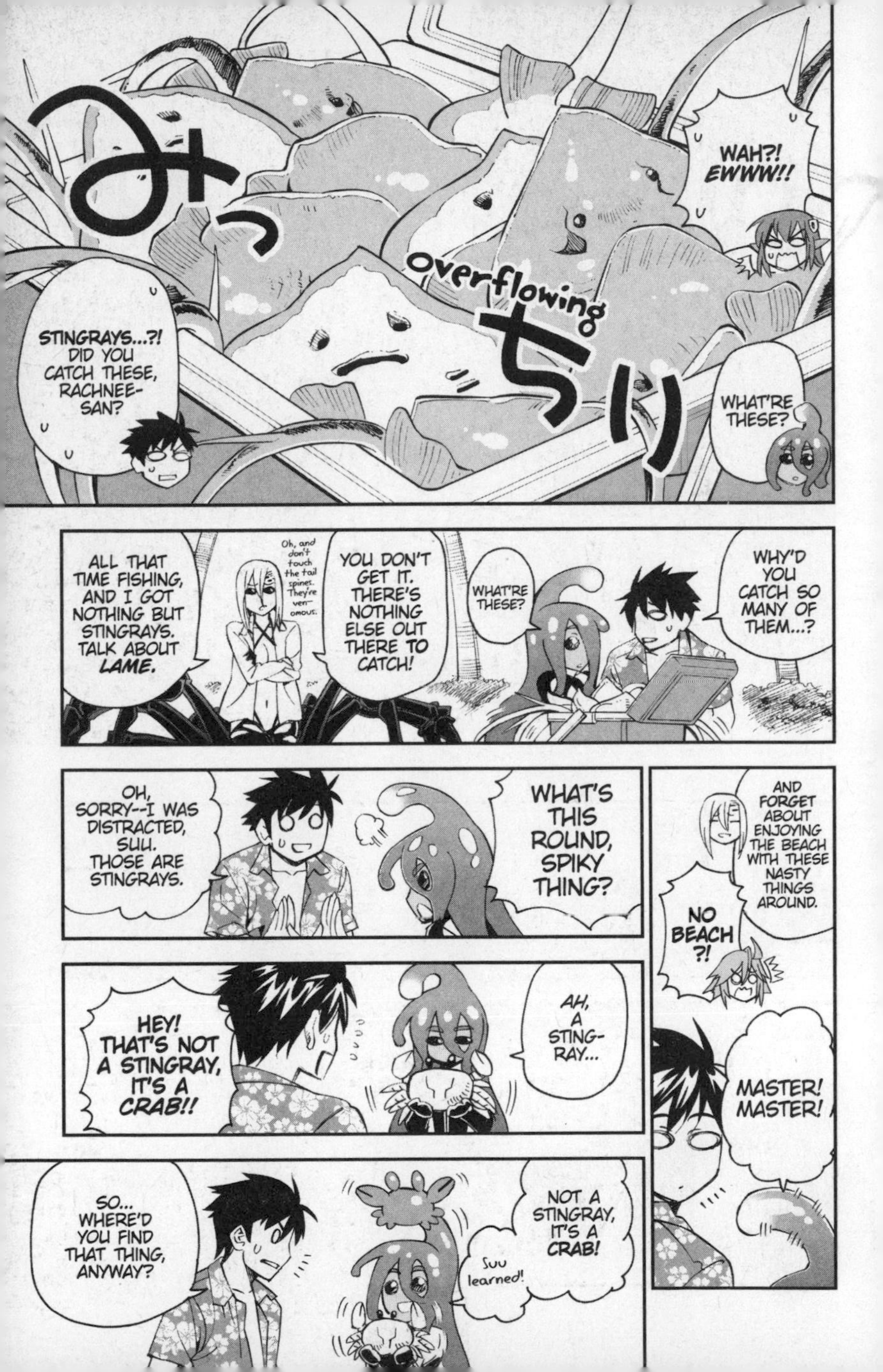
WAH?! EWWW!!
WHAT'RE THESE?
overflowing
みっ
ちり
STINGRAYS...?! DID YOU CATCH THESE, RACHNEE-SAN?
WHY'D YOU CATCH SO MANY OF THEM...?
WHAT'RE THESE?
YOU DON'T GET IT. THERE'S NOTHING ELSE OUT THERE TO CATCH!
Oh, and don't touch the tail spines. They're venomous.
ALL THAT TIME FISHING, AND I GOT NOTHING BUT STINGRAYS. TALK ABOUT LAME.
AND FORGET ABOUT ENJOYING THE BEACH WITH THESE NASTY THINGS AROUND.
NO BEACH?!
MASTER! MASTER!
WHAT'S THIS ROUND, SPIKY THING?
OH, SORRY--I WAS DISTRACTED, SUU. THOSE ARE STINGRAYS.
AH, A STING-RAY...
HEY! THAT'S NOT A STINGRAY, IT'S A CRAB!!
NOT A STINGRAY, IT'S A CRAB!
Suu learned!
SO... WHERE'D YOU FIND THAT THING, ANYWAY?

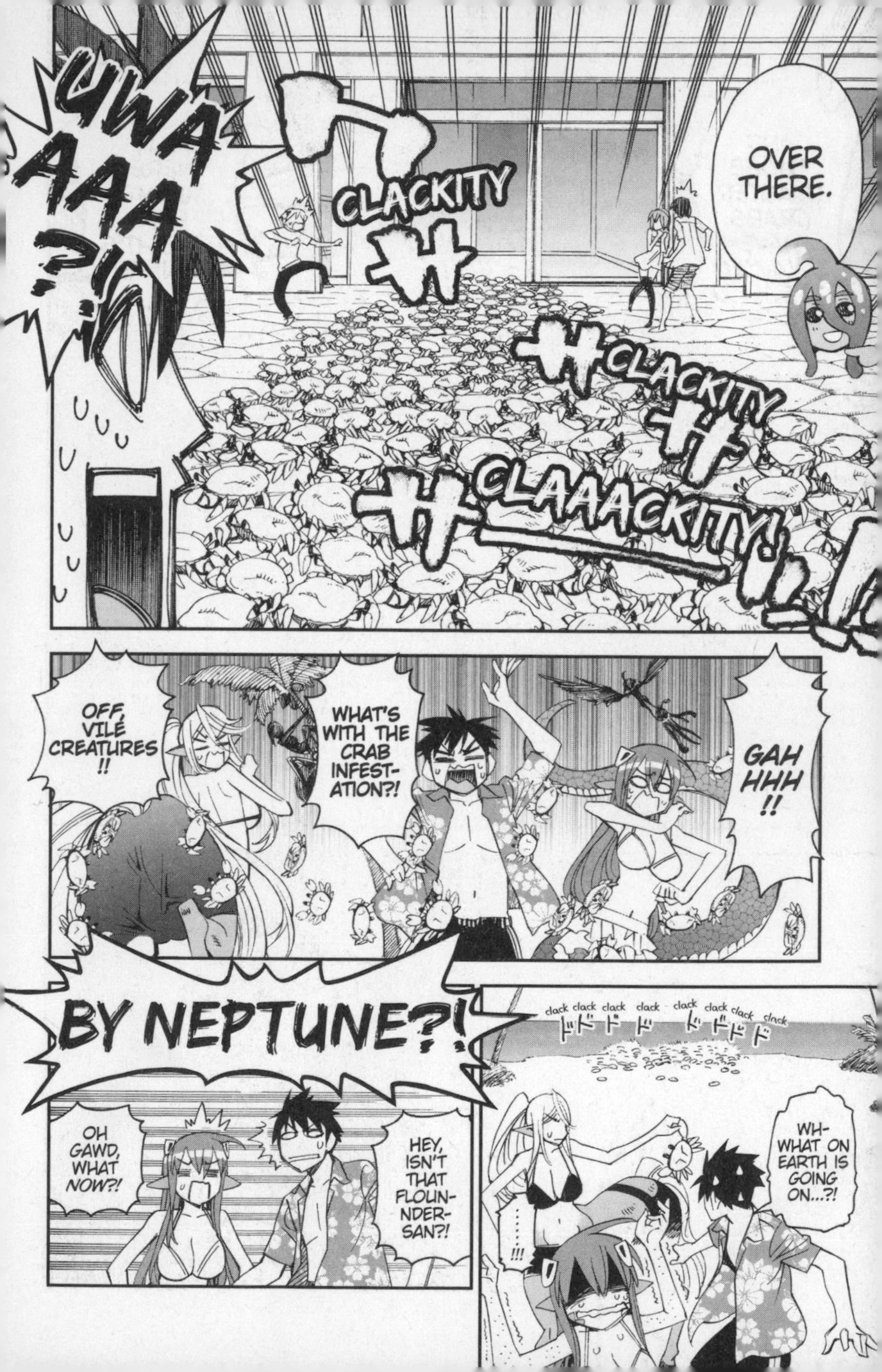
OVER THERE.
CLACKITY
CLACKITY
CLAAACKITY!!
CLACKITY
UWAAAA?!
GAHHHH!!
WHAT'S WITH THE CRAB INFESTATION?!
OFF, VILE CREATURES!!
clack clack clack clack clack clack clack clack
ドドドド ドドドド
WH-WHAT ON EARTH IS GOING ON...?!
......!!!
BY NEPTUNE?!
HEY, ISN'T THAT FLOUNNDER-SAN?!
OH GAWD, WHAT NOW?!

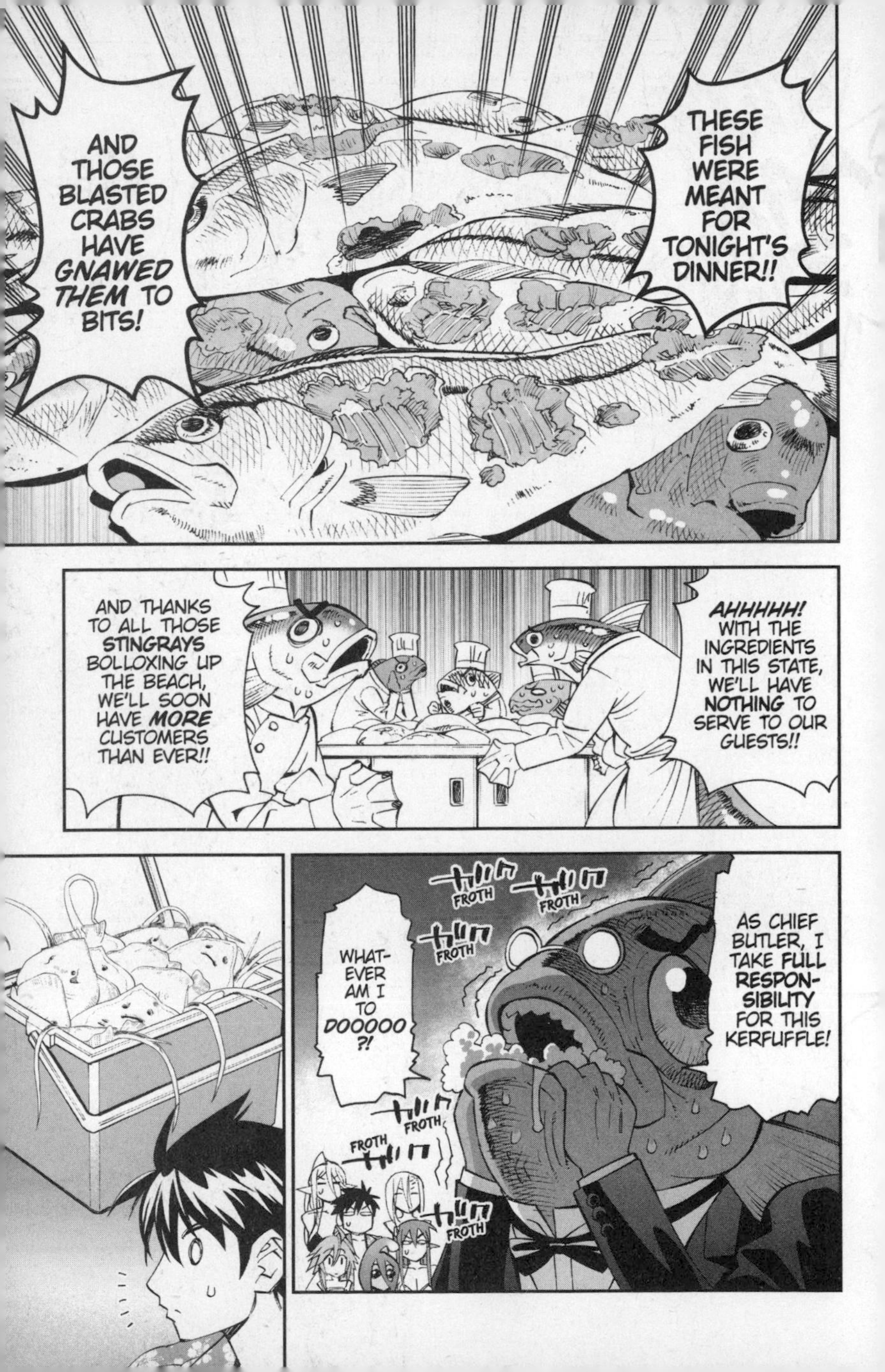
THESE FISH WERE MEANT FOR TONIGHT'S DINNER!!
AND THOSE BLASTED CRABS HAVE *GNAWED THEM* TO BITS!
AHHHHH! WITH THE INGREDIENTS IN THIS STATE, WE'LL HAVE **NOTHING** TO SERVE TO OUR GUESTS!!
AND THANKS TO ALL THOSE **STINGRAYS** BOLLOXING UP THE BEACH, WE'LL SOON HAVE ***MORE*** CUSTOMERS THAN EVER!!
FROTH
FROTH
FROTH
AS CHIEF BUTLER, I TAKE **FULL** RESPON-SIBILITY FOR THIS KERFUFFLE!
WHAT-EVER AM I TO *DOOOOO ?!*
FROTH
FROTH
FROTH

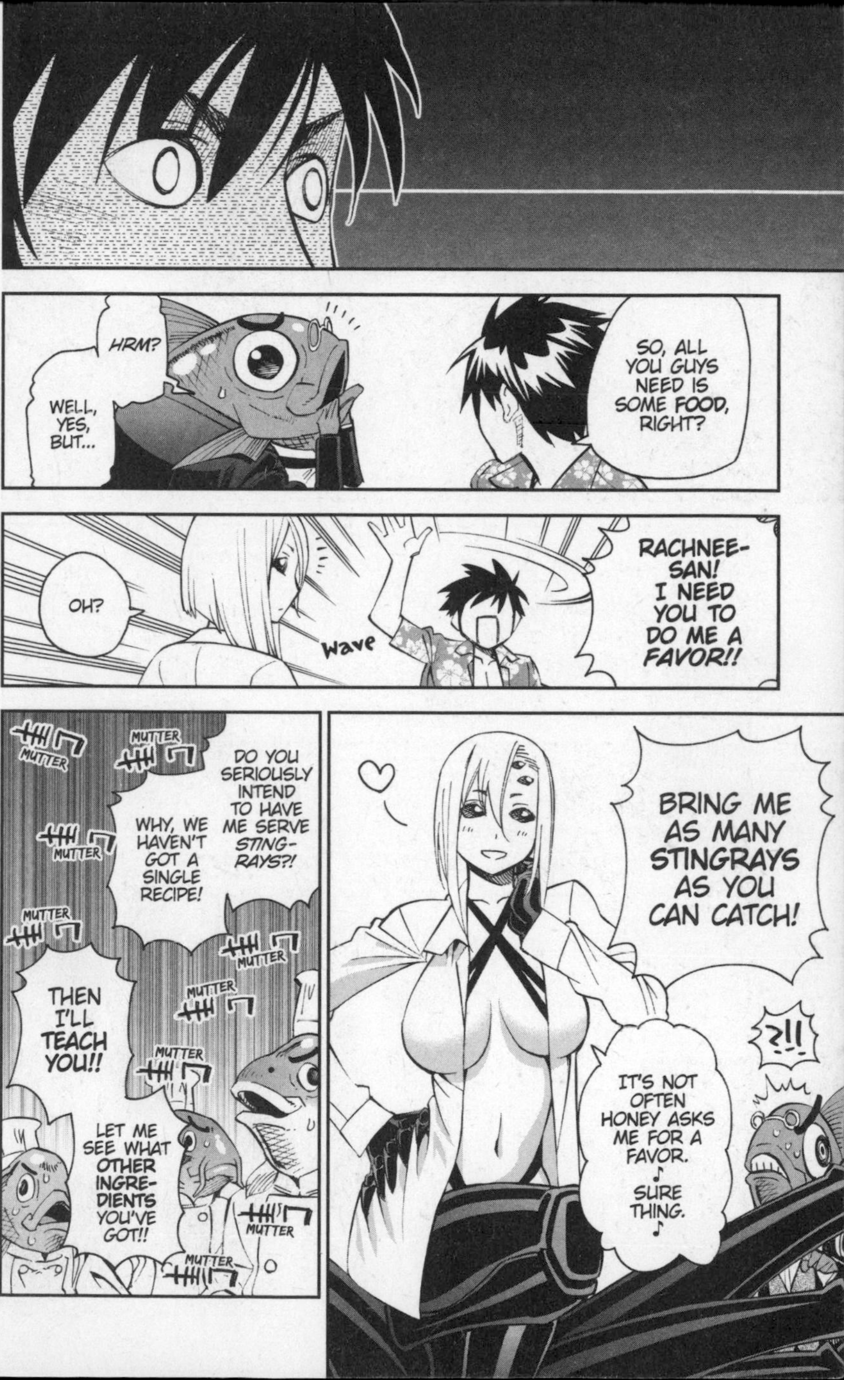
SO, ALL YOU GUYS NEED IS SOME FOOD, RIGHT?
HRM?
WELL, YES, BUT...
RACHNEE-SAN! I NEED YOU TO DO ME A FAVOR!!
Wave
OH?
BRING ME AS MANY STINGRAYS AS YOU CAN CATCH!
?!!
IT'S NOT OFTEN HONEY ASKS ME FOR A FAVOR. ♪ SURE THING. ♪
DO YOU SERIOUSLY INTEND TO HAVE ME SERVE STINGRAYS?!
WHY, WE HAVEN'T GOT A SINGLE RECIPE!
MUTTER
MUTTER
MUTTER
MUTTER
MUTTER
THEN I'LL TEACH YOU!!
MUTTER
MUTTER
LET ME SEE WHAT OTHER INGREDIENTS YOU'VE GOT!!
MUTTER
MUTTER

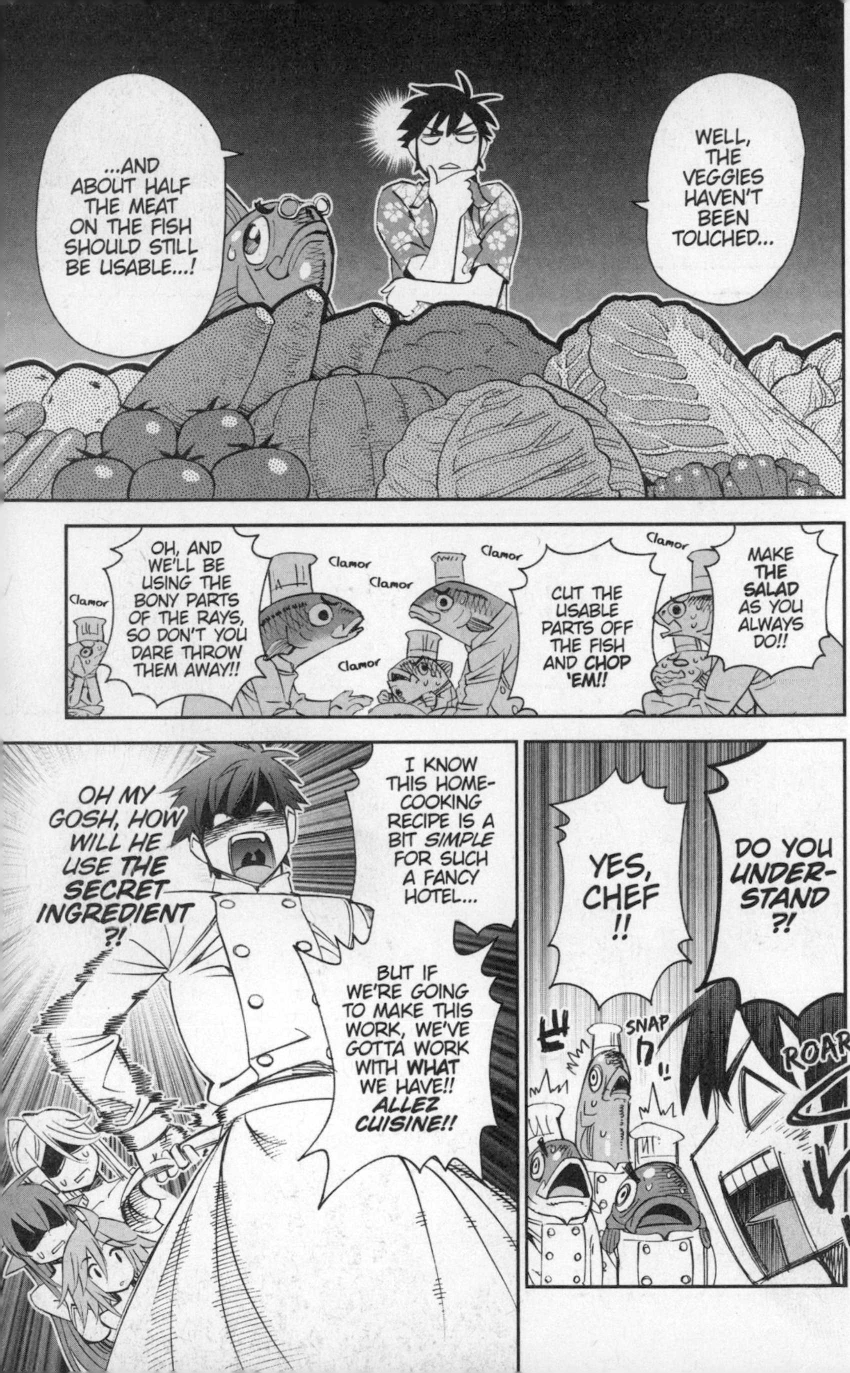
WELL, THE VEGGIES HAVEN'T BEEN TOUCHED...
...AND ABOUT HALF THE MEAT ON THE FISH SHOULD STILL BE USABLE...!
Clamor
MAKE THE SALAD AS YOU ALWAYS DO!!
Clamor
CUT THE USABLE PARTS OFF THE FISH AND CHOP 'EM!!
Clamor
Clamor
Clamor
OH, AND WE'LL BE USING THE BONY PARTS OF THE RAYS, SO DON'T YOU DARE THROW THEM AWAY!!
Clamor
DO YOU UNDERSTAND?!
ROAR!
YES, CHEF!!
SNAP
I KNOW THIS HOME-COOKING RECIPE IS A BIT SIMPLE FOR SUCH A FANCY HOTEL...
BUT IF WE'RE GOING TO MAKE THIS WORK, WE'VE GOTTA WORK WITH WHAT WE HAVE!! ALLEZ CUISINE!!
OH MY GOSH, HOW WILL HE USE THE SECRET INGREDIENT?!

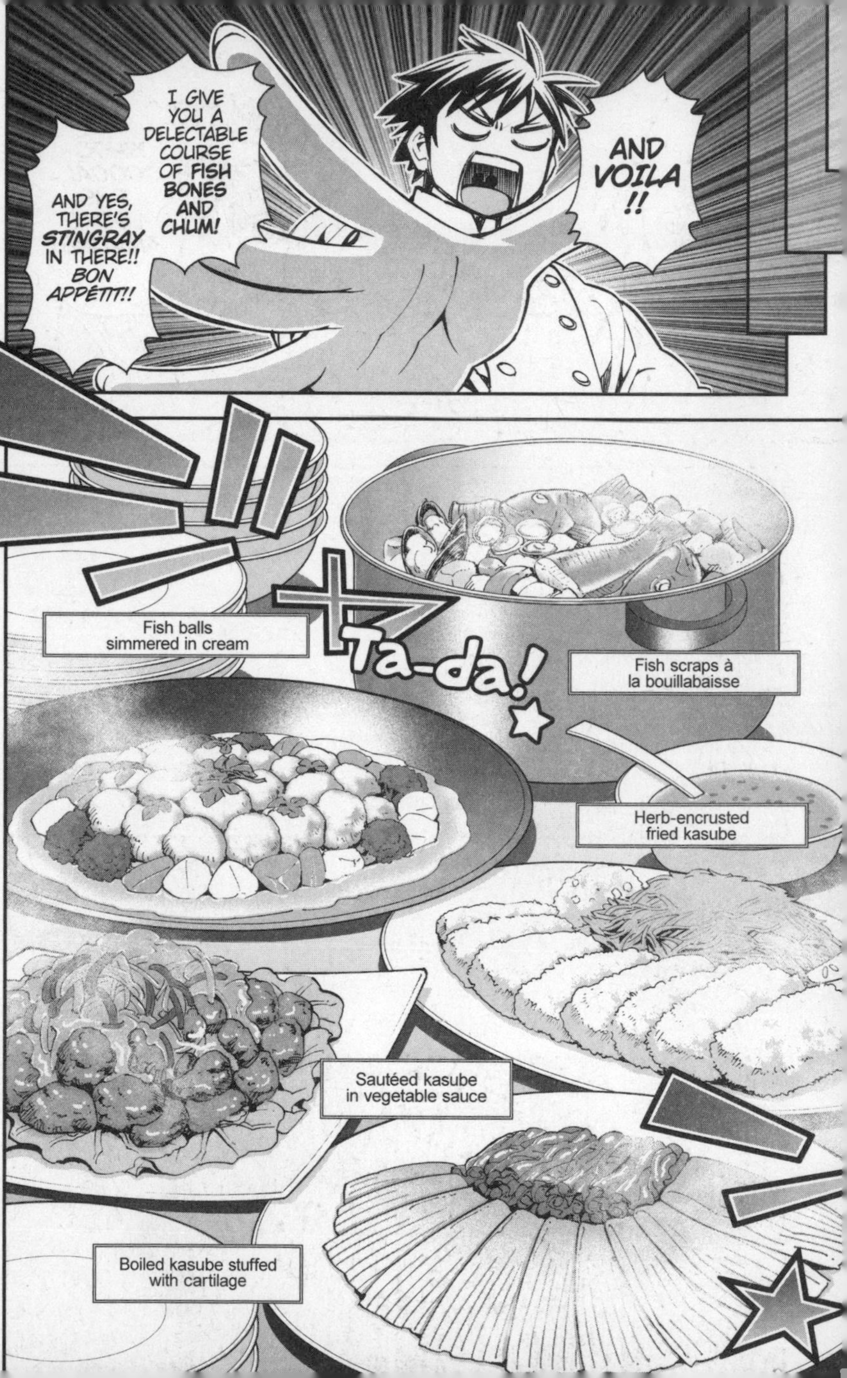
AND VOILA!!
I GIVE YOU A DELECTABLE COURSE OF FISH BONES AND CHUM!
AND YES, THERE'S STINGRAY IN THERE!! BON APPÉTIT!!
Ta-da!
Fish scraps à la bouillabaisse
Fish balls simmered in cream
Herb-encrusted fried kasube
Sautéed kasube in vegetable sauce
Boiled kasube stuffed with cartilage

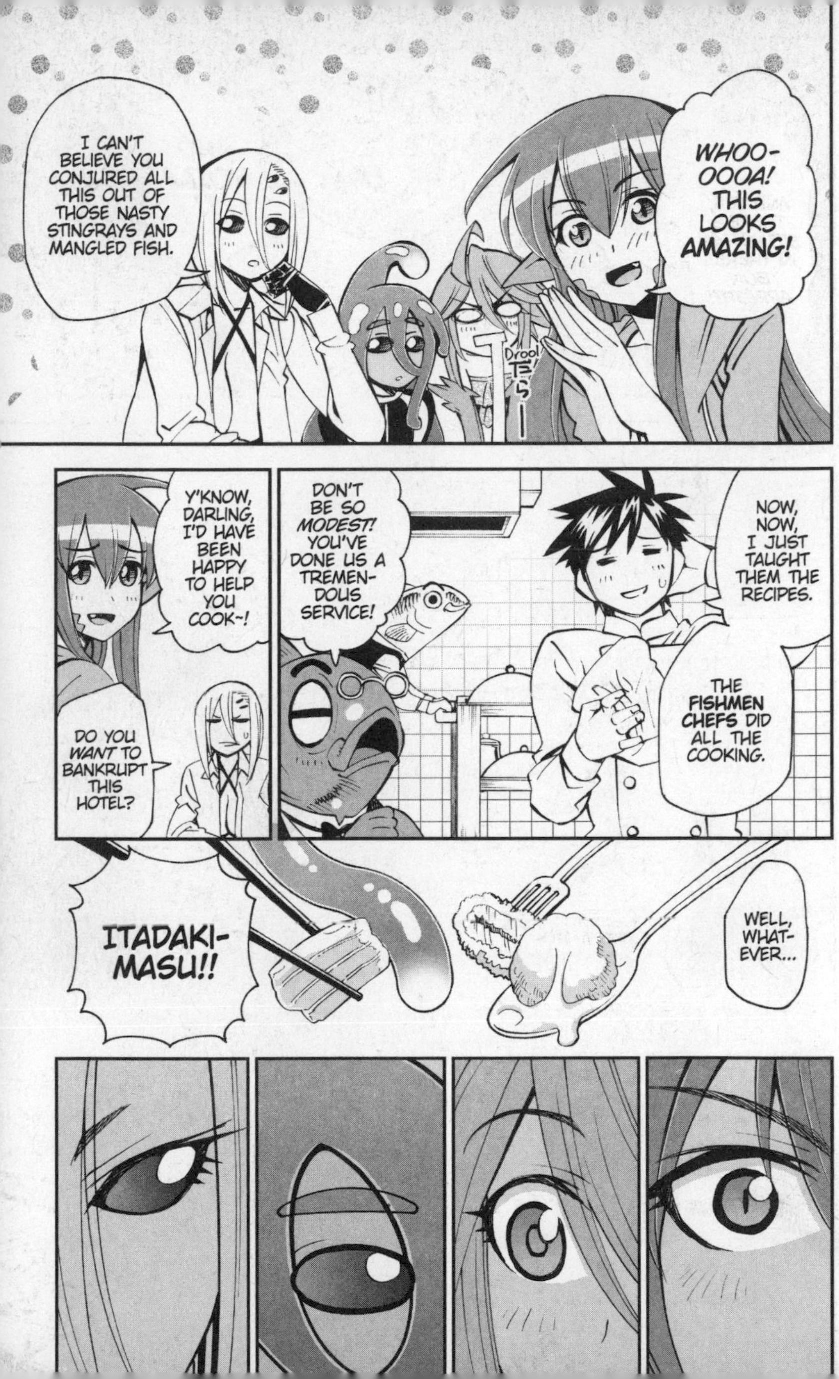
WHOO-OOOA! THIS LOOKS AMAZING!
Drool!
I CAN'T BELIEVE YOU CONJURED ALL THIS OUT OF THOSE NASTY STINGRAYS AND MANGLED FISH.
NOW, NOW, I JUST TAUGHT THEM THE RECIPES.
THE FISHMEN CHEFS DID ALL THE COOKING.
DON'T BE SO *MODEST*! YOU'VE DONE US A TREMEN-DOUS SERVICE!
Y'KNOW, DARLING, I'D HAVE BEEN HAPPY TO HELP YOU COOK~!
DO YOU *WANT* TO BANKRUPT THIS HOTEL?
WELL, WHAT-EVER...
ITADAKI-MASU!!

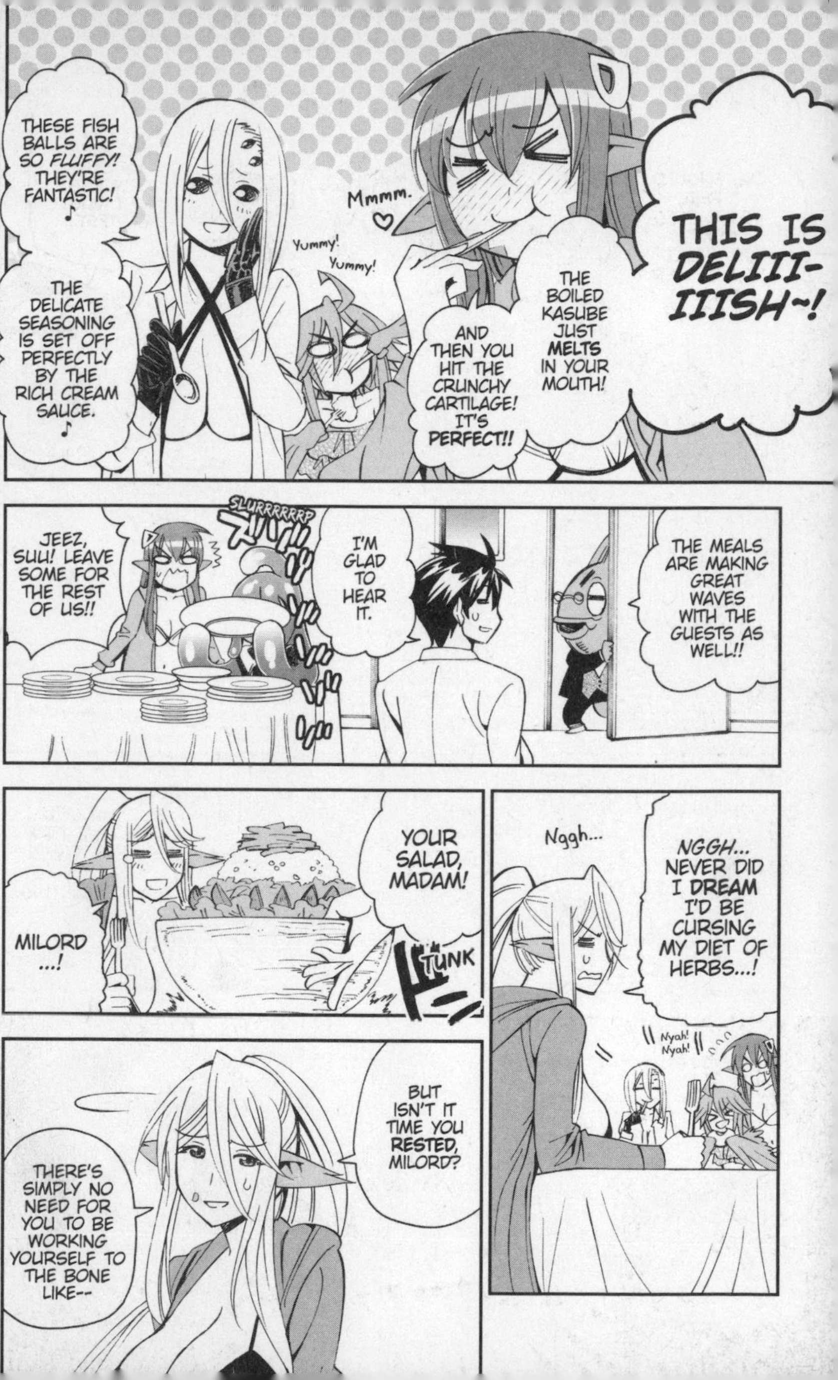
THIS IS DELIIII-IIISH~!
THE BOILED KASUBE JUST MELTS IN YOUR MOUTH!
AND THEN YOU HIT THE CRUNCHY CARTILAGE! IT'S PERFECT!!
Mmmm. ♡
Yummy! Yummy!
THESE FISH BALLS ARE SO FLUFFY! THEY'RE FANTASTIC! ♪
THE DELICATE SEASONING IS SET OFF PERFECTLY BY THE RICH CREAM SAUCE. ♪
THE MEALS ARE MAKING GREAT WAVES WITH THE GUESTS AS WELL!!
I'M GLAD TO HEAR IT.
SLURRRRRRP
JEEZ, SUU! LEAVE SOME FOR THE REST OF US!!
Nggh...
NGGH... NEVER DID I DREAM I'D BE CURSING MY DIET OF HERBS...!
Nyah! Nyah!
YOUR SALAD, MADAM!
TUNK
MILORD ...!
BUT ISN'T IT TIME YOU RESTED, MILORD?
THERE'S SIMPLY NO NEED FOR YOU TO BE WORKING YOURSELF TO THE BONE LIKE--

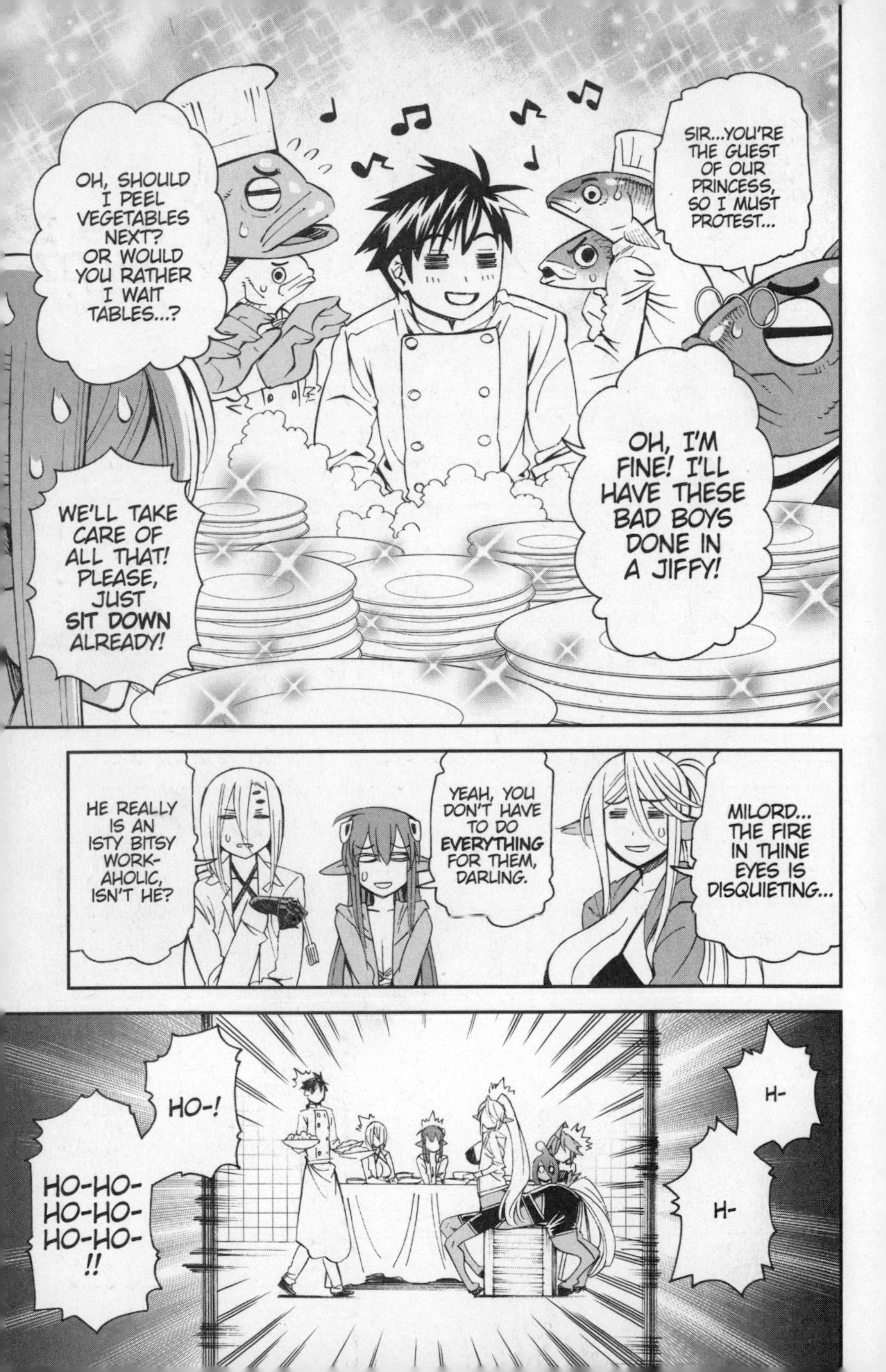
SIR...YOU'RE THE GUEST OF OUR PRINCESS, SO I MUST PROTEST...
OH, SHOULD I PEEL VEGETABLES NEXT? OR WOULD YOU RATHER I WAIT TABLES...?
WE'LL TAKE CARE OF ALL THAT! PLEASE, JUST SIT DOWN ALREADY!
OH, I'M FINE! I'LL HAVE THESE BAD BOYS DONE IN A JIFFY!
MILORD... THE FIRE IN THINE EYES IS DISQUIETING...
YEAH, YOU DON'T HAVE TO DO EVERYTHING FOR THEM, DARLING.
HE REALLY IS AN ISTY BITSY WORK-AHOLIC, ISN'T HE?
H-
H-
HO-!
HO-HO-HO-HO-HO-HO-!!

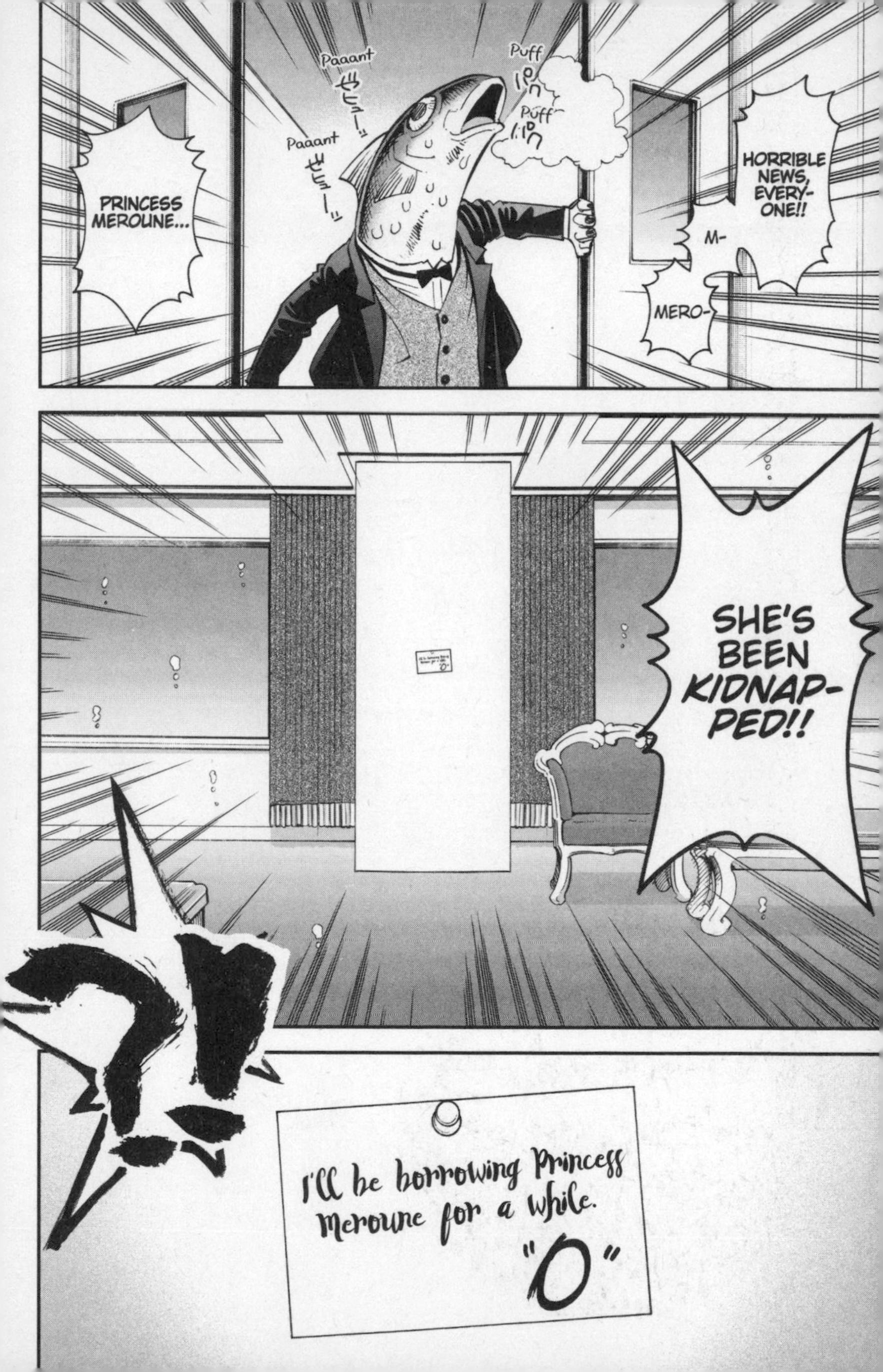
HORRIBLE NEWS, EVERYONE!!
M-
MERO-
Puff
Puff
Paaant
Paaant
PRINCESS MEROUNE...
SHE'S BEEN KIDNAPPED!!
?!
I'll be borrowing Princess Meroune for a while.
"O"

Monster Musume

Everyday Life with Monster Girls

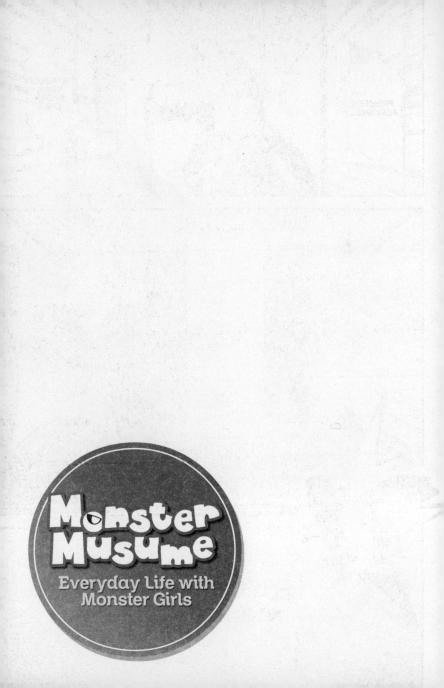

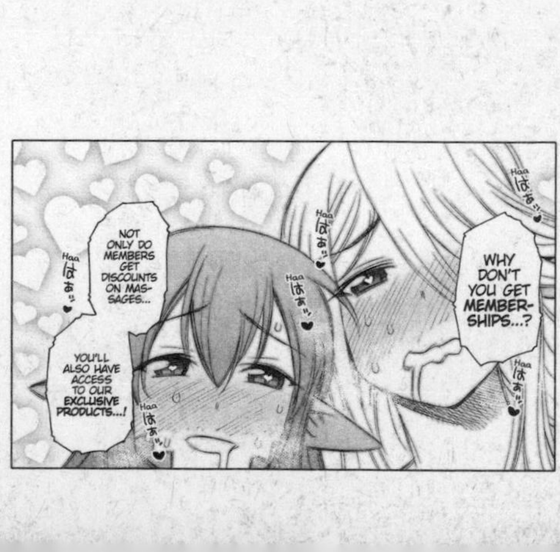
WHY DON'T YOU GET MEMBERSHIPS...?
NOT ONLY DO MEMBERS GET DISCOUNTS ON MASSAGES...
YOU'LL ALSO HAVE ACCESS TO OUR EXCLUSIVE PRODUCTS...!

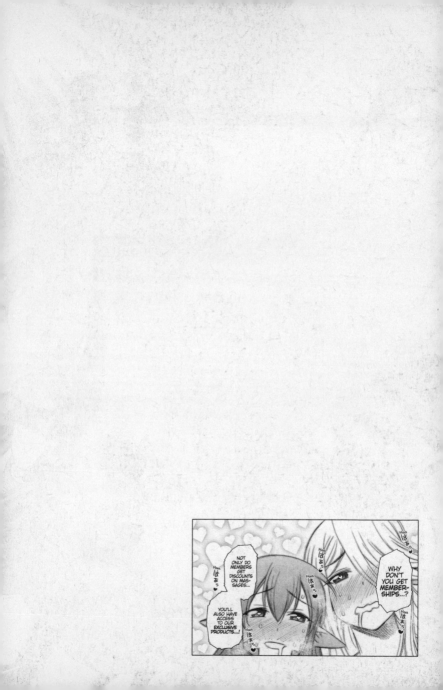

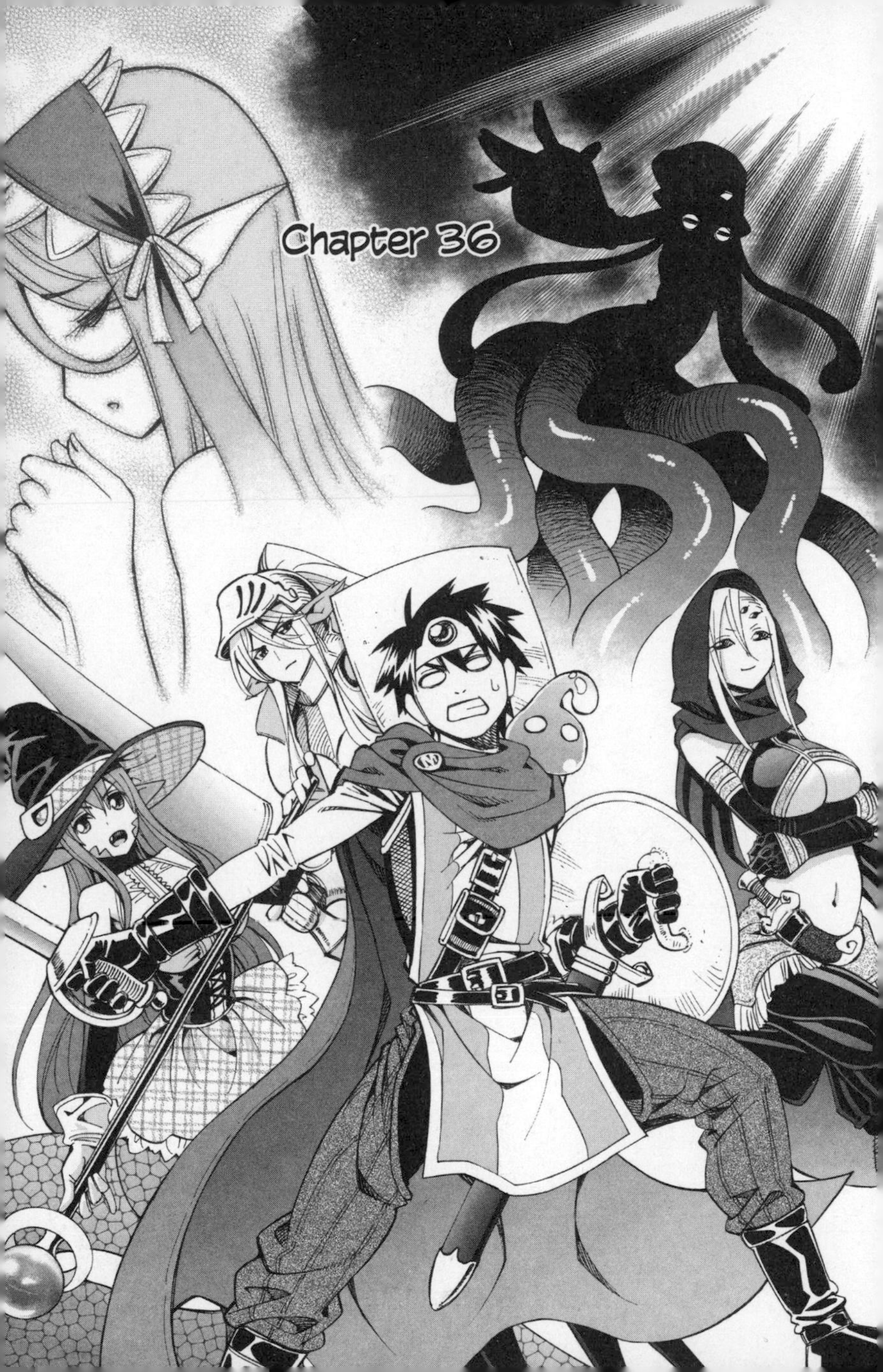
Chapter 36

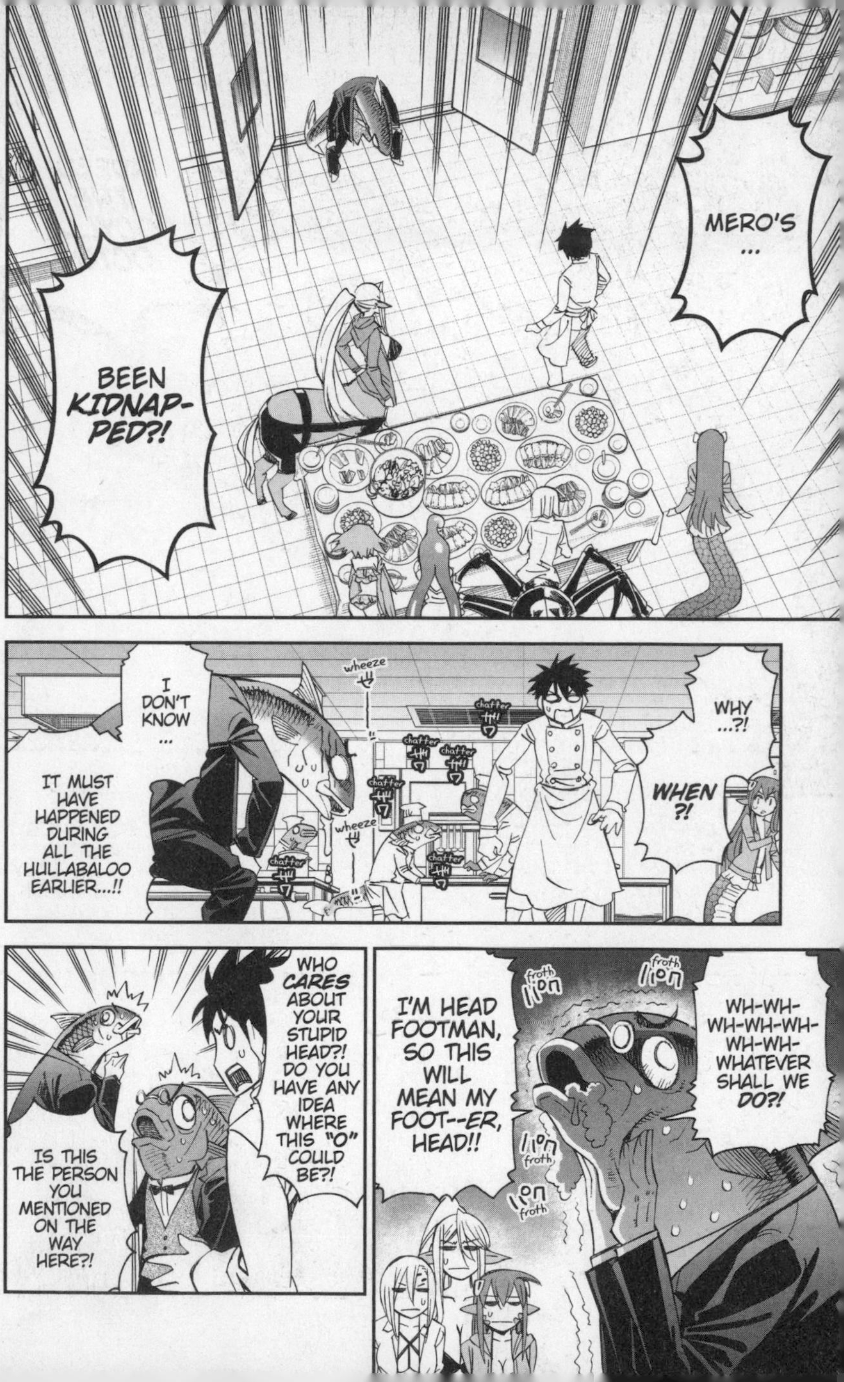
MERO'S ...
BEEN KIDNAPPED?!
WHY ...?!
WHEN ?!
chatter
chatter
chatter
wheeze
chatter
chatter
wheeze
I DON'T KNOW ...
IT MUST HAVE HAPPENED DURING ALL THE HULLABALOO EARLIER...!!
froth
froth
WH-WH-WH-WH-WH-WH-WH-WHATEVER SHALL WE DO?!
I'M HEAD FOOTMAN, SO THIS WILL MEAN MY FOOT--ER, HEAD!!
froth
froth
WHO CARES ABOUT YOUR STUPID HEAD?! DO YOU HAVE ANY IDEA WHERE THIS "O" COULD BE?!
IS THIS THE PERSON YOU MENTIONED ON THE WAY HERE?!

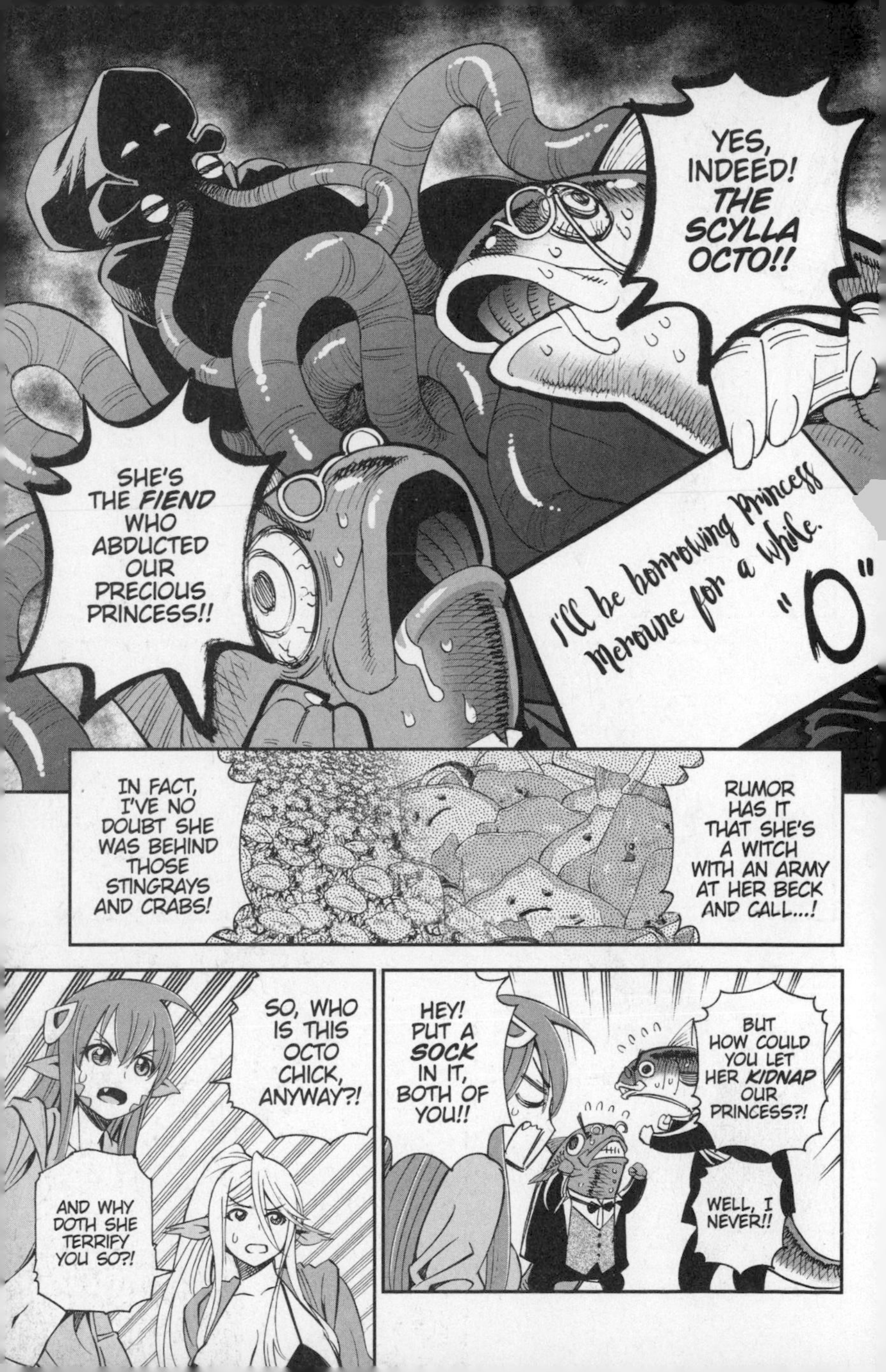
YES, INDEED! THE SCYLLA OCTO!!
I'll be borrowing Princess Meroune for a while. "O"
SHE'S THE FIEND WHO ABDUCTED OUR PRECIOUS PRINCESS!!
RUMOR HAS IT THAT SHE'S A WITCH WITH AN ARMY AT HER BECK AND CALL...!
IN FACT, I'VE NO DOUBT SHE WAS BEHIND THOSE STINGRAYS AND CRABS!
BUT HOW COULD YOU LET HER KIDNAP OUR PRINCESS?!
HEY! PUT A SOCK IN IT, BOTH OF YOU!!
WELL, I NEVER!!
SO, WHO IS THIS OCTO CHICK, ANYWAY?!
AND WHY DOTH SHE TERRIFY YOU SO?!

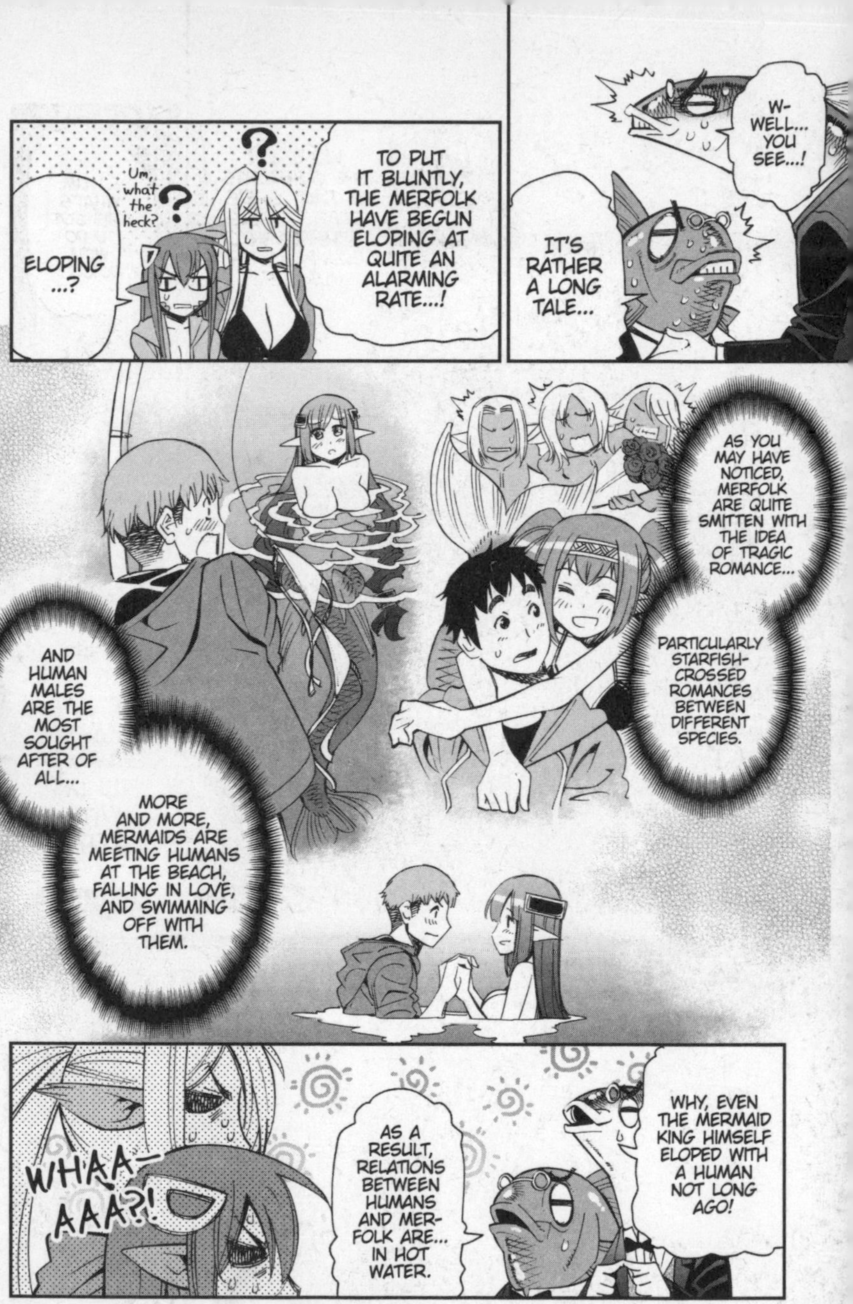
W-WELL... YOU SEE...!
IT'S RATHER A LONG TALE...
TO PUT IT BLUNTLY, THE MERFOLK HAVE BEGUN ELOPING AT QUITE AN ALARMING RATE...!
Um, what the heck?
ELOPING ...?
AS YOU MAY HAVE NOTICED, MERFOLK ARE QUITE SMITTEN WITH THE IDEA OF TRAGIC ROMANCE...
PARTICULARLY STARFISH-CROSSED ROMANCES BETWEEN DIFFERENT SPECIES.
AND HUMAN MALES ARE THE MOST SOUGHT AFTER OF ALL...
MORE AND MORE, MERMAIDS ARE MEETING HUMANS AT THE BEACH, FALLING IN LOVE, AND SWIMMING OFF WITH THEM.
WHY, EVEN THE MERMAID KING HIMSELF ELOPED WITH A HUMAN NOT LONG AGO!
AS A RESULT, RELATIONS BETWEEN HUMANS AND MER-FOLK ARE... IN HOT WATER.
WHAA—AAA?!

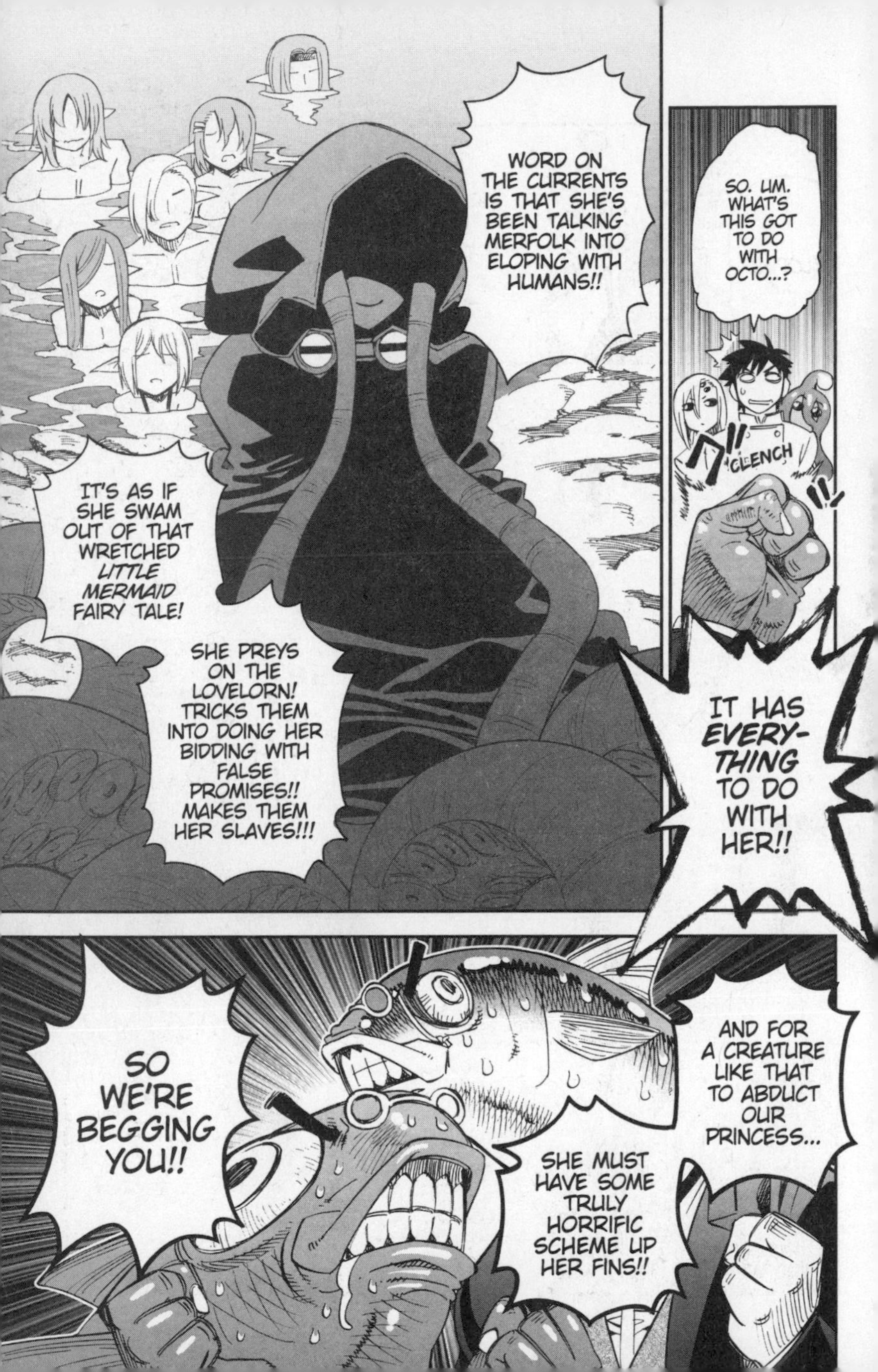
SO. UM. WHAT'S THIS GOT TO DO WITH OCTO...?
CLENCH
IT HAS EVERYTHING TO DO WITH HER!!
WORD ON THE CURRENTS IS THAT SHE'S BEEN TALKING MERFOLK INTO ELOPING WITH HUMANS!!
IT'S AS IF SHE SWAM OUT OF THAT WRETCHED *LITTLE MERMAID* FAIRY TALE!
SHE PREYS ON THE LOVELORN! TRICKS THEM INTO DOING HER BIDDING WITH FALSE PROMISES!! MAKES THEM HER SLAVES!!!
AND FOR A CREATURE LIKE THAT TO ABDUCT OUR PRINCESS...
SHE MUST HAVE SOME TRULY HORRIFIC SCHEME UP HER FINS!!
SO WE'RE BEGGING YOU!!

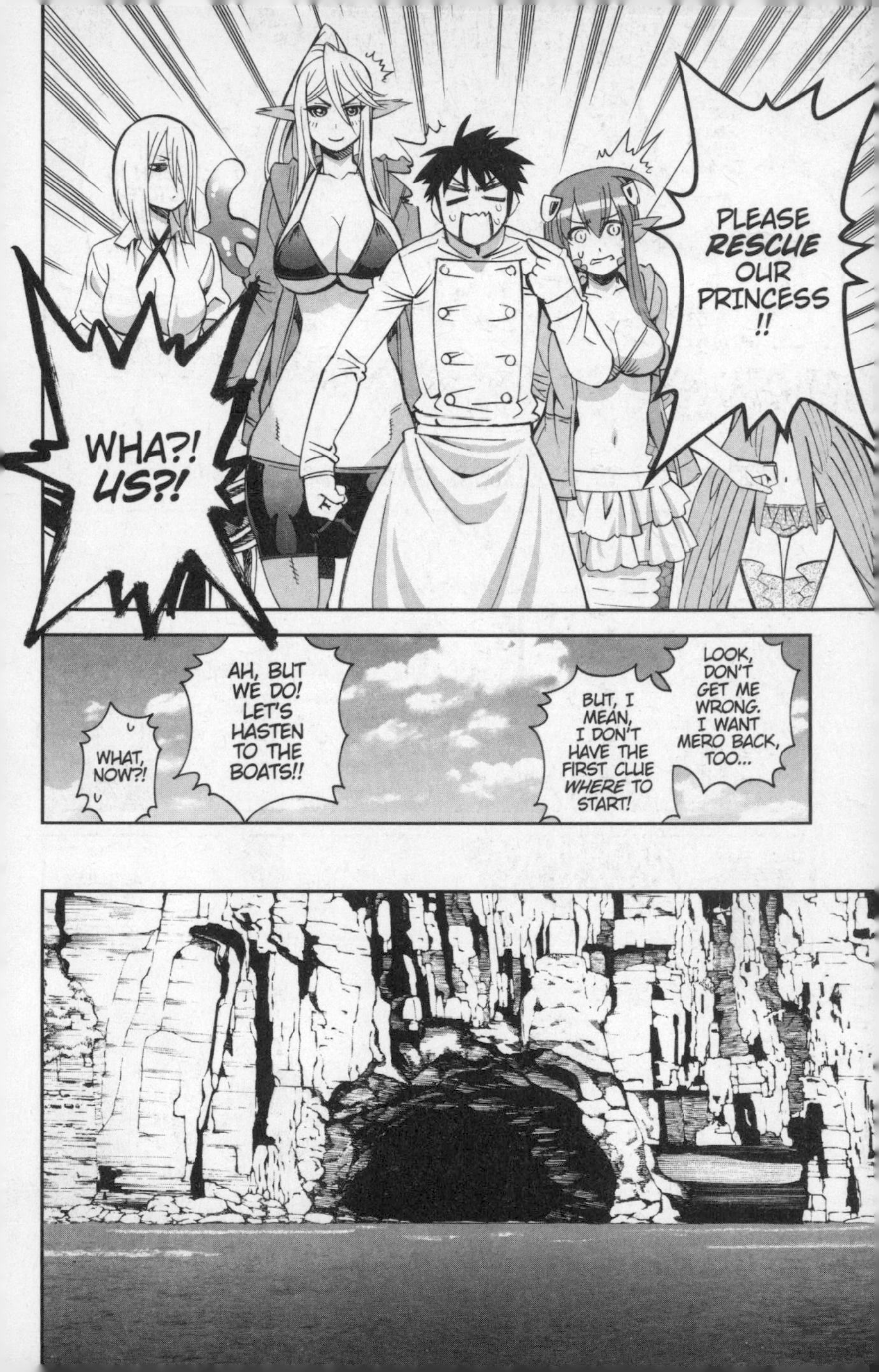
PLEASE RESCUE OUR PRINCESS!!
WHA?! US?!
LOOK, DON'T GET ME WRONG. I WANT MERO BACK, TOO...
BUT, I MEAN, I DON'T HAVE THE FIRST CLUE WHERE TO START!
AH, BUT WE DO! LET'S HASTEN TO THE BOATS!!
WHAT, NOW?!

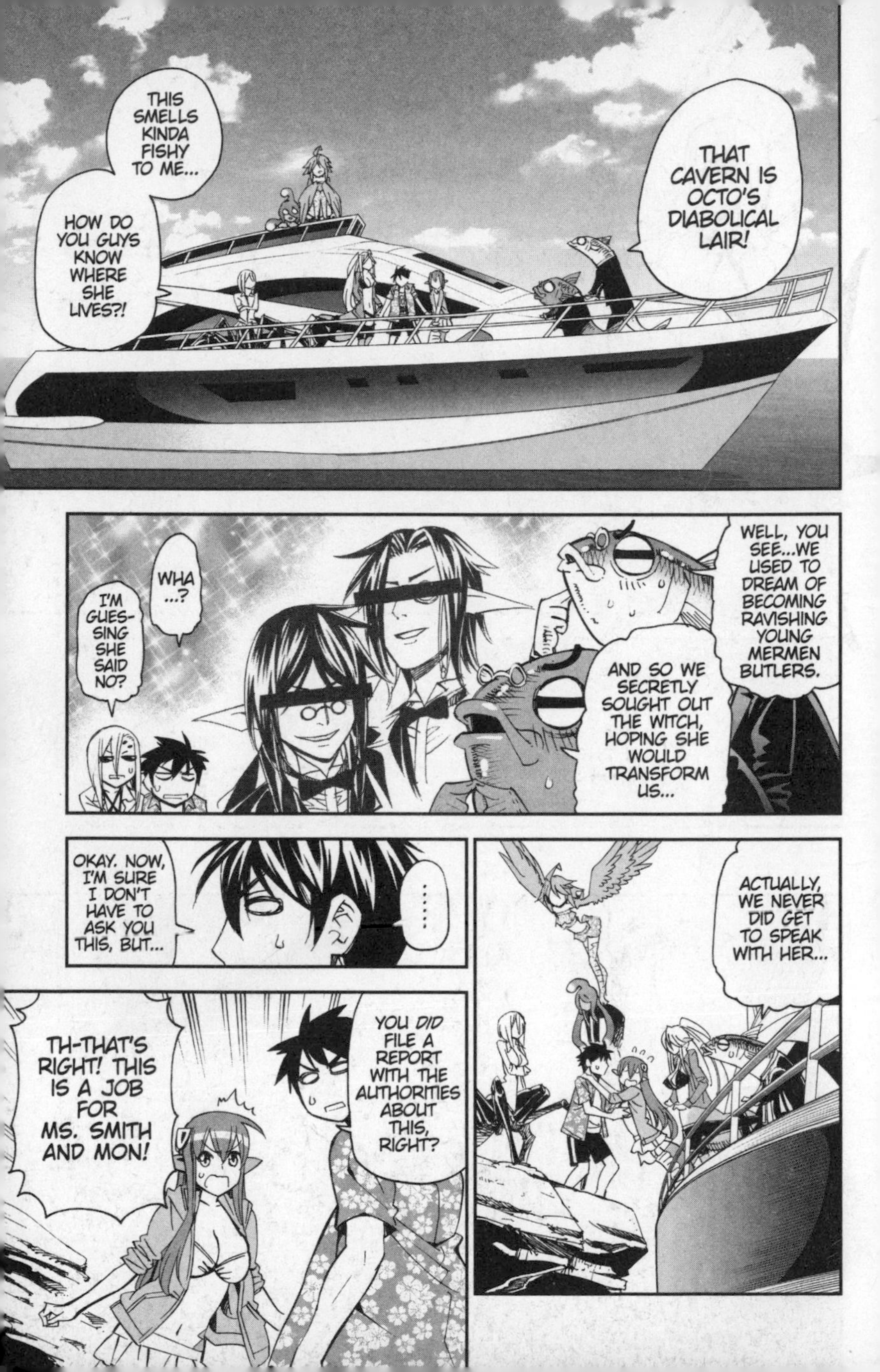
THAT CAVERN IS OCTO'S DIABOLICAL LAIR!
THIS SMELLS KINDA FISHY TO ME...
HOW DO YOU GUYS KNOW WHERE SHE LIVES?!
WELL, YOU SEE...WE USED TO DREAM OF BECOMING RAVISHING YOUNG MERMEN BUTLERS.
AND SO WE SECRETLY SOUGHT OUT THE WITCH, HOPING SHE WOULD TRANSFORM US...
WHA...?
I'M GUES-SING SHE SAID NO?
ACTUALLY, WE NEVER DID GET TO SPEAK WITH HER...
OKAY. NOW, I'M SURE I DON'T HAVE TO ASK YOU THIS, BUT...
......
YOU *DID* FILE A REPORT WITH THE AUTHORITIES ABOUT THIS, RIGHT?
TH-THAT'S RIGHT! THIS IS A JOB FOR MS. SMITH AND MON!

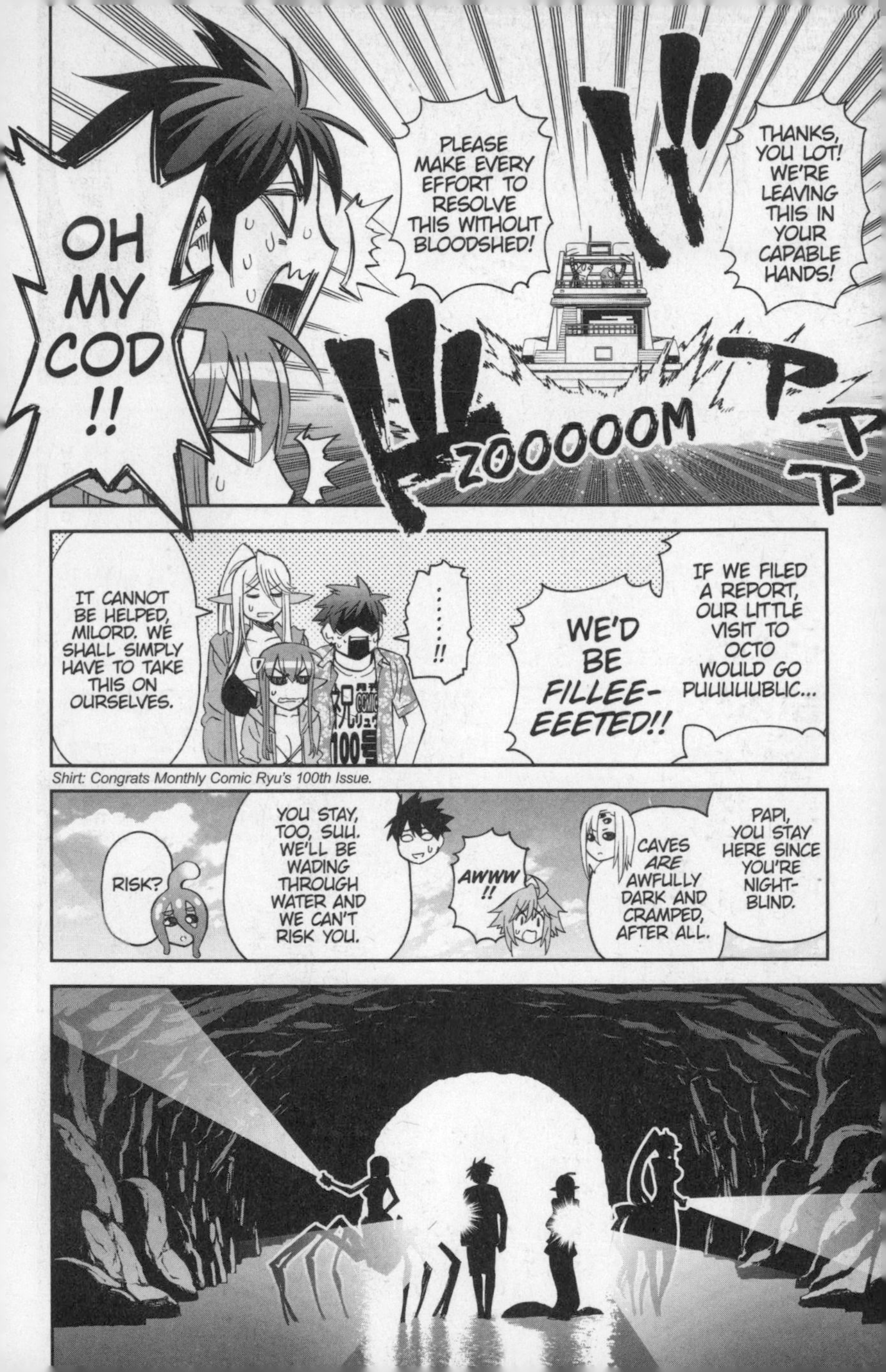
THANKS, YOU LOT! WE'RE LEAVING THIS IN YOUR CAPABLE HANDS!
P P P
ZOOOOOM
PLEASE MAKE EVERY EFFORT TO RESOLVE THIS WITHOUT BLOODSHED!
OH MY COD!!
IF WE FILED A REPORT, OUR LITTLE VISIT TO OCTO WOULD GO PUUUUUBLIC...
WE'D BE FILLEE-EEETED!!
......!!
IT CANNOT BE HELPED, MILORD. WE SHALL SIMPLY HAVE TO TAKE THIS ON OURSELVES.
PAPI, YOU STAY HERE SINCE YOU'RE NIGHT-BLIND.
CAVES ARE AWFULLY DARK AND CRAMPED, AFTER ALL.
AWWW!!
YOU STAY, TOO, SUU. WE'LL BE WADING THROUGH WATER AND WE CAN'T RISK YOU.
RISK?
Shirt: Congrats Monthly Comic Ryu's 100th Issue.

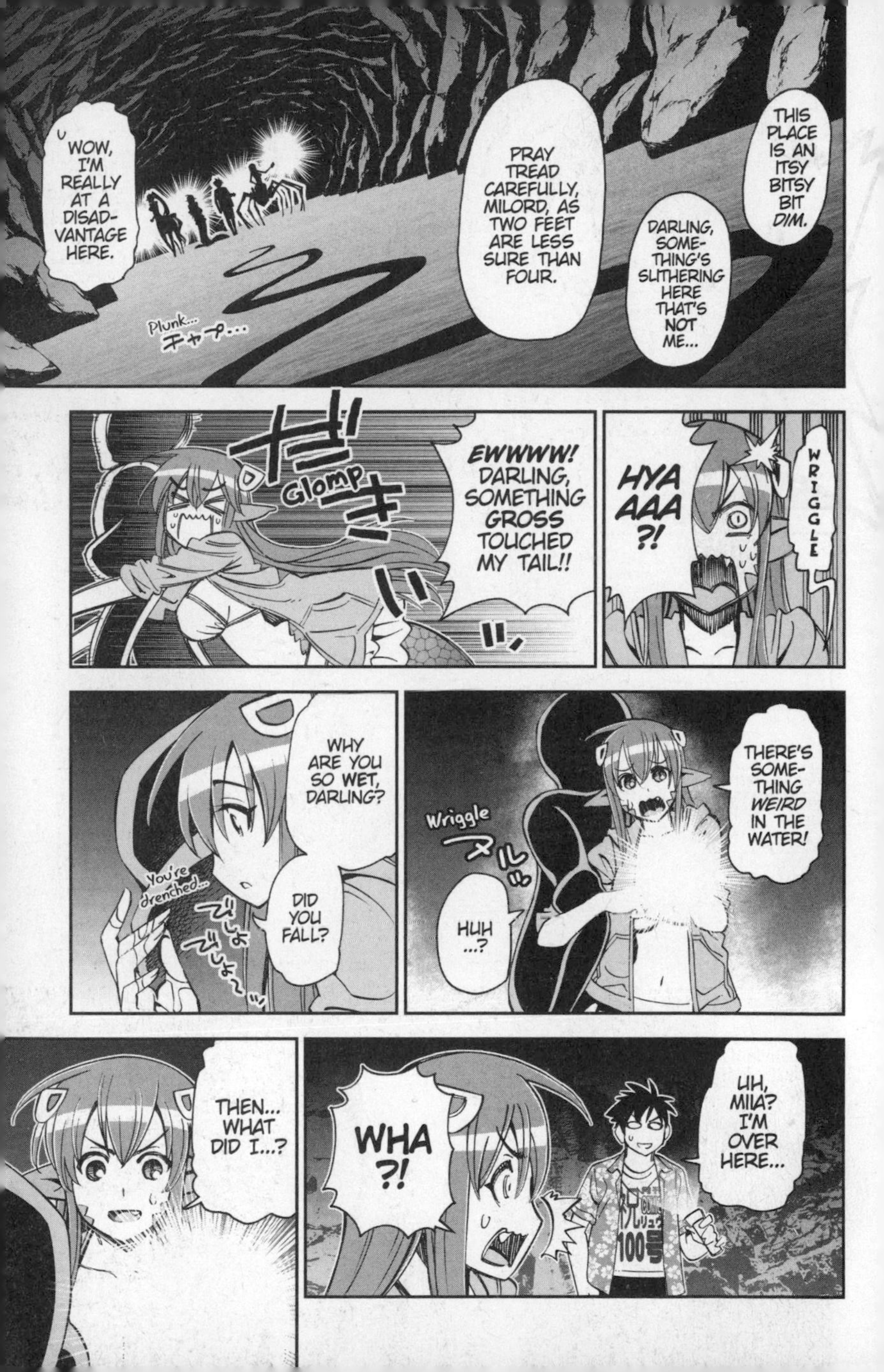
THIS PLACE IS AN ITSY BITSY BIT *DIM.*
DARLING, SOMETHING'S SLITHERING HERE THAT'S NOT ME...
PRAY TREAD CAREFULLY, MILORD, AS TWO FEET ARE LESS SURE THAN FOUR.
WOW, I'M REALLY AT A DISADVANTAGE HERE.
Plunk... チャプ...
WRIGGLE
HYAAAA?!
EWWWW! DARLING, SOMETHING GROSS TOUCHED MY TAIL!!
Glomp
THERE'S SOMETHING *WEIRD* IN THE WATER!
Wriggle ヌル
HUH...?
WHY ARE YOU SO WET, DARLING?
DID YOU FALL?
You're drenched... びしょびしょ~ッ
UH, MIIA? I'M OVER HERE...
WHA?!
THEN... WHAT DID I...?

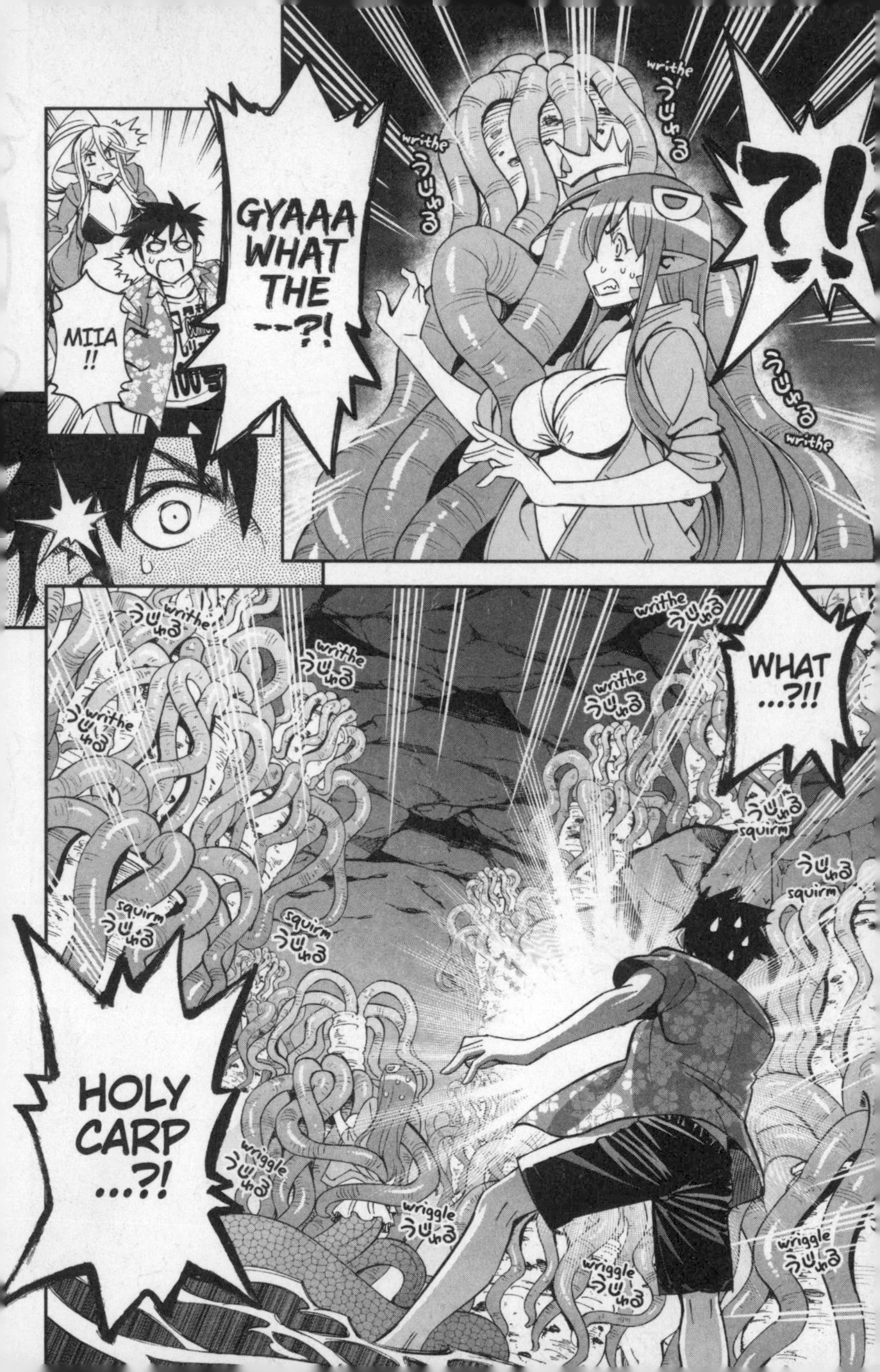
writhe うじゅる
writhe うじゅる
?!
うじゅる writhe
GYAAA WHAT THE --?!
MIIA!!
WHAT ...?!!
writhe うじゅる
writhe うじゅる
writhe うじゅる
うじゅる squirm
うじゅる squirm
writhe うじゅる
writhe うじゅる
squirm うじゅる
squirm うじゅる
wriggle うじゅる
wriggle うじゅる
wriggle うじゅる
wriggle うじゅる
HOLY CARP ...?!

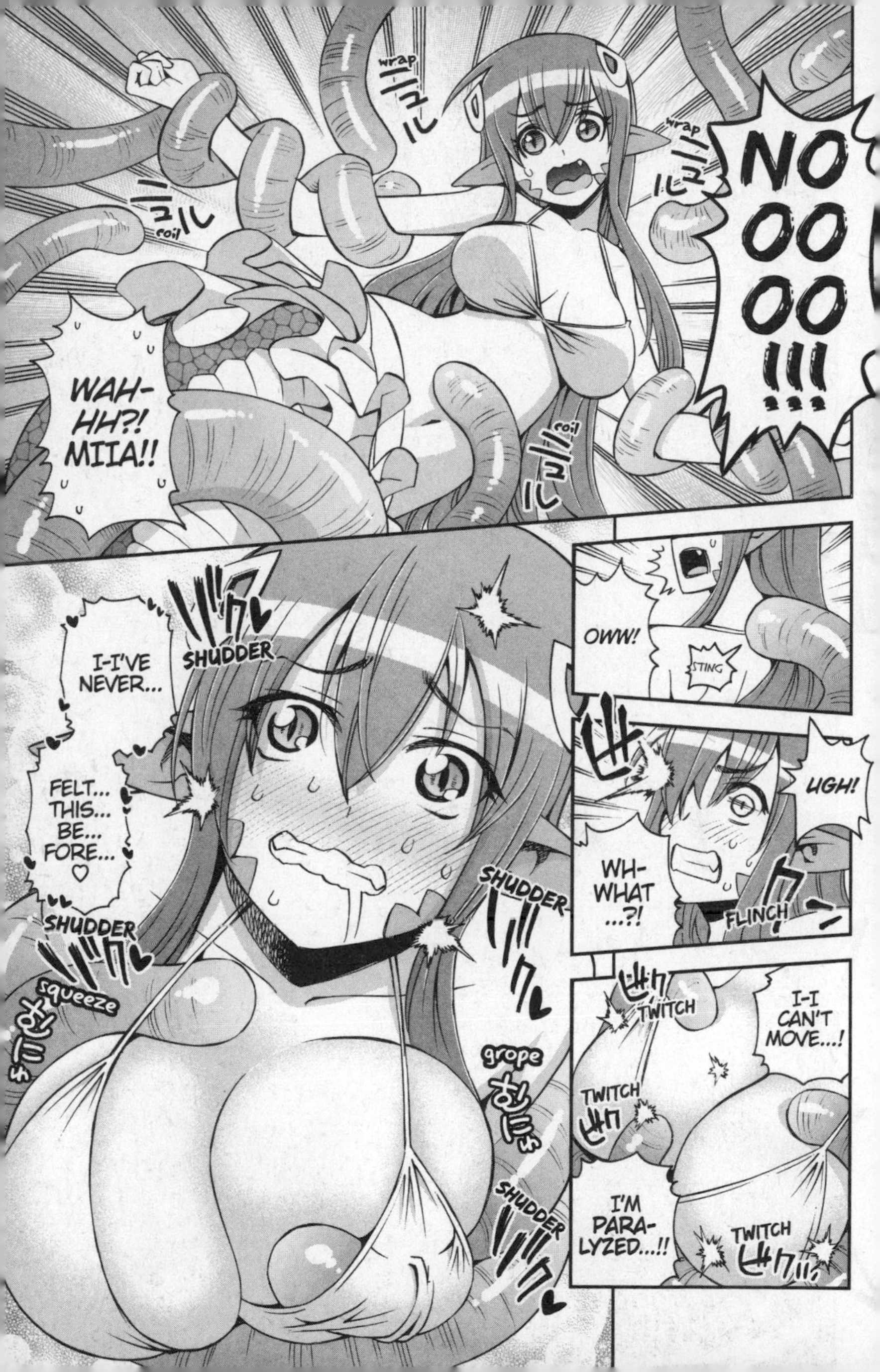
NOOOOOOO!!!!!!
wrap
wrap
coil
coil
WAH-HH?! MIIA!!
OWW!
STING
UGH!
WH-WHAT...?!
FLINCH
I-I CAN'T MOVE...!
TWITCH
TWITCH
I'M PARA-LYZED...!!
TWITCH
SHUDDER
I-I'VE NEVER...
FELT... THIS... BE... FORE... ♡
SHUDDER
SHUDDER
squeeze
grope
SHUDDER

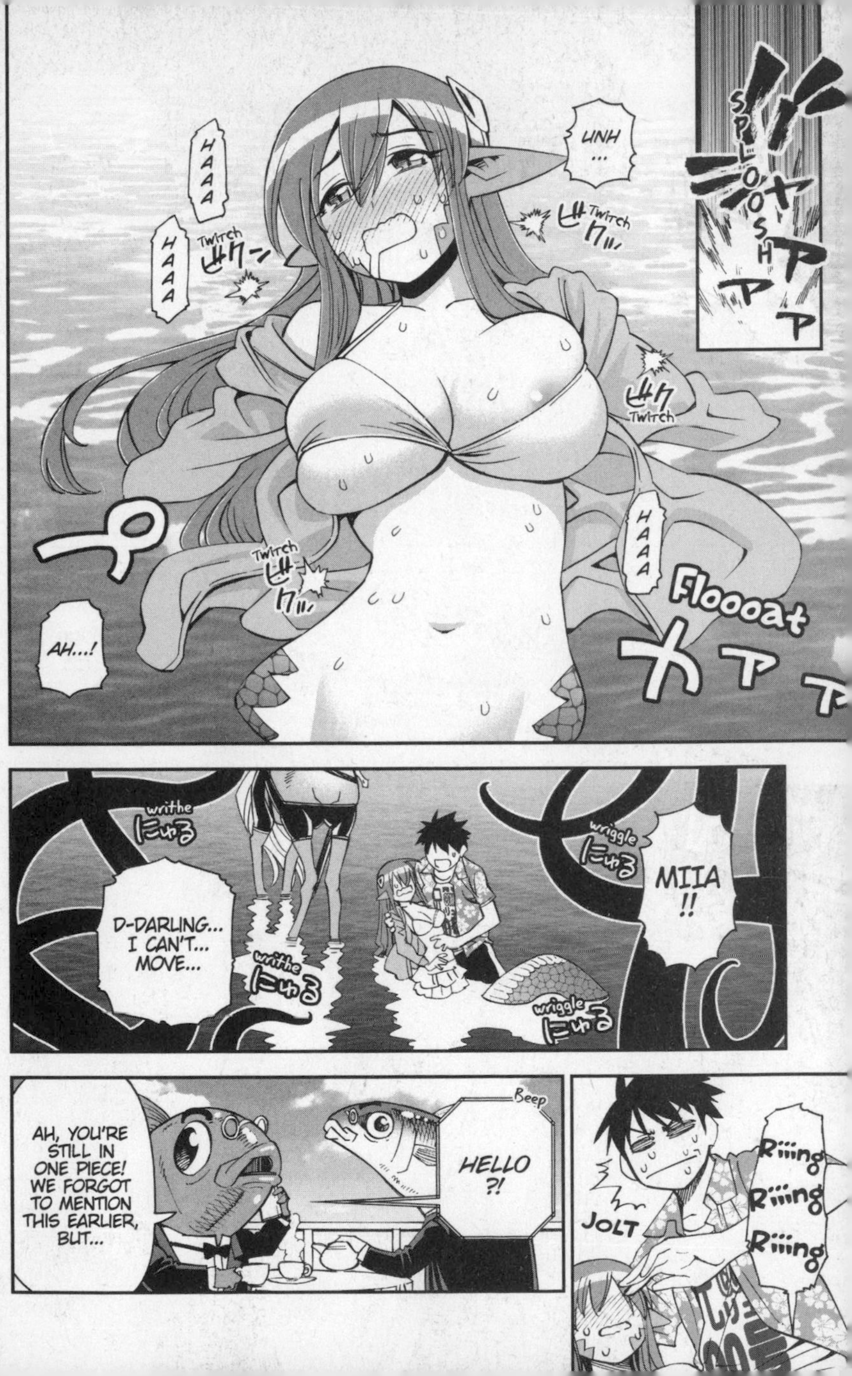
SPLOOSH
UNH ...
Twitch
HAAA
HAAA
Twitch
Twitch
HAAA
Floooat
Twitch
AH...!
MIIA !!
wriggle
にゅる
writhe
にゅる
D-DARLING... I CAN'T... MOVE...
writhe
にゅる
wriggle
にゅる
Riiing
Riiing
Riiing
JOLT
Beep
HELLO ?!
AH, YOU'RE STILL IN ONE PIECE! WE FORGOT TO MENTION THIS EARLIER, BUT...

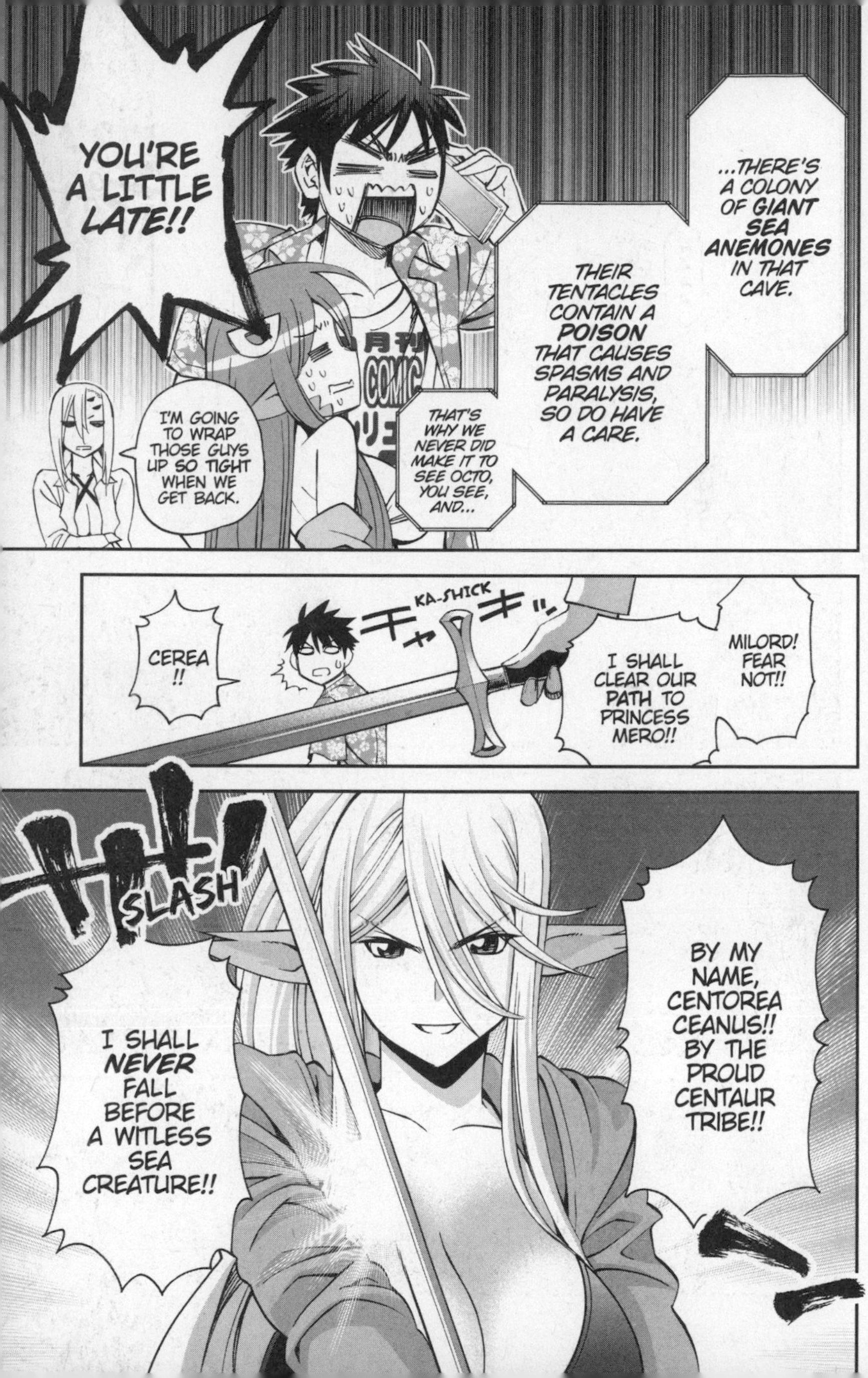
...THERE'S A COLONY OF GIANT SEA ANEMONES IN THAT CAVE.
THEIR TENTACLES CONTAIN A POISON THAT CAUSES SPASMS AND PARALYSIS, SO DO HAVE A CARE.
THAT'S WHY WE NEVER DID MAKE IT TO SEE OCTO, YOU SEE, AND...
YOU'RE A LITTLE LATE!!
I'M GOING TO WRAP THOSE GUYS UP SO TIGHT WHEN WE GET BACK.
MILORD! FEAR NOT!!
I SHALL CLEAR OUR PATH TO PRINCESS MERO!!
KA-SHICK
CEREA !!
BY MY NAME, CENTOREA CEANUS!! BY THE PROUD CENTAUR TRIBE!!
SLASH
I SHALL NEVER FALL BEFORE A WITLESS SEA CREATURE!!

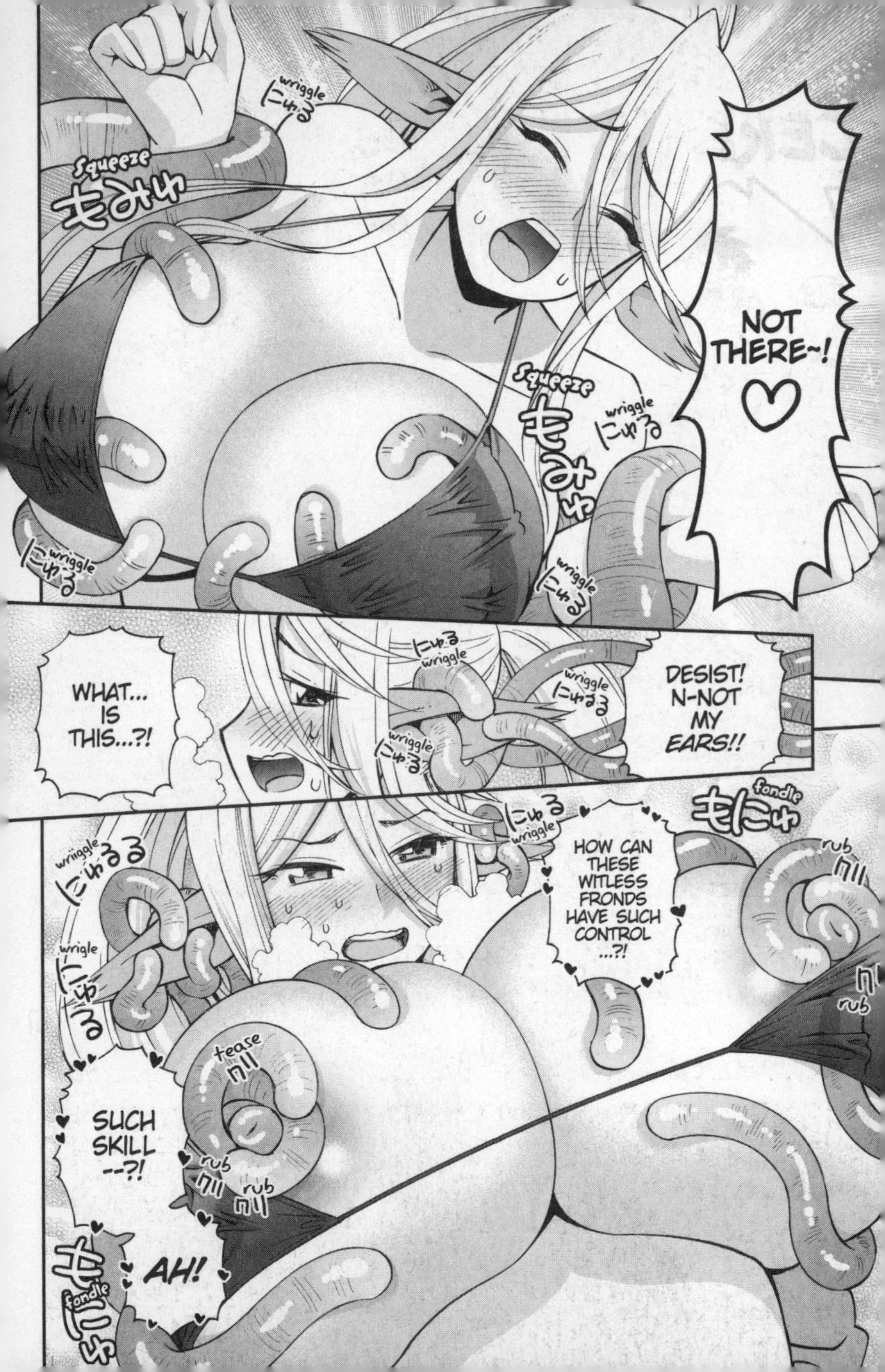
NOT THERE~! ♥
wriggle にゅる
squeeze もみゅ
squeeze もみゅ
wriggle にゅる
wriggle にゅる
wriggle にゅる
DESIST! N-NOT MY EARS!!
にゅる wriggle
wriggle にゅるる
wriggle にゅる
WHAT... IS THIS...?!
fondle もにゅ
にゅる wriggle
HOW CAN THESE WITLESS FRONDS HAVE SUCH CONTROL ...?!
rub クリ
クリ rub
wriggle にゅるる
wrigle にゅるる
tease クリ
SUCH SKILL --?!
rub クリ
rub クリ
AH!
fondle もにゅ

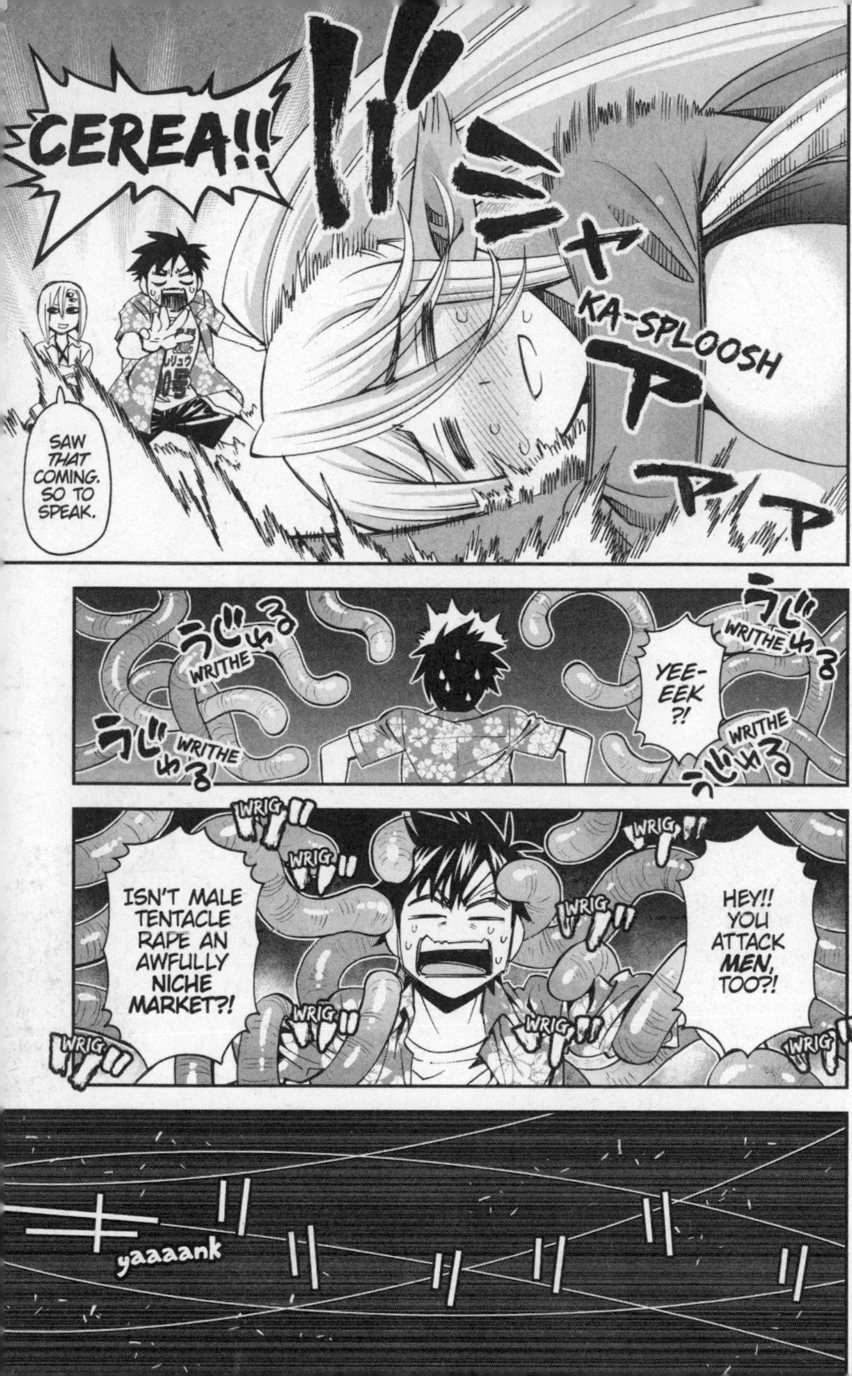
CEREA!!
KA-SPLOOSH
SAW THAT COMING. SO TO SPEAK.
うじゅる
WRITHE
YEEE-EEK?!
WRITHE
うじゅる
WRITHE
うじゅる
WRITHE
HEY!! YOU ATTACK MEN, TOO?!
ISN'T MALE TENTACLE RAPE AN AWFULLY NICHE MARKET?!
WRIG
WRIG
WRIG
WRIG
WRIG
WRIG
WRIG
yaaaank

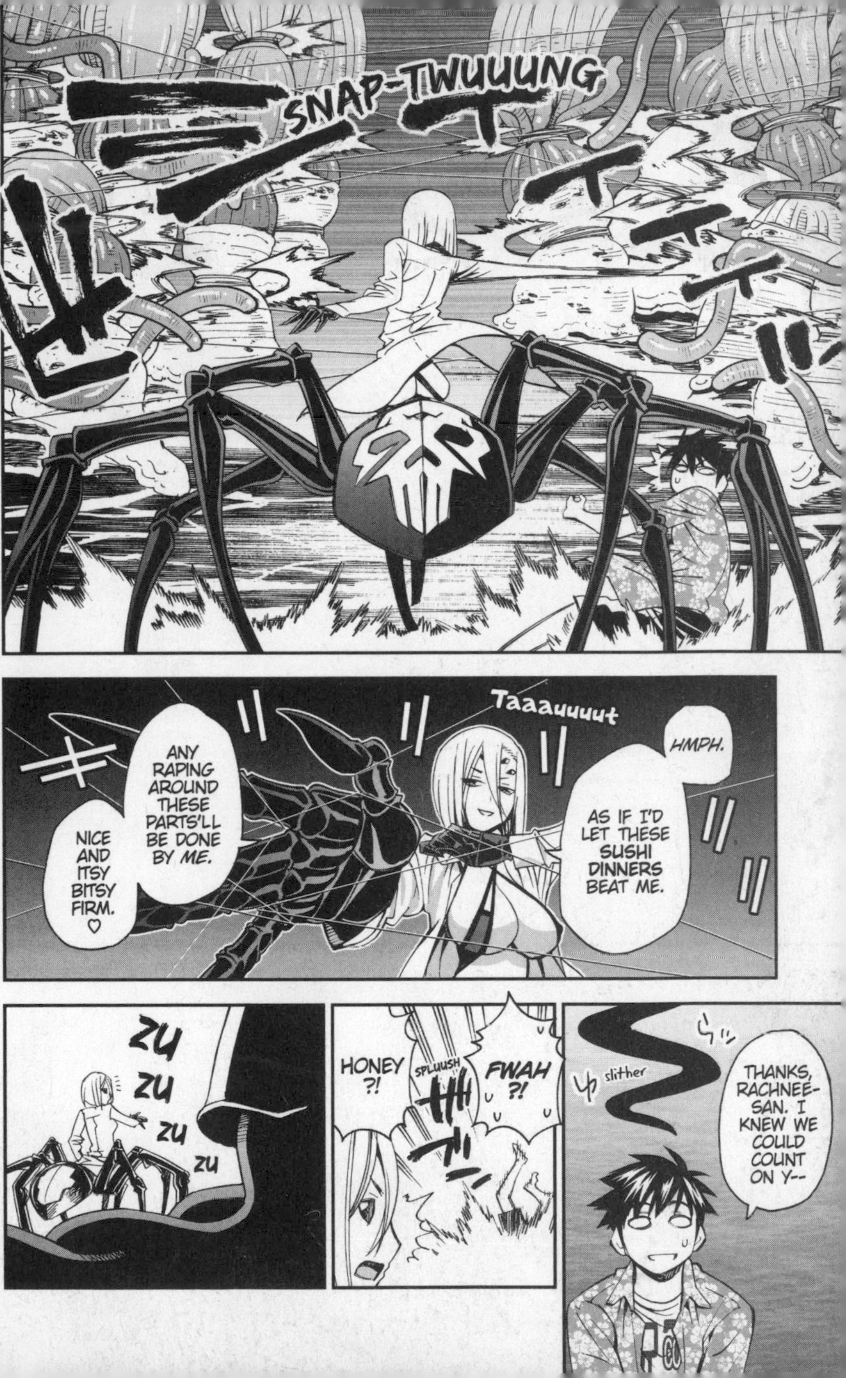
SNAP-TWUUUNG
Taaauuuut
HMPH.
AS IF I'D LET THESE SUSHI DINNERS BEAT ME.
ANY RAPING AROUND THESE PARTS'LL BE DONE BY ME.
NICE AND ITSY BITSY FIRM. ♡
slither
THANKS, RACHNEE-SAN. I KNEW WE COULD COUNT ON Y--
FWAH ?!
SPLUUSH
HONEY ?!
ZU
ZU
ZU
ZU

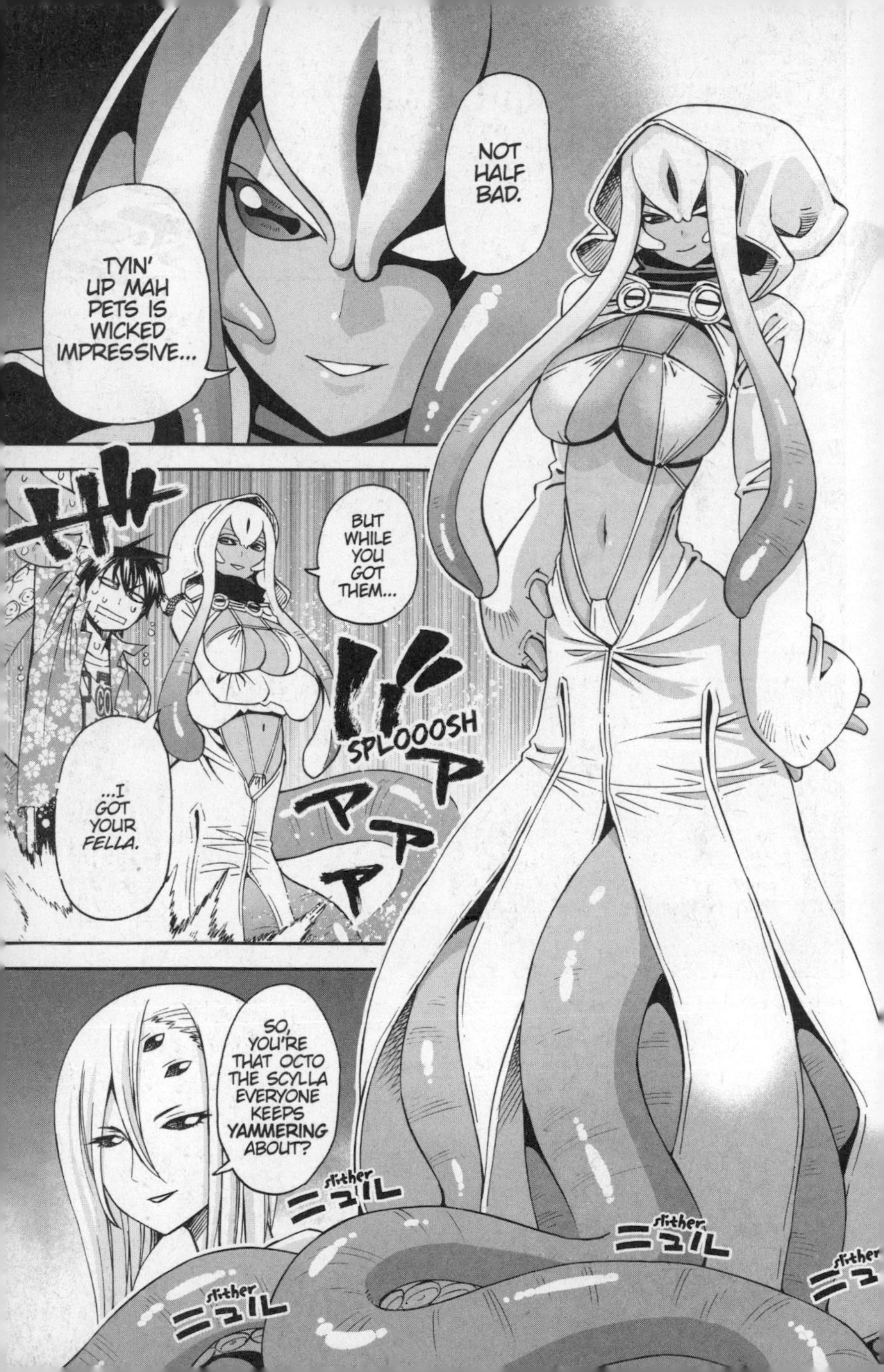
NOT HALF BAD.
TYIN' UP MAH PETS IS WICKED IMPRESSIVE...
BUT WHILE YOU GOT THEM...
SPLOOOSH
...I GOT YOUR FELLA.
SO, YOU'RE THAT OCTO THE SCYLLA EVERYONE KEEPS YAMMERING ABOUT?
slither ニュル
slither ニュル
slither ニュル
slither

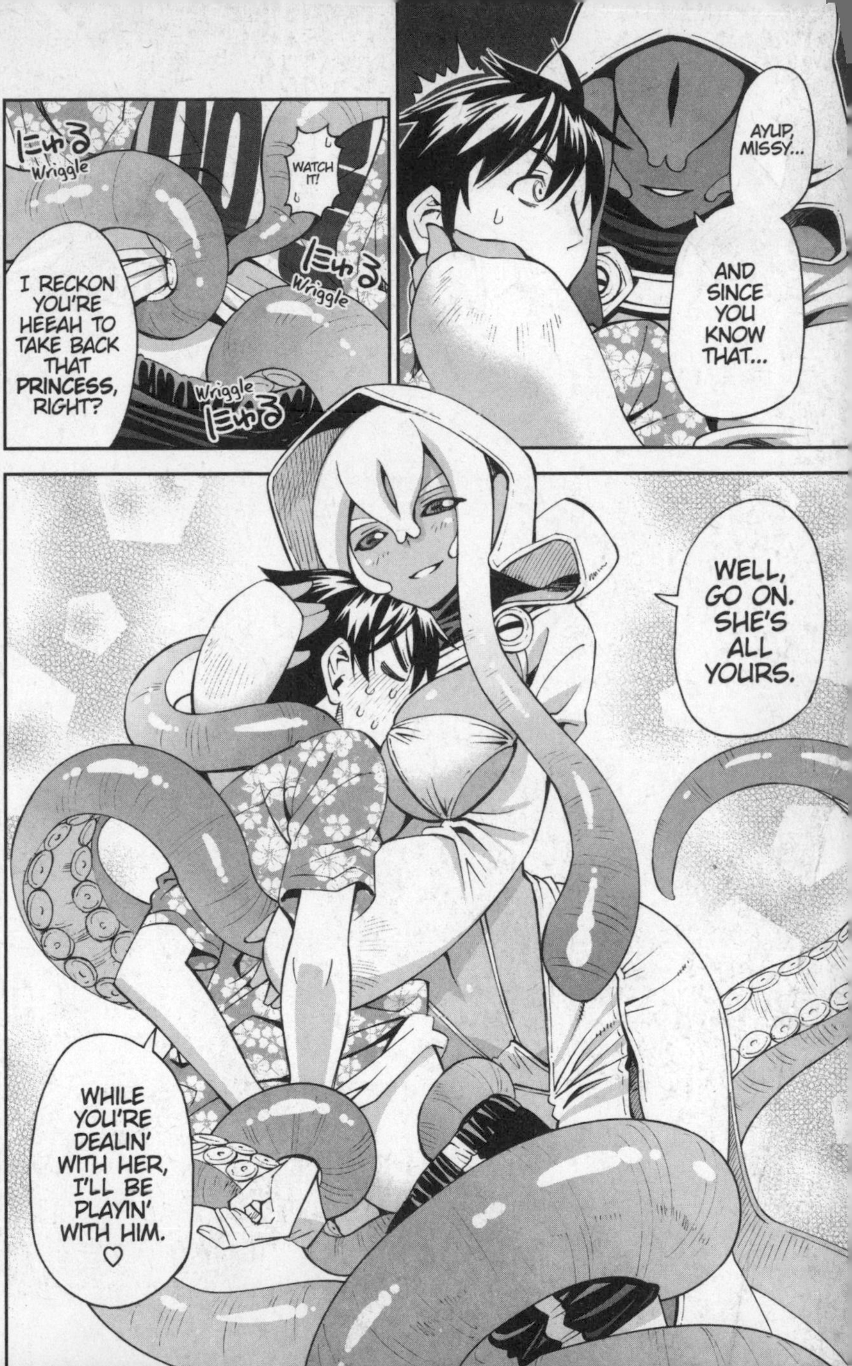
AYUP, MISSY...
AND SINCE YOU KNOW THAT...
にゅる
Wriggle
WATCH IT!
にゅる
Wriggle
I RECKON YOU'RE HEEAH TO TAKE BACK THAT PRINCESS, RIGHT?
Wriggle
にゅる
WELL, GO ON. SHE'S ALL YOURS.
WHILE YOU'RE DEALIN' WITH HER, I'LL BE PLAYIN' WITH HIM. ♡

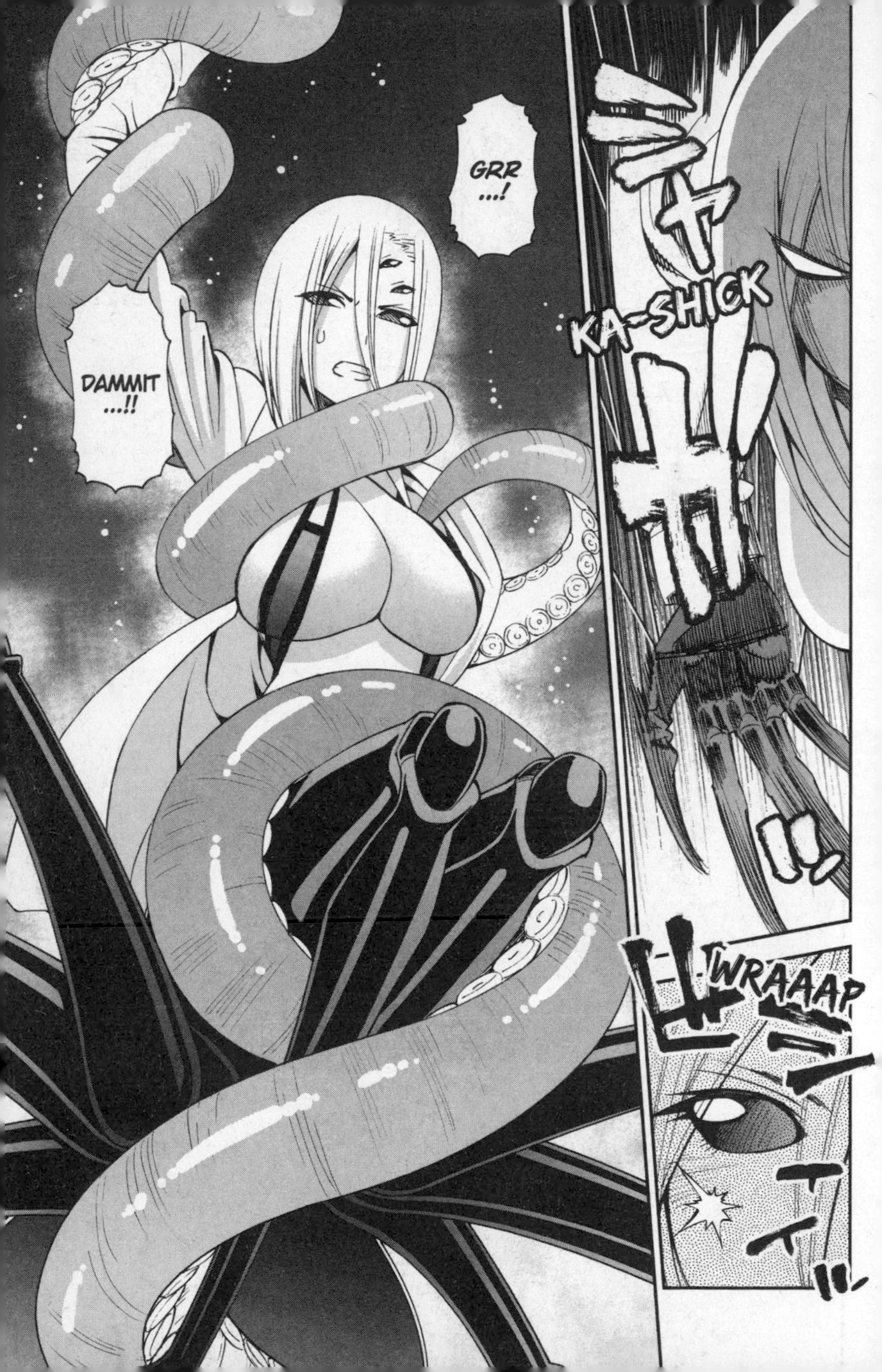
KA-SHICK
WRAAAP
GRR ...!
DAMMIT ...!!

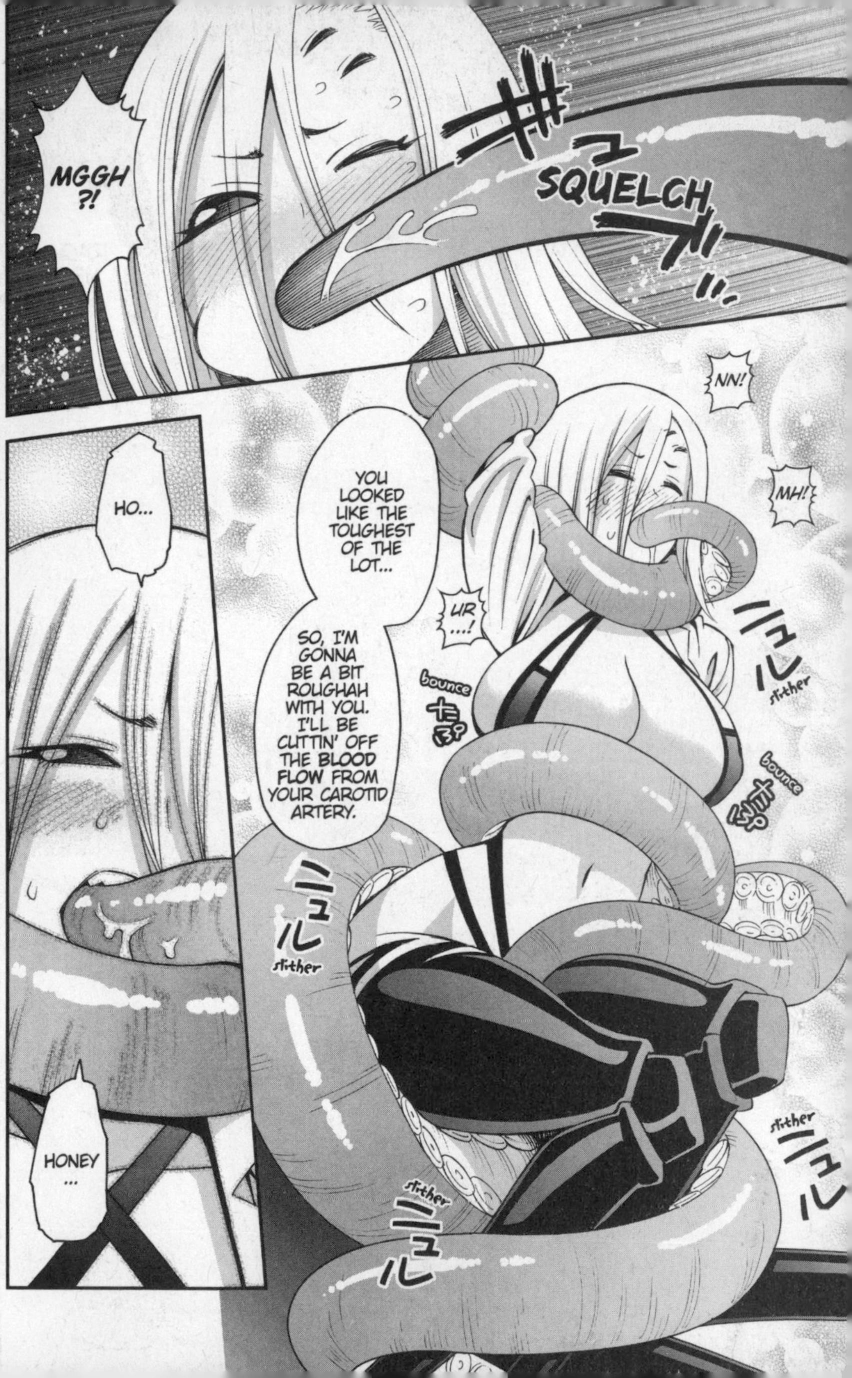
MGGH ?!
SQUELCH
NN!
MH!
YOU LOOKED LIKE THE TOUGHEST OF THE LOT...
UR ...!
SO, I'M GONNA BE A BIT ROUGHAH WITH YOU. I'LL BE CUTTIN' OFF THE BLOOD FLOW FROM YOUR CAROTID ARTERY.
ニュル slither
bounce
bounce
ニュル slither
slither ニュル
slither ニュル
HO...
HONEY ...

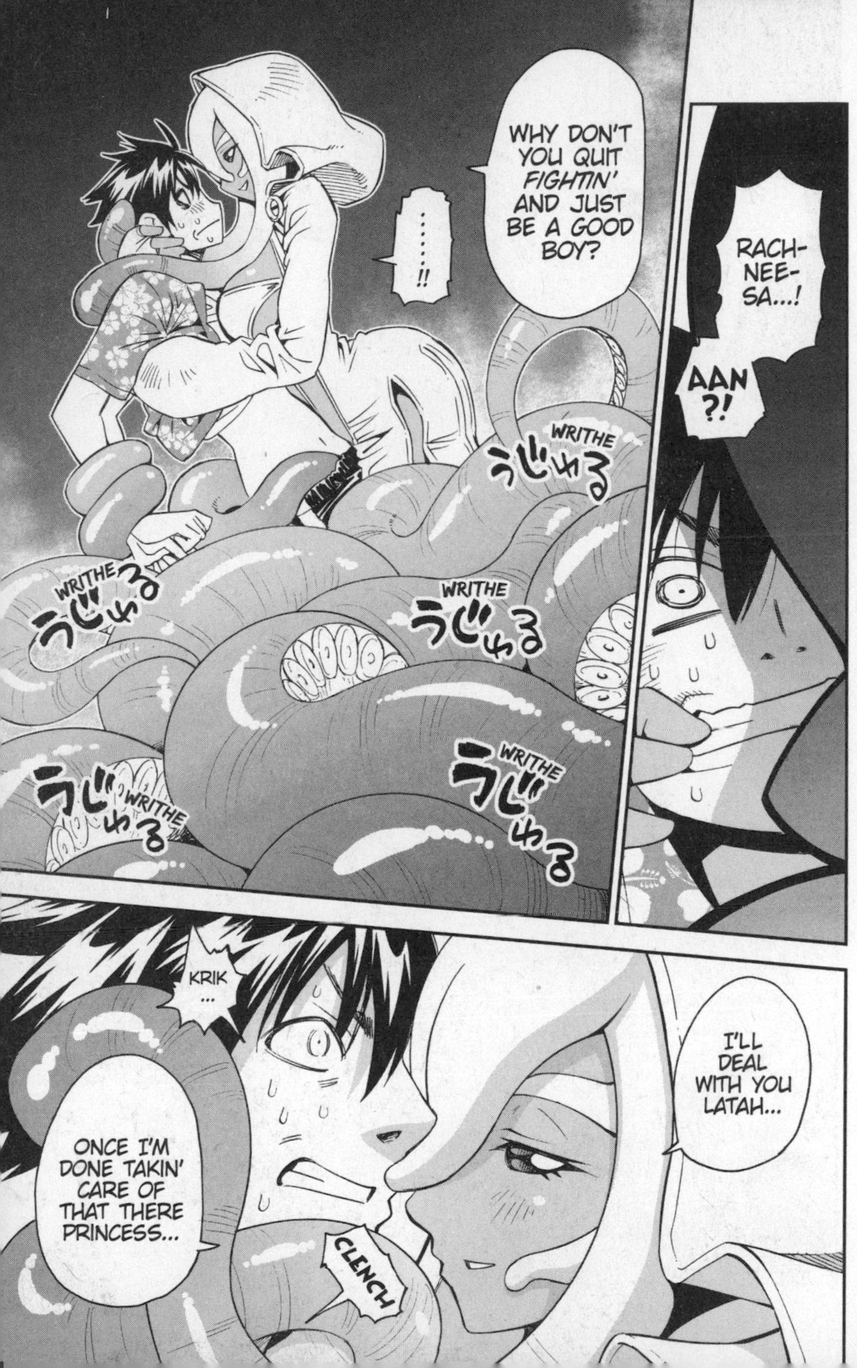
RACH-NEE-SA...!
AAN ?!
WHY DON'T YOU QUIT *FIGHTIN'* AND JUST BE A GOOD BOY?
......!!
WRITHE
うじゅる
WRITHE
うじゅる
WRITHE
うじゅる
WRITHE
うじゅる
WRITHE
うじゅる
I'LL DEAL WITH YOU LATAH...
KRIK...
ONCE I'M DONE TAKIN' CARE OF THAT THERE PRINCESS...
CLENCH

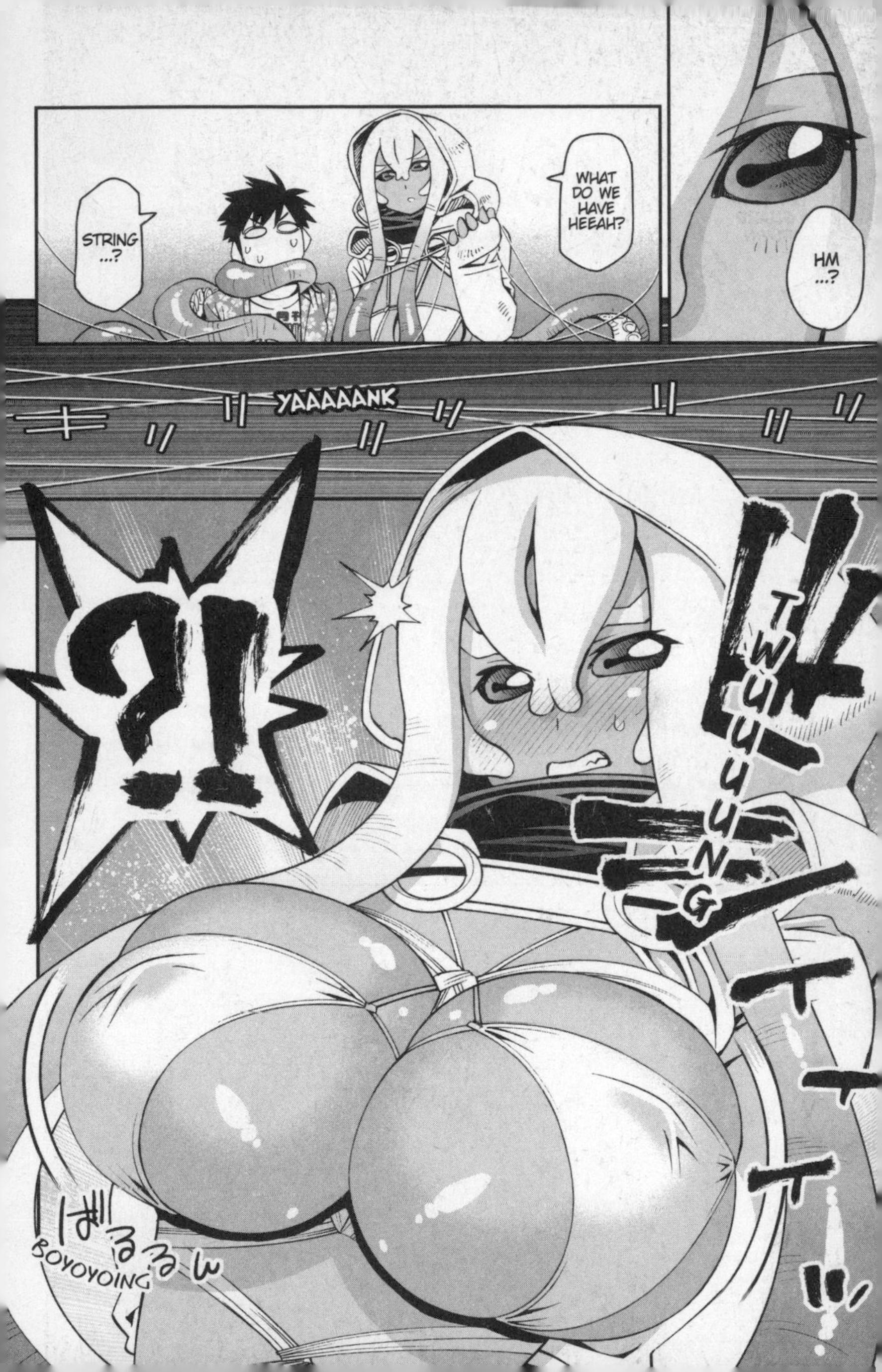
HM ...?
WHAT DO WE HAVE HEEAH?
STRING ...?
YAAAAANK
TWUUUUUNG
?!
BOYOYOING

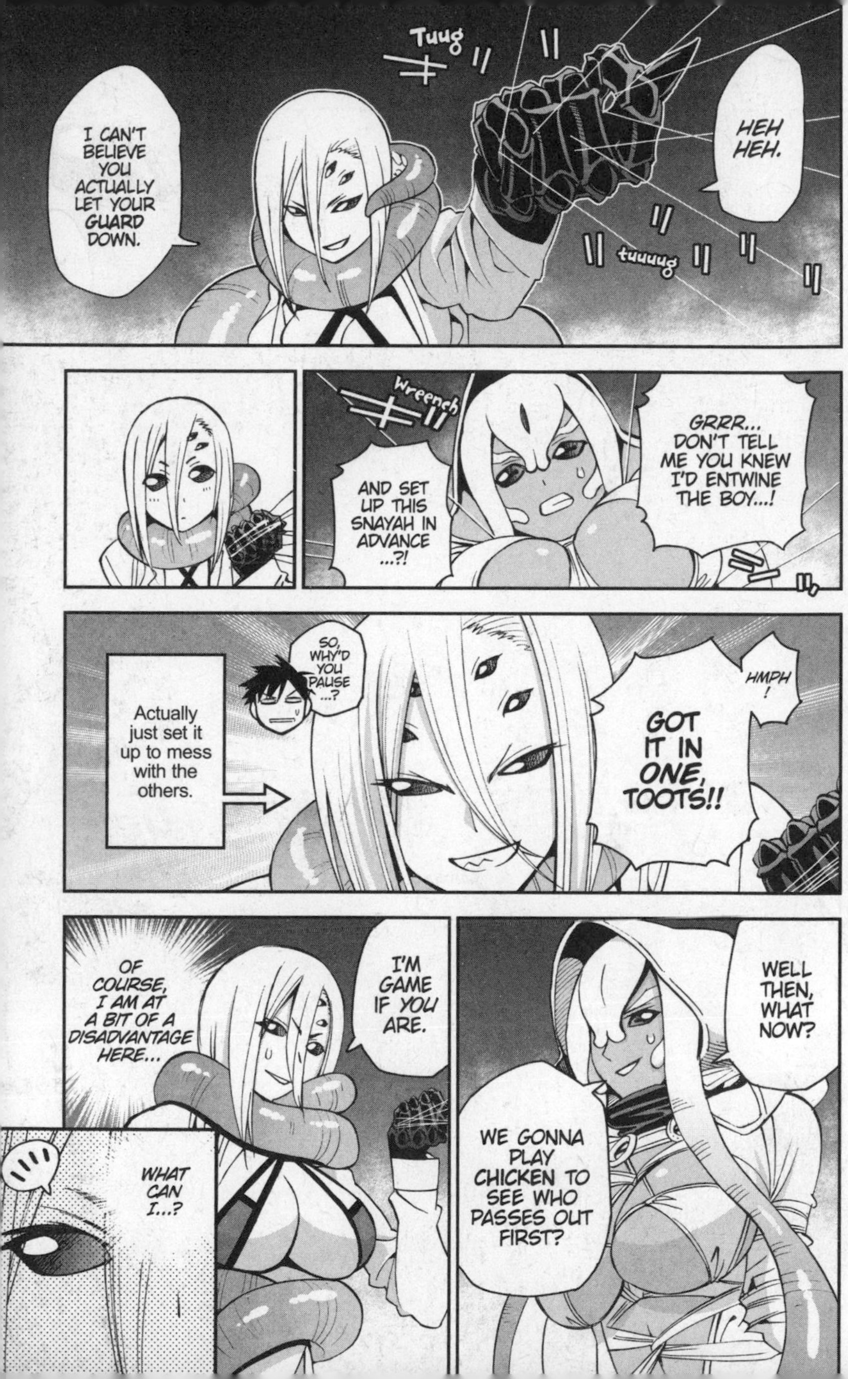
HEH HEH.
Tuug
tuuuug
I CAN'T BELIEVE YOU ACTUALLY LET YOUR GUARD DOWN.
GRRR... DON'T TELL ME YOU KNEW I'D ENTWINE THE BOY...!
Wreench
AND SET UP THIS SNAYAH IN ADVANCE ...?!
HMPH!
GOT IT IN ONE, TOOTS!!
SO, WHY'D YOU PAUSE ...?
Actually just set it up to mess with the others.
WELL THEN, WHAT NOW?
WE GONNA PLAY CHICKEN TO SEE WHO PASSES OUT FIRST?
I'M GAME IF YOU ARE.
OF COURSE, I AM AT A BIT OF A DISADVANTAGE HERE...
WHAT CAN I...?

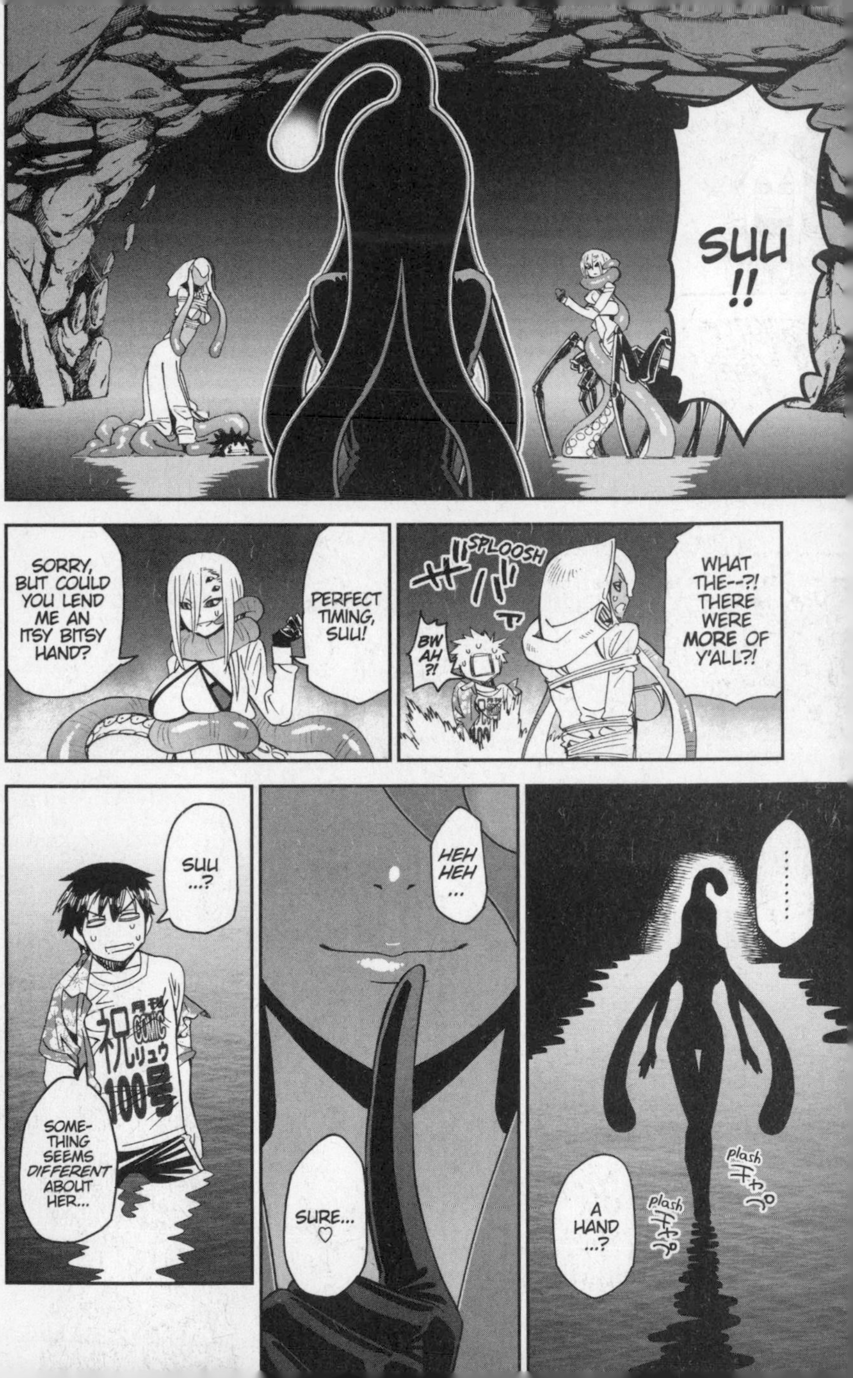
SUU !!
WHAT THE--?! THERE WERE MORE OF Y'ALL?!
SPLOOSH
BWAH ?!
PERFECT TIMING, SUU!
SORRY, BUT COULD YOU LEND ME AN ITSY BITSY HAND?
......
plash
チャプ
plash
チャプ
A HAND ...?
HEH HEH ...
SURE... ♡
SUU ...?
月刊
COMIC
祝
リュウ
100号
SOME-THING SEEMS DIFFERENT ABOUT HER...

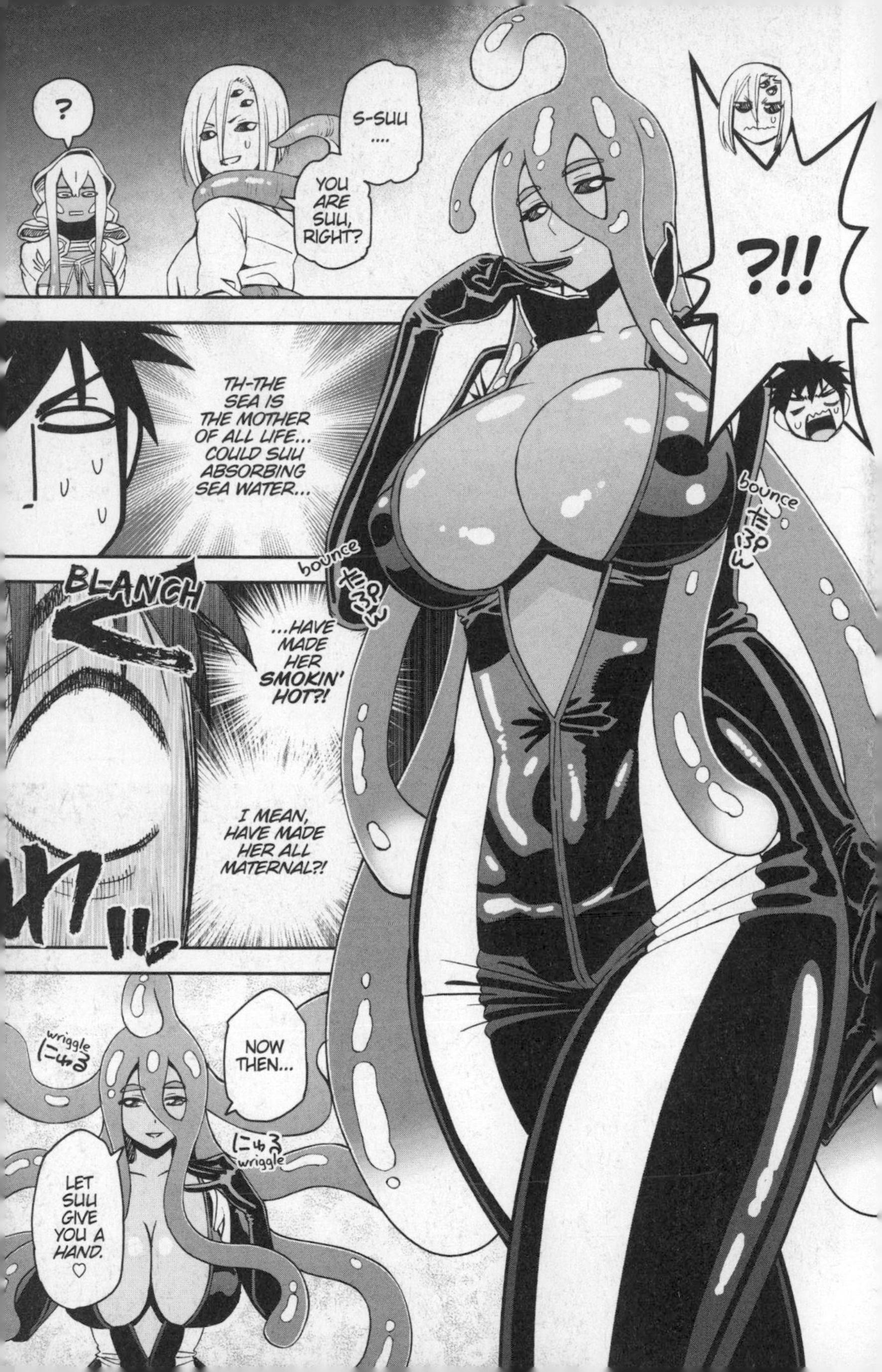
?!!
bounce
たぷん
bounce
たぷん
S-SUU ....
YOU ARE SUU, RIGHT?
?
TH-THE SEA IS THE MOTHER OF ALL LIFE... COULD SUU ABSORBING SEA WATER...
BLANCH
...HAVE MADE HER SMOKIN' HOT?!
I MEAN, HAVE MADE HER ALL MATERNAL?!
NOW THEN...
にゅる
wriggle
wriggle
にゅる
LET SUU GIVE YOU A HAND. ♡

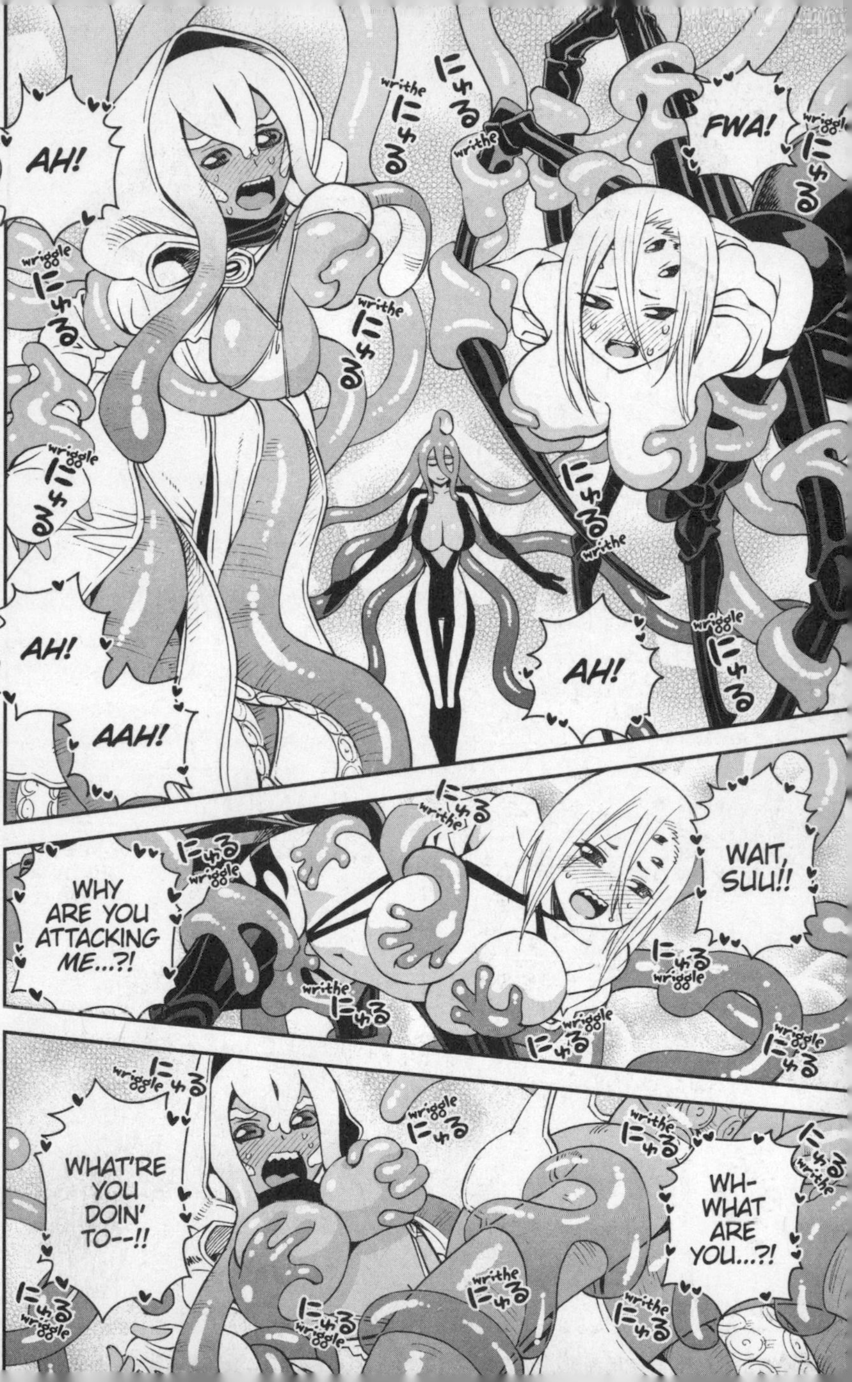
wriggle
にゅる
FWA!
にゅる
writhe
にゅる
writhe
AH!
wriggle
にゅる
writhe
にゅる
wriggle
にゅる
にゅる
writhe
wriggle
にゅる
AH!
AH!
AAH!
WAIT, SUU!!
にゅる
writhe
にゅる
wriggle
wriggle
にゅる
wriggle
にゅる
にゅる
wriggle
WHY ARE YOU ATTACKING ME...?!
writhe
にゅる
にゅる
writhe
writhe
にゅる
WH- WHAT ARE YOU...?!
wriggle
にゅる
wriggle
にゅる
WHAT'RE YOU DOIN' TO--!!
writhe
にゅる
writhe
にゅる
にゅる
wriggle
にゅる
wriggle

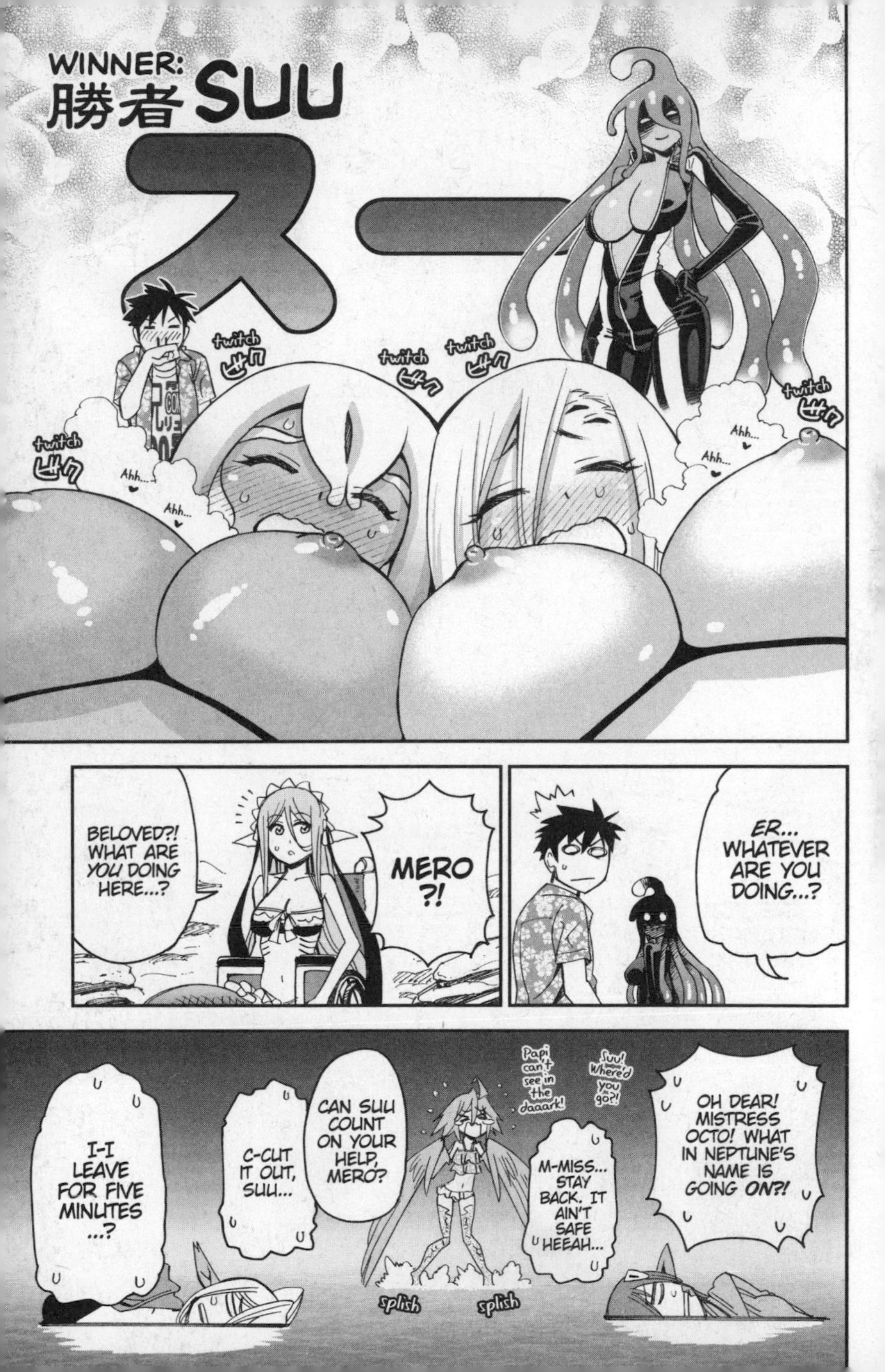
WINNER:
勝者 SUU
スー
twitch ビクッ
Ahh...♥
Ahh...♥
twitch ビクッ
twitch ビクッ
twitch ビクッ
Ahh...♥
Ahh...♥
twitch ビクッ
ER... WHATEVER ARE YOU DOING...?
MERO ?!
BELOVED?! WHAT ARE YOU DOING HERE...?
OH DEAR! MISTRESS OCTO! WHAT IN NEPTUNE'S NAME IS GOING ON?!
Suu! Where'd you go?!
Papi can't see in the daaark!
M-MISS... STAY BACK. IT AIN'T SAFE HEEAH...
CAN SUU COUNT ON YOUR HELP, MERO?
C-CUT IT OUT, SUU...
I-I LEAVE FOR FIVE MINUTES ...?
splish
splish

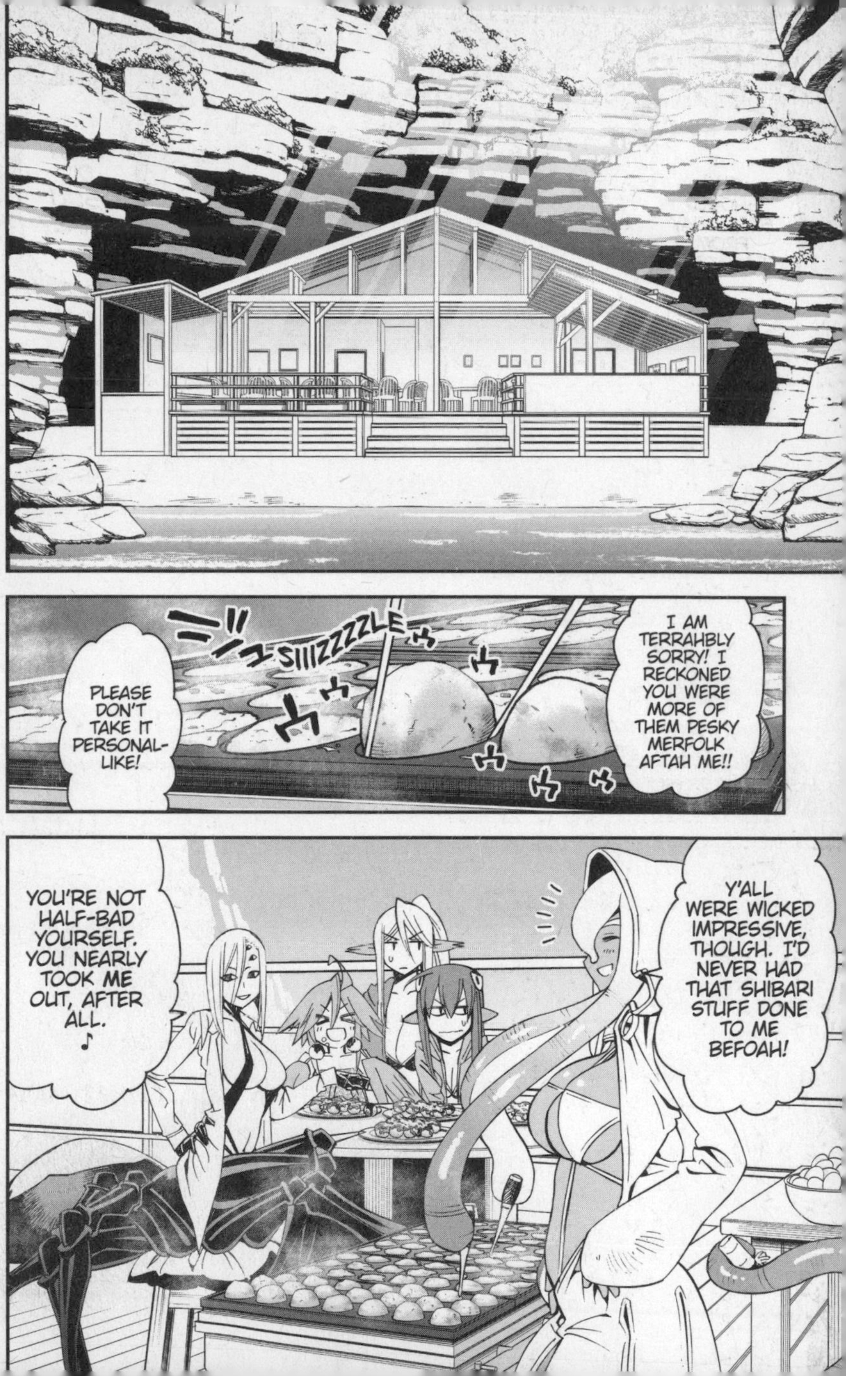
I AM TERRAHBLY SORRY! I RECKONED YOU WERE MORE OF THEM PESKY MERFOLK AFTAH ME!!
SIIIZZZZLE
PLEASE DON'T TAKE IT PERSONAL-LIKE!
Y'ALL WERE WICKED IMPRESSIVE, THOUGH. I'D NEVER HAD THAT SHIBARI STUFF DONE TO ME BEFOAH!
YOU'RE NOT HALF-BAD YOURSELF. YOU NEARLY TOOK ME OUT, AFTER ALL. ♪

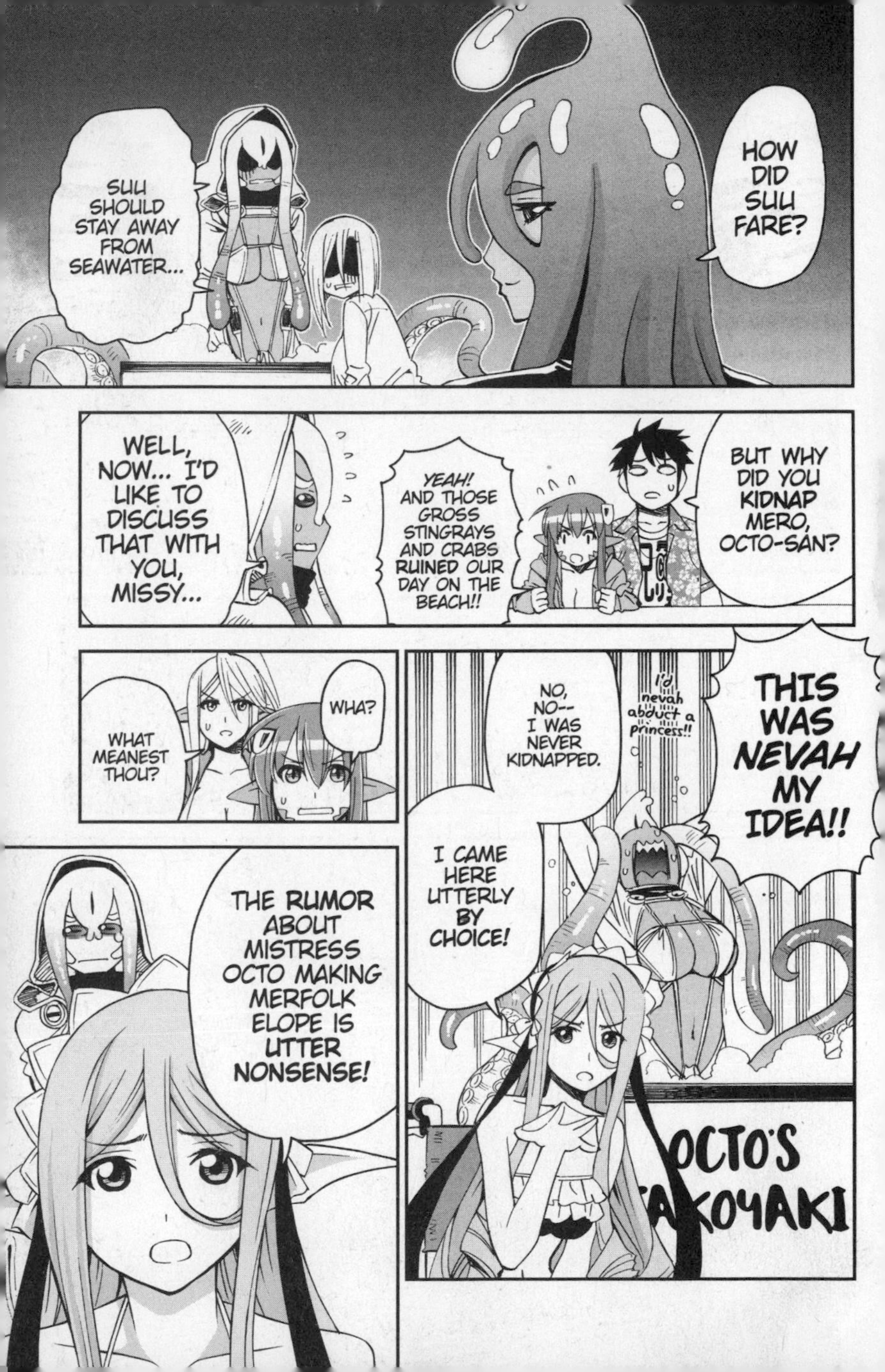
HOW DID SUU FARE?
SUU SHOULD STAY AWAY FROM SEAWATER...
BUT WHY DID YOU KIDNAP MERO, OCTO-SAN?
YEAH! AND THOSE GROSS STINGRAYS AND CRABS RUINED OUR DAY ON THE BEACH!!
WELL, NOW... I'D LIKE TO DISCUSS THAT WITH YOU, MISSY...
THIS WAS NEVAH MY IDEA!!
I'd nevah abduct a princess!!
NO, NO-- I WAS NEVER KIDNAPPED.
I CAME HERE UTTERLY BY CHOICE!
OCTO'S
AKOYAKI
WHA?
WHAT MEANEST THOU?
THE RUMOR ABOUT MISTRESS OCTO MAKING MERFOLK ELOPE IS UTTER NONSENSE!

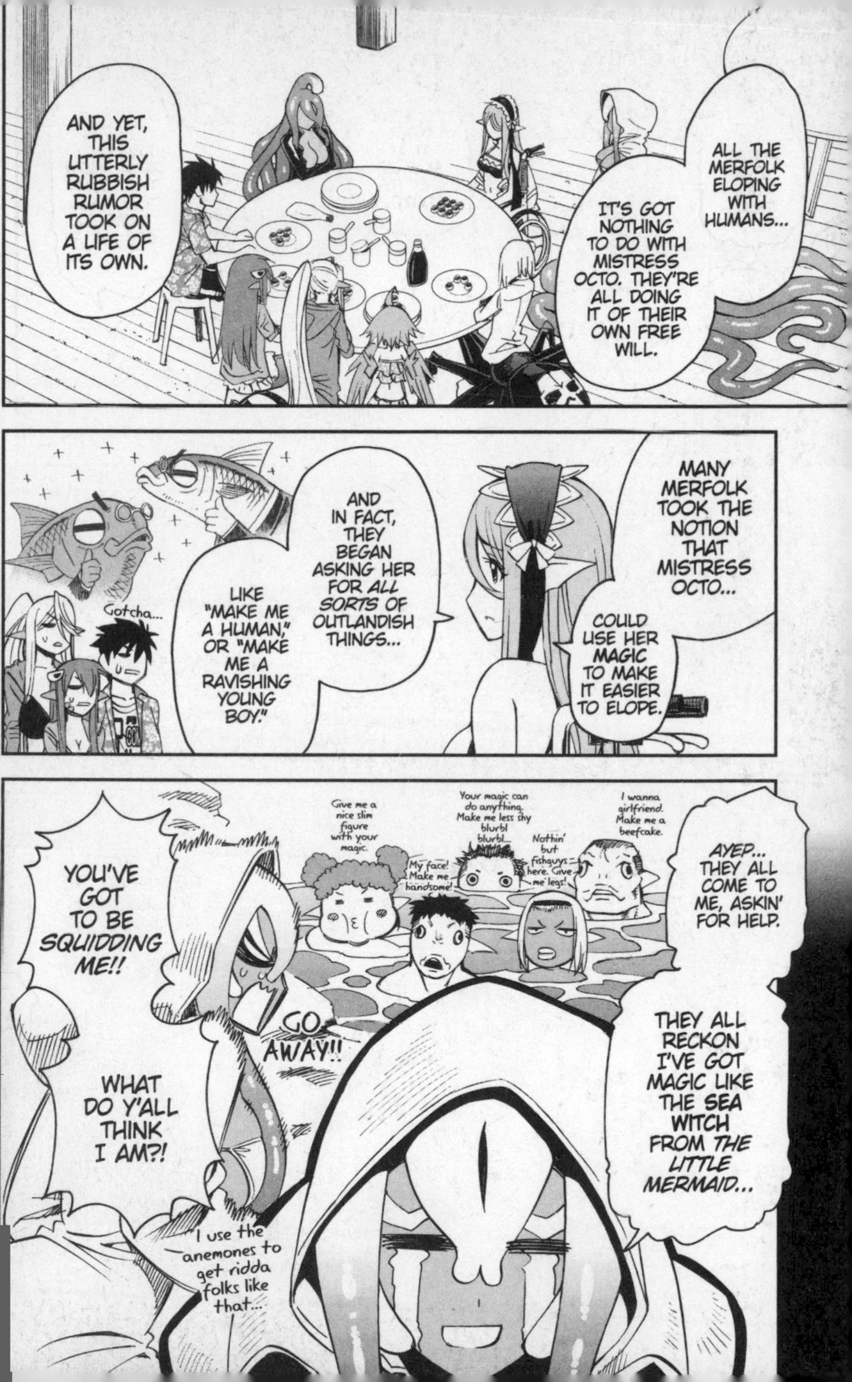
ALL THE MERFOLK ELOPING WITH HUMANS...
IT'S GOT NOTHING TO DO WITH MISTRESS OCTO. THEY'RE ALL DOING IT OF THEIR OWN FREE WILL.
AND YET, THIS UTTERLY RUBBISH RUMOR TOOK ON A LIFE OF ITS OWN.
MANY MERFOLK TOOK THE NOTION THAT MISTRESS OCTO...
COULD USE HER *MAGIC* TO MAKE IT EASIER TO ELOPE.
AND IN FACT, THEY BEGAN ASKING HER FOR *ALL SORTS* OF OUTLANDISH THINGS...
LIKE "MAKE ME A HUMAN," OR "MAKE ME A RAVISHING YOUNG BOY."
Gotcha...
AYEP... THEY ALL COME TO ME, ASKIN' FOR HELP.
I wanna girlfriend. Make me a beefcake.
Nothin' but fishguys here. Give me legs!
Your magic can do anything. Make me less shy blurbl blurbl...
My face! Make me handsome!
Give me a nice slim figure with your magic.
THEY ALL RECKON I'VE GOT MAGIC LIKE THE SEA WITCH FROM *THE LITTLE MERMAID*...
YOU'VE GOT TO BE *SQUIDDING* ME!!
GO AWAY!!
WHAT DO Y'ALL THINK I AM?!
I use the anemones to get ridda folks like that...

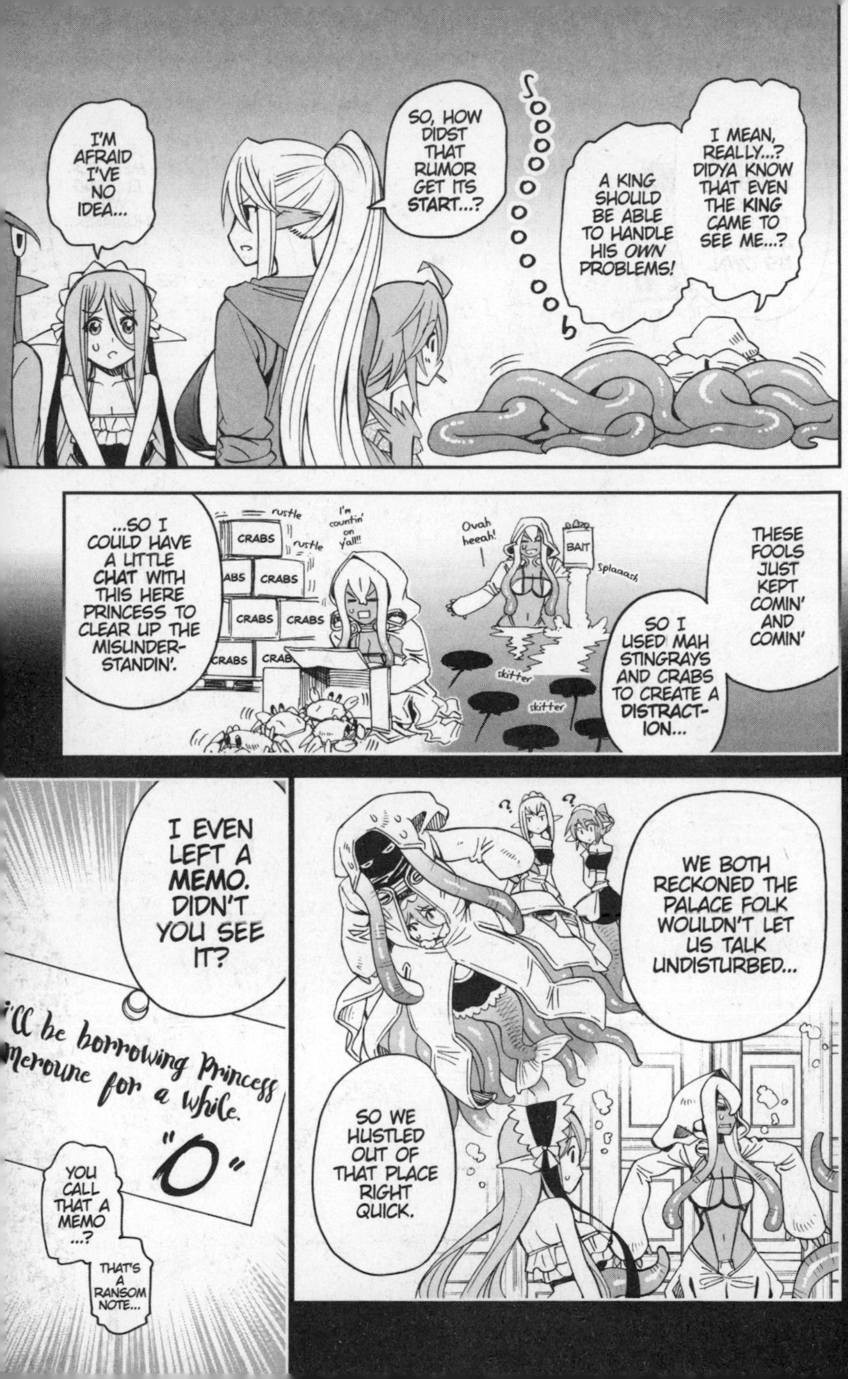
I MEAN, REALLY...? DIDYA KNOW THAT EVEN THE KING CAME TO SEE ME...?
A KING SHOULD BE ABLE TO HANDLE HIS *OWN* PROBLEMS!
Sooooooooooob
SO, HOW DIDST THAT RUMOR GET ITS START...?
I'M AFRAID I'VE NO IDEA...
THESE FOOLS JUST KEPT COMIN' AND COMIN'
SO I USED MAH STINGRAYS AND CRABS TO CREATE A DISTRACTION...
Ovah heeah!
BAIT
Splaaash
skitter
skitter
I'm countin' on y'all!!
rustle
rustle
CRABS
CRABS
ABS
CRABS
CRABS
CRABS
CRAB
...SO I COULD HAVE A LITTLE CHAT WITH THIS HERE PRINCESS TO CLEAR UP THE MISUNDERSTANDIN'.
WE BOTH RECKONED THE PALACE FOLK WOULDN'T LET US TALK UNDISTURBED...
SO WE HUSTLED OUT OF THAT PLACE RIGHT QUICK.
I EVEN LEFT A MEMO. DIDN'T YOU SEE IT?
'll be borrowing Princess
eroune for a while.
"O"
YOU CALL THAT A MEMO...?
THAT'S A RANSOM NOTE...

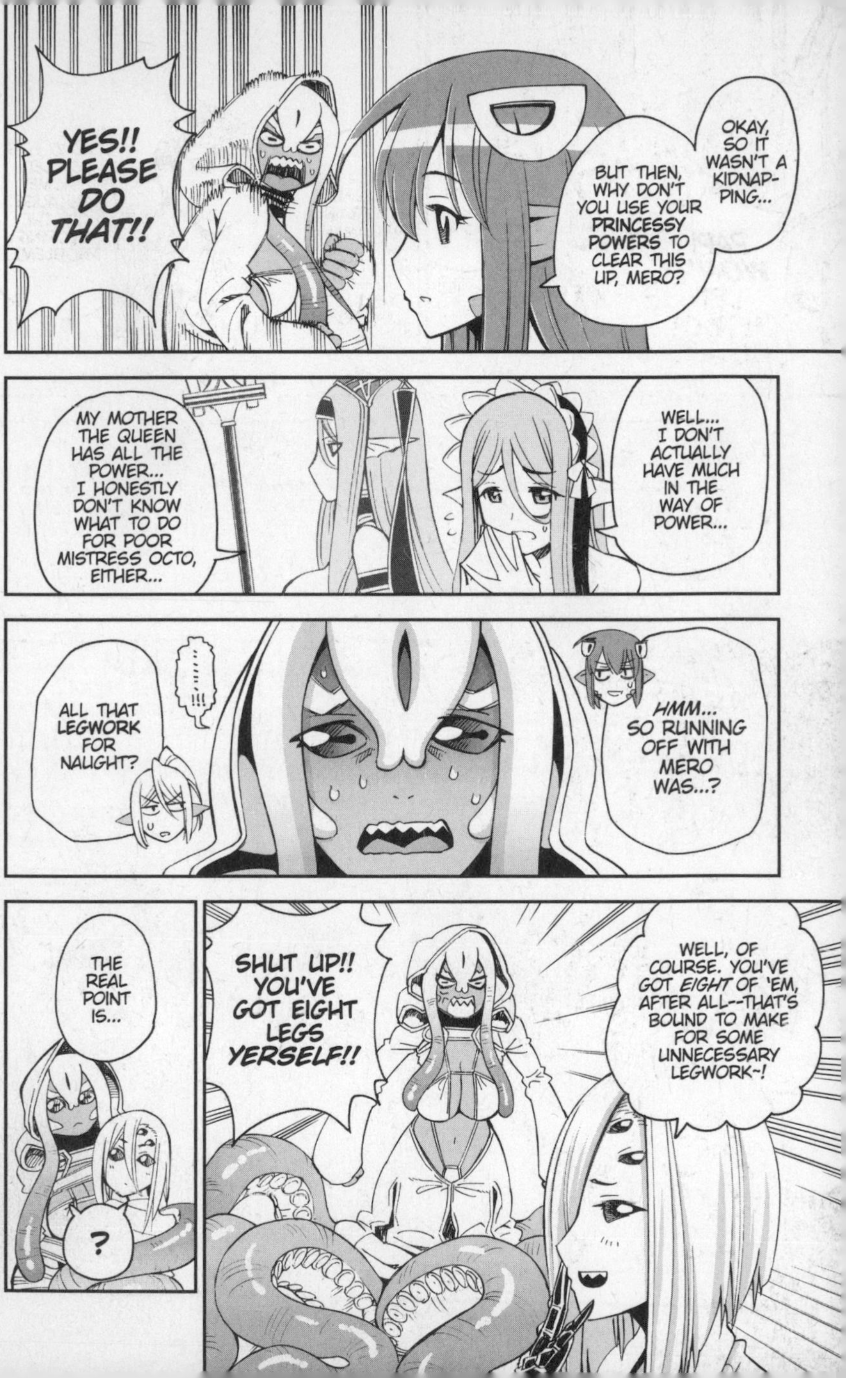
OKAY, SO IT WASN'T A KIDNAP-PING...
BUT THEN, WHY DON'T YOU USE YOUR PRINCESSY POWERS TO CLEAR THIS UP, MERO?
YES!! PLEASE DO THAT!!
WELL... I DON'T ACTUALLY HAVE MUCH IN THE WAY OF POWER...
MY MOTHER THE QUEEN HAS ALL THE POWER... I HONESTLY DON'T KNOW WHAT TO DO FOR POOR MISTRESS OCTO, EITHER...
HMM... SO RUNNING OFF WITH MERO WAS...?
......!!!
ALL THAT LEGWORK FOR NAUGHT?
WELL, OF COURSE. YOU'VE GOT *EIGHT* OF 'EM, AFTER ALL--THAT'S BOUND TO MAKE FOR SOME UNNECESSARY LEGWORK~!
SHUT UP!! YOU'VE GOT EIGHT LEGS *YERSELF!!*
THE REAL POINT IS...
?

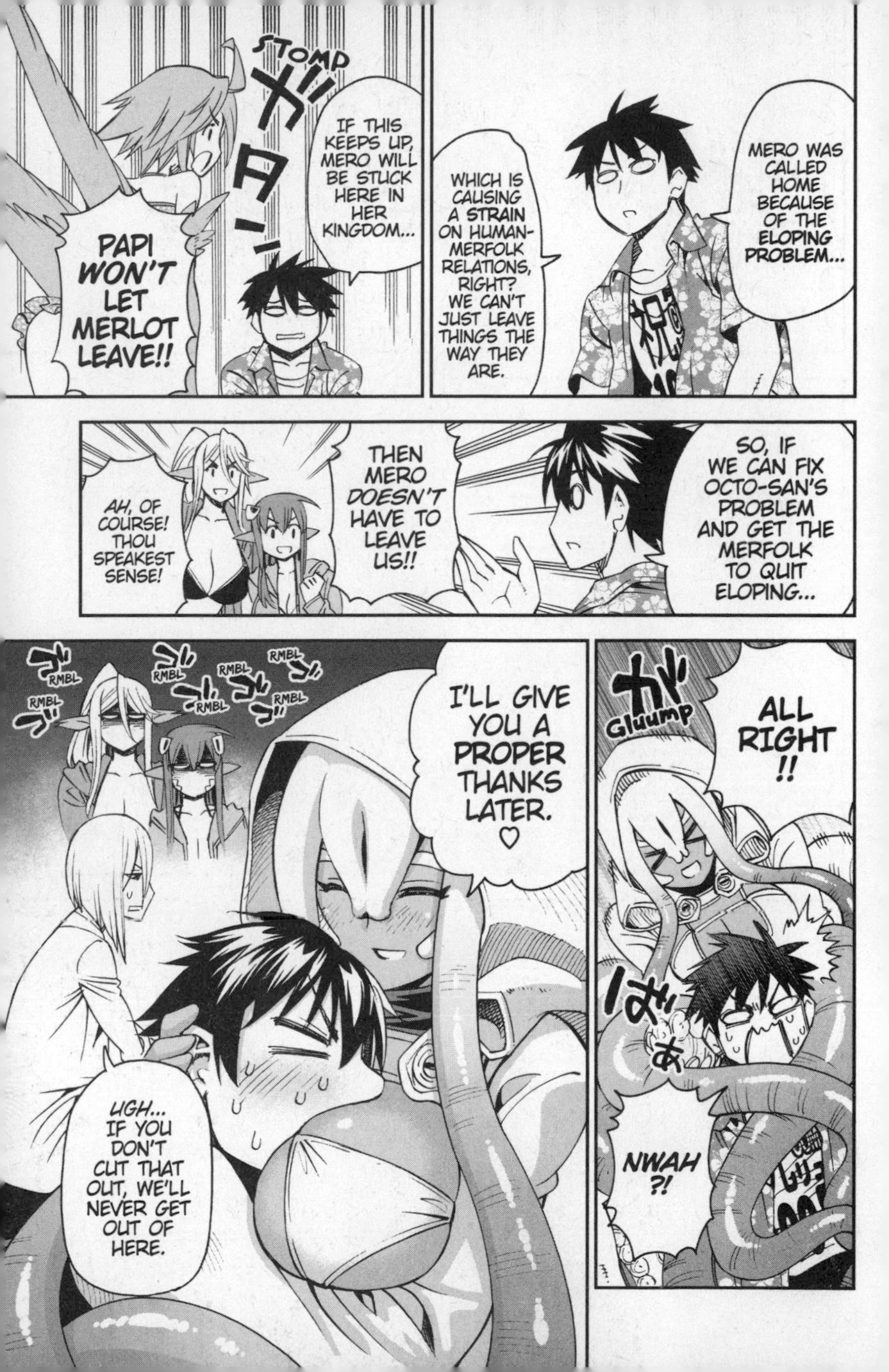
MERO WAS CALLED HOME BECAUSE OF THE ELOPING PROBLEM...
WHICH IS CAUSING A STRAIN ON HUMAN-MERFOLK RELATIONS, RIGHT? WE CAN'T JUST LEAVE THINGS THE WAY THEY ARE.
STOMP
IF THIS KEEPS UP, MERO WILL BE STUCK HERE IN HER KINGDOM...
PAPI WON'T LET MERLOT LEAVE!!
SO, IF WE CAN FIX OCTO-SAN'S PROBLEM AND GET THE MERFOLK TO QUIT ELOPING...
THEN MERO DOESN'T HAVE TO LEAVE US!!
AH, OF COURSE! THOU SPEAKEST SENSE!
Gluump
ALL RIGHT!!
NWAH?!
I'LL GIVE YOU A PROPER THANKS LATER. ♡
RMBL RMBL RMBL RMBL RMBL RMBL
UGH... IF YOU DON'T CUT THAT OUT, WE'LL NEVER GET OUT OF HERE.

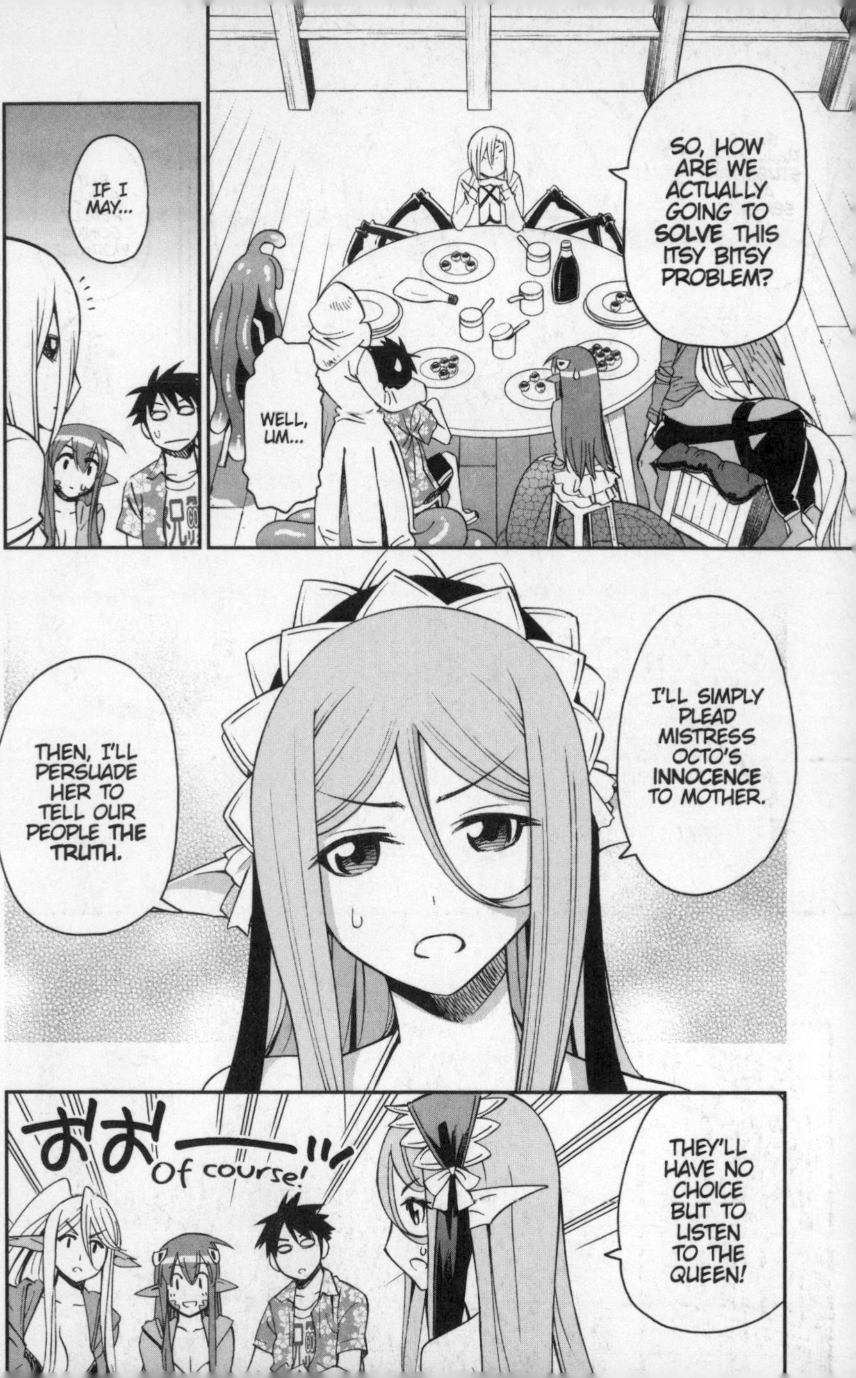
SO, HOW ARE WE ACTUALLY GOING TO SOLVE THIS ITSY BITSY PROBLEM?
WELL, UM...
IF I MAY...
I'LL SIMPLY PLEAD MISTRESS OCTO'S INNOCENCE TO MOTHER.
THEN, I'LL PERSUADE HER TO TELL OUR PEOPLE THE TRUTH.
THEY'LL HAVE NO CHOICE BUT TO LISTEN TO THE QUEEN!
おお――!!
Of course!

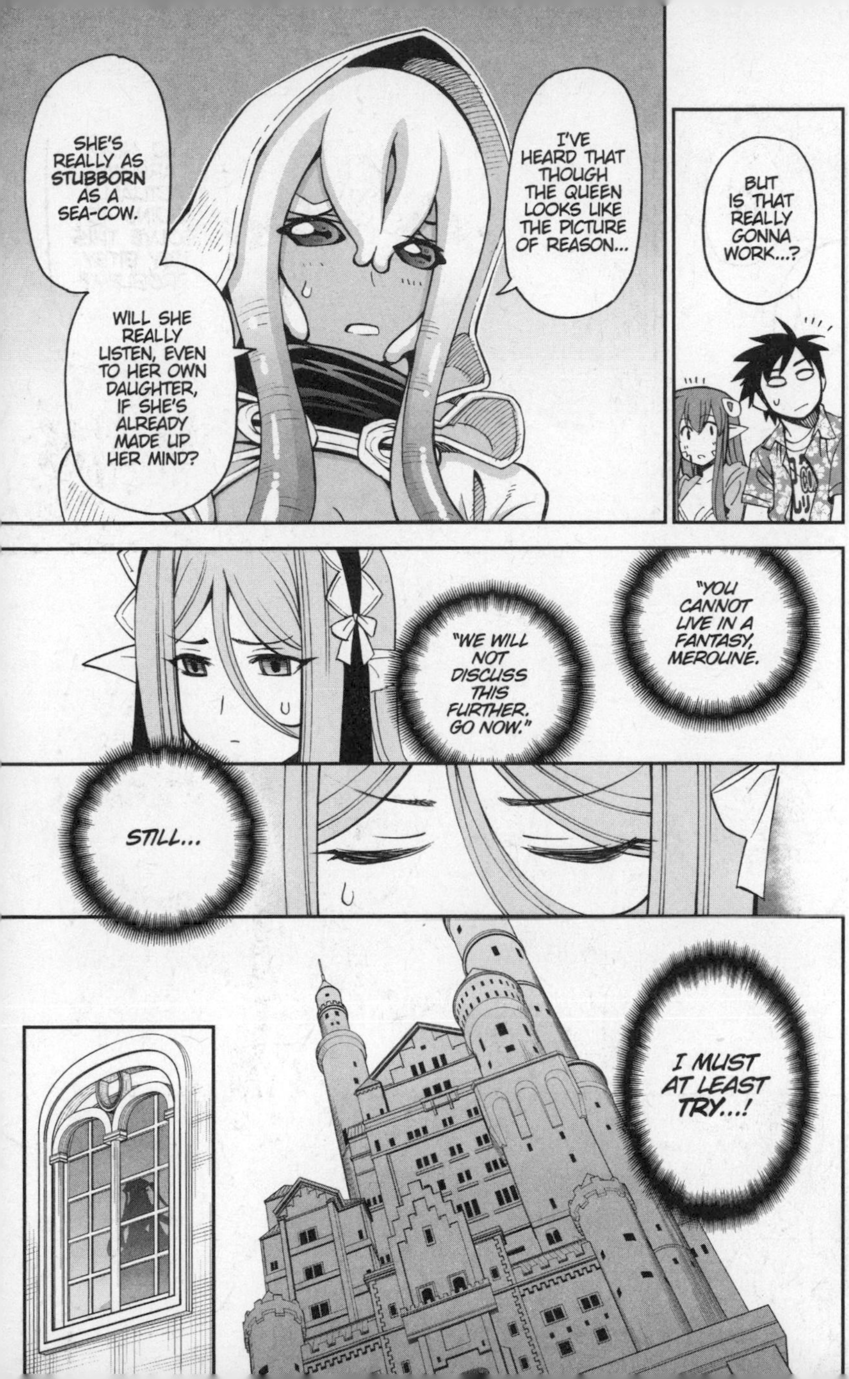
BUT IS THAT REALLY GONNA WORK...?
I'VE HEARD THAT THOUGH THE QUEEN LOOKS LIKE THE PICTURE OF REASON...
SHE'S REALLY AS STUBBORN AS A SEA-COW.
WILL SHE REALLY LISTEN, EVEN TO HER OWN DAUGHTER, IF SHE'S ALREADY MADE UP HER MIND?
"YOU CANNOT LIVE IN A FANTASY, MEROUNE.
"WE WILL NOT DISCUSS THIS FURTHER. GO NOW."
STILL...
I MUST AT LEAST TRY...!

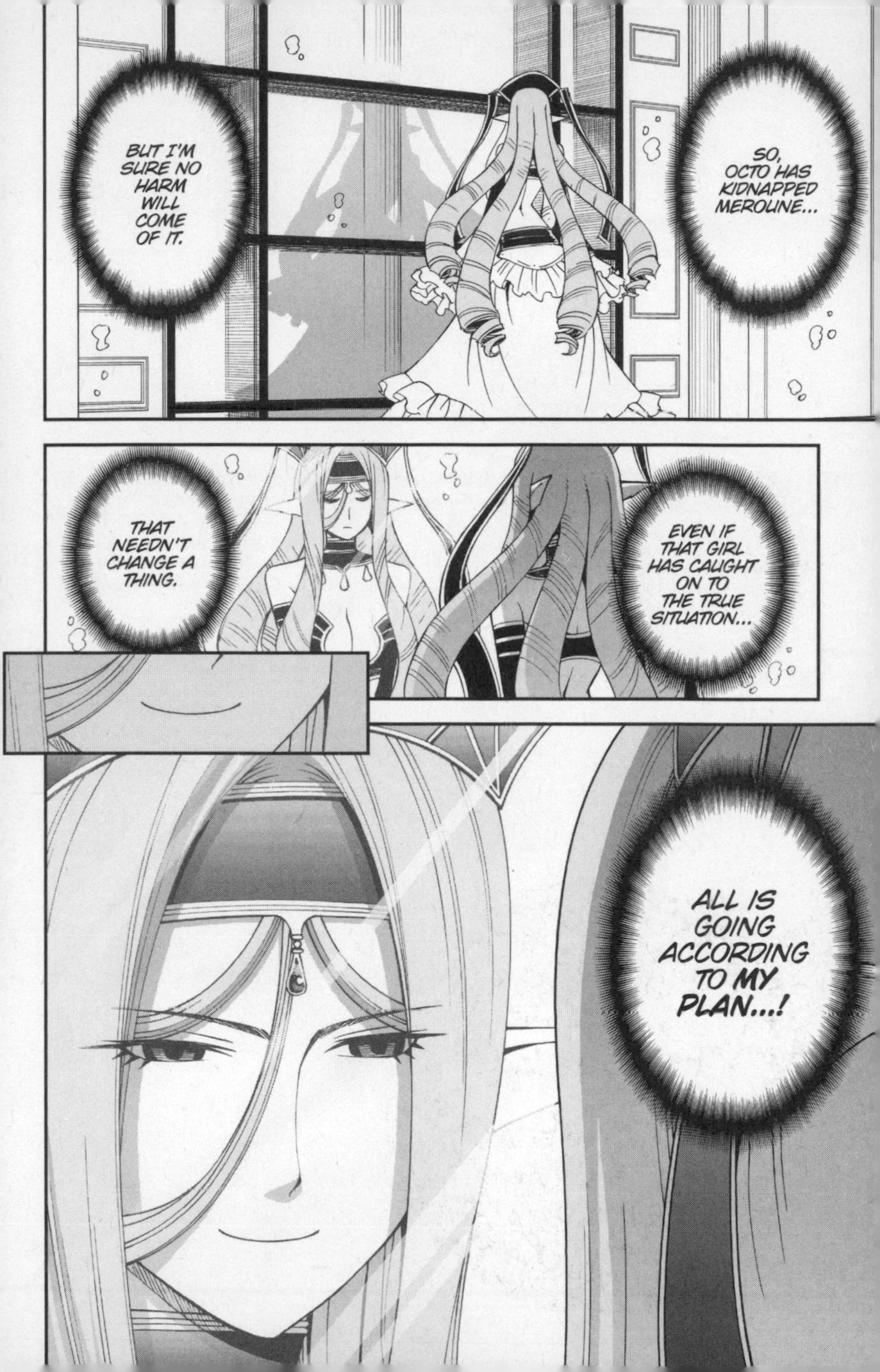
SO, OCTO HAS KIDNAPPED MEROUNE...
BUT I'M SURE NO HARM WILL COME OF IT.
EVEN IF THAT GIRL HAS CAUGHT ON TO THE TRUE SITUATION...
THAT NEEDN'T CHANGE A THING.
ALL IS GOING ACCORDING TO MY PLAN...!

Monster Musume

Everyday Life with Monster Girls

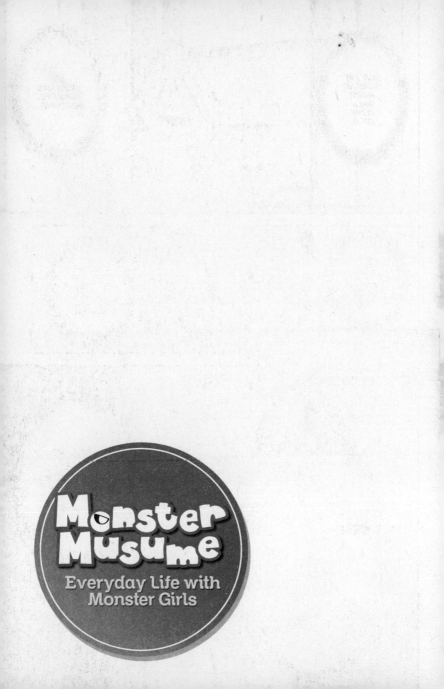

WELL, YOU SEE...WE USED TO DREAM OF BECOMING RAVISHING YOUNG MERMEN BUTLERS.
AND SO WE SECRETLY SOUGHT OUT THE WITCH, HOPING SHE WOULD TRANSFORM US...
WHA ...?
I'M GUES-SING SHE SAID NO?

Chapter 37

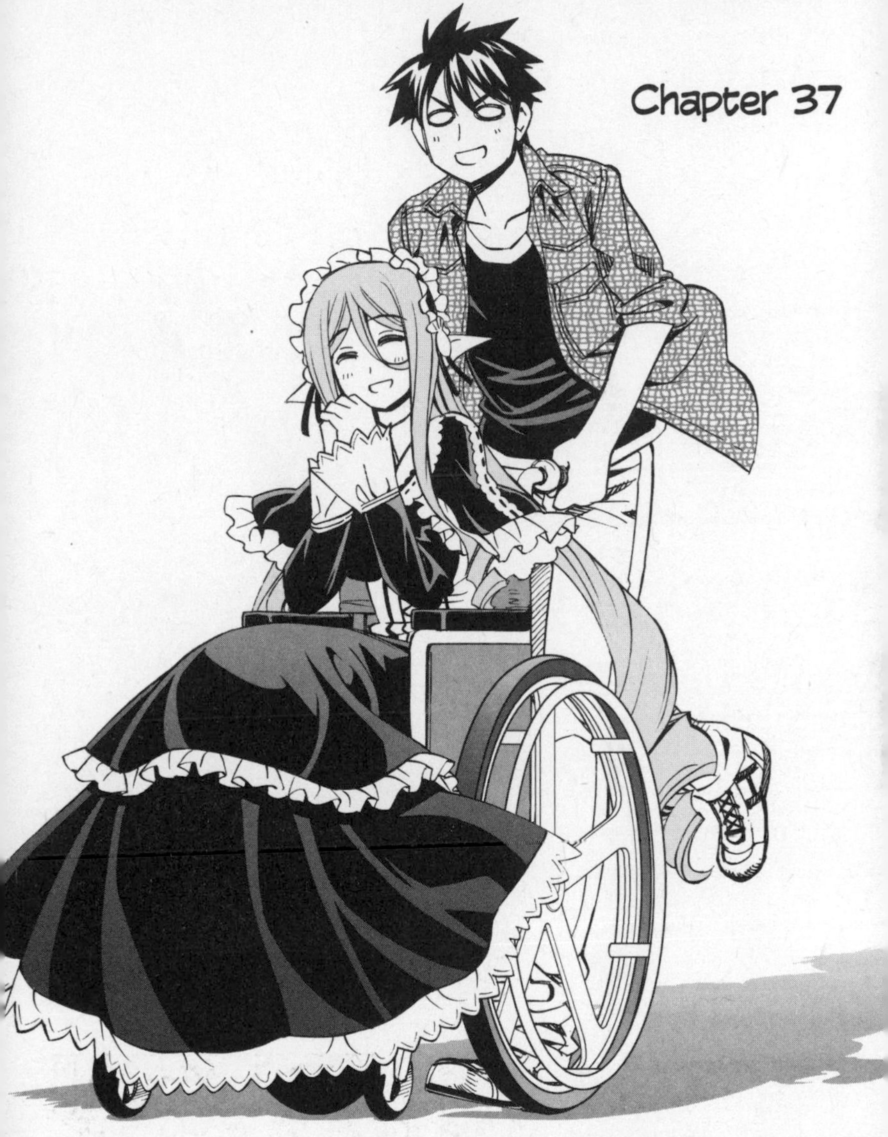

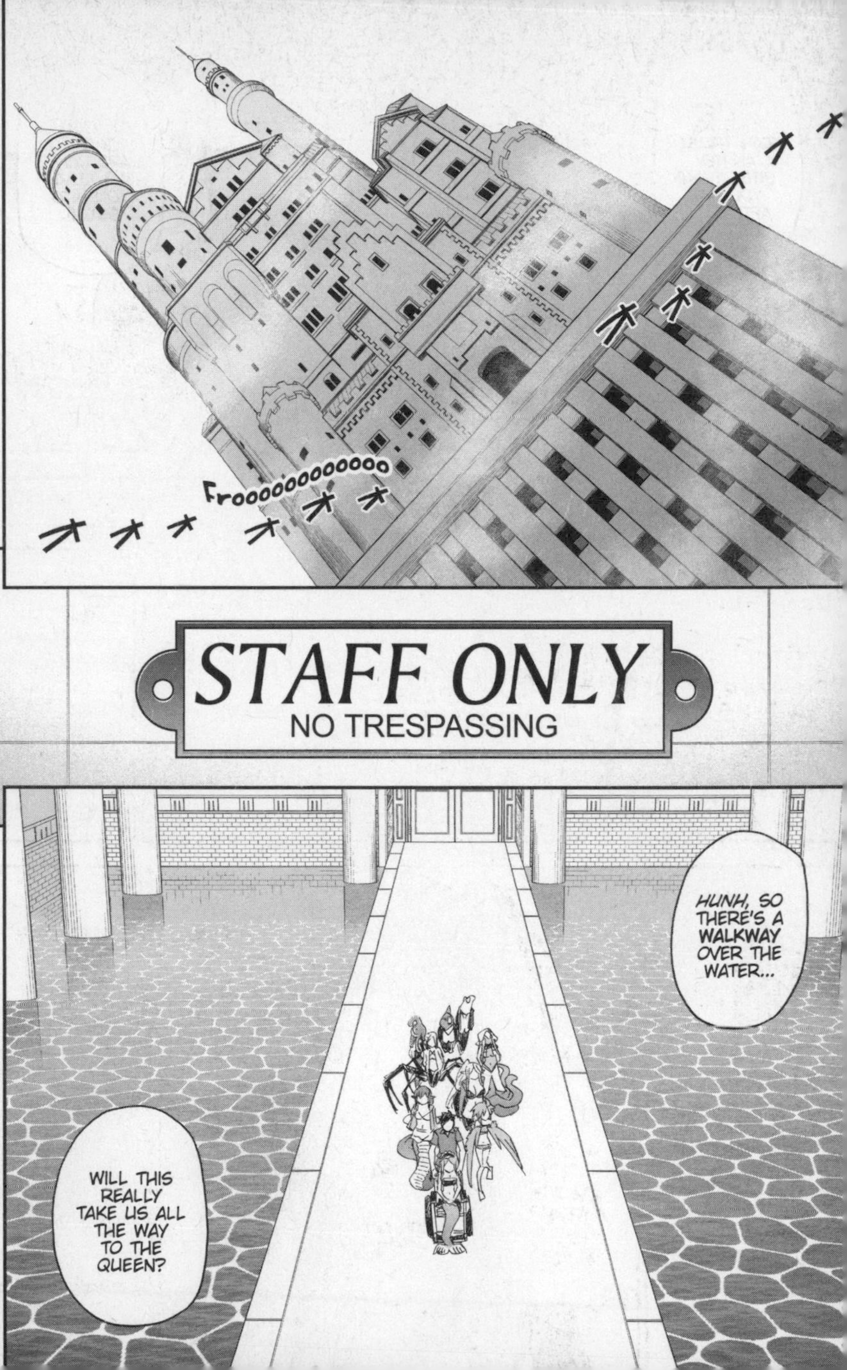
Froooooooooooo
STAFF ONLY
NO TRESPASSING
HUNH, SO THERE'S A WALKWAY OVER THE WATER...
WILL THIS REALLY TAKE US ALL THE WAY TO THE QUEEN?

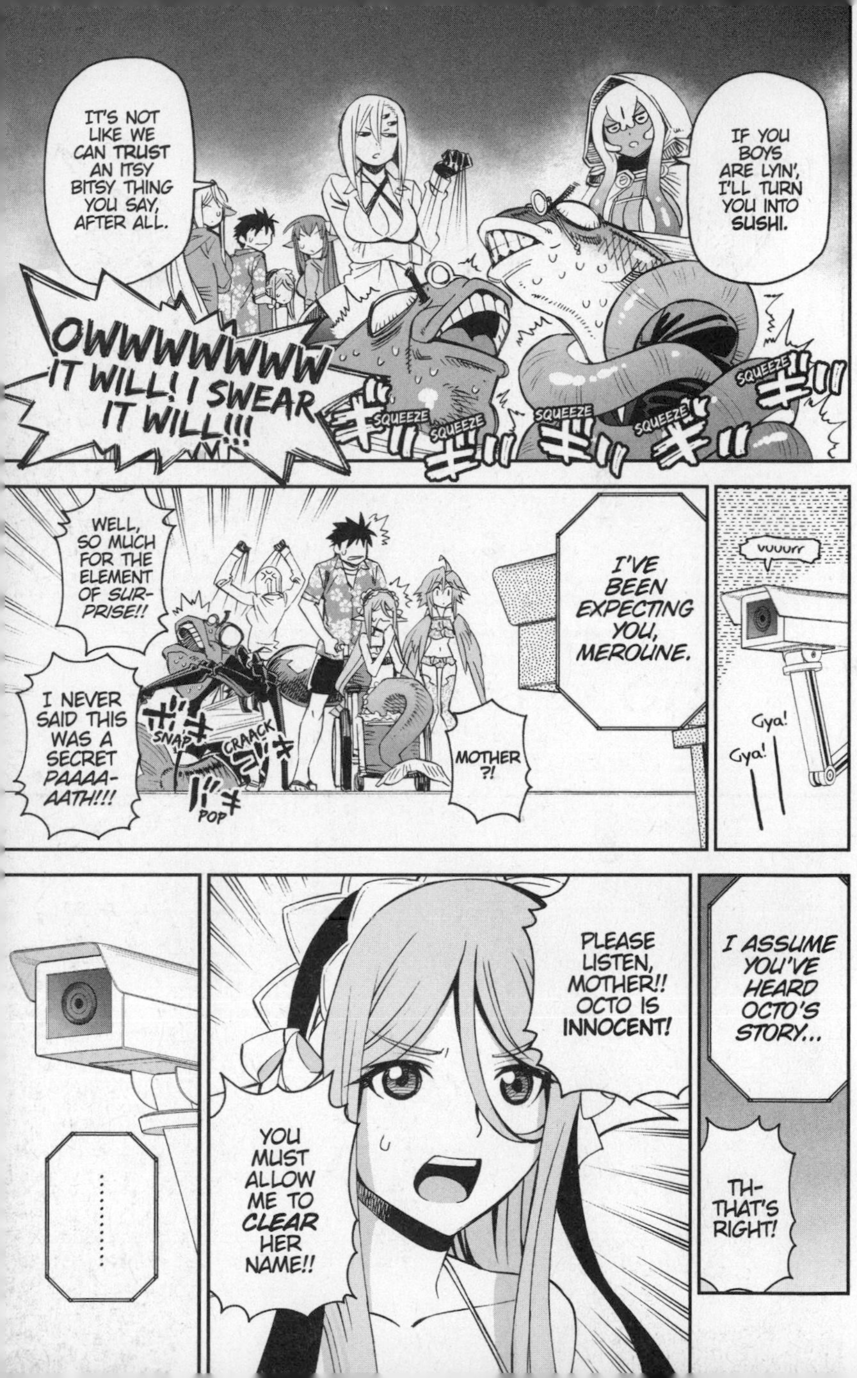
IF YOU BOYS ARE LYIN', I'LL TURN YOU INTO SUSHI.
IT'S NOT LIKE WE CAN TRUST AN ITSY BITSY THING YOU SAY, AFTER ALL.
OWWWWWWWW
IT WILL! I SWEAR IT WILL!!!
SQUEEZE
SQUEEZE
SQUEEZE
SQUEEZE
SQUEEZE
vuuurr
Gya!
Gya!
I'VE BEEN EXPECTING YOU, MEROUNE.
MOTHER ?!
WELL, SO MUCH FOR THE ELEMENT OF SUR-PRISE!!
I NEVER SAID THIS WAS A SECRET PAAAA-AATH!!!
SNAP
CRAACK
POP
I ASSUME YOU'VE HEARD OCTO'S STORY...
TH-THAT'S RIGHT!
PLEASE LISTEN, MOTHER!! OCTO IS INNOCENT!
YOU MUST ALLOW ME TO CLEAR HER NAME!!
......

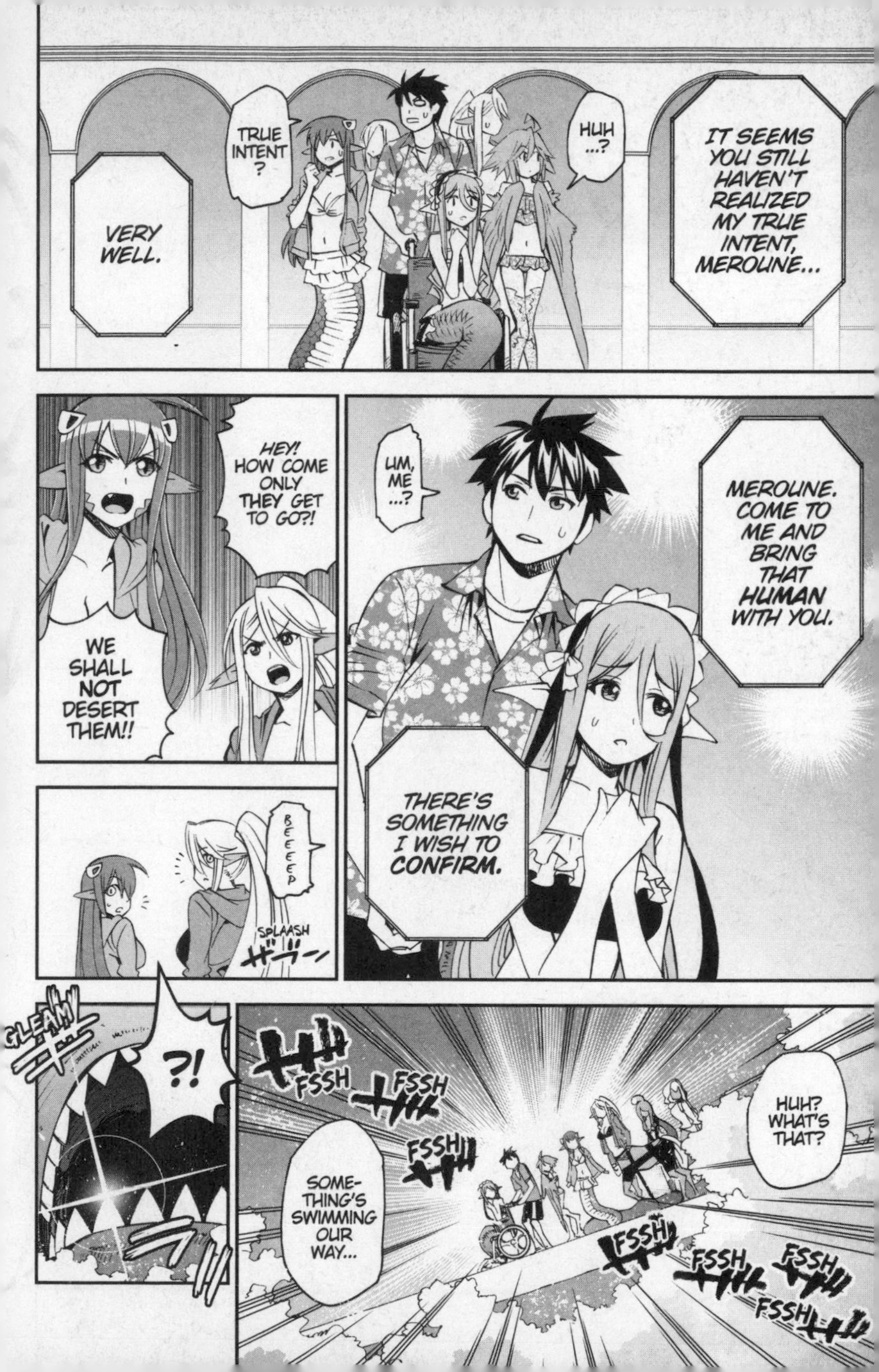
IT SEEMS YOU STILL HAVEN'T REALIZED MY TRUE INTENT, MEROUNE...
HUH ...?
TRUE INTENT ?
VERY WELL.
MEROUNE. COME TO ME AND BRING THAT HUMAN WITH YOU.
UM, ME ...?
THERE'S SOMETHING I WISH TO CONFIRM.
HEY! HOW COME ONLY THEY GET TO GO?!
WE SHALL NOT DESERT THEM!!
BEEEEP
SPLAASH
HUH? WHAT'S THAT?
FSSH
FSSH
FSSH
SOME-THING'S SWIMMING OUR WAY...
FSSH
FSSH
FSSH
FSSH
?!
GLEAM

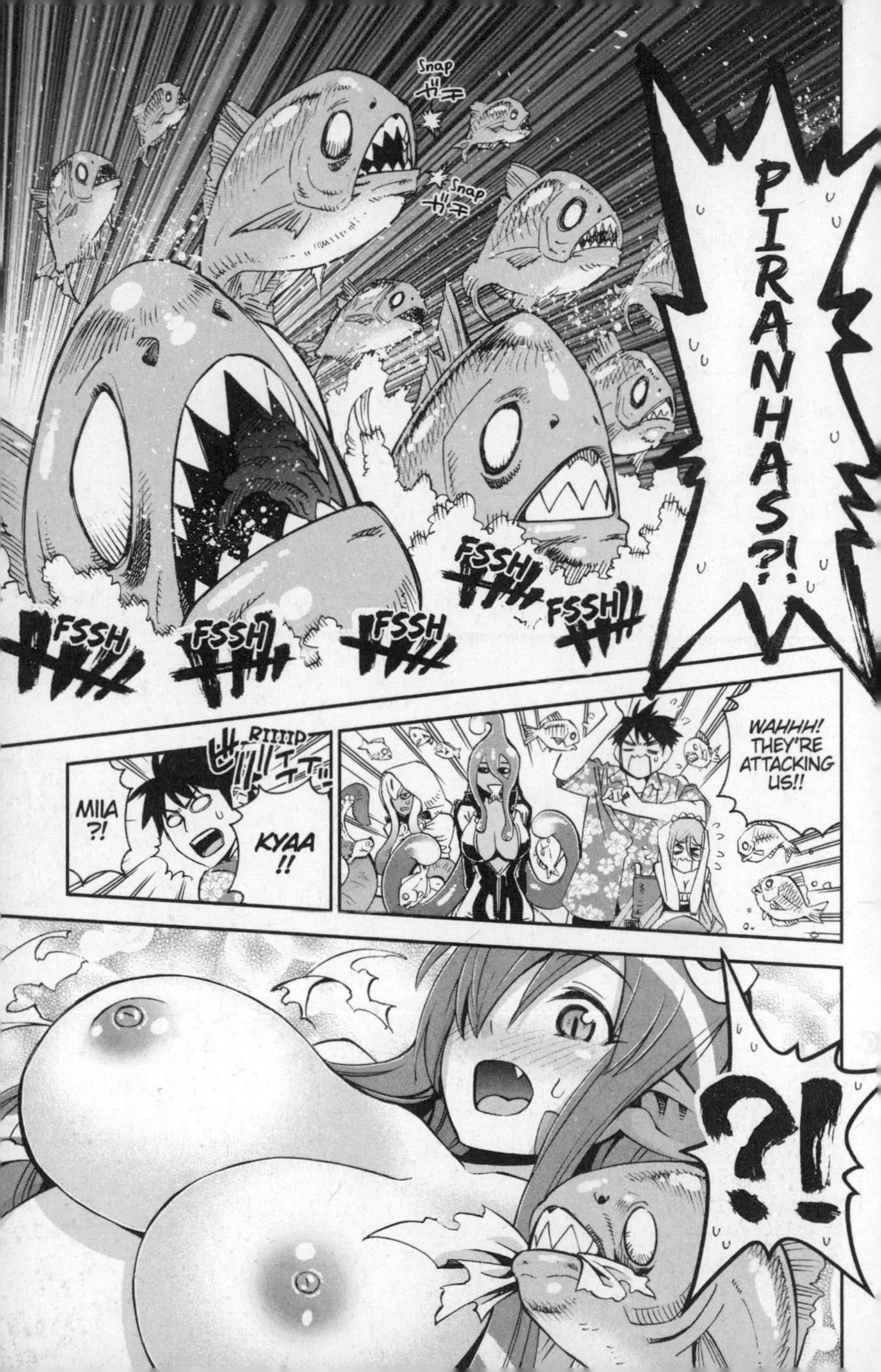
PIRANHAS?!
Snap
ガチ
Snap
ガチ
FSSH
FSSH
FSSH
FSSH
FSSH
WAHHH! THEY'RE ATTACKING US!!
RIIIIP
MIIA ?!
KYAA !!
?!

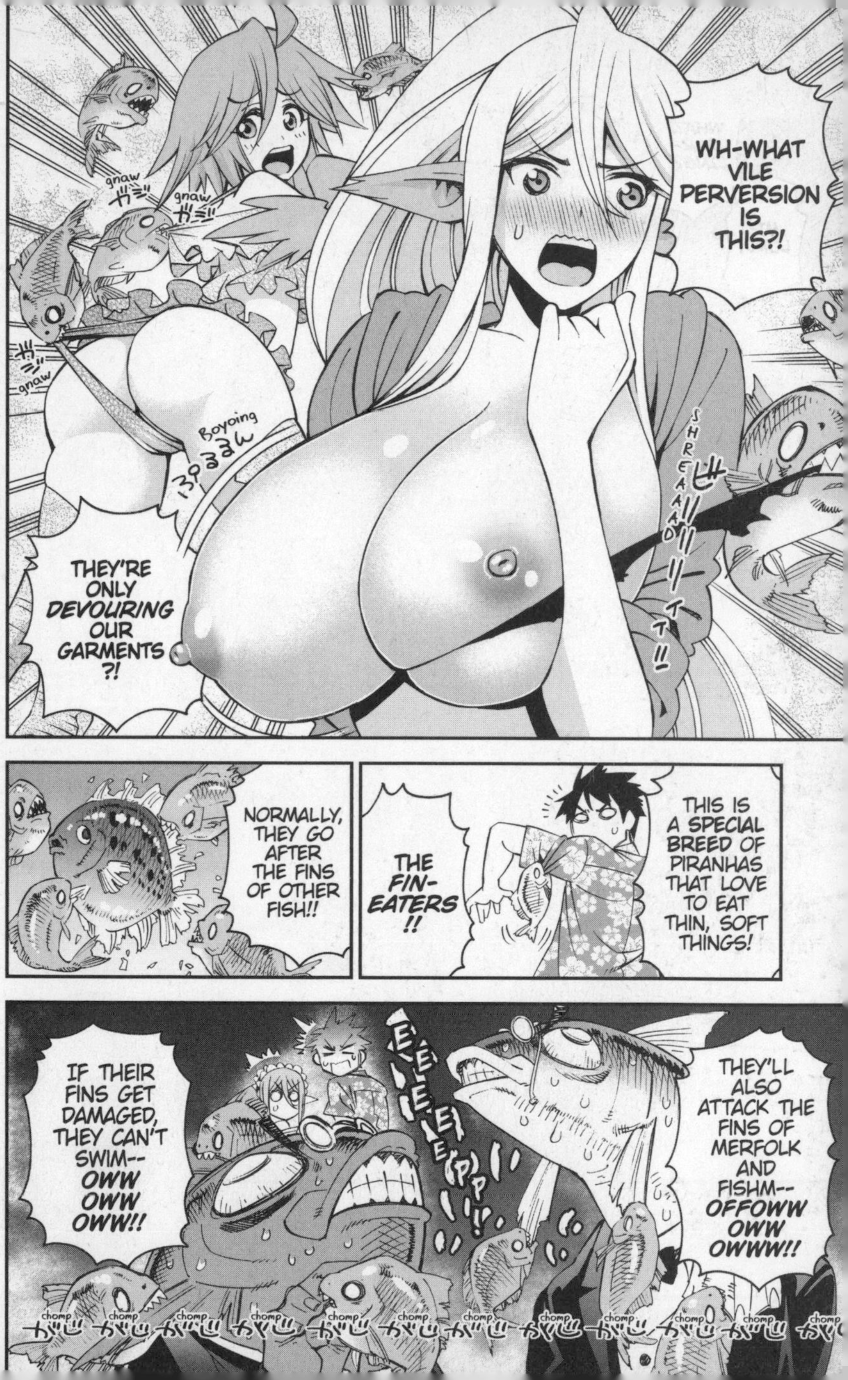
WH-WHAT VILE PERVERSION IS THIS?!
SHREAAAD
Boyoing
gnaw
gnaw
gnaw
THEY'RE ONLY DEVOURING OUR GARMENTS?!
THIS IS A SPECIAL BREED OF PIRANHAS THAT LOVE TO EAT THIN, SOFT THINGS!
THE FIN-EATERS!!
NORMALLY, THEY GO AFTER THE FINS OF OTHER FISH!!
THEY'LL ALSO ATTACK THE FINS OF MERFOLK AND FISHM-- OFFOWW OWW OWWW!!
EEEEEEEPP!!
IF THEIR FINS GET DAMAGED, THEY CAN'T SWIM-- OWW OWW OWW!!
chomp chomp chomp chomp chomp chomp chomp chomp chomp chomp chomp

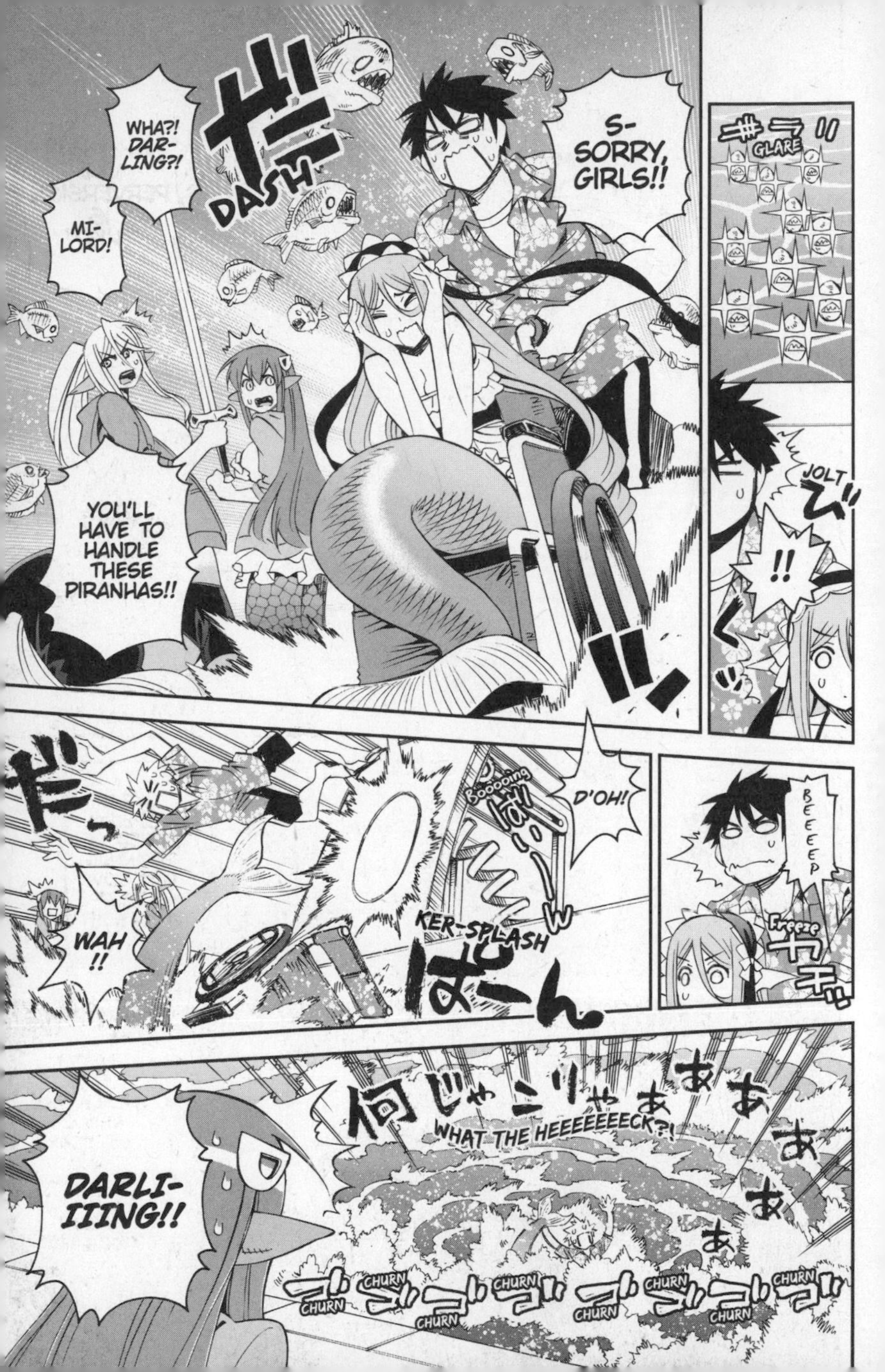
GLARE
JOLT
!!
S-SORRY, GIRLS!!
DASH
WHA?! DAR-LING?!
MI-LORD!
YOU'LL HAVE TO HANDLE THESE PIRANHAS!!
BEEEEP
Freeze
D'OH!
Booooing
KER-SPLASH
WAH!!
WHAT THE HEEEEEEECK?!
DARLI-IIING!!
CHURN
CHURN
CHURN
CHURN
CHURN
CHURN
CHURN
CHURN

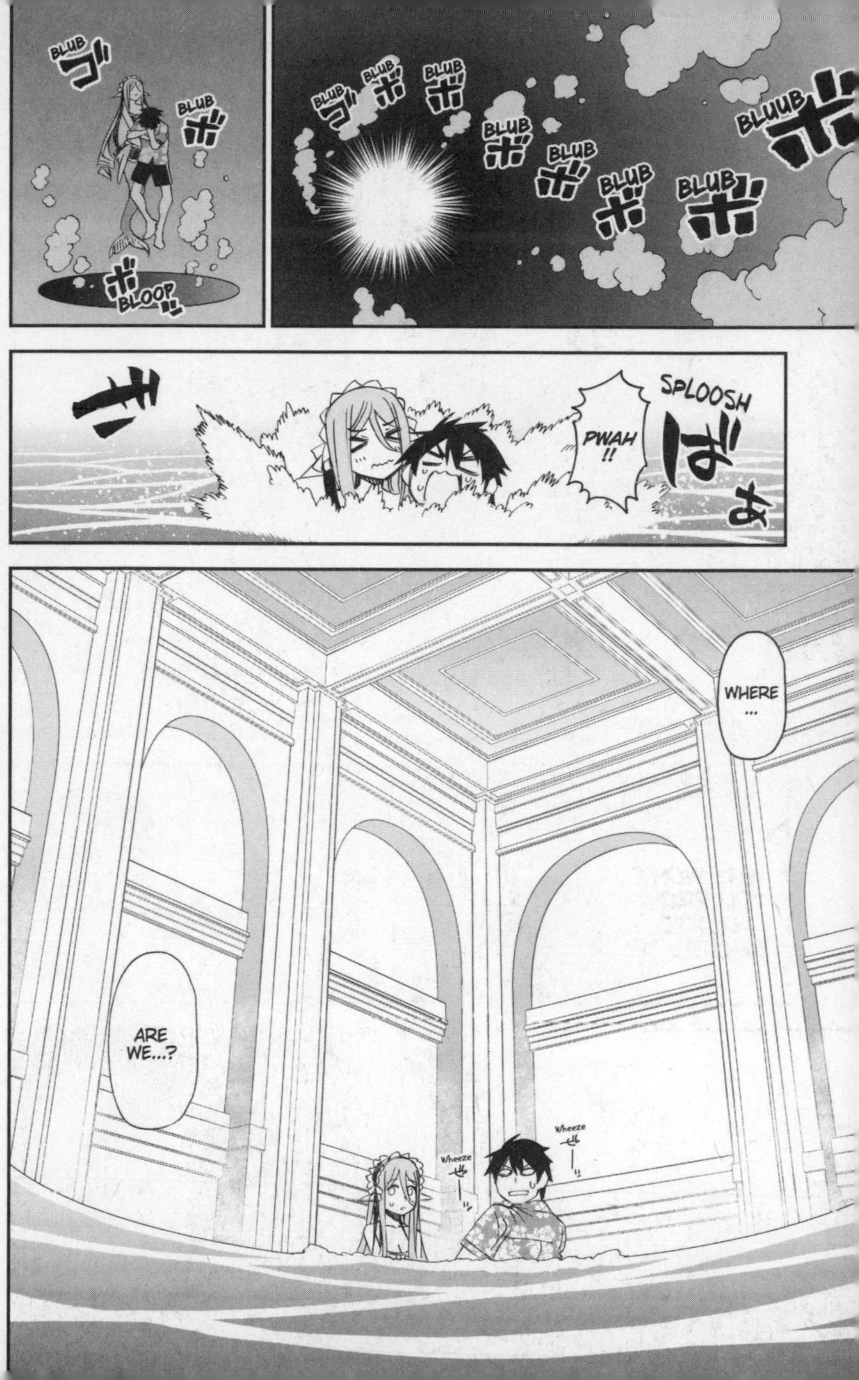
BLUUB
ボ
BLUB
ボ
BLUB
ボ
BLUB
ボ
BLUB
ボ
BLUB
ボ
BLUB
ボ
BLUB
ゴ
BLUB
ゴ
BLUB
ボ
ボ
BLOOP
SPLOOSH
ばあ
PWAH!!
ざ
WHERE...
ARE WE...?
Wheeze
ぜー!!
Wheeze
ぜー!!

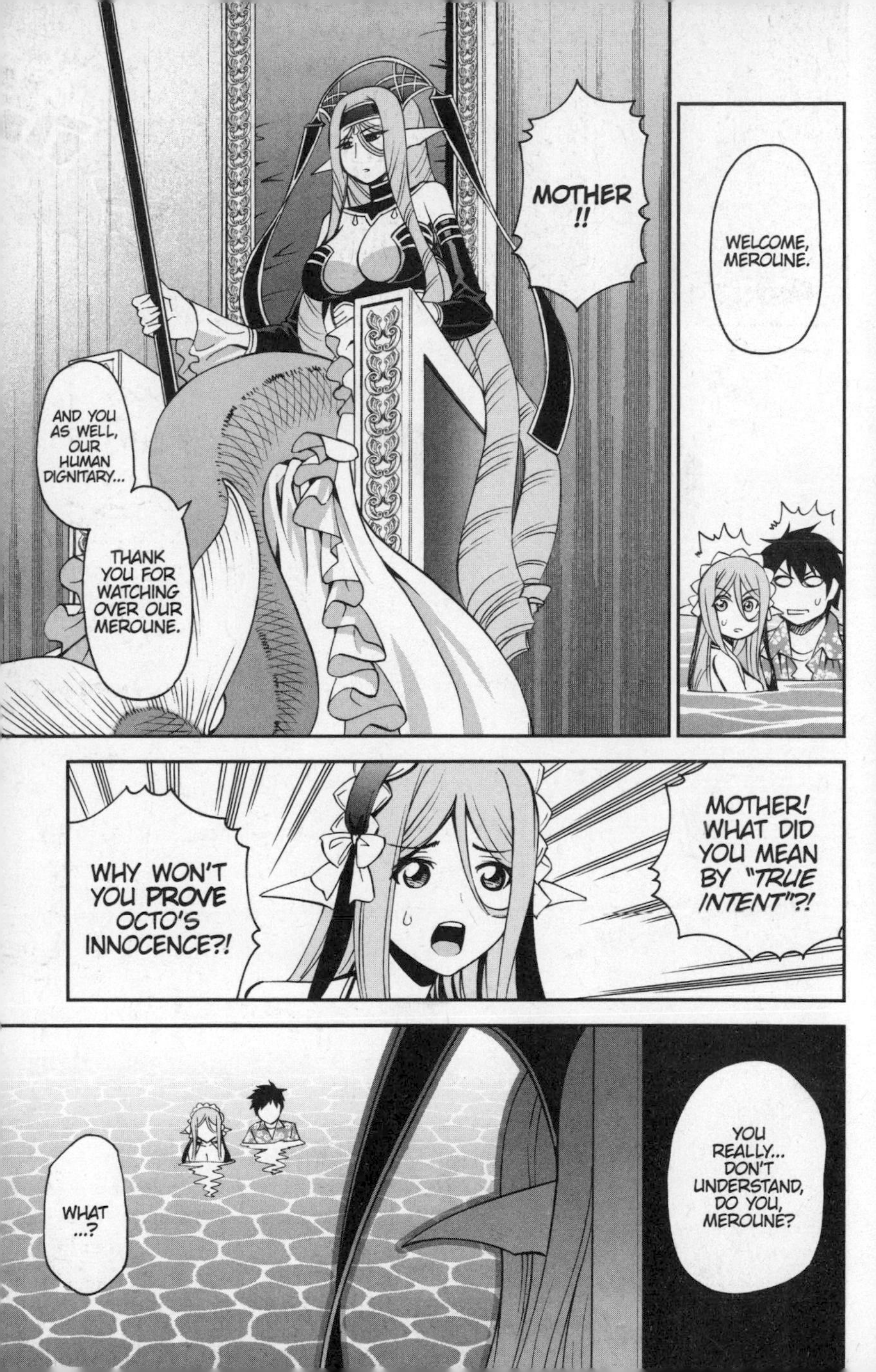
WELCOME, MEROUNE.
MOTHER !!
AND YOU AS WELL, OUR HUMAN DIGNITARY...
THANK YOU FOR WATCHING OVER OUR MEROUNE.
MOTHER! WHAT DID YOU MEAN BY "TRUE INTENT"?!
WHY WON'T YOU PROVE OCTO'S INNOCENCE?!
YOU REALLY... DON'T UNDERSTAND, DO YOU, MEROUNE?
WHAT ...?

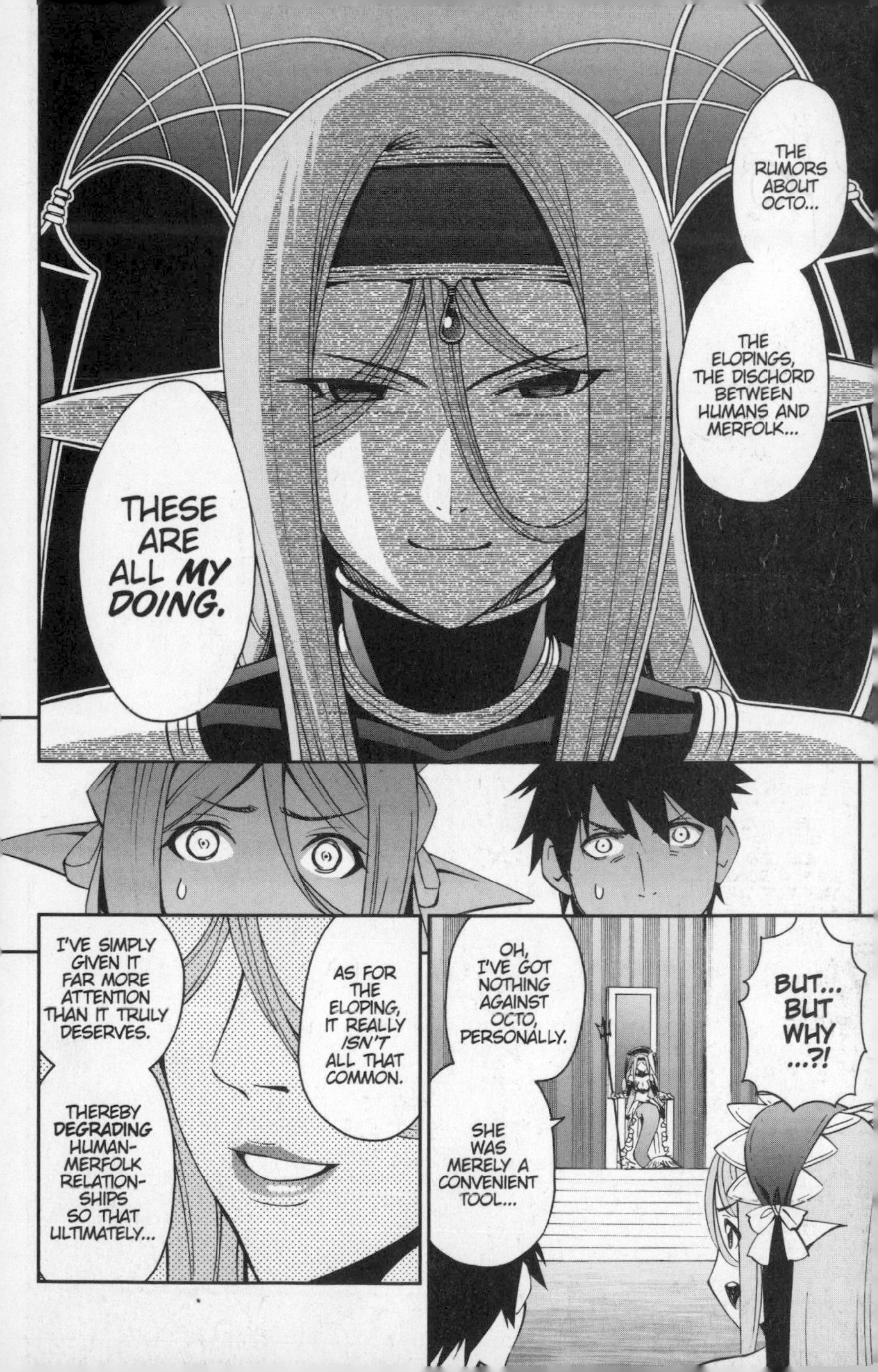
THE RUMORS ABOUT OCTO...
THE ELOPINGS, THE DISCHORD BETWEEN HUMANS AND MERFOLK...
THESE ARE ALL *MY DOING.*
BUT... BUT WHY ...?!
OH, I'VE GOT NOTHING AGAINST OCTO, PERSONALLY.
SHE WAS MERELY A CONVENIENT TOOL...
AS FOR THE ELOPING, IT REALLY *ISN'T* ALL THAT COMMON.
I'VE SIMPLY GIVEN IT FAR MORE ATTENTION THAN IT TRULY DESERVES.
THEREBY **DEGRADING** HUMAN-MERFOLK RELATIONSHIPS SO THAT ULTIMATELY...

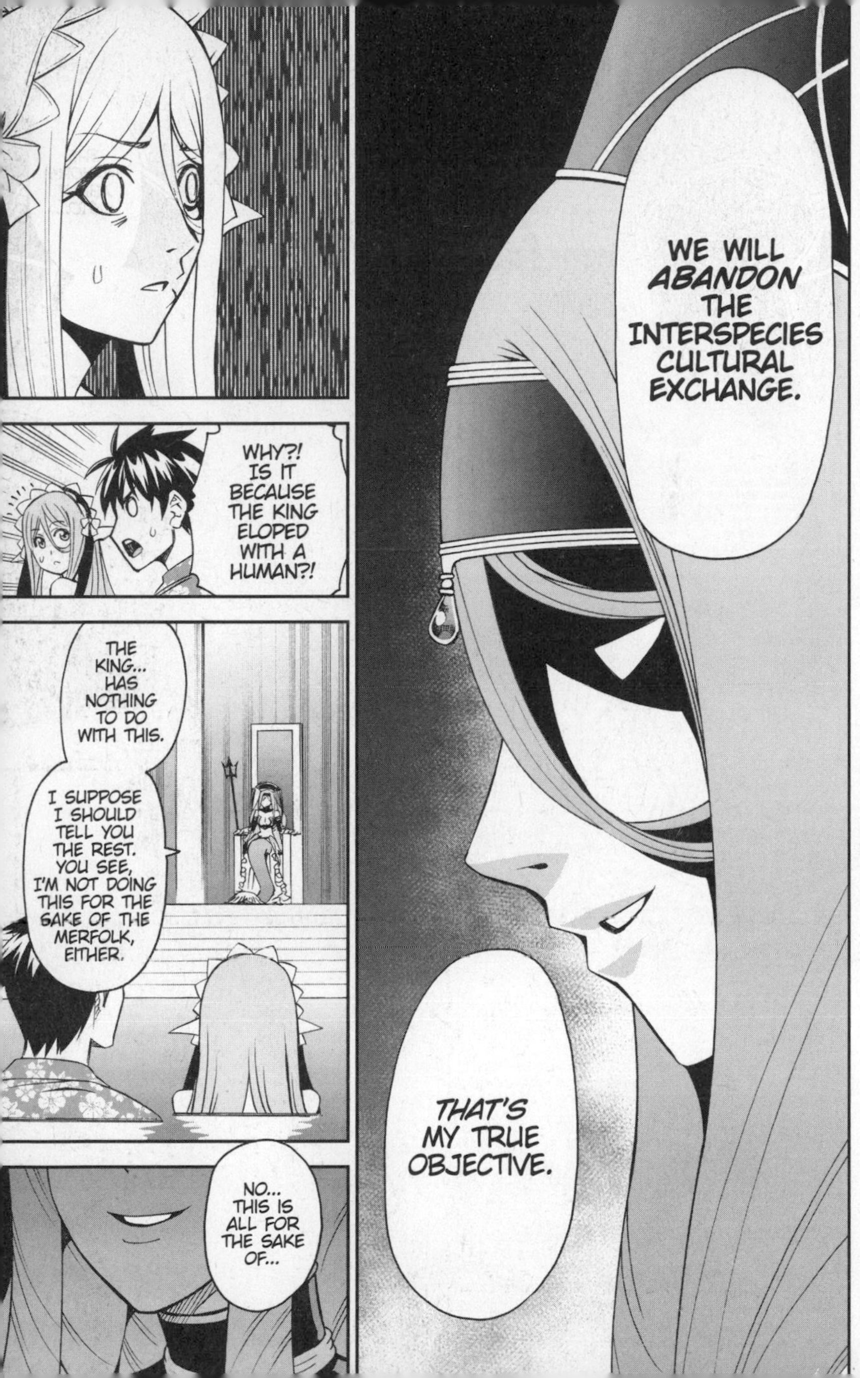
WE WILL *ABANDON* THE INTERSPECIES CULTURAL EXCHANGE.
THAT'S MY TRUE OBJECTIVE.
WHY?! IS IT BECAUSE THE KING ELOPED WITH A HUMAN?!
THE KING... HAS NOTHING TO DO WITH THIS.
I SUPPOSE I SHOULD TELL YOU THE REST. YOU SEE, I'M NOT DOING THIS FOR THE SAKE OF THE MERFOLK, EITHER.
NO... THIS IS ALL FOR THE SAKE OF...

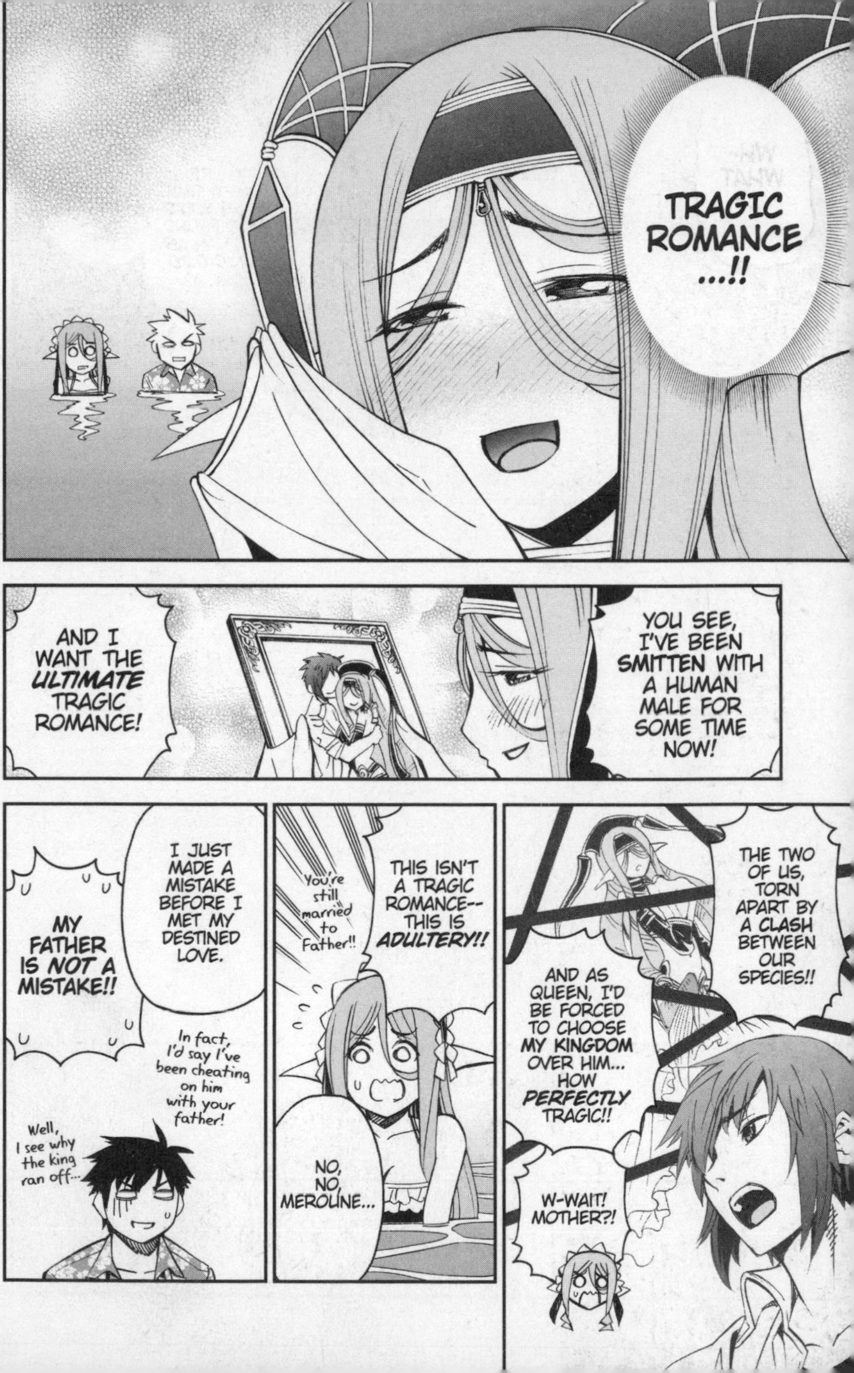
TRAGIC ROMANCE ....!!
YOU SEE, I'VE BEEN SMITTEN WITH A HUMAN MALE FOR SOME TIME NOW!
AND I WANT THE ULTIMATE TRAGIC ROMANCE!
THE TWO OF US, TORN APART BY A CLASH BETWEEN OUR SPECIES!!
AND AS QUEEN, I'D BE FORCED TO CHOOSE MY KINGDOM OVER HIM... HOW PERFECTLY TRAGIC!!
W-WAIT! MOTHER?!
THIS ISN'T A TRAGIC ROMANCE-- THIS IS ADULTERY!!
You're still married to Father!!
NO, NO, MEROUNE...
I JUST MADE A MISTAKE BEFORE I MET MY DESTINED LOVE.
MY FATHER IS NOT A MISTAKE!!
In fact, I'd say I've been cheating on him with your father!
Well, I see why the king ran off...

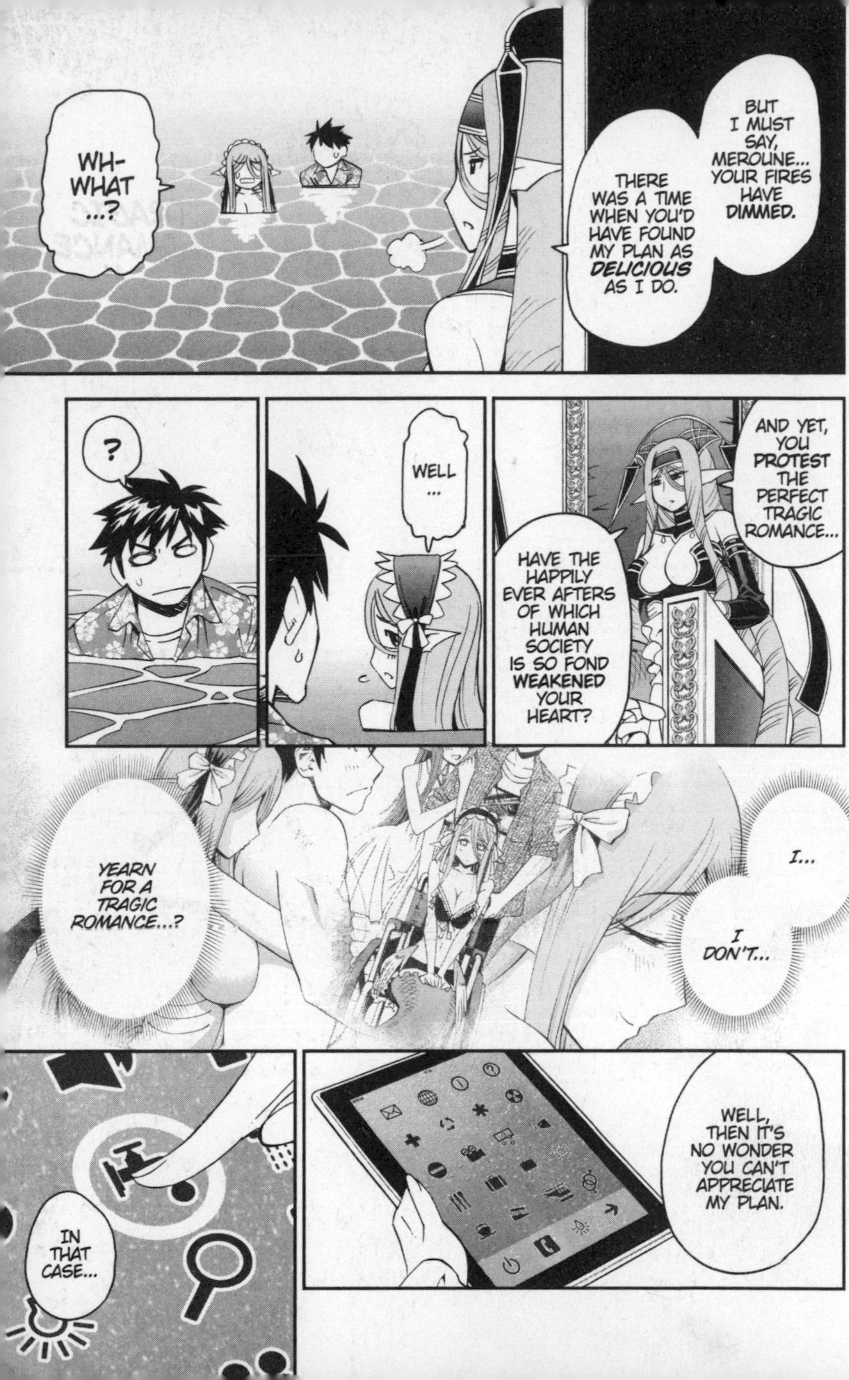
BUT I MUST SAY, MEROUNE... YOUR FIRES HAVE DIMMED.
THERE WAS A TIME WHEN YOU'D HAVE FOUND MY PLAN AS DELICIOUS AS I DO.
WH-WHAT ...?
AND YET, YOU PROTEST THE PERFECT TRAGIC ROMANCE...
HAVE THE HAPPILY EVER AFTERS OF WHICH HUMAN SOCIETY IS SO FOND WEAKENED YOUR HEART?
WELL ...
?
I...
I DON'T...
YEARN FOR A TRAGIC ROMANCE...?
WELL, THEN IT'S NO WONDER YOU CAN'T APPRECIATE MY PLAN.
IN THAT CASE...

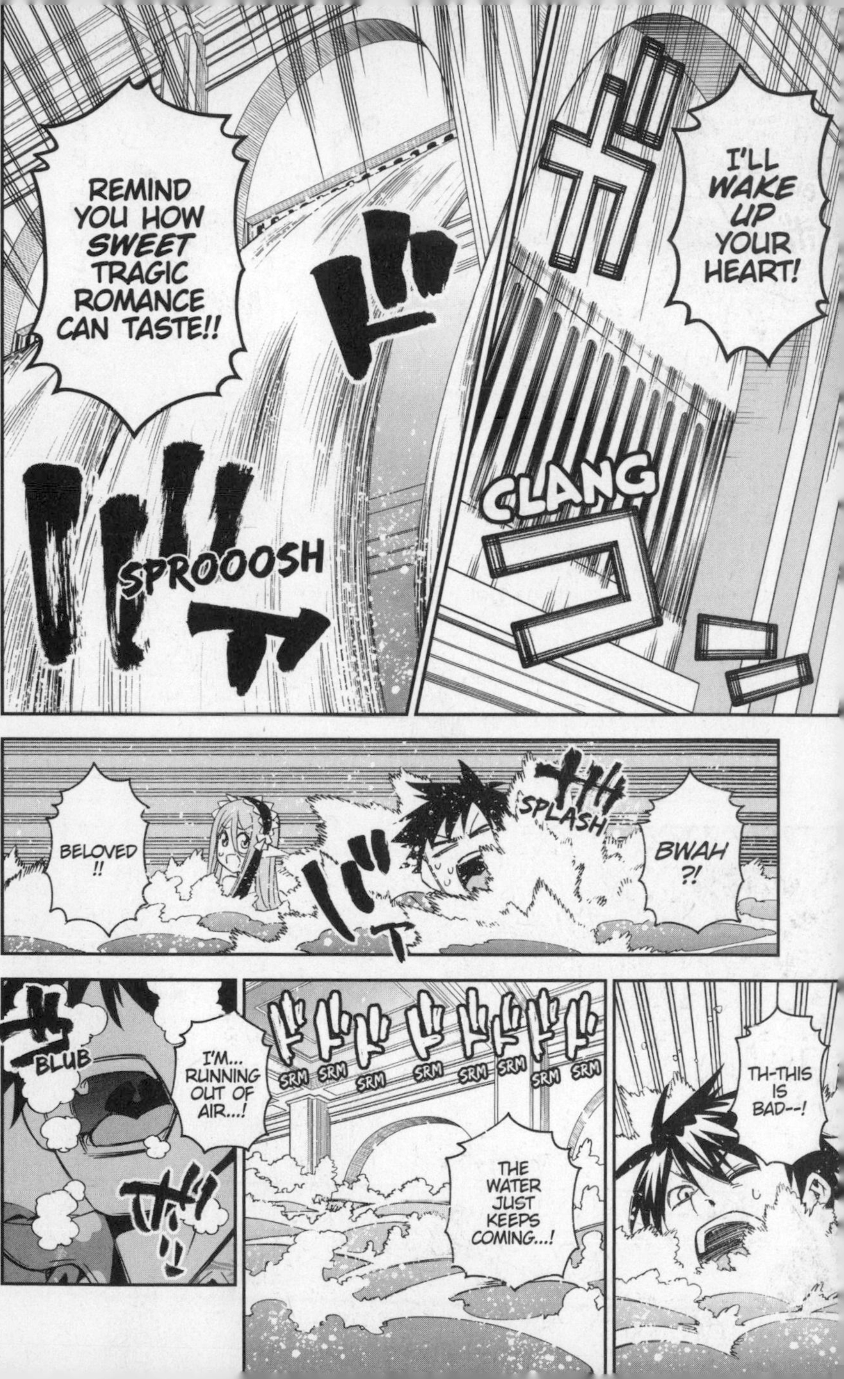
I'LL WAKE UP YOUR HEART!
REMIND YOU HOW SWEET TRAGIC ROMANCE CAN TASTE!!
CLANG
SPROOOSH
BWAH ?!
SPLASH
BELOVED !!
TH-THIS IS BAD--!
SRM SRM SRM SRM SRM SRM SRM SRM
THE WATER JUST KEEPS COMING...!
I'M... RUNNING OUT OF AIR...!
BLUB

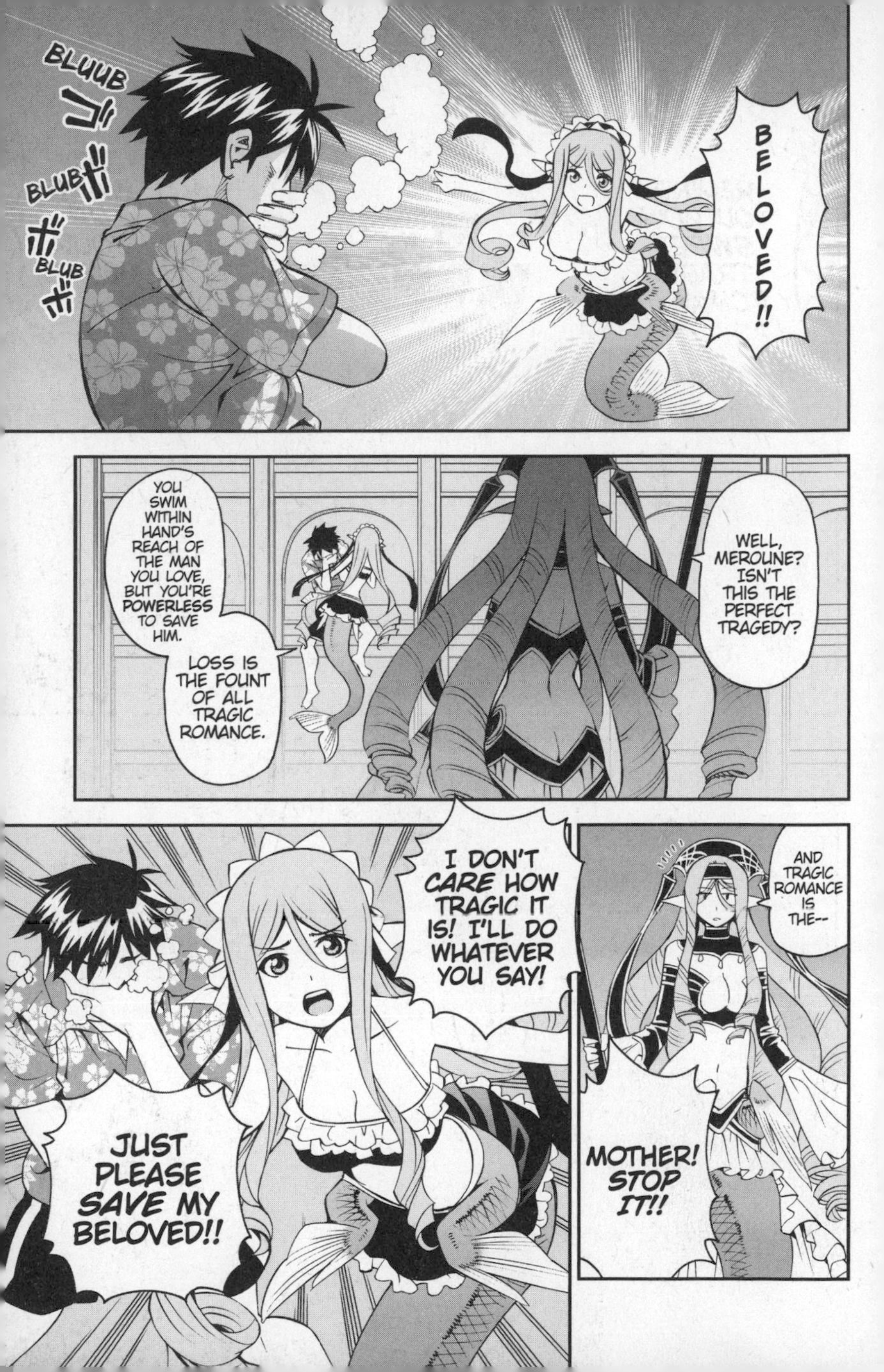
BELOVED!!
BLUUB
BLUB
BLUB
WELL, MEROUNE? ISN'T THIS THE PERFECT TRAGEDY?
YOU SWIM WITHIN HAND'S REACH OF THE MAN YOU LOVE, BUT YOU'RE POWERLESS TO SAVE HIM.
LOSS IS THE FOUNT OF ALL TRAGIC ROMANCE.
AND TRAGIC ROMANCE IS THE--
MOTHER! STOP IT!!
I DON'T CARE HOW TRAGIC IT IS! I'LL DO WHATEVER YOU SAY!
JUST PLEASE SAVE MY BELOVED!!

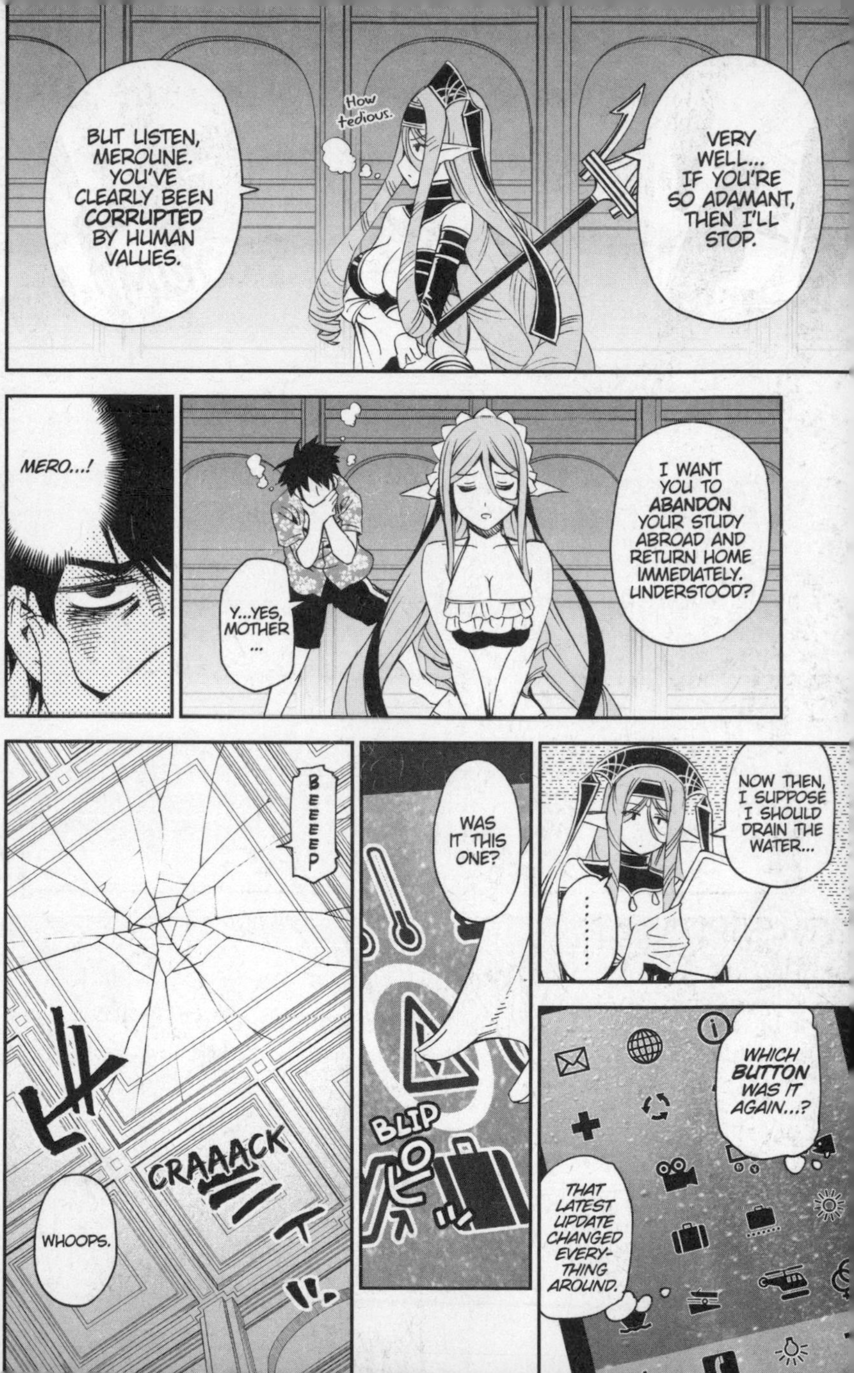
VERY WELL... IF YOU'RE SO ADAMANT, THEN I'LL STOP.
How tedious.
BUT LISTEN, MEROUNE. YOU'VE CLEARLY BEEN CORRUPTED BY HUMAN VALUES.
I WANT YOU TO ABANDON YOUR STUDY ABROAD AND RETURN HOME IMMEDIATELY. UNDERSTOOD?
Y...YES, MOTHER...
MERO...!
NOW THEN, I SUPPOSE I SHOULD DRAIN THE WATER...
......
WHICH BUTTON WAS IT AGAIN...?
THAT LATEST UPDATE CHANGED EVERYTHING AROUND.
WAS IT THIS ONE?
BLIP
BEEEEEP
CRAAACK
WHOOPS.

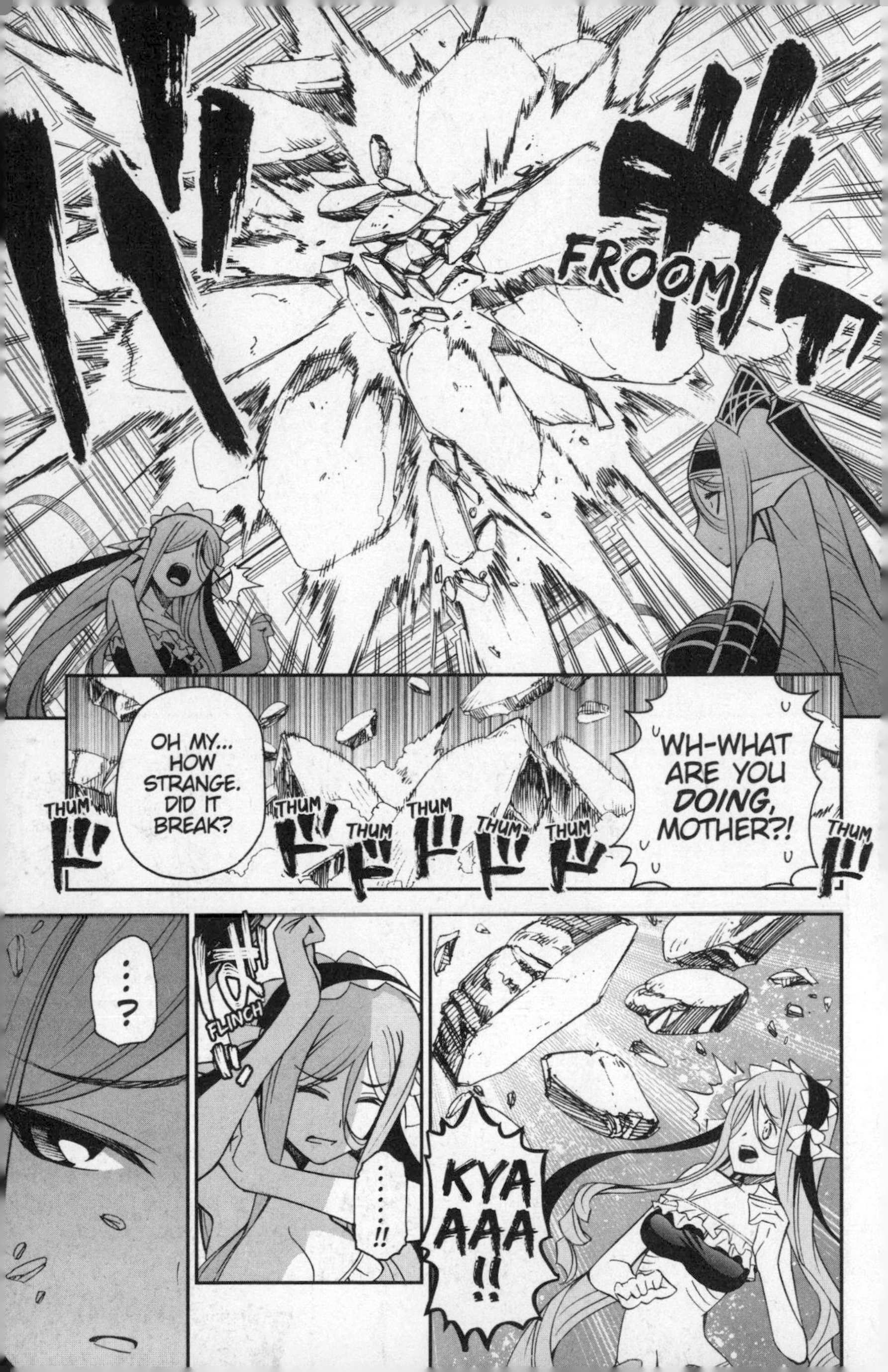
FROOM
THUM
WH-WHAT ARE YOU DOING, MOTHER?!
THUM
THUM
THUM
THUM
THUM
OH MY... HOW STRANGE. DID IT BREAK?
THUM
KYAAAA!!
FLINCH
......!!
...?

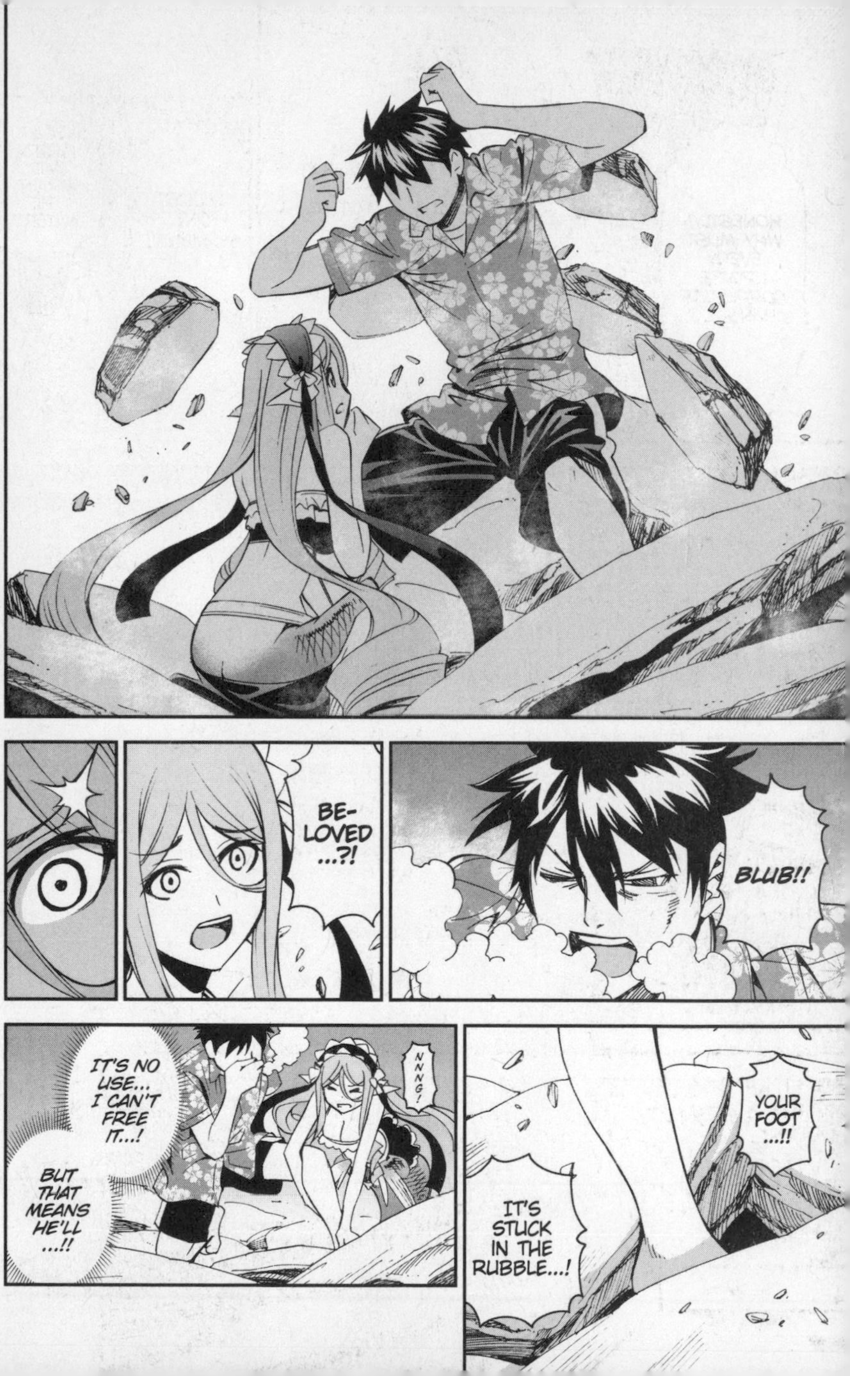
BLUB!!
BE-LOVED ...?!
YOUR FOOT ...!!
IT'S STUCK IN THE RUBBLE...!
NNNG!
IT'S NO USE... I CAN'T FREE IT...!
BUT THAT MEANS HE'LL ...!!

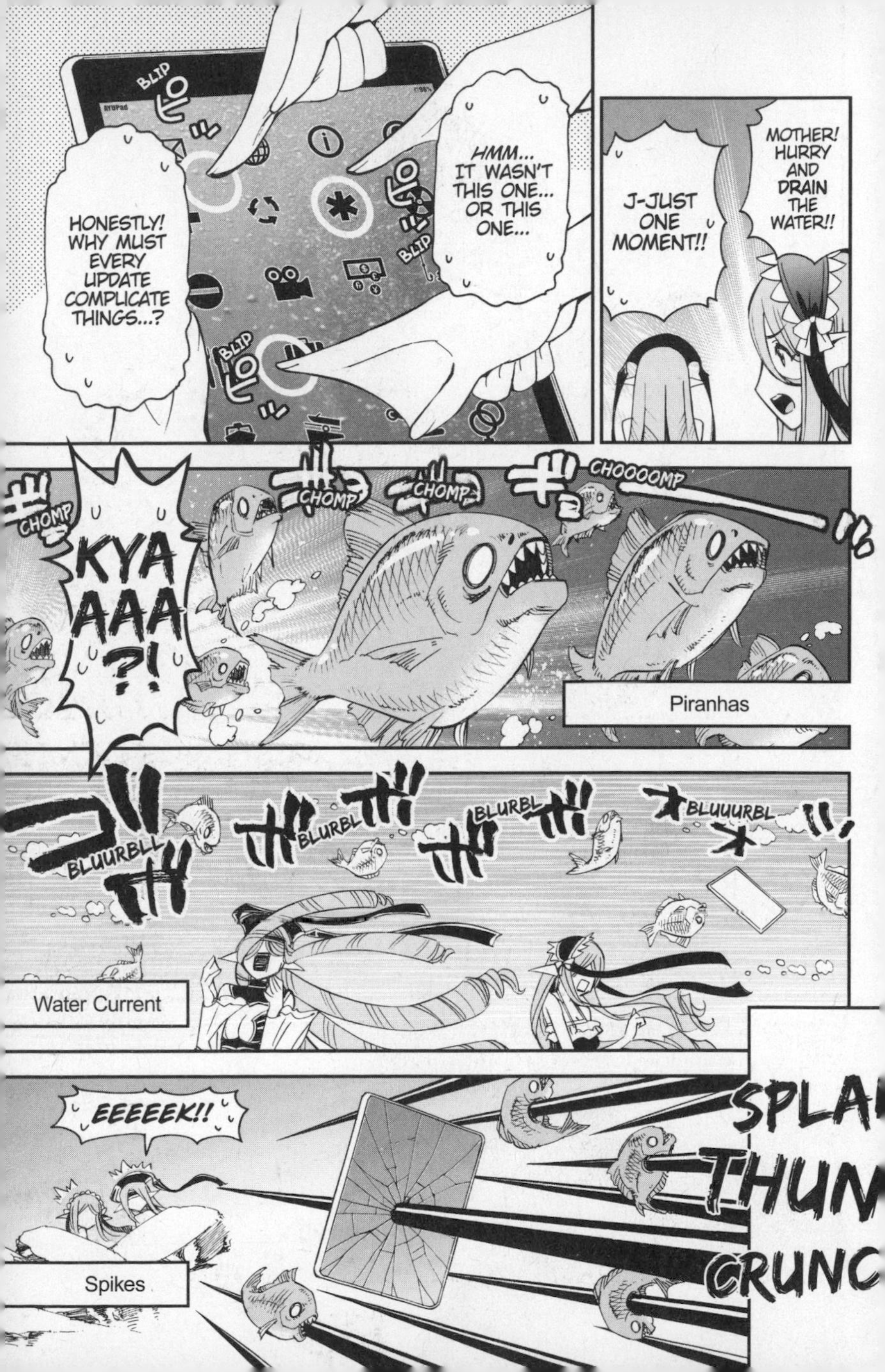
MOTHER! HURRY AND DRAIN THE WATER!!
J-JUST ONE MOMENT!!
HMM... IT WASN'T THIS ONE... OR THIS ONE...
BLIP
BLIP
HONESTLY! WHY MUST EVERY UPDATE COMPLICATE THINGS...?
BLIP
CHOOOOMP
CHOMP
CHOMP
KYAAAA?!
CHOMP
Piranhas
BLUUURBL
BLURBL
BLURBL
BLUURBLL
Water Current
SPLA
THUM
CRUNC
EEEEEK!!
Spikes

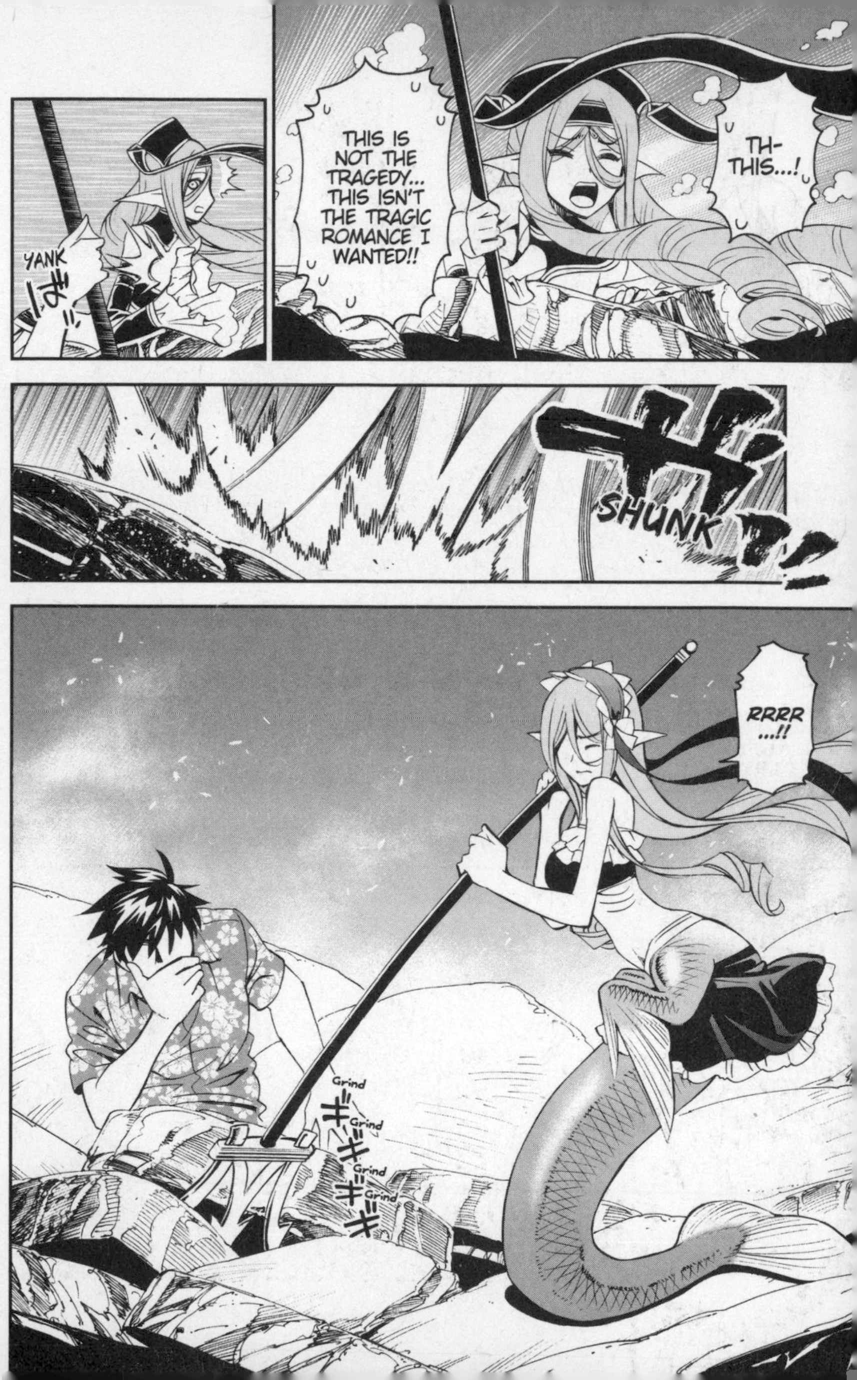
TH-THIS...!
THIS IS NOT THE TRAGEDY... THIS ISN'T THE TRAGIC ROMANCE I WANTED!!
YANK
SHUNK
RRRR...!!
Grind
Grind
Grind
Grind

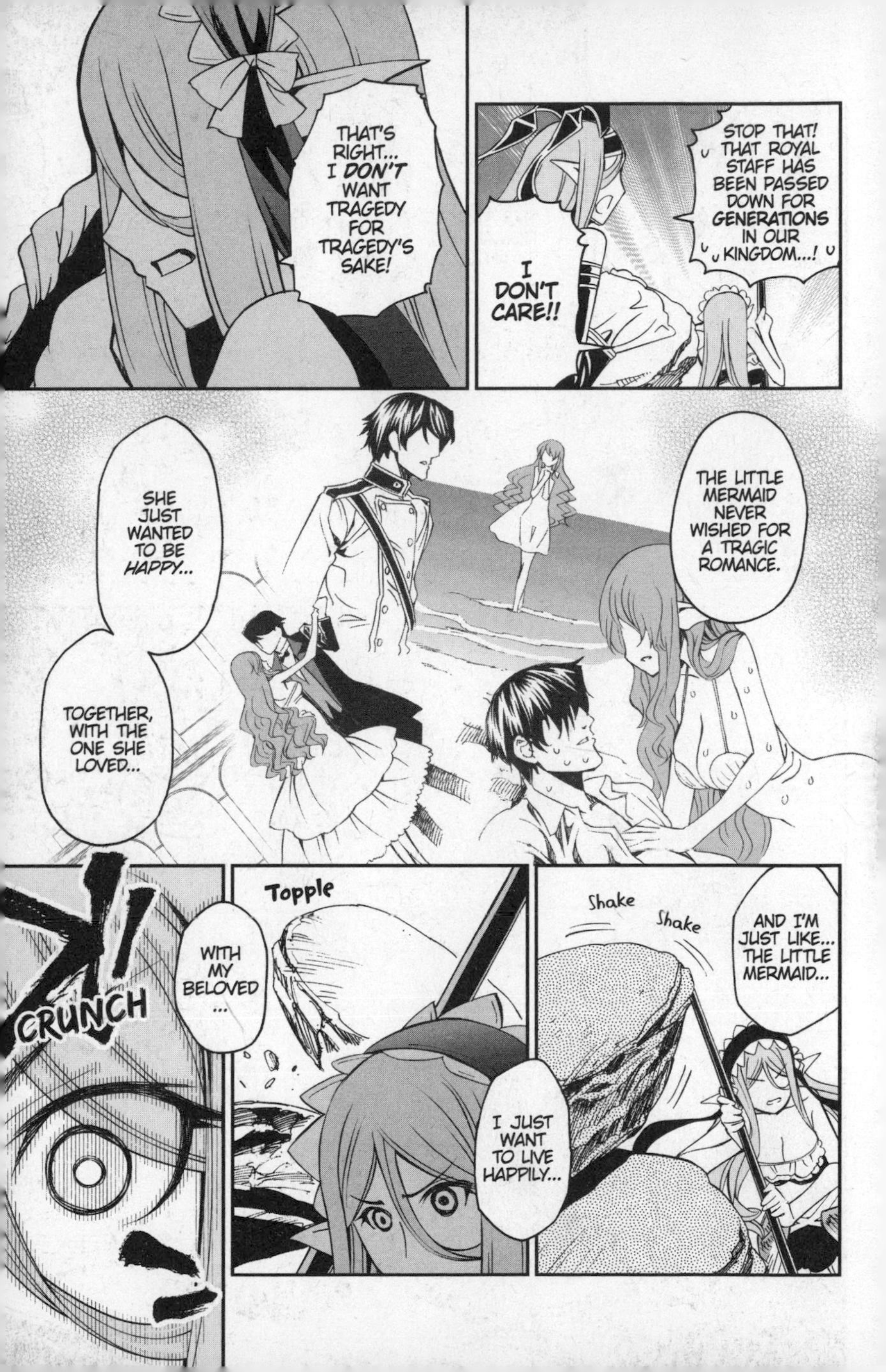
STOP THAT! THAT ROYAL STAFF HAS BEEN PASSED DOWN FOR GENERATIONS IN OUR KINGDOM...!
I DON'T CARE!!
THAT'S RIGHT... I *DON'T* WANT TRAGEDY FOR TRAGEDY'S SAKE!
THE LITTLE MERMAID NEVER WISHED FOR A TRAGIC ROMANCE.
SHE JUST WANTED TO BE *HAPPY*...
TOGETHER, WITH THE ONE SHE LOVED...
Shake
Shake
AND I'M JUST LIKE... THE LITTLE MERMAID...
Topple
I JUST WANT TO LIVE HAPPILY...
WITH MY BELOVED ...
CRUNCH

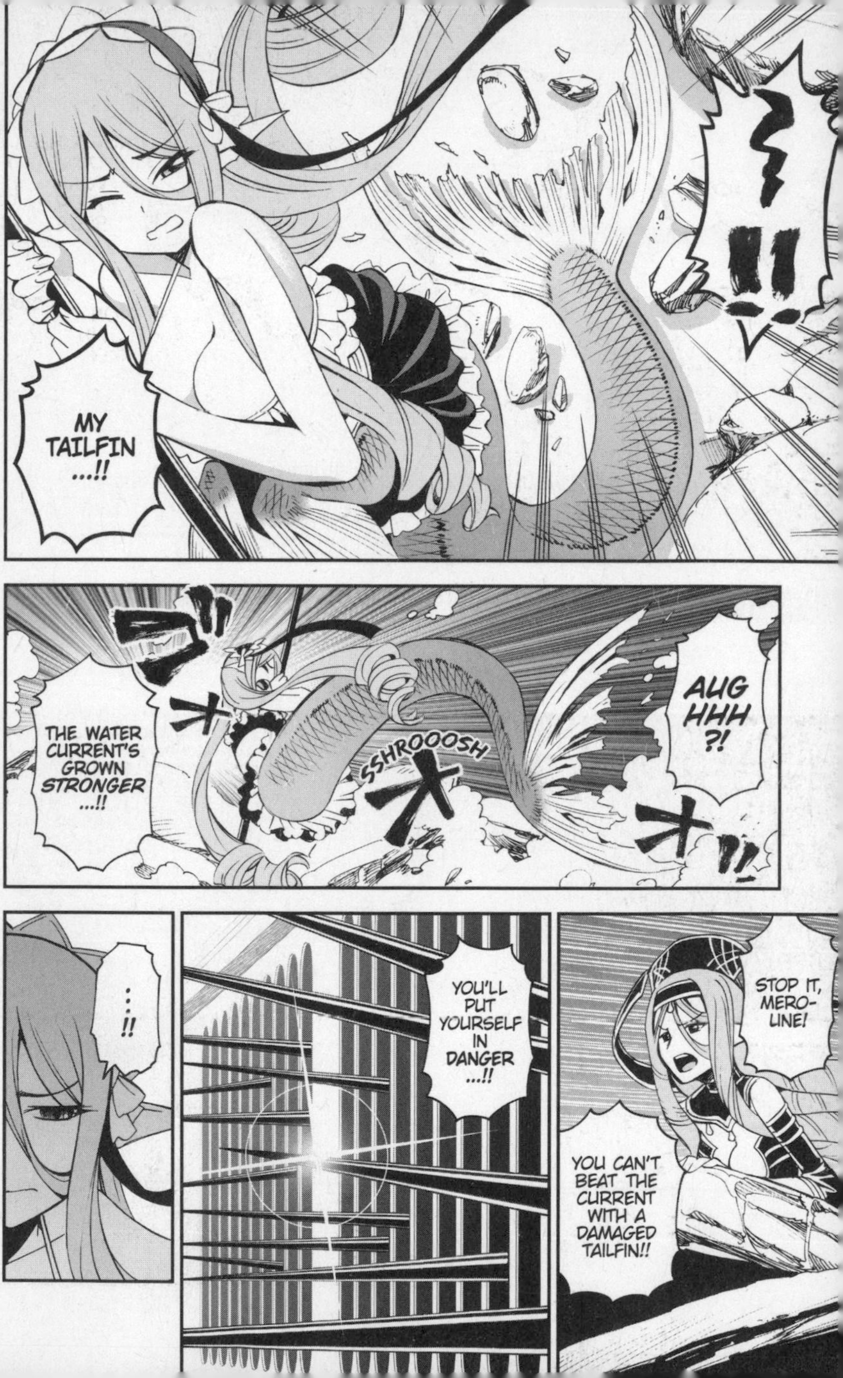
!!
MY TAILFIN ...!!
AUGH HHH?!
SSHROOOSH
THE WATER CURRENT'S GROWN STRONGER ...!!
STOP IT, MERO-LINE!
YOU CAN'T BEAT THE CURRENT WITH A DAMAGED TAILFIN!!
YOU'LL PUT YOURSELF IN DANGER ...!!
...!!

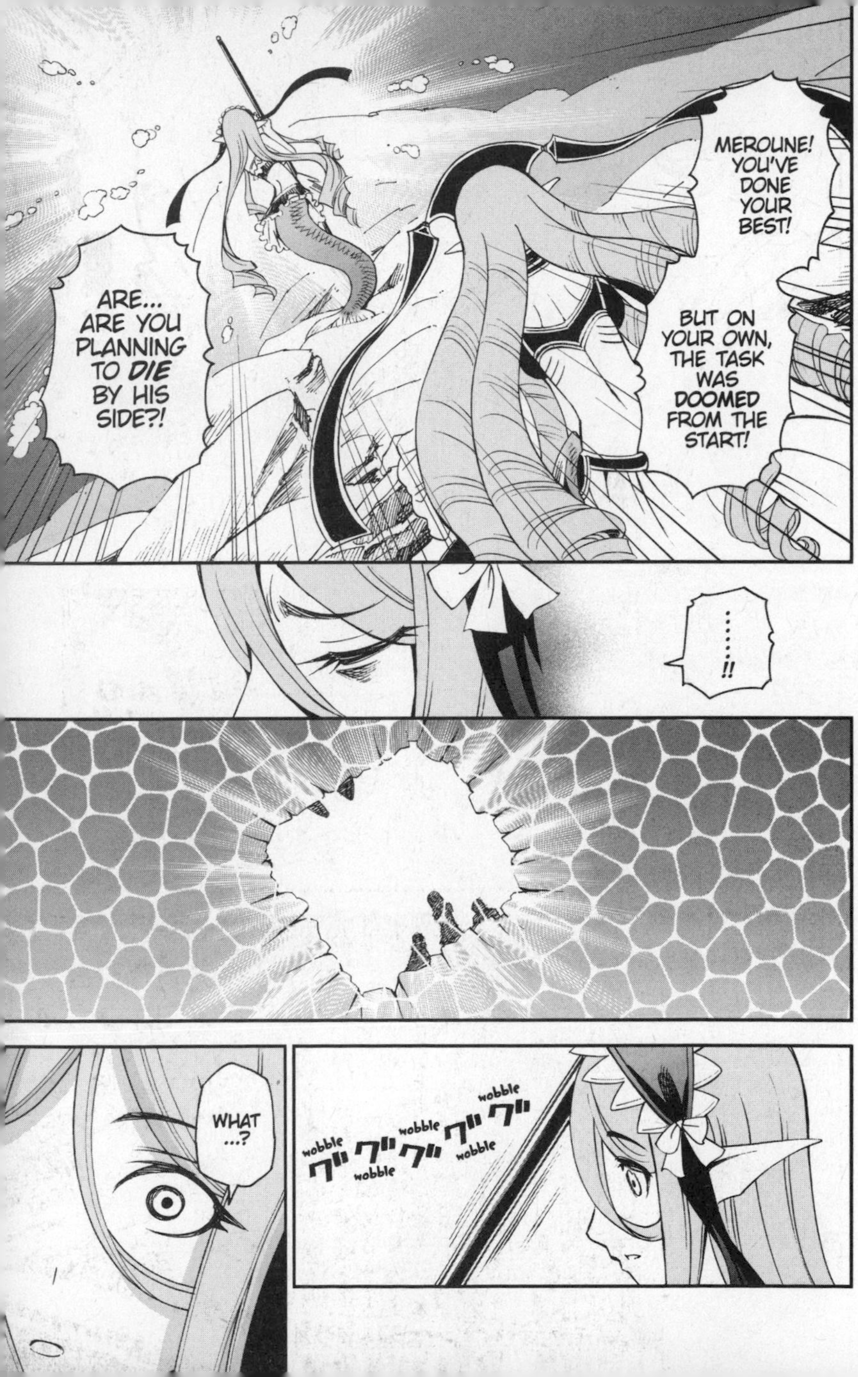
MEROUNE! YOU'VE DONE YOUR BEST!
BUT ON YOUR OWN, THE TASK WAS DOOMED FROM THE START!
ARE... ARE YOU PLANNING TO *DIE* BY HIS SIDE?!
......!!
wobble グ
wobble グ
wobble グ
wobble グ
wobble グ
WHAT ...?

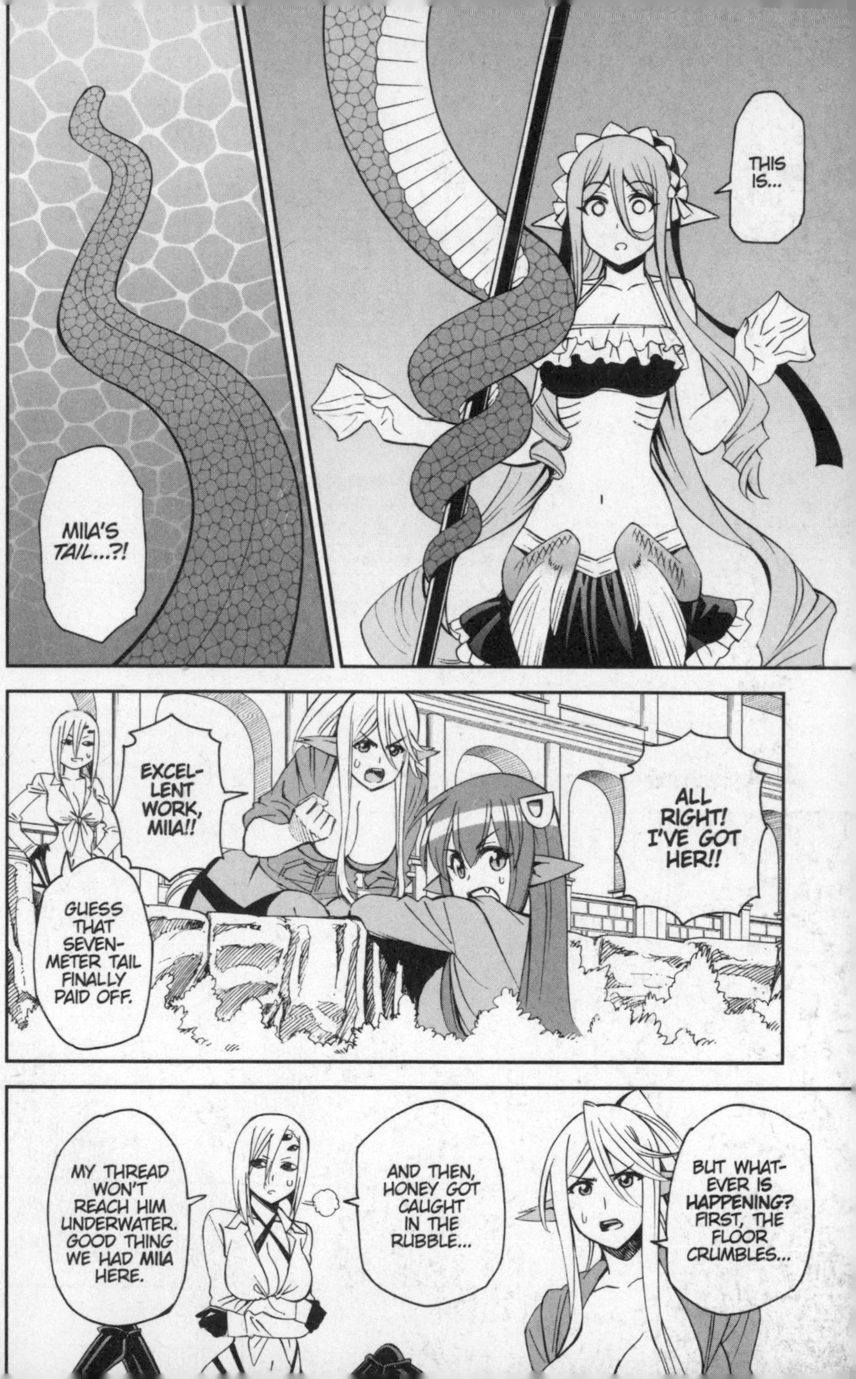
THIS IS...
MIIA'S TAIL...?!
ALL RIGHT! I'VE GOT HER!!
EXCEL-LENT WORK, MIIA!!
GUESS THAT SEVEN-METER TAIL FINALLY PAID OFF.
BUT WHAT-EVER IS HAPPENING? FIRST, THE FLOOR CRUMBLES...
AND THEN, HONEY GOT CAUGHT IN THE RUBBLE...
MY THREAD WON'T REACH HIM UNDERWATER. GOOD THING WE HAD MIIA HERE.

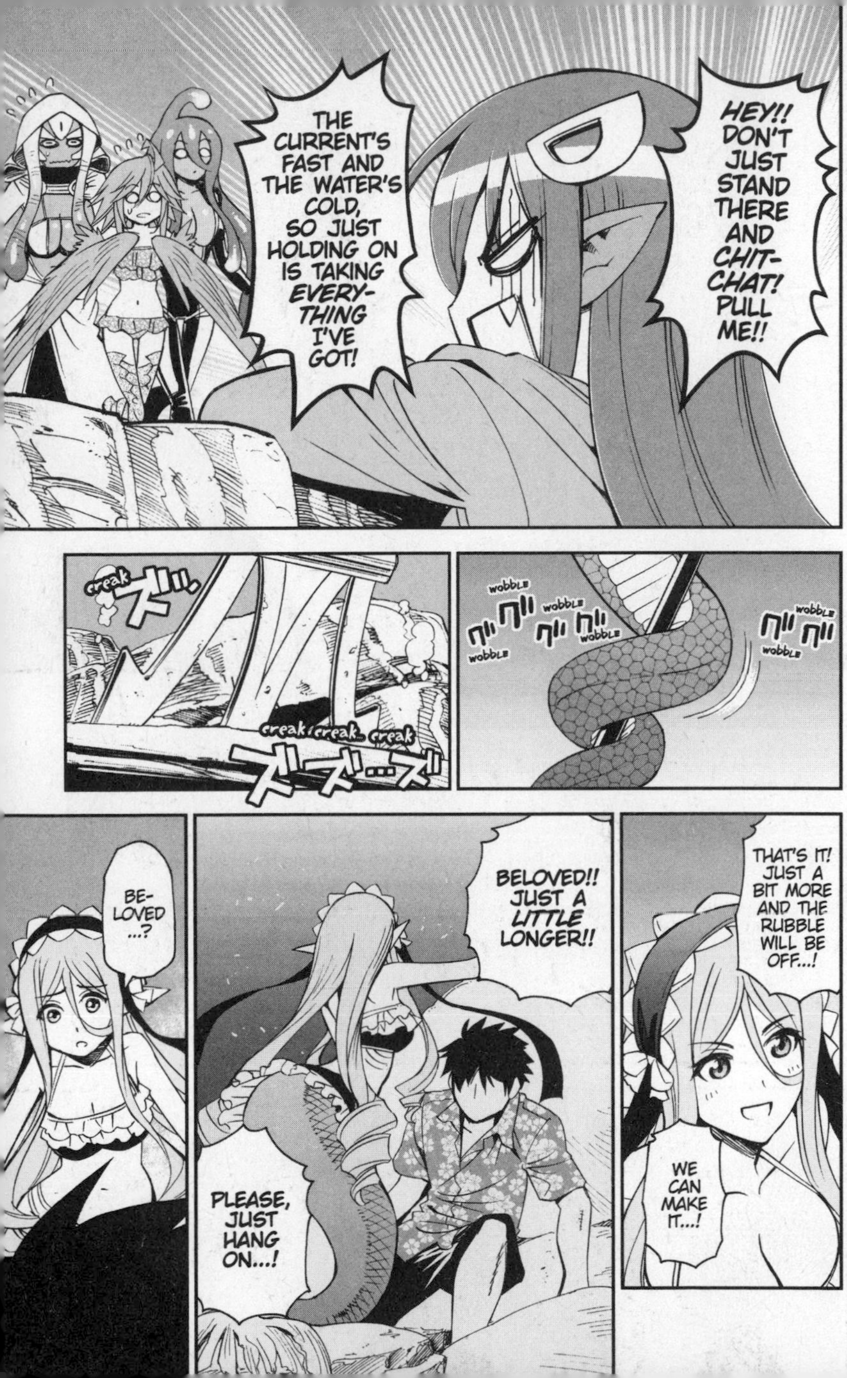
HEY!! DON'T JUST STAND THERE AND CHIT-CHAT! PULL ME!!
THE CURRENT'S FAST AND THE WATER'S COLD, SO JUST HOLDING ON IS TAKING EVERYTHING I'VE GOT!
wobble wobble wobble wobble wobble wobble
creak
creak creak... creak
THAT'S IT! JUST A BIT MORE AND THE RUBBLE WILL BE OFF...!
WE CAN MAKE IT...!
BELOVED!! JUST A LITTLE LONGER!!
PLEASE, JUST HANG ON...!
BE-LOVED ...?

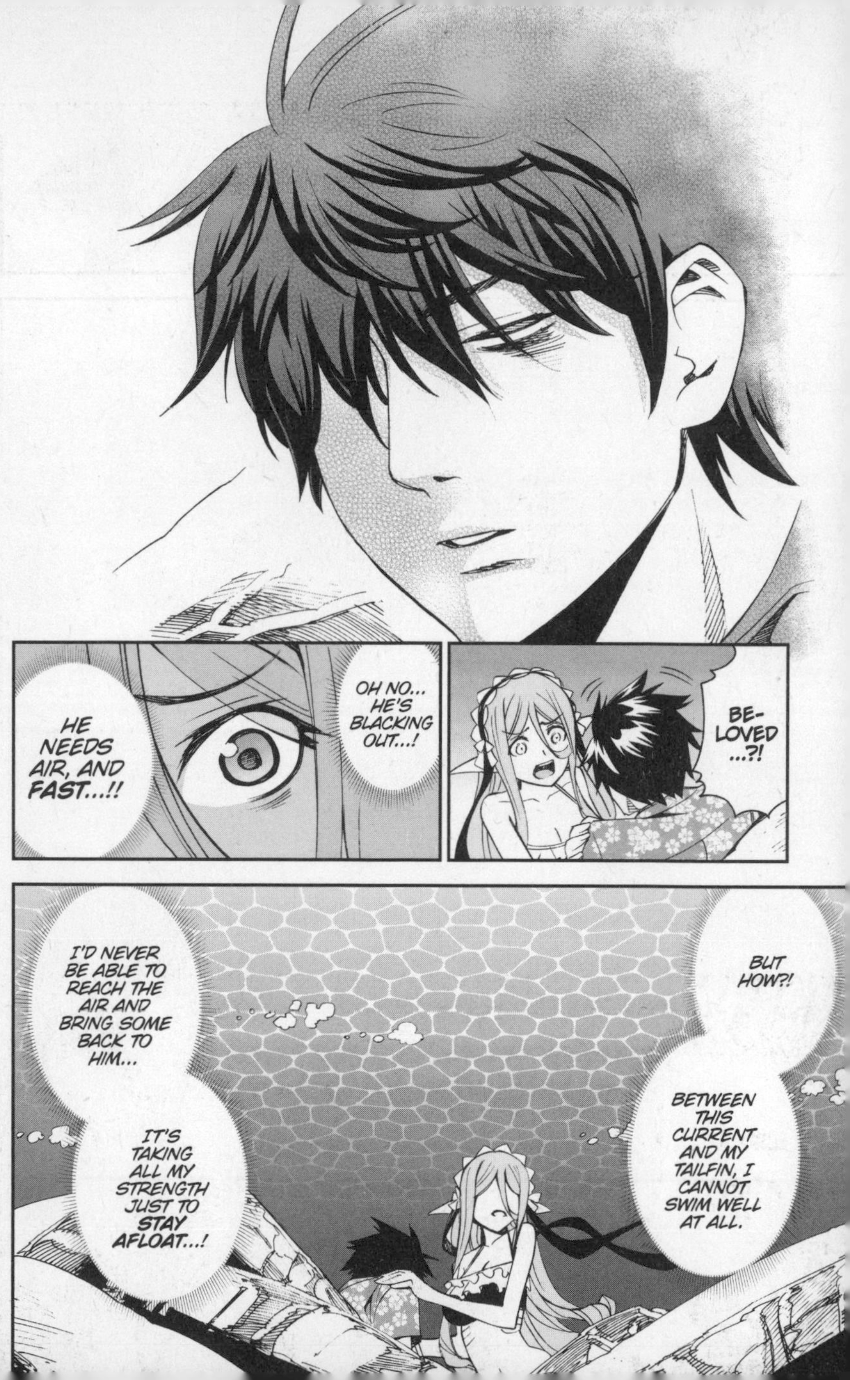
BE-LOVED ...?!
OH NO... HE'S BLACKING OUT...!
HE NEEDS AIR, AND FAST...!!
BUT HOW?!
BETWEEN THIS CURRENT AND MY TAILFIN, I CANNOT SWIM WELL AT ALL.
I'D NEVER BE ABLE TO REACH THE AIR AND BRING SOME BACK TO HIM...
IT'S TAKING ALL MY STRENGTH JUST TO STAY AFLOAT...!

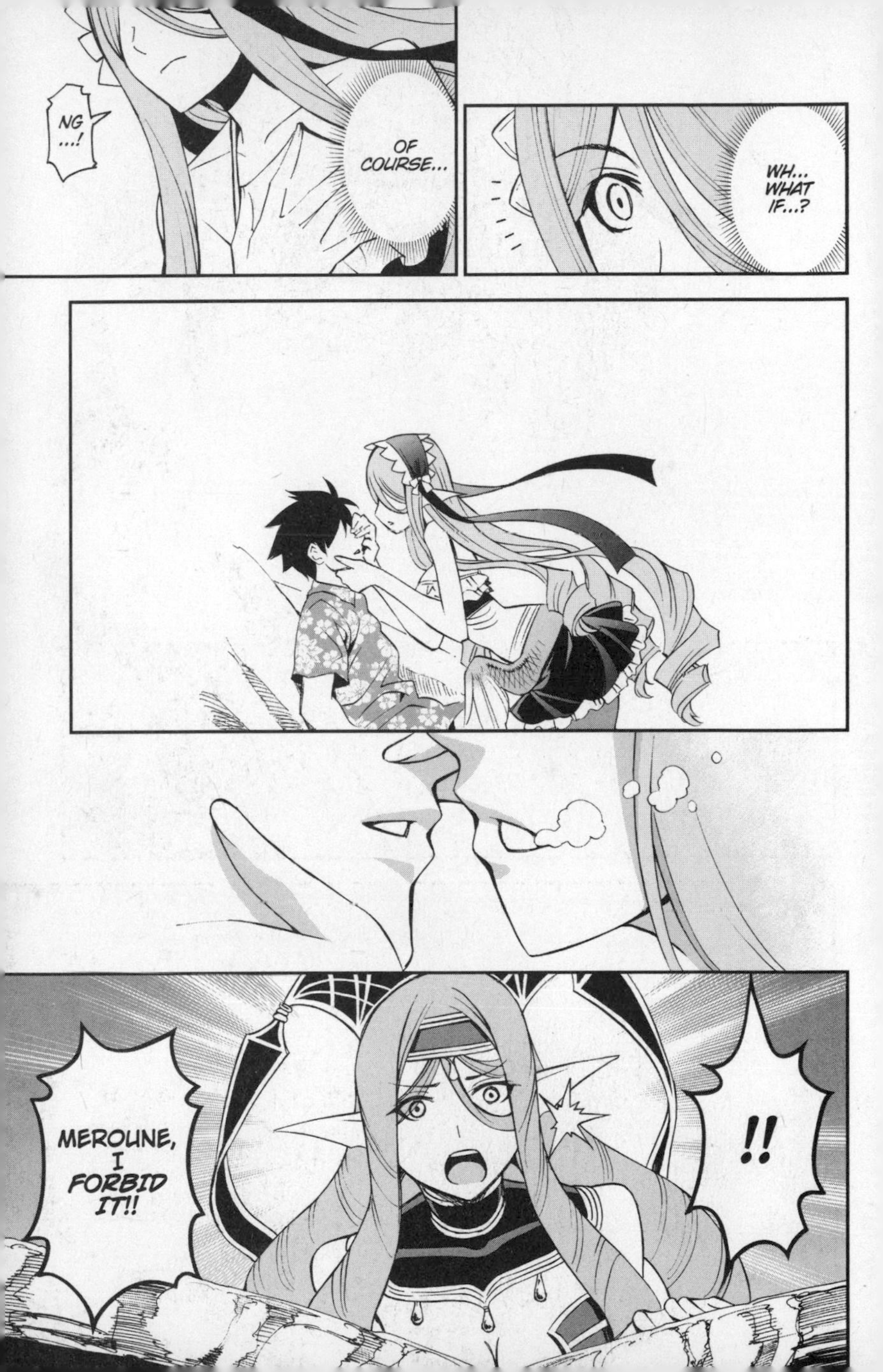
WH... WHAT IF...?
OF COURSE...
NG ...!
!!
MEROUNE, I FORBID IT!!

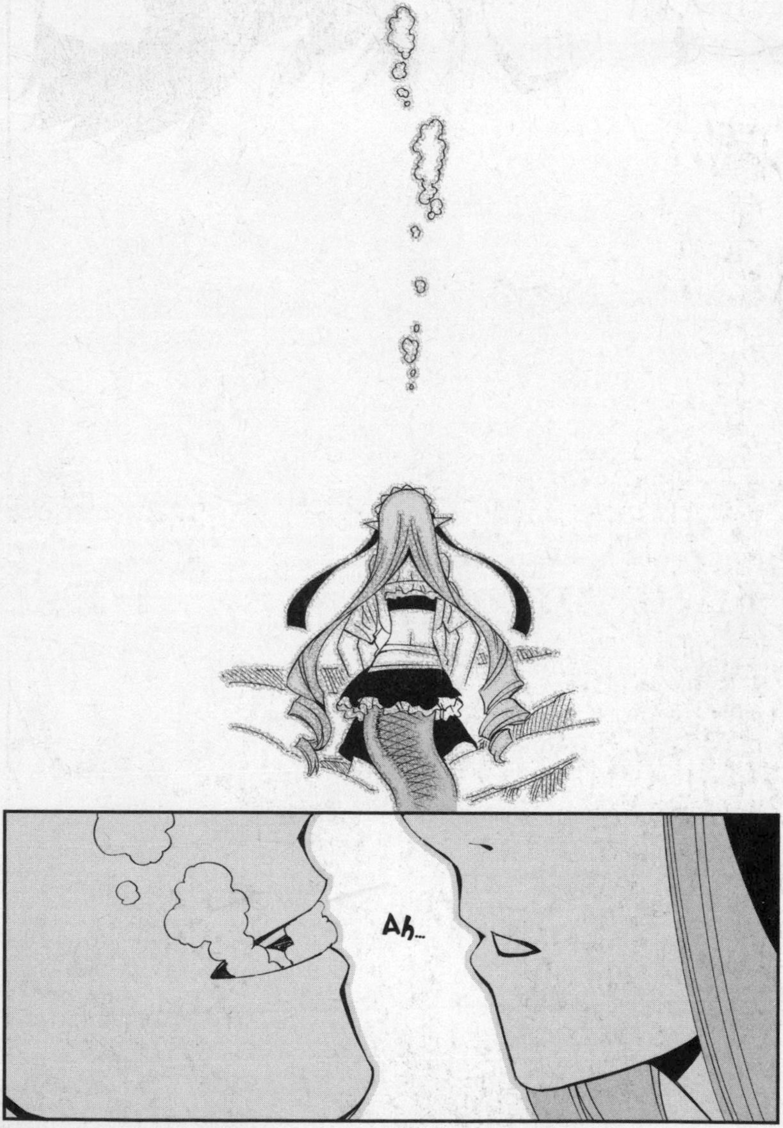
Ah...

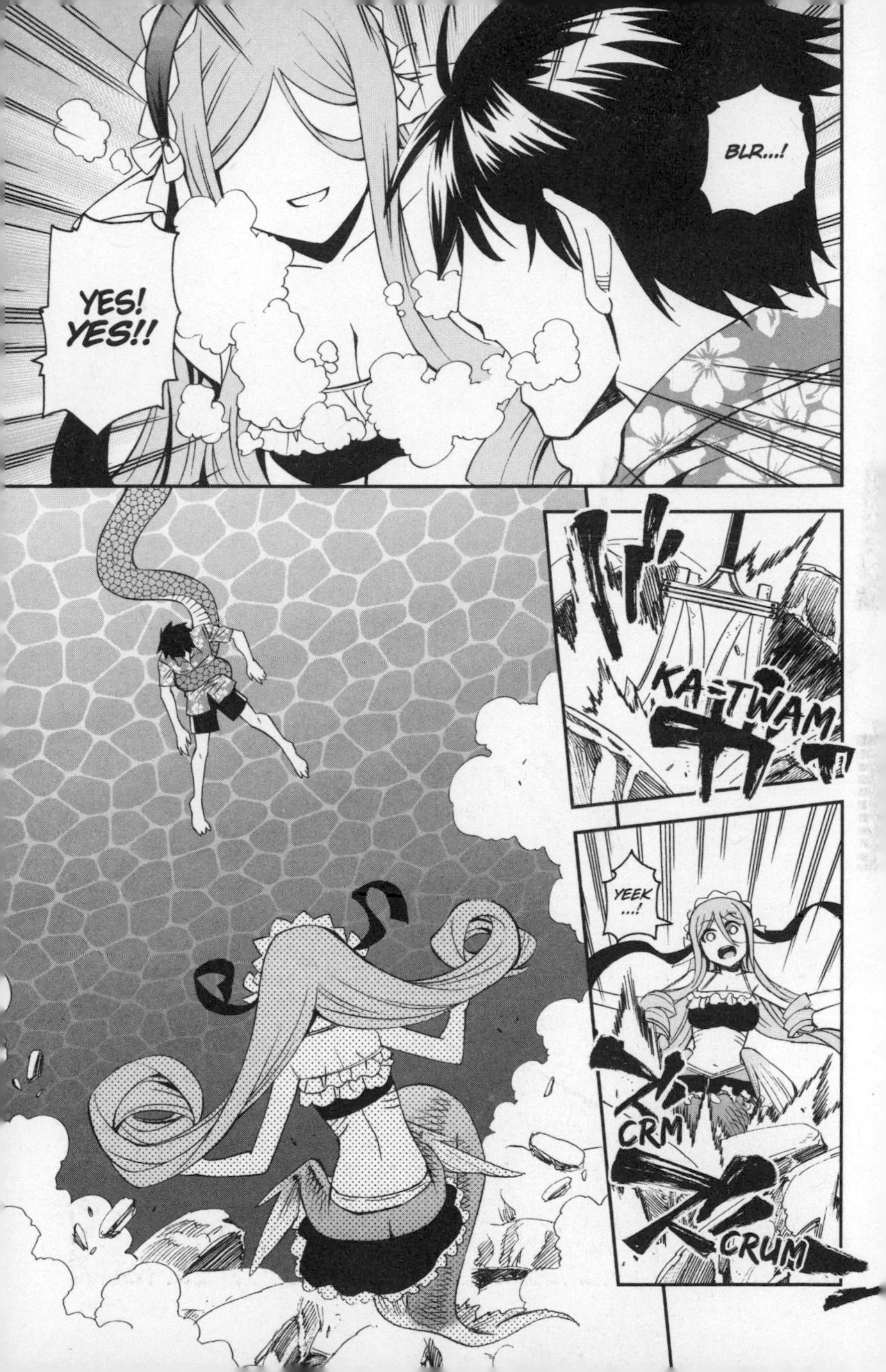
BLR...!
YES! YES!!
KA-TWAM
YEEK ...!
CRM
CRUM

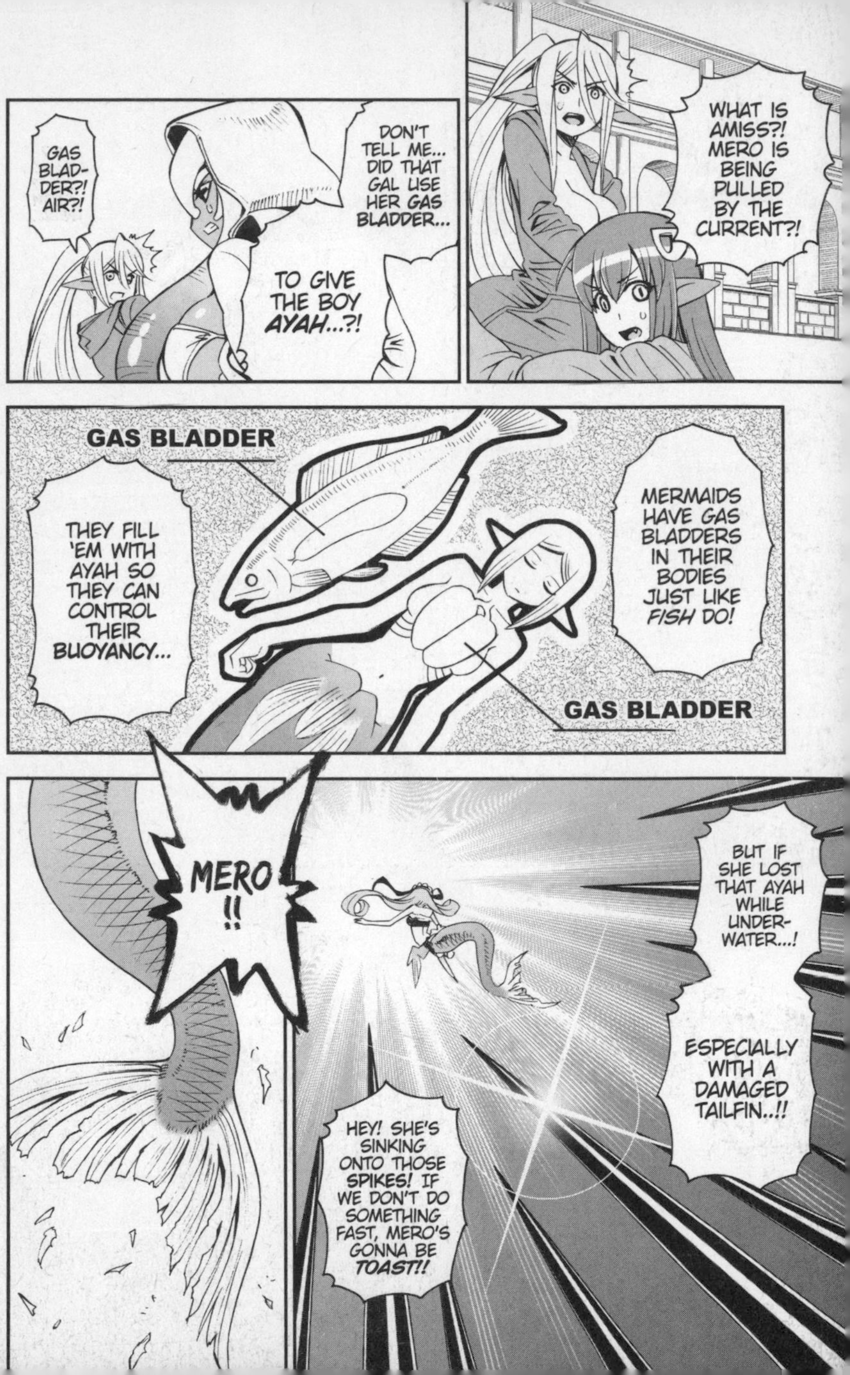
WHAT IS AMISS?! MERO IS BEING PULLED BY THE CURRENT?!
DON'T TELL ME... DID THAT GAL USE HER GAS BLADDER...
TO GIVE THE BOY *AYAH*...?!
GAS BLAD-DER?! AIR?!
MERMAIDS HAVE GAS BLADDERS IN THEIR BODIES JUST LIKE *FISH* DO!
GAS BLADDER
THEY FILL 'EM WITH AYAH SO THEY CAN CONTROL THEIR BUOYANCY...
GAS BLADDER
BUT IF SHE LOST THAT AYAH WHILE UNDER-WATER...!
ESPECIALLY WITH A DAMAGED TAILFIN..!!
MERO !!
HEY! SHE'S SINKING ONTO THOSE *SPIKES!* IF WE DON'T DO SOMETHING FAST, MERO'S GONNA BE *TOAST!!*

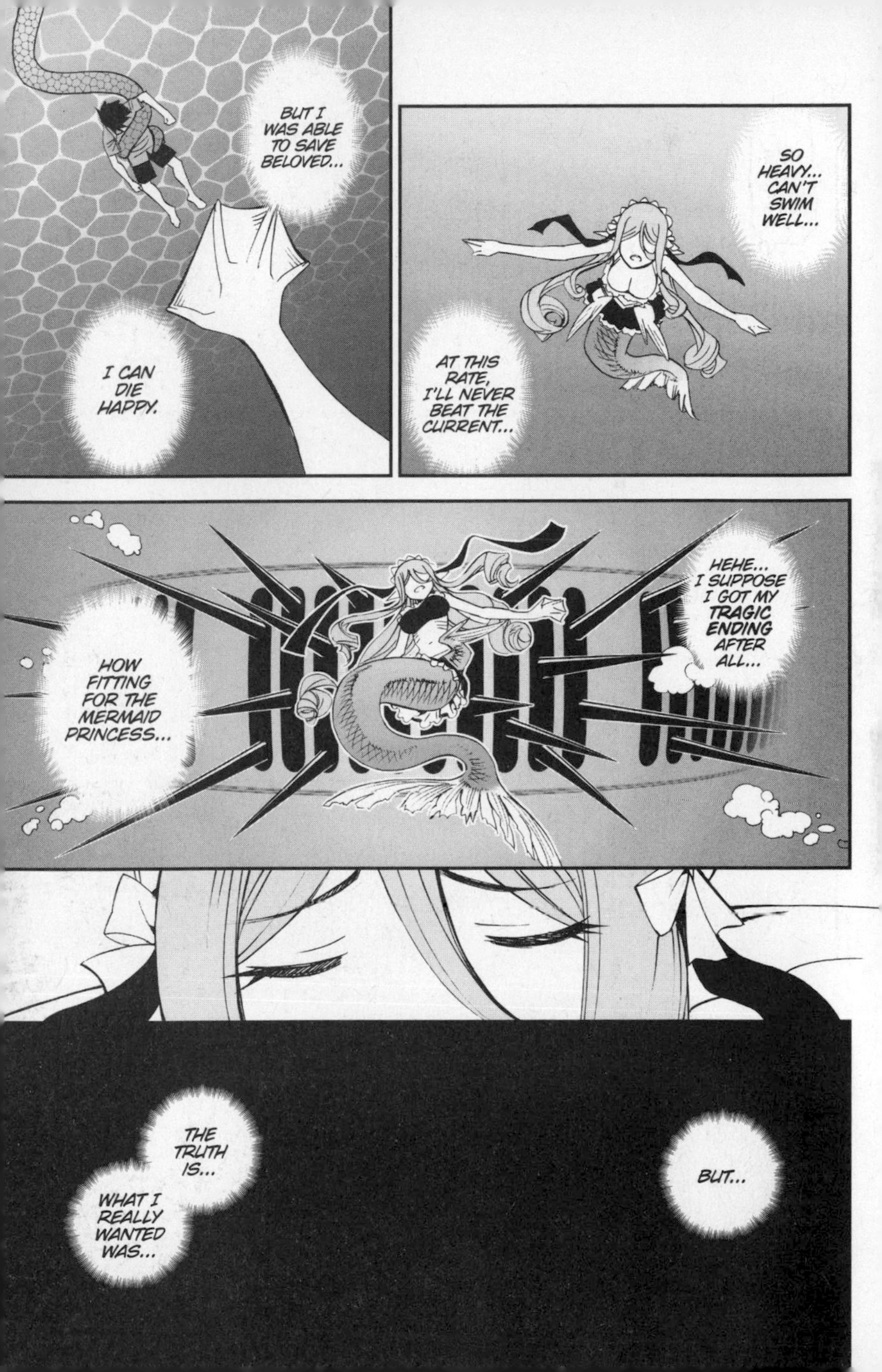
SO HEAVY... CAN'T SWIM WELL...
AT THIS RATE, I'LL NEVER BEAT THE CURRENT...
BUT I WAS ABLE TO SAVE BELOVED...
I CAN DIE HAPPY.
HEHE... I SUPPOSE I GOT MY TRAGIC ENDING AFTER ALL...
HOW FITTING FOR THE MERMAID PRINCESS...
BUT...
THE TRUTH IS...
WHAT I REALLY WANTED WAS...

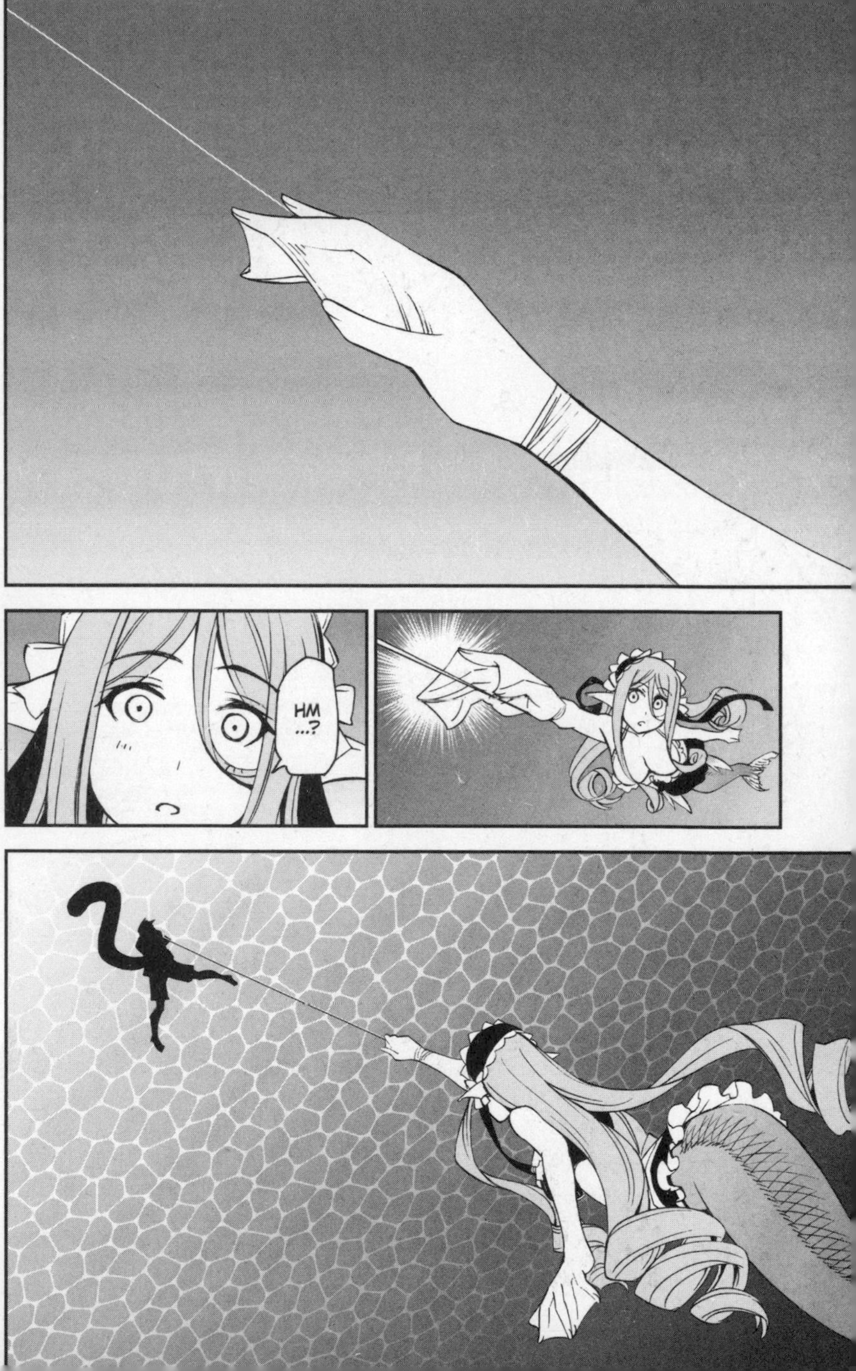
HM ...?

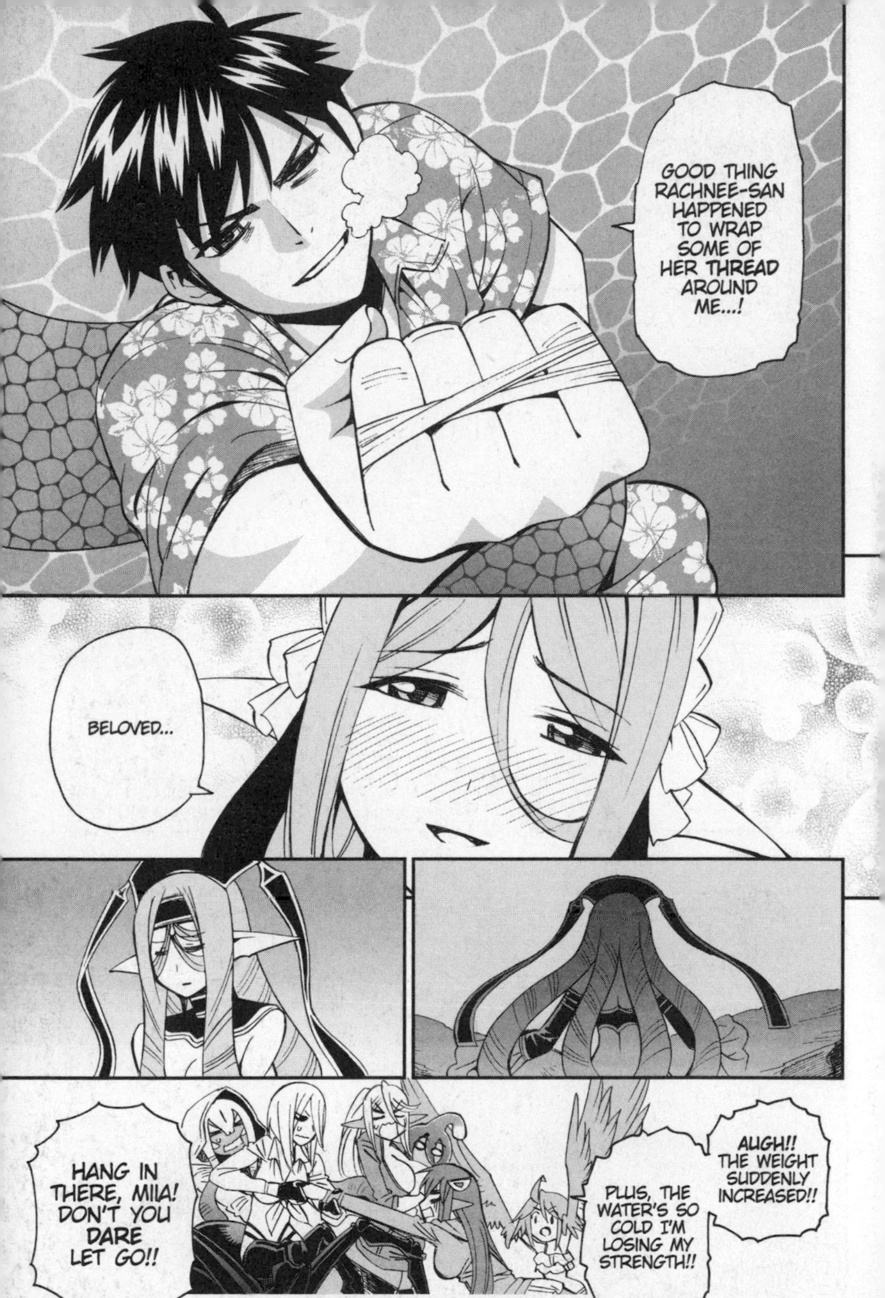
GOOD THING RACHNEE-SAN HAPPENED TO WRAP SOME OF HER THREAD AROUND ME...!
BELOVED...
AUGH!! THE WEIGHT SUDDENLY INCREASED!!
PLUS, THE WATER'S SO COLD I'M LOSING MY STRENGTH!!
HANG IN THERE, MIIA! DON'T YOU DARE LET GO!!

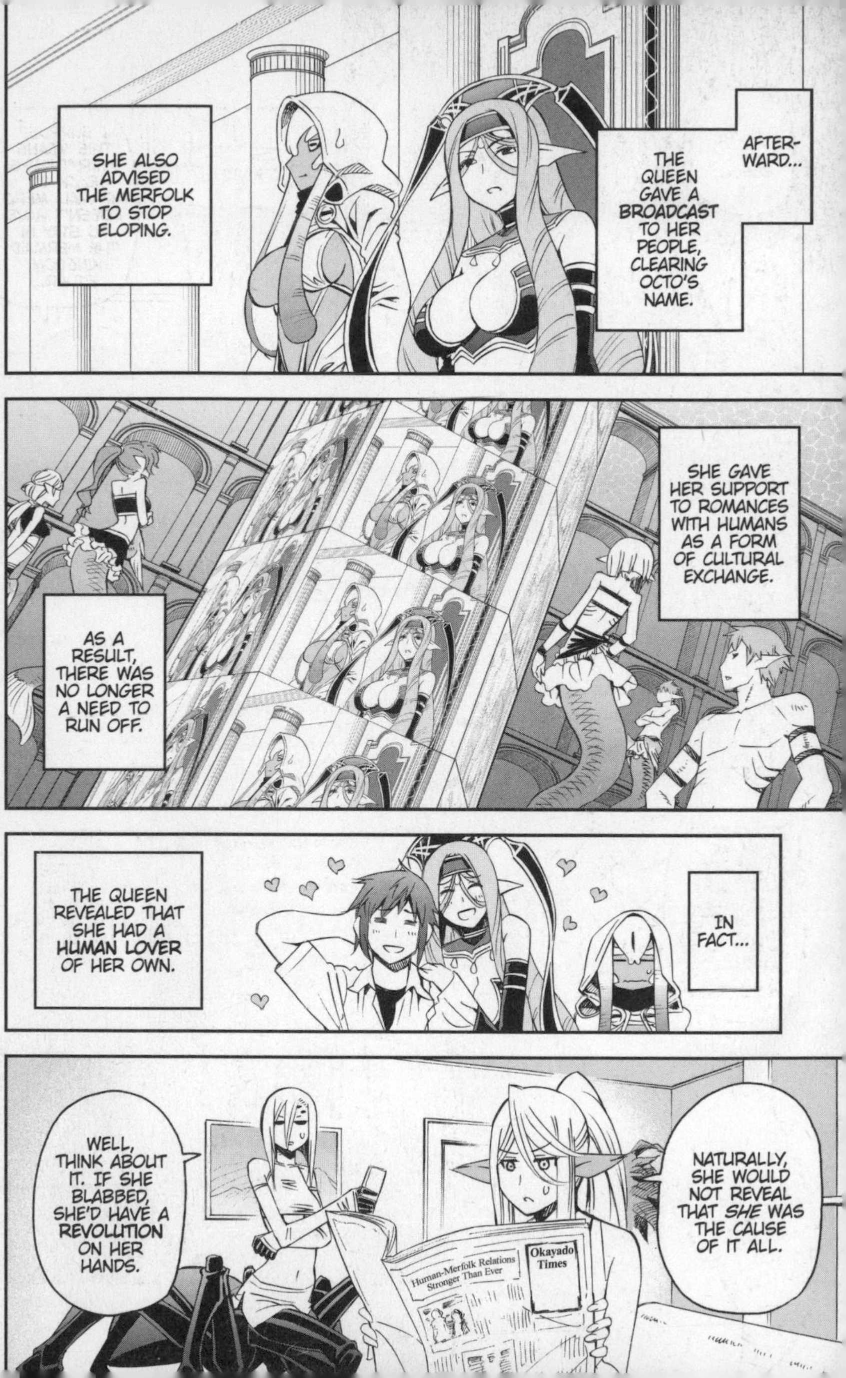
AFTERWARD... THE QUEEN GAVE A BROADCAST TO HER PEOPLE, CLEARING OCTO'S NAME.
SHE ALSO ADVISED THE MERFOLK TO STOP ELOPING.
SHE GAVE HER SUPPORT TO ROMANCES WITH HUMANS AS A FORM OF CULTURAL EXCHANGE.
AS A RESULT, THERE WAS NO LONGER A NEED TO RUN OFF.
IN FACT...
THE QUEEN REVEALED THAT SHE HAD A HUMAN LOVER OF HER OWN.
NATURALLY, SHE WOULD NOT REVEAL THAT *SHE* WAS THE CAUSE OF IT ALL.
Okayado Times
Human-Merfolk Relations Stronger Than Ever
WELL, THINK ABOUT IT. IF SHE BLABBED, SHE'D HAVE A REVOLUTION ON HER HANDS.

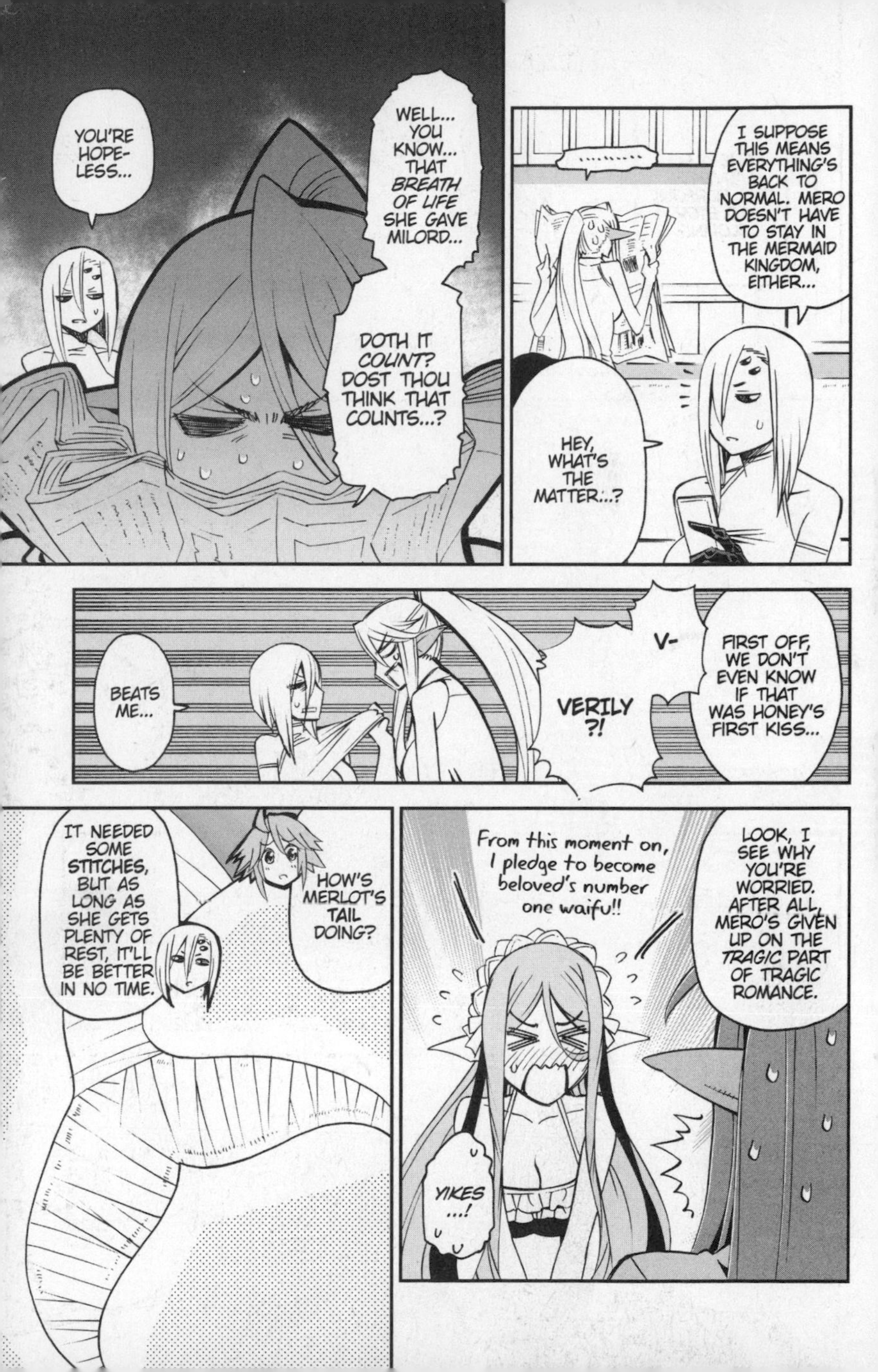
I SUPPOSE THIS MEANS EVERYTHING'S BACK TO NORMAL. MERO DOESN'T HAVE TO STAY IN THE MERMAID KINGDOM, EITHER...
......
HEY, WHAT'S THE MATTER...?
WELL... YOU KNOW... THAT *BREATH OF LIFE* SHE GAVE MILORD...
DOTH IT *COUNT?* DOST THOU THINK THAT COUNTS...?
YOU'RE HOPE-LESS...
FIRST OFF, WE DON'T EVEN KNOW IF THAT WAS HONEY'S FIRST KISS...
V-
VERILY ?!
BEATS ME...
LOOK, I SEE WHY YOU'RE WORRIED. AFTER ALL, MERO'S GIVEN UP ON THE *TRAGIC* PART OF TRAGIC ROMANCE.
From this moment on, I pledge to become beloved's number one waifu!!
YIKES ...!
HOW'S MERLOT'S TAIL DOING?
IT NEEDED SOME STITCHES, BUT AS LONG AS SHE GETS PLENTY OF REST, IT'LL BE BETTER IN NO TIME.

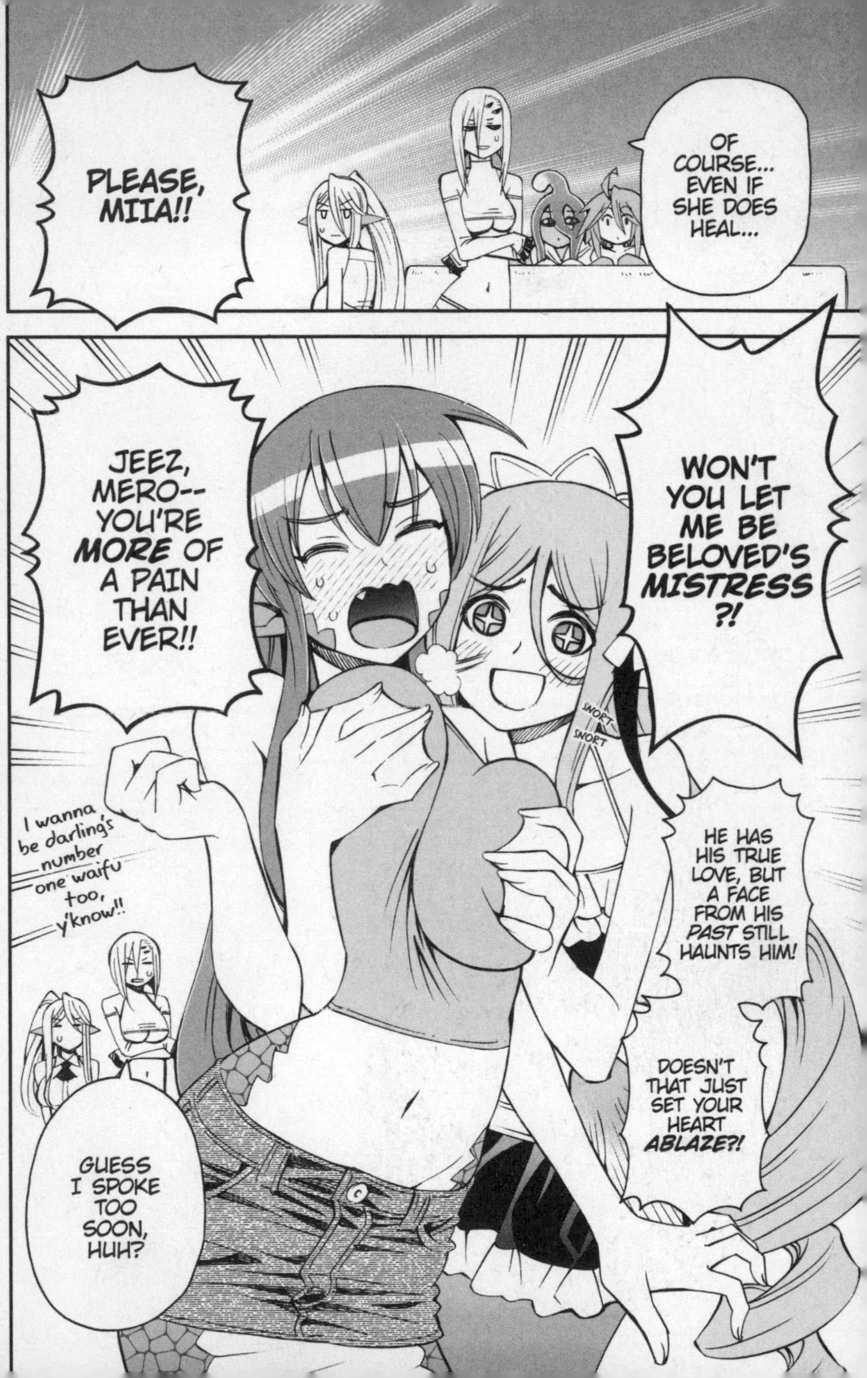
OF COURSE... EVEN IF SHE DOES HEAL...
PLEASE, MIIA!!
WON'T YOU LET ME BE BELOVED'S *MISTRESS*?!
JEEZ, MERO-- YOU'RE *MORE* OF A PAIN THAN EVER!!
SNORT SNORT
HE HAS HIS TRUE LOVE, BUT A FACE FROM HIS *PAST* STILL HAUNTS HIM!
DOESN'T THAT JUST SET YOUR HEART *ABLAZE*?!
I wanna be darling's number one waifu too, y'know!!
GUESS I SPOKE TOO SOON, HUH?

Monster Musume

Everyday Life with Monster Girls

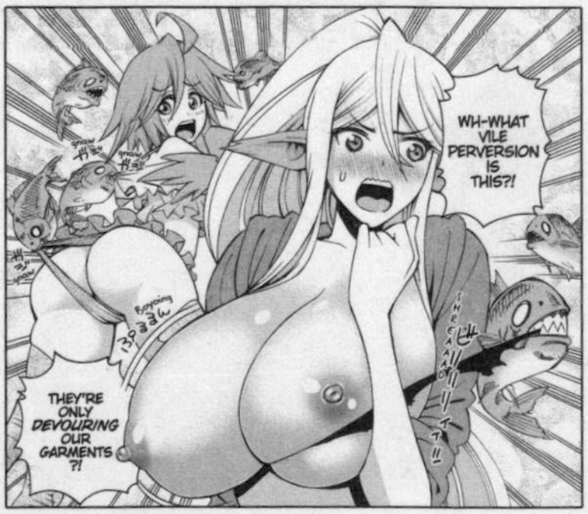
WH-WHAT VILE PERVERSION IS THIS?!
THEY'RE ONLY *DEVOURING* OUR GARMENTS?!

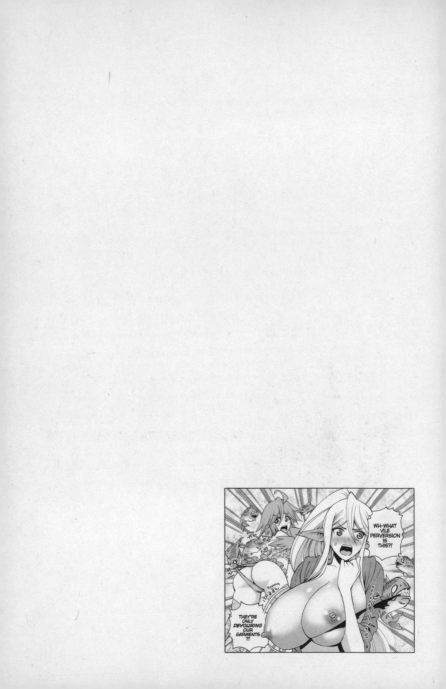

Chapter 38

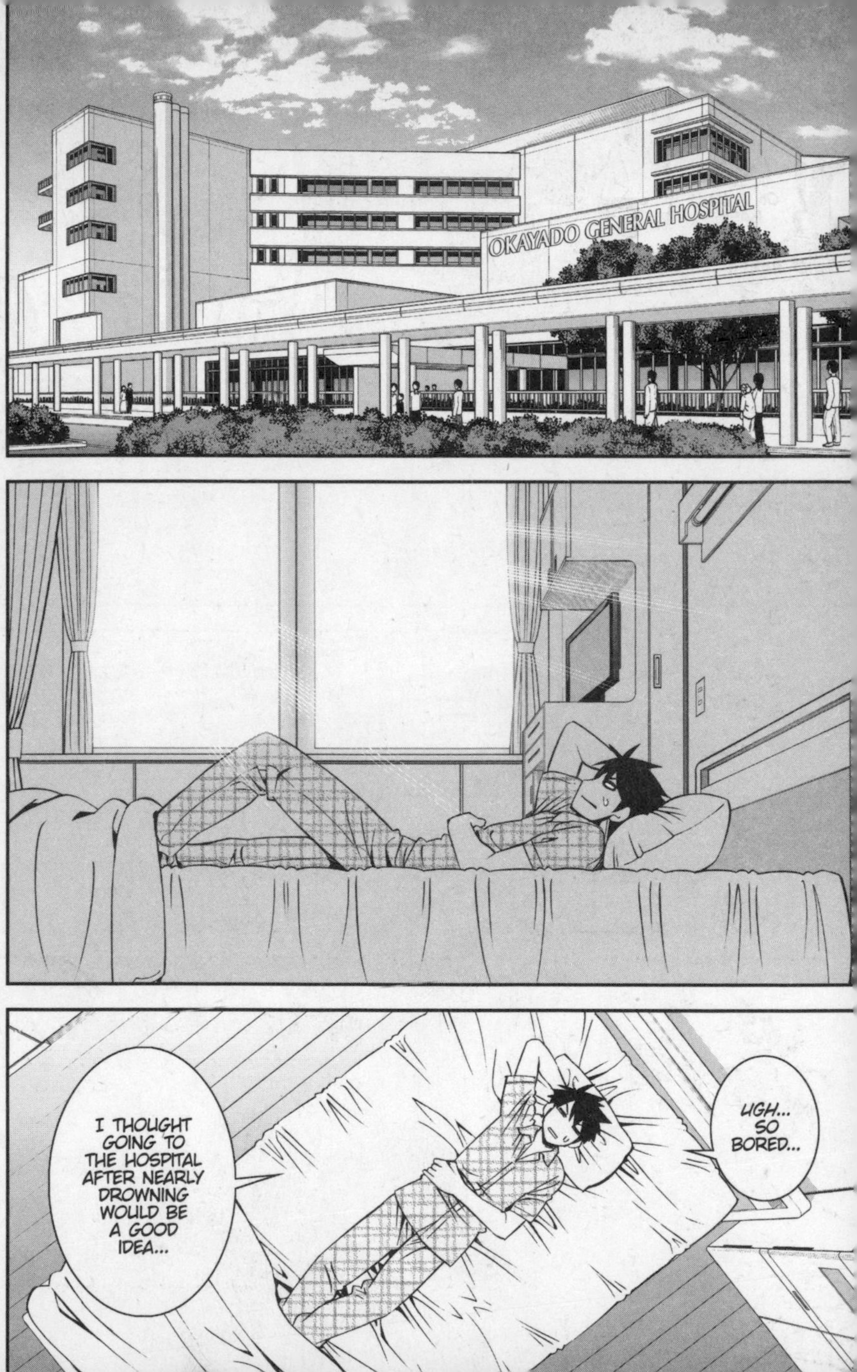
OKAYADO GENERAL HOSPITAL
UGH... SO BORED...
I THOUGHT GOING TO THE HOSPITAL AFTER NEARLY DROWNING WOULD BE A GOOD IDEA...

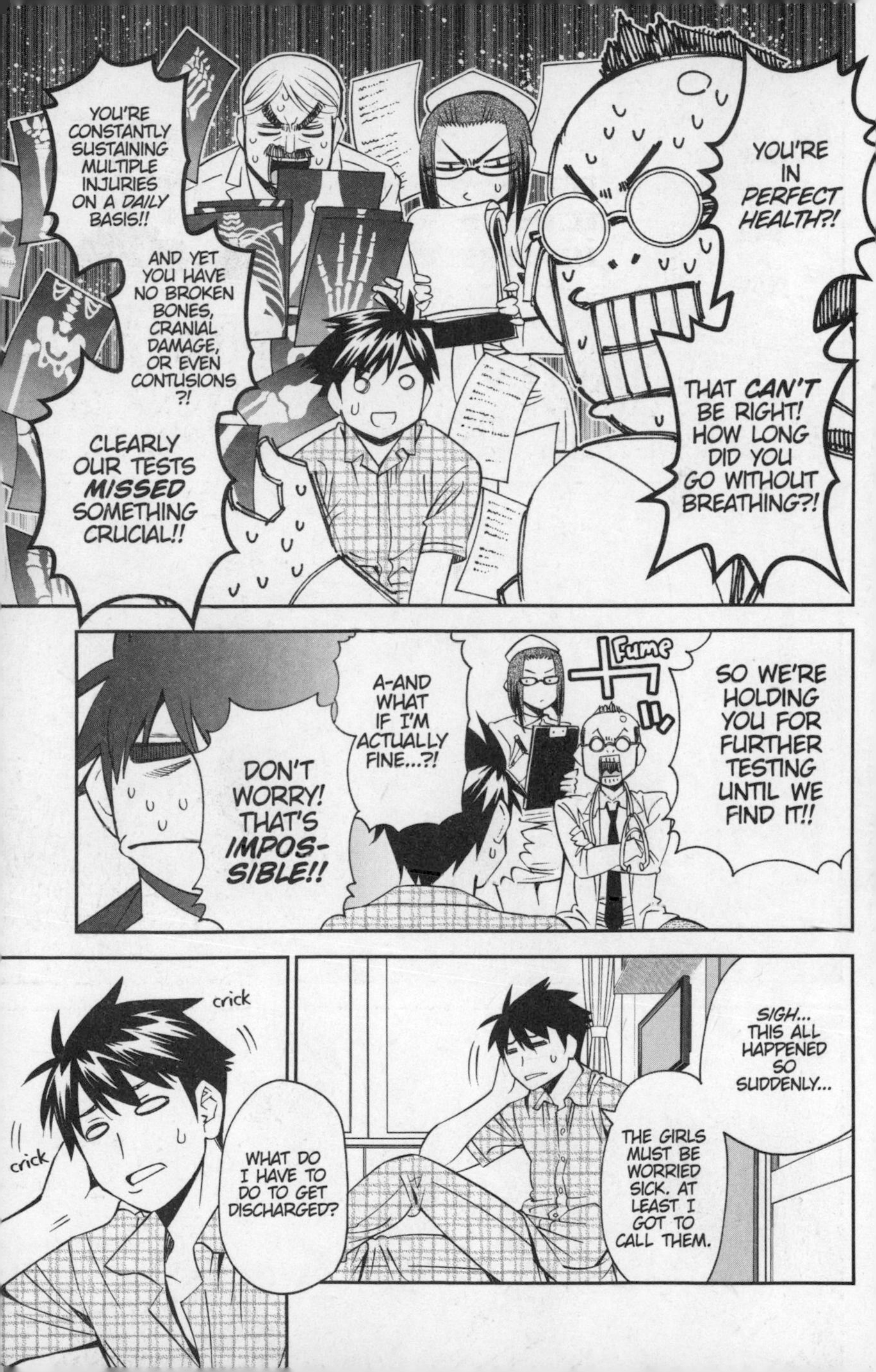
YOU'RE IN PERFECT HEALTH?!
THAT CAN'T BE RIGHT! HOW LONG DID YOU GO WITHOUT BREATHING?!
YOU'RE CONSTANTLY SUSTAINING MULTIPLE INJURIES ON A DAILY BASIS!!
AND YET YOU HAVE NO BROKEN BONES, CRANIAL DAMAGE, OR EVEN CONTUSIONS?!
CLEARLY OUR TESTS MISSED SOMETHING CRUCIAL!!
SO WE'RE HOLDING YOU FOR FURTHER TESTING UNTIL WE FIND IT!!
Fume
A-AND WHAT IF I'M ACTUALLY FINE...?!
DON'T WORRY! THAT'S IMPOSSIBLE!!
SIGH... THIS ALL HAPPENED SO SUDDENLY...
THE GIRLS MUST BE WORRIED SICK. AT LEAST I GOT TO CALL THEM.
crick
WHAT DO I HAVE TO DO TO GET DISCHARGED?
crick

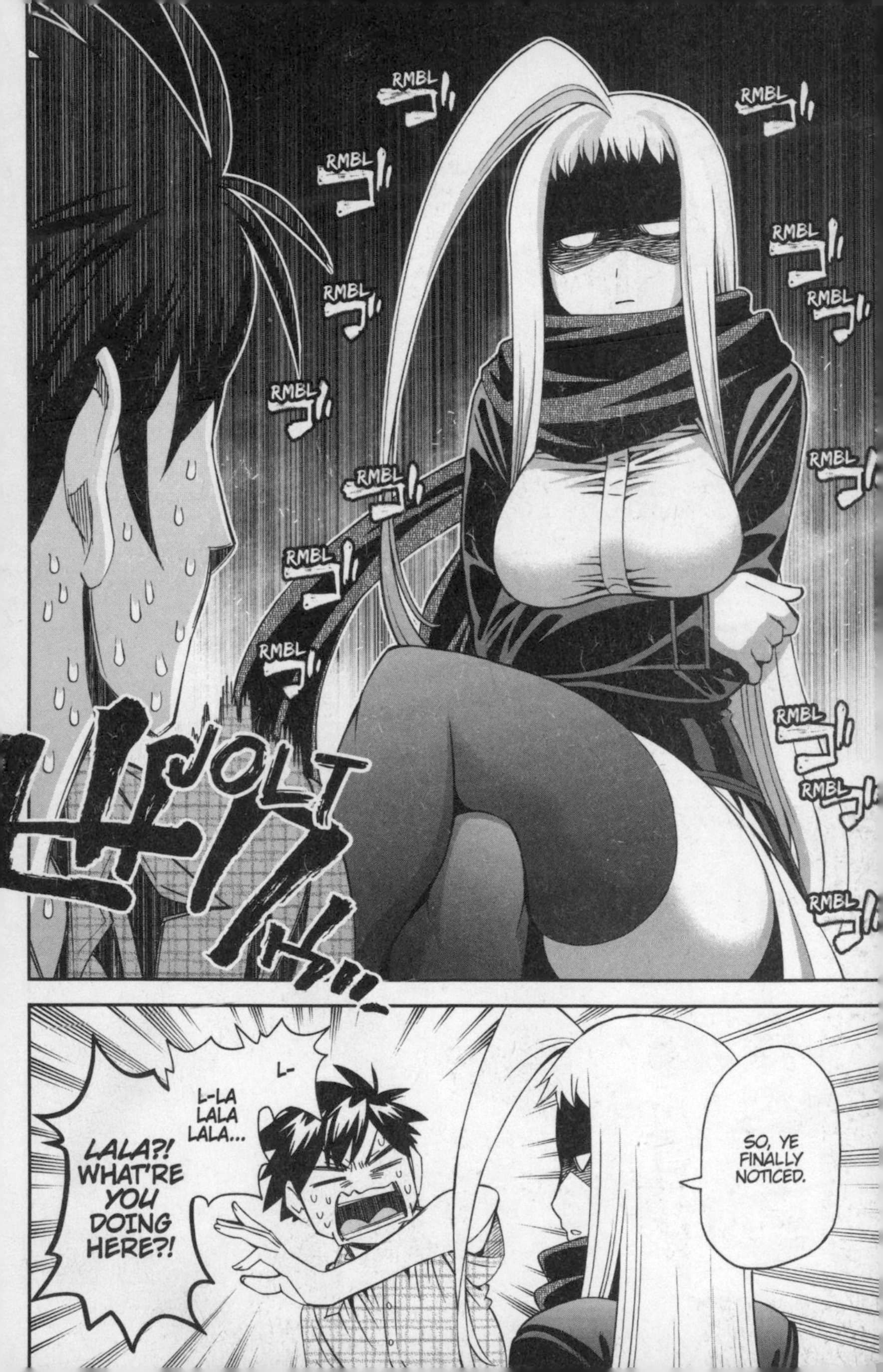
RMBL
RMBL
RMBL
RMBL
RMBL
RMBL
RMBL
RMBL
RMBL
RMBL
RMBL
RMBL
RMBL
RMBL
JOLT
SO, YE FINALLY NOTICED.
L-
L-LA LALA LALA...
LALA?! WHAT'RE YOU DOING HERE?!

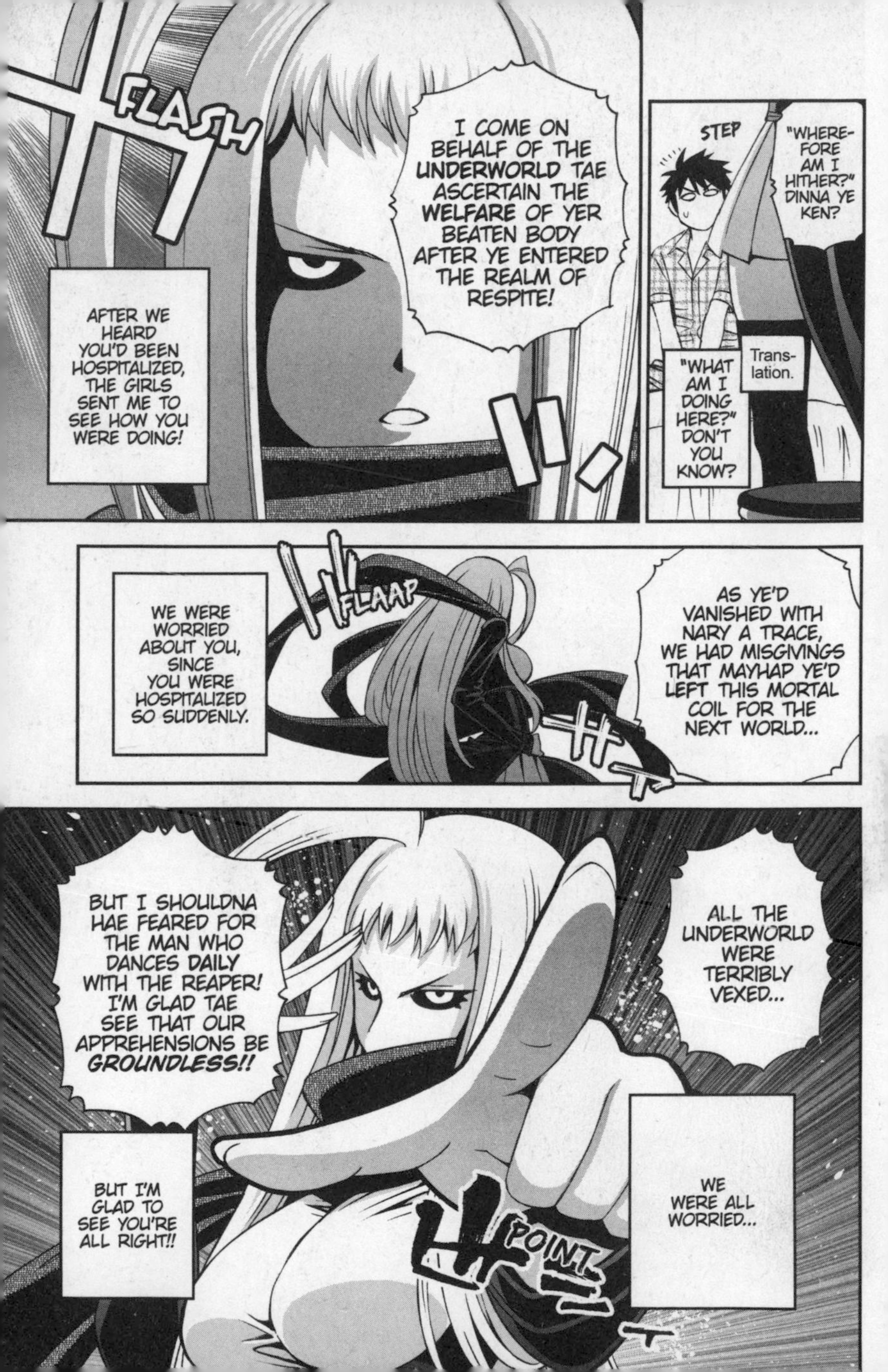
STEP
"WHEREFORE AM I HITHER?" DINNA YE KEN?
Trans-lation.
"WHAT AM I DOING HERE?" DON'T YOU KNOW?
FLASH
I COME ON BEHALF OF THE UNDERWORLD TAE ASCERTAIN THE WELFARE OF YER BEATEN BODY AFTER YE ENTERED THE REALM OF RESPITE!
AFTER WE HEARD YOU'D BEEN HOSPITALIZED, THE GIRLS SENT ME TO SEE HOW YOU WERE DOING!
FLAAP
AS YE'D VANISHED WITH NARY A TRACE, WE HAD MISGIVINGS THAT MAYHAP YE'D LEFT THIS MORTAL COIL FOR THE NEXT WORLD...
WE WERE WORRIED ABOUT YOU, SINCE YOU WERE HOSPITALIZED SO SUDDENLY.
ALL THE UNDERWORLD WERE TERRIBLY VEXED...
WE WERE ALL WORRIED...
BUT I SHOULDNA HAE FEARED FOR THE MAN WHO DANCES DAILY WITH THE REAPER! I'M GLAD TAE SEE THAT OUR APPREHENSIONS BE GROUNDLESS!!
BUT I'M GLAD TO SEE YOU'RE ALL RIGHT!!
POINT

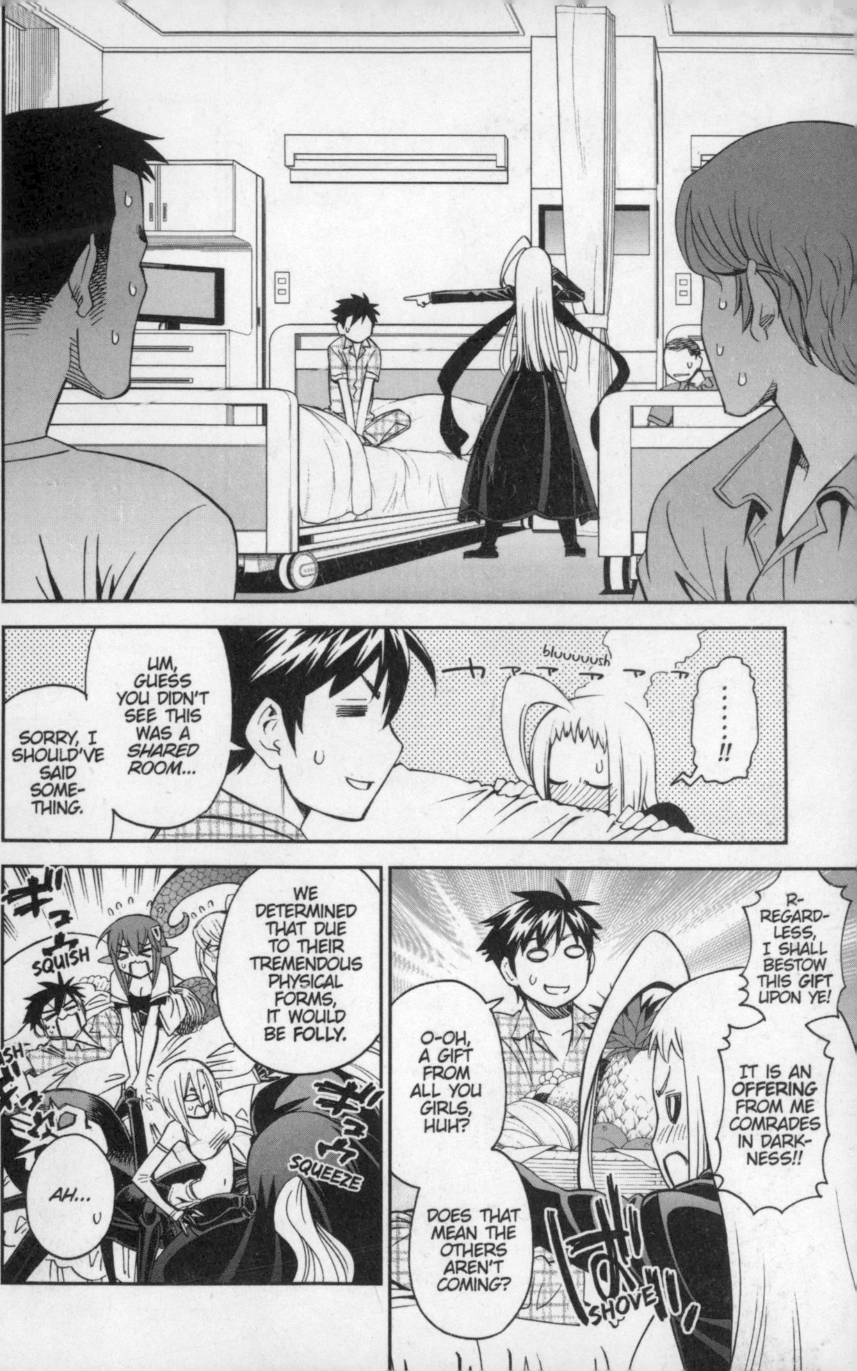
......!!
bluuuuush
UM, GUESS YOU DIDN'T SEE THIS WAS A *SHARED* ROOM...
SORRY, I SHOULD'VE SAID SOMETHING.
R-REGARDLESS, I SHALL BESTOW THIS GIFT UPON YE!
IT IS AN OFFERING FROM ME COMRADES IN DARKNESS!!
O-OH, A GIFT FROM ALL YOU GIRLS, HUH?
DOES THAT MEAN THE OTHERS AREN'T COMING?
SHOVE
WE DETERMINED THAT DUE TO THEIR TREMENDOUS PHYSICAL FORMS, IT WOULD BE FOLLY.
SQUISH
SQUEEZE
CRUSH
AH...

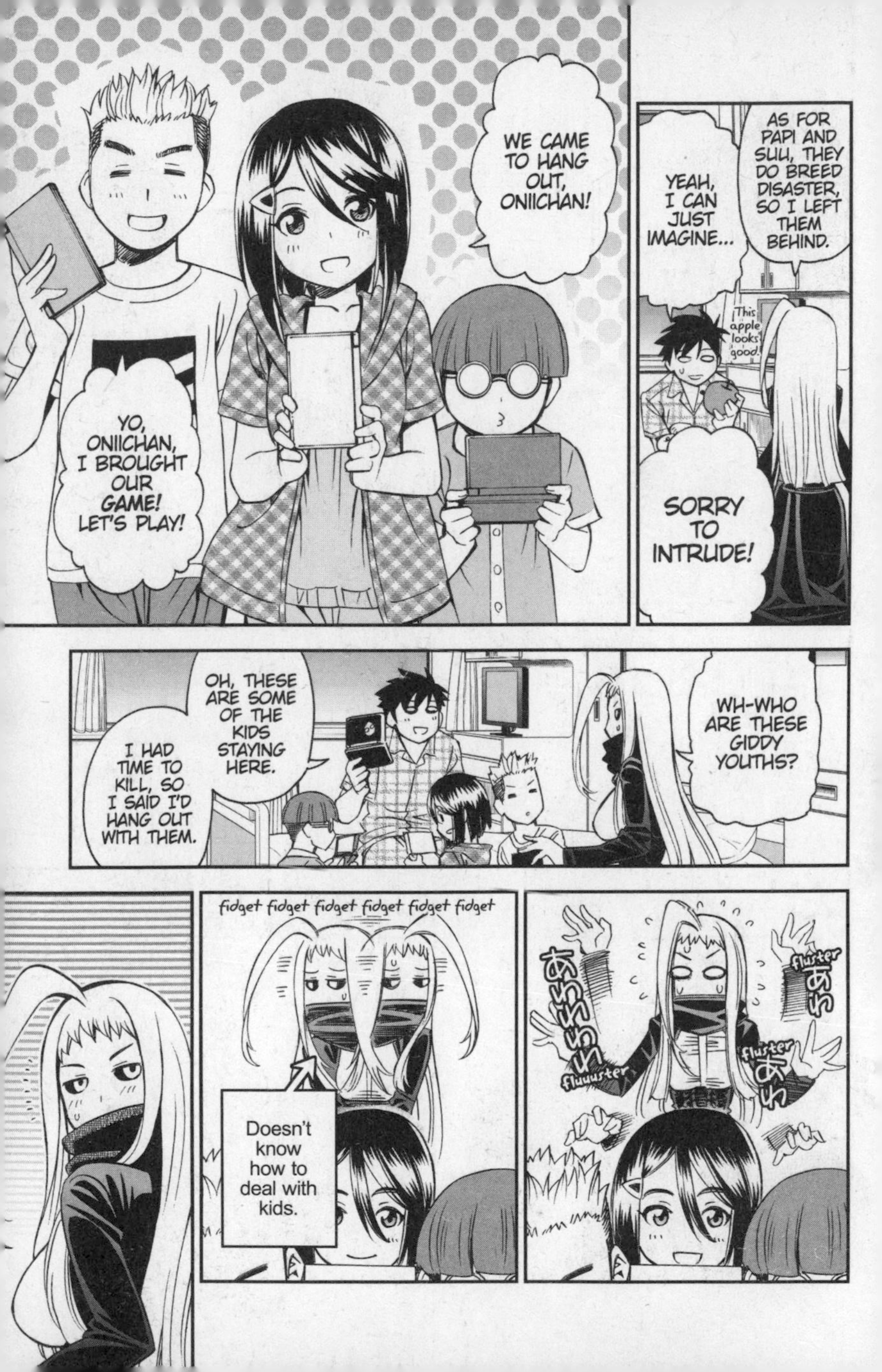
AS FOR PAPI AND SUU, THEY DO BREED DISASTER, SO I LEFT THEM BEHIND.
YEAH, I CAN JUST IMAGINE...
This apple looks good.
SORRY TO INTRUDE!
WE CAME TO HANG OUT, ONIICHAN!
YO, ONIICHAN, I BROUGHT OUR GAME! LET'S PLAY!
WH-WHO ARE THESE GIDDY YOUTHS?
OH, THESE ARE SOME OF THE KIDS STAYING HERE.
I HAD TIME TO KILL, SO I SAID I'D HANG OUT WITH THEM.
fluster あわ
fluster あわ
あわわわ fluuuster
fidget fidget fidget fidget fidget fidget
Doesn't know how to deal with kids.

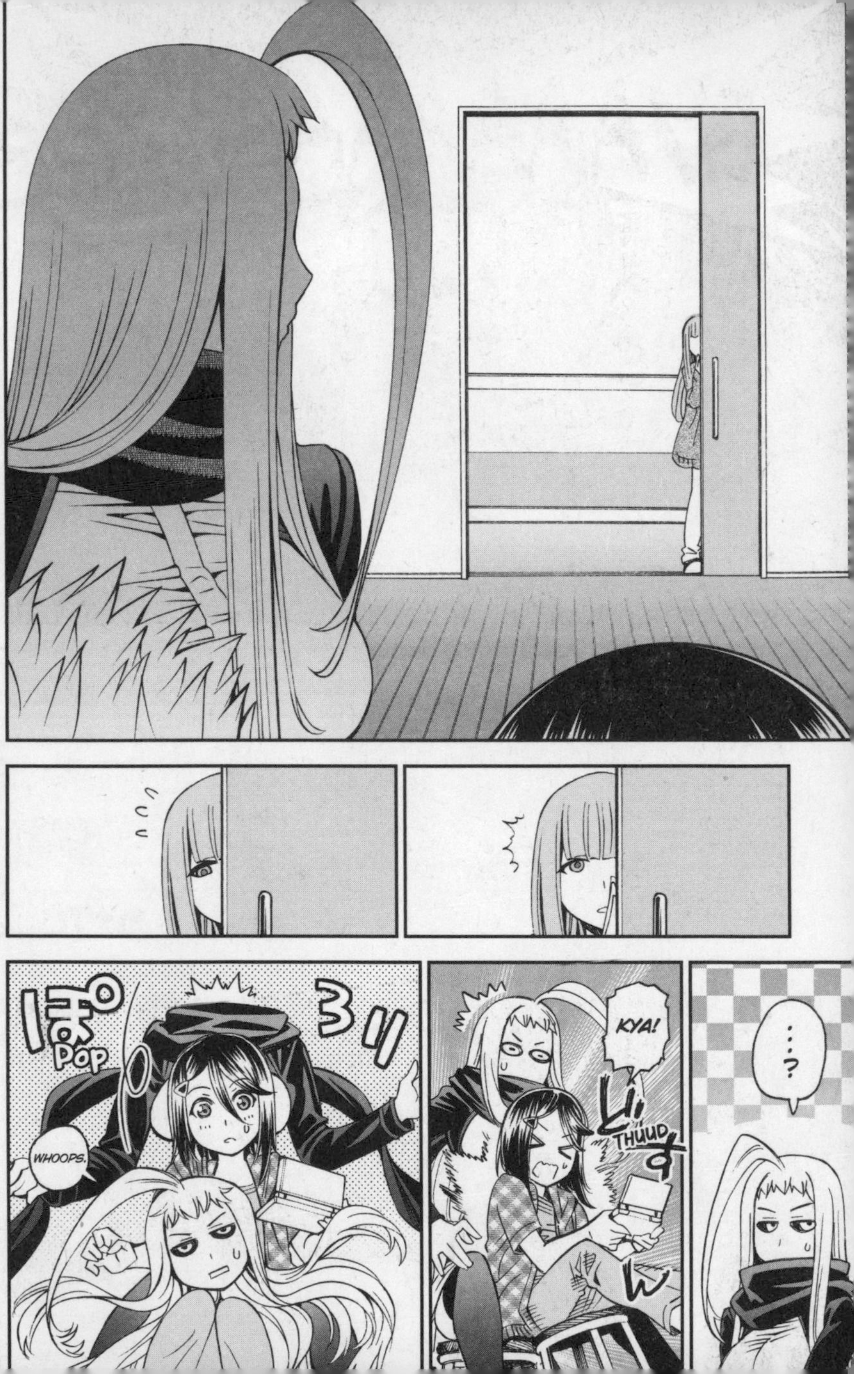

...?
KYA!
THUUD
WHOOPS.
POP

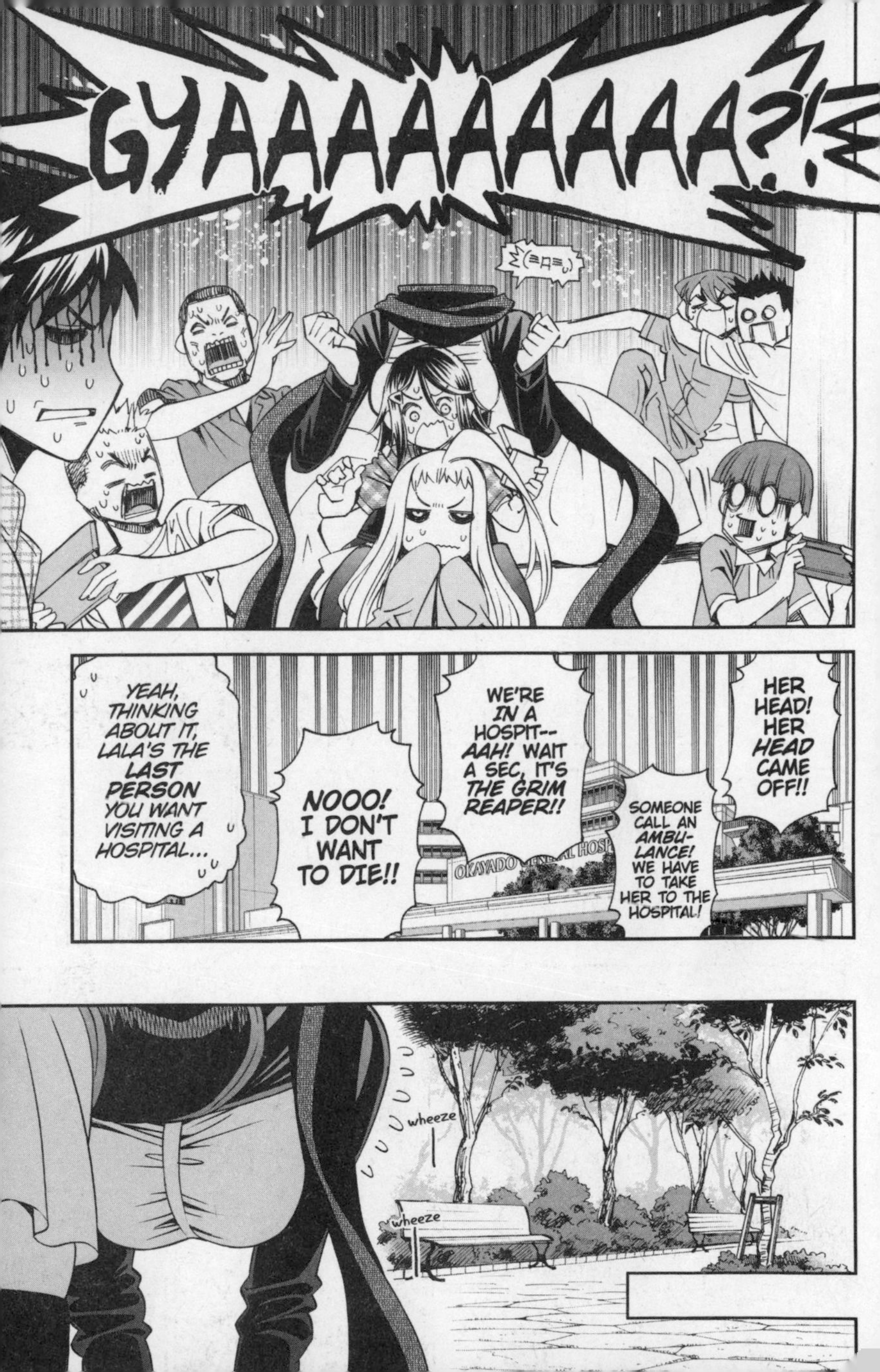
GYAAAAAAAAA?!
Σ(≡Д≡υ)
HER HEAD! HER HEAD CAME OFF!!
SOMEONE CALL AN AMBULANCE! WE HAVE TO TAKE HER TO THE HOSPITAL!
WE'RE IN A HOSPIT-- AAH! WAIT A SEC, IT'S THE GRIM REAPER!!
NOOO! I DON'T WANT TO DIE!!
YEAH, THINKING ABOUT IT, LALA'S THE LAST PERSON YOU WANT VISITING A HOSPITAL...
wheeze
wheeze

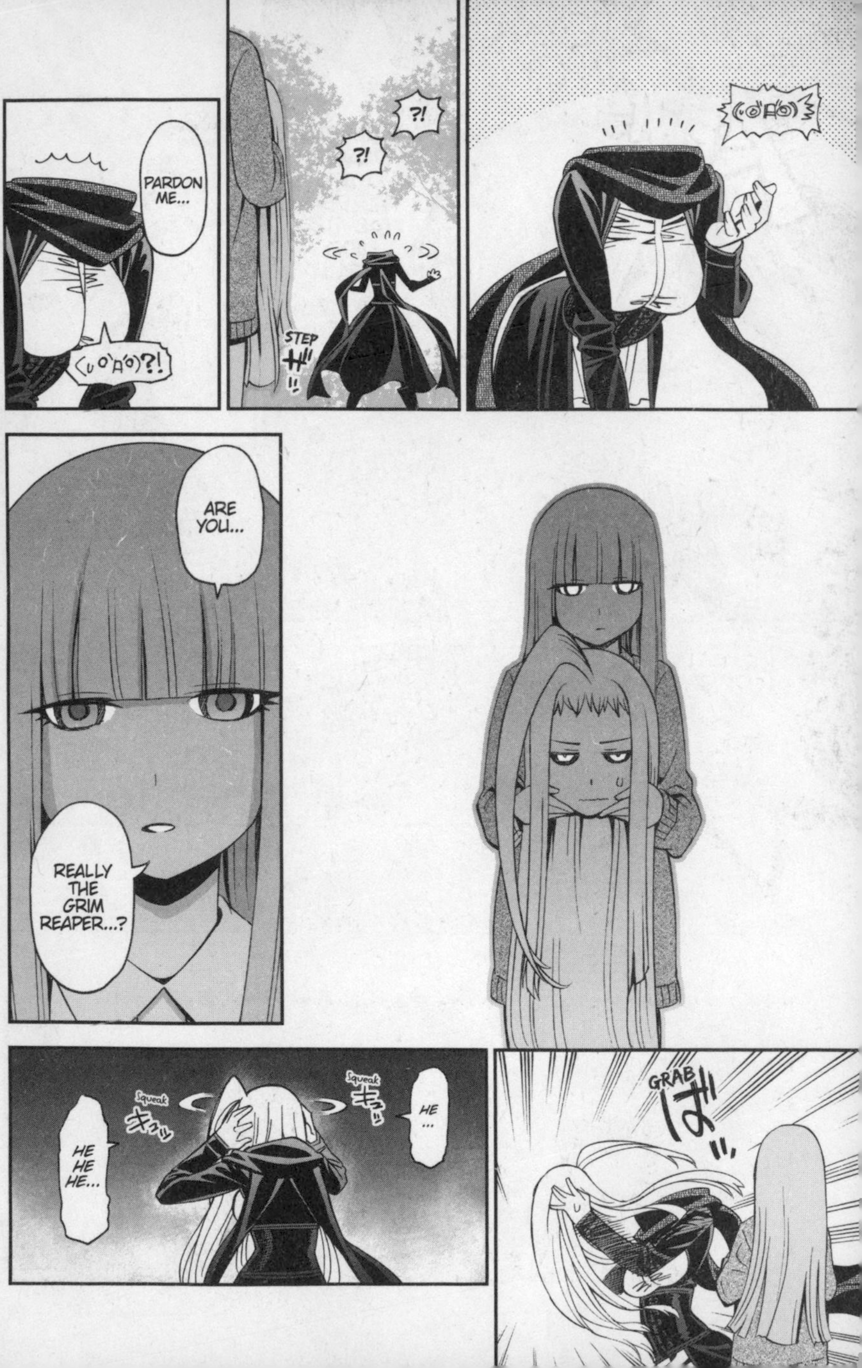

?!
?!
STEP
PARDON ME...
ARE YOU...
REALLY THE GRIM REAPER...?
GRAB
ばッ
HE ...
Squeak
Squeak
HE HE HE...

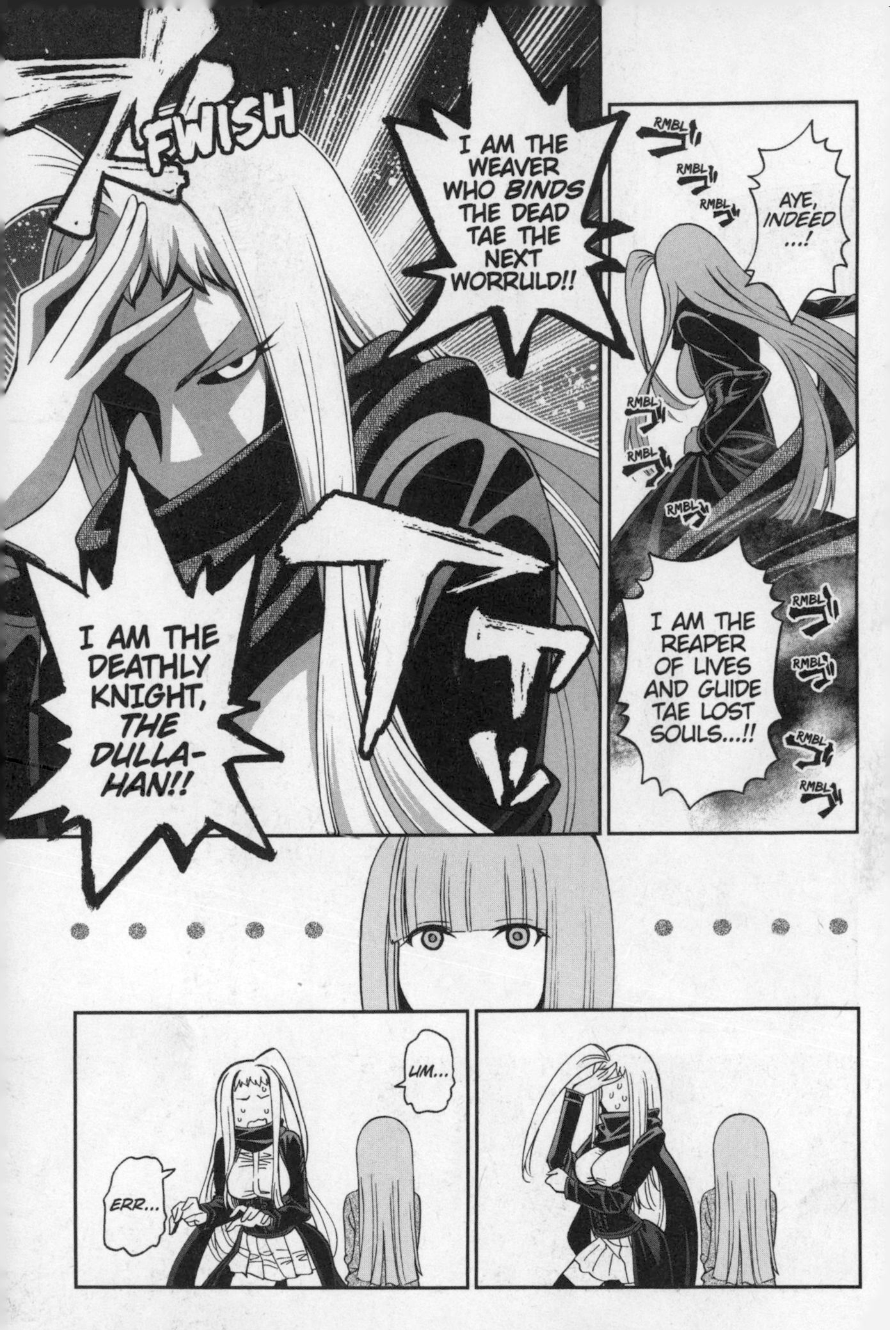
RMBL
RMBL
RMBL
AYE, INDEED ...!
RMBL
RMBL
RMBL
I AM THE REAPER OF LIVES AND GUIDE TAE LOST SOULS...!!
RMBL
RMBL
RMBL
RMBL
FWISH
I AM THE WEAVER WHO *BINDS* THE DEAD TAE THE NEXT WORRULD!!
I AM THE DEATHLY KNIGHT, *THE DULLA-HAN!!*
UM...
ERR...

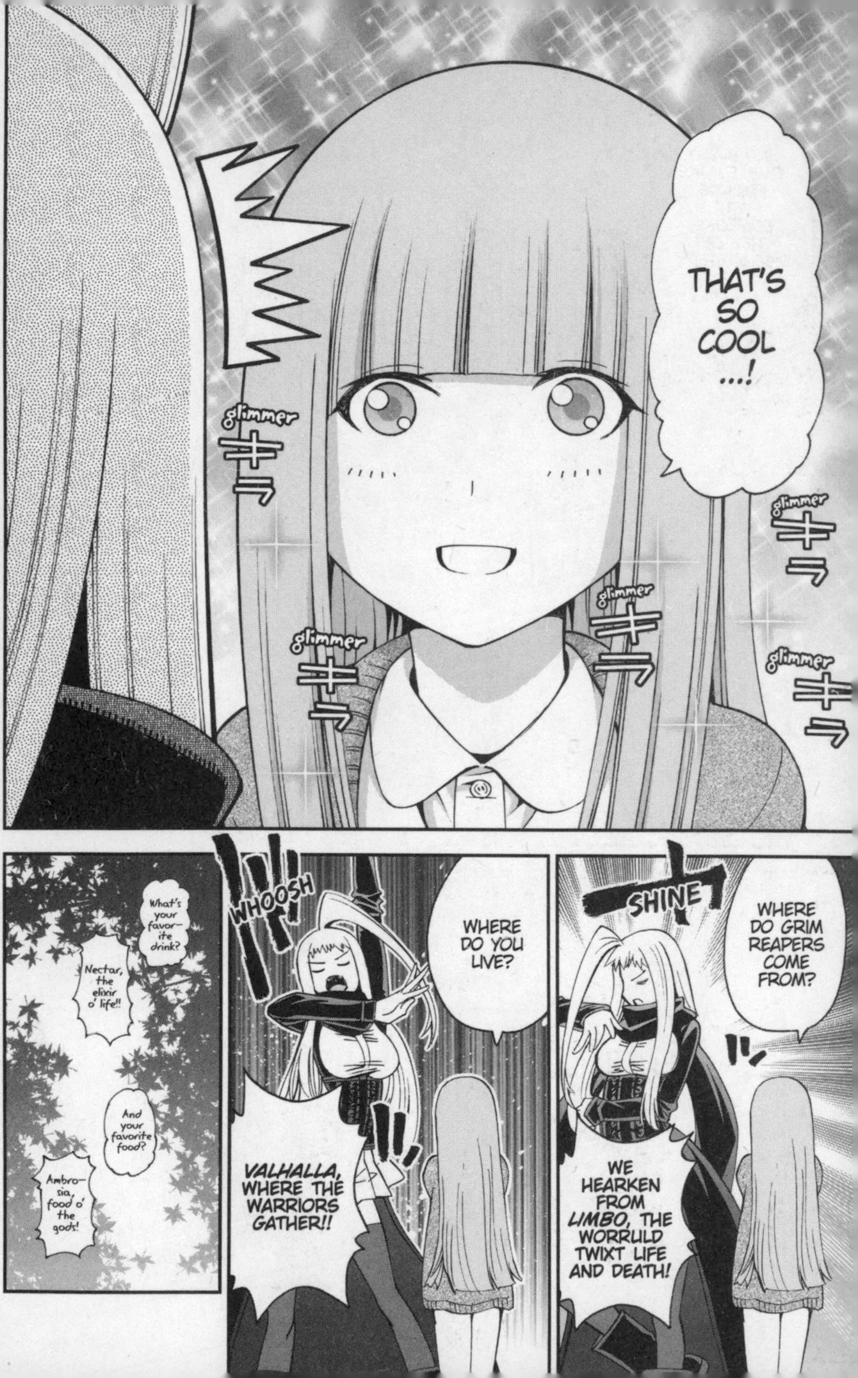
THAT'S SO COOL ...!
glimmer キラ
glimmer キラ
glimmer キラ
glimmer キラ
glimmer キラ
SHINE
WHERE DO GRIM REAPERS COME FROM?
WE HEARKEN FROM *LIMBO*, THE WORRULD TWIXT LIFE AND DEATH!
WHOOSH
WHERE DO YOU LIVE?
VALHALLA, WHERE THE WARRIORS GATHER!!
What's your favor-ite drink?
Nectar, the elixir o' life!!
And your favorite food?
Ambro-sia, food o' the gods!

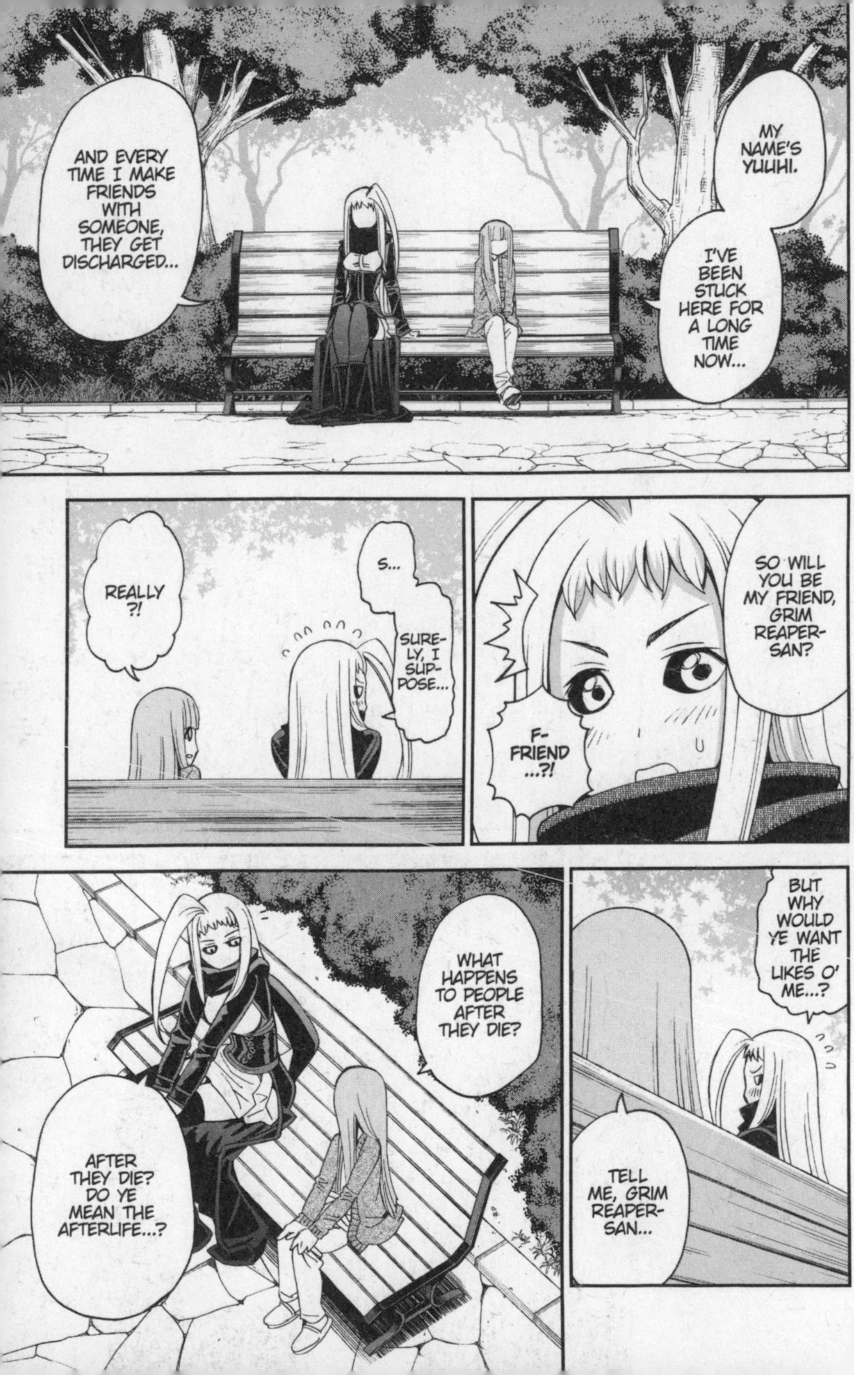
MY NAME'S YUUHI.
I'VE BEEN STUCK HERE FOR A LONG TIME NOW...
AND EVERY TIME I MAKE FRIENDS WITH SOMEONE, THEY GET DISCHARGED...
SO WILL YOU BE MY FRIEND, GRIM REAPER-SAN?
F-FRIEND...?!
S...
SURELY, I SUPPOSE...
REALLY?!
BUT WHY WOULD YE WANT THE LIKES O' ME...?
TELL ME, GRIM REAPER-SAN...
WHAT HAPPENS TO PEOPLE AFTER THEY DIE?
AFTER THEY DIE? DO YE MEAN THE AFTERLIFE...?

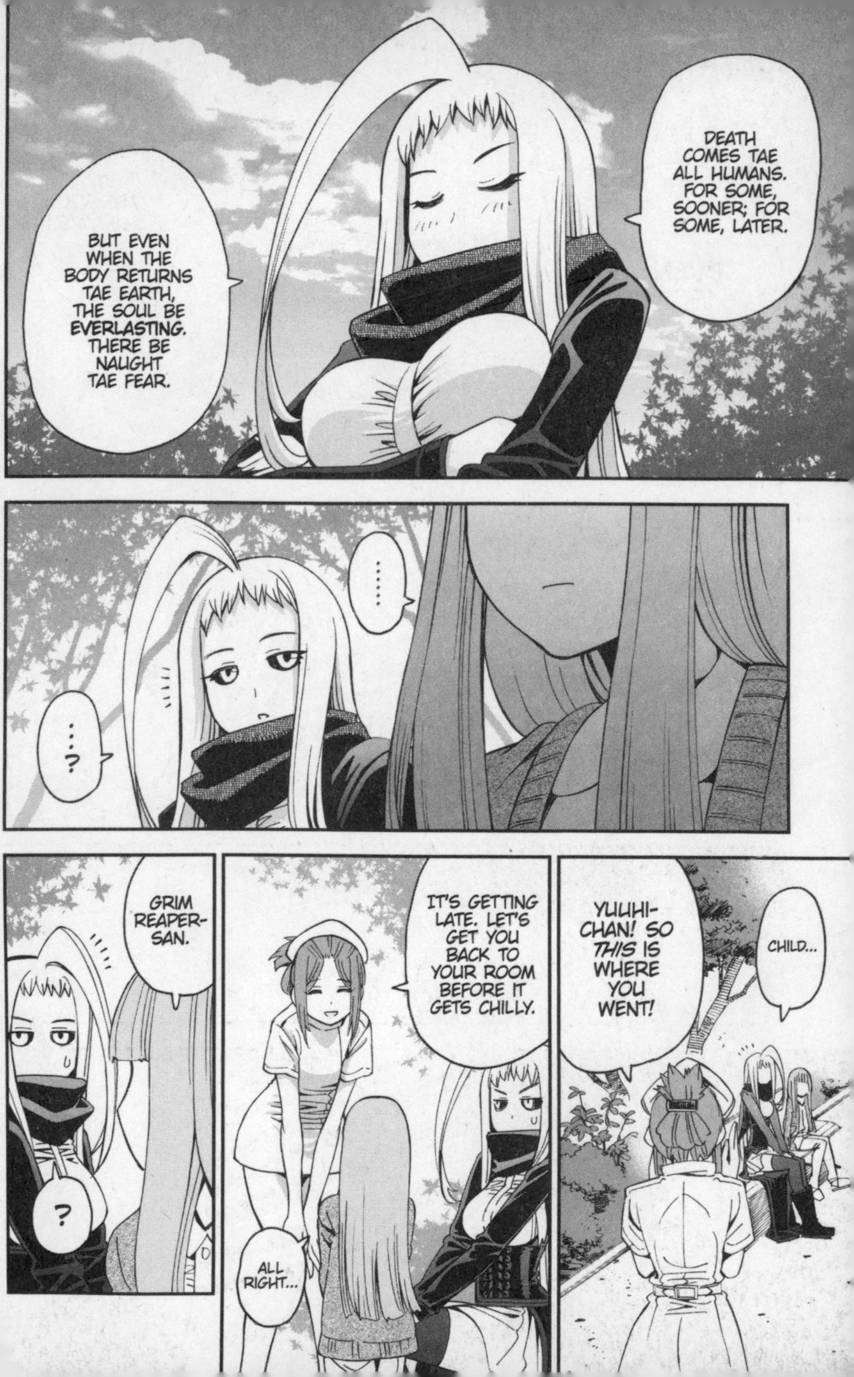
DEATH COMES TAE ALL HUMANS. FOR SOME, SOONER; FOR SOME, LATER.
BUT EVEN WHEN THE BODY RETURNS TAE EARTH, THE SOUL BE EVERLASTING. THERE BE NAUGHT TAE FEAR.
......
...?
CHILD...
YUUHI-CHAN! SO *THIS* IS WHERE YOU WENT!
IT'S GETTING LATE. LET'S GET YOU BACK TO YOUR ROOM BEFORE IT GETS CHILLY.
ALL RIGHT...
GRIM REAPER-SAN.
?

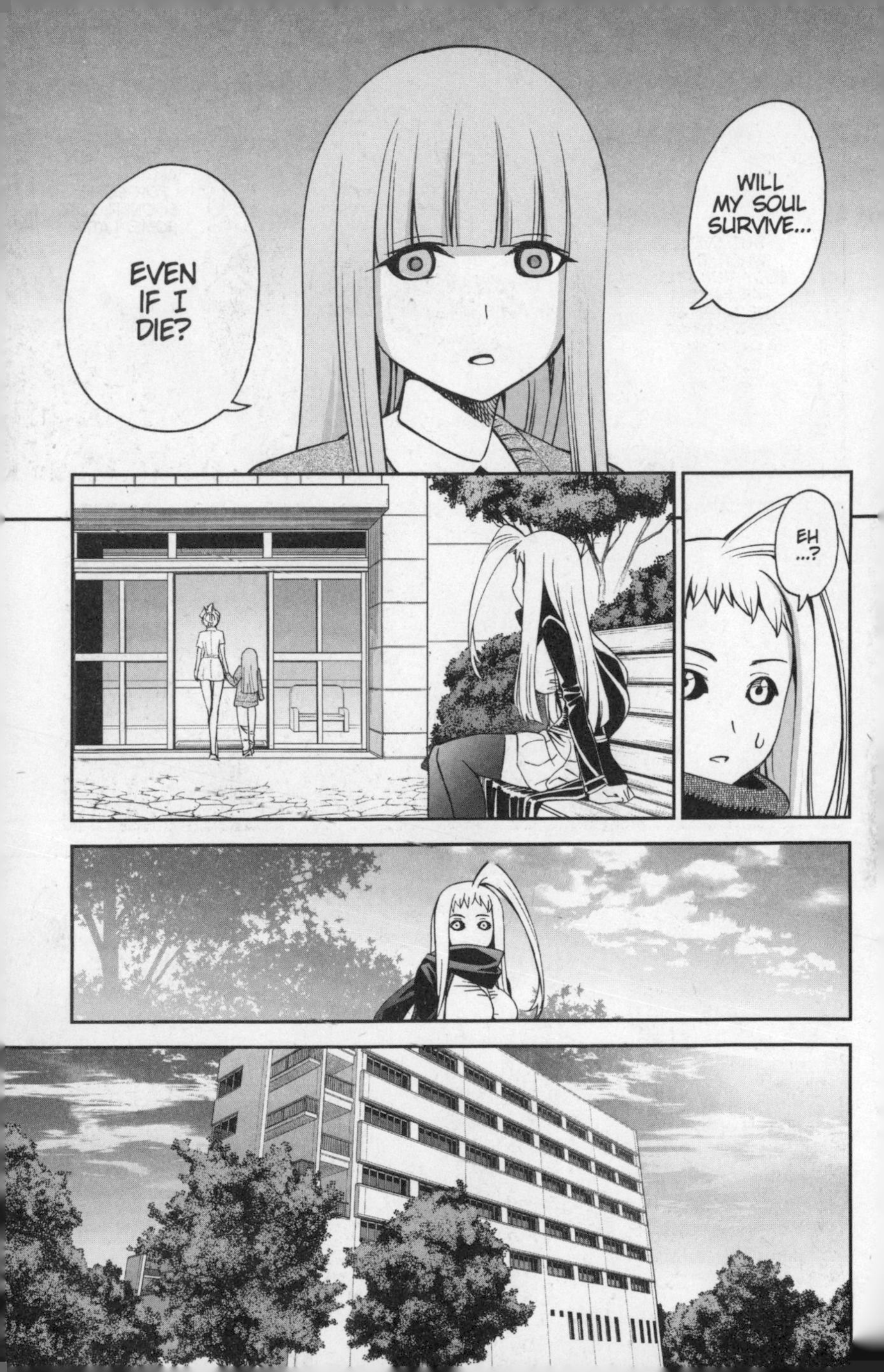
WILL MY SOUL SURVIVE...
EVEN IF I DIE?
EH ...?

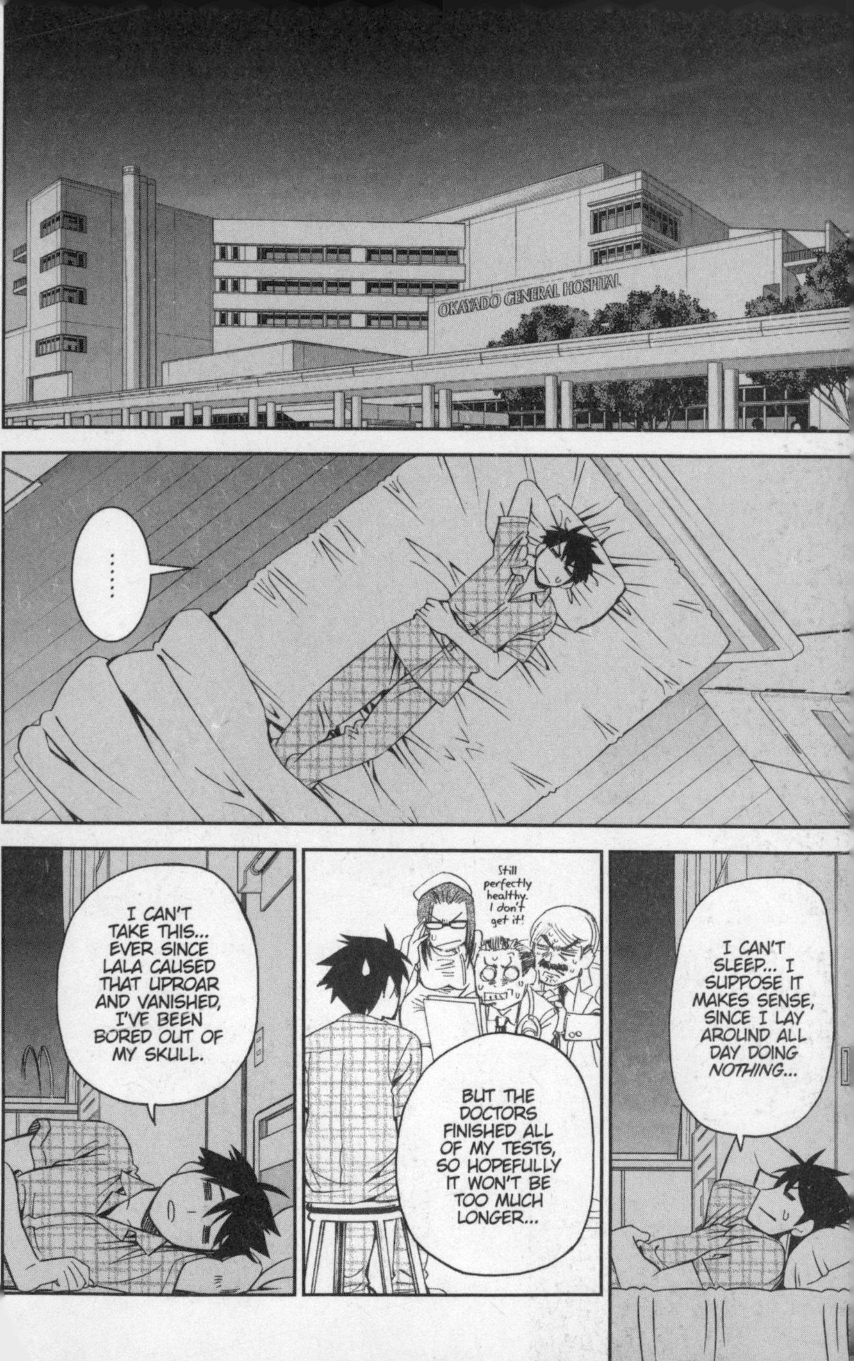
OKAYADO GENERAL HOSPITAL
......
I CAN'T SLEEP... I SUPPOSE IT MAKES SENSE, SINCE I LAY AROUND ALL DAY DOING *NOTHING*...
Still perfectly healthy. I don't get it!
BUT THE DOCTORS FINISHED ALL OF MY TESTS, SO HOPEFULLY IT WON'T BE TOO MUCH LONGER...
I CAN'T TAKE THIS... EVER SINCE LALA CAUSED THAT UPROAR AND VANISHED, I'VE BEEN BORED OUT OF MY SKULL.

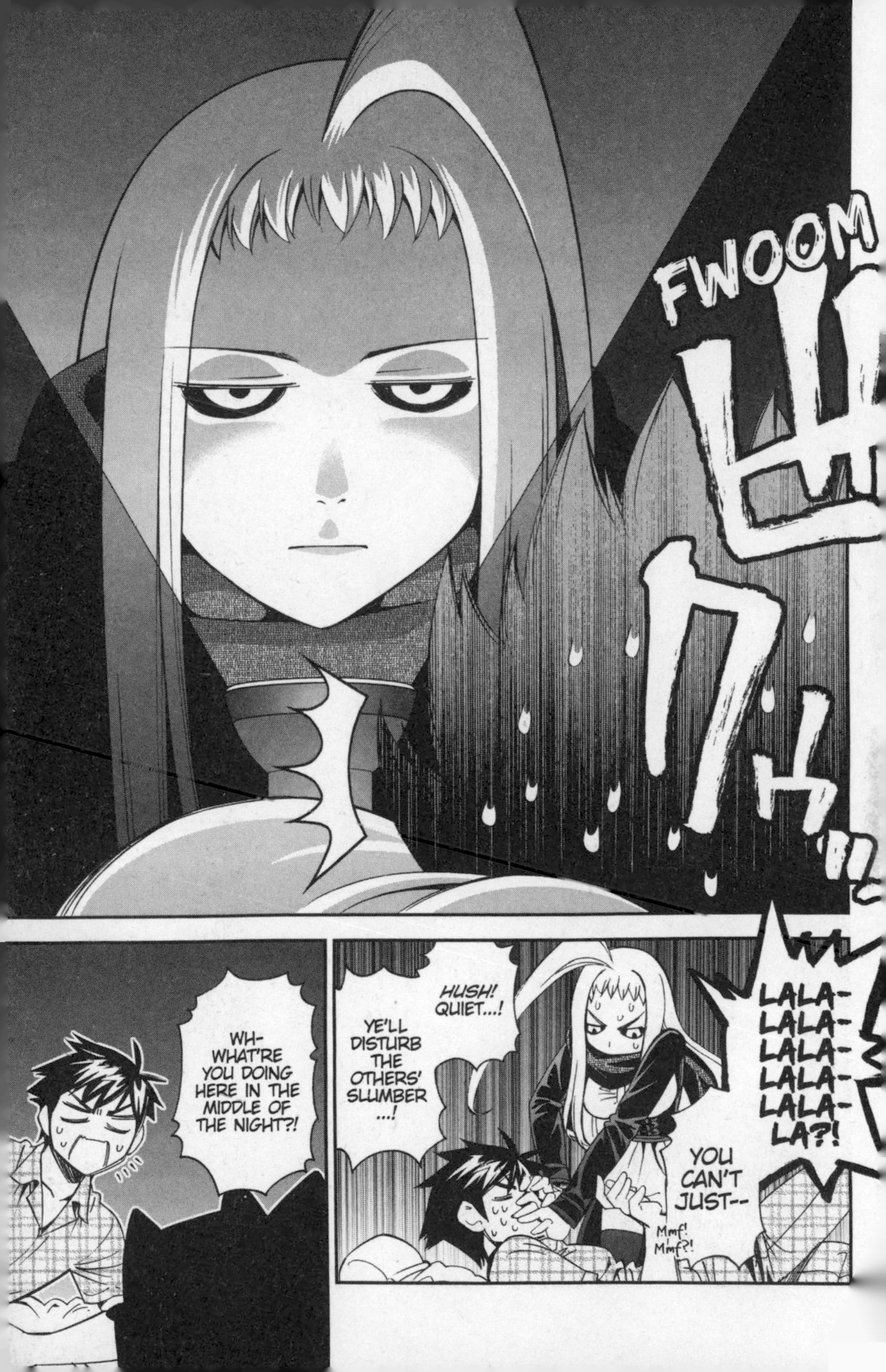
FWOOM
LALA-LALA-LALA-LALA-LALA-LA?!
YOU CAN'T JUST--
HUSH! QUIET...!
YE'LL DISTURB THE OTHERS' SLUMBER...!
Mmf! Mmf?!
WH- WHAT'RE YOU DOING HERE IN THE MIDDLE OF THE NIGHT?!

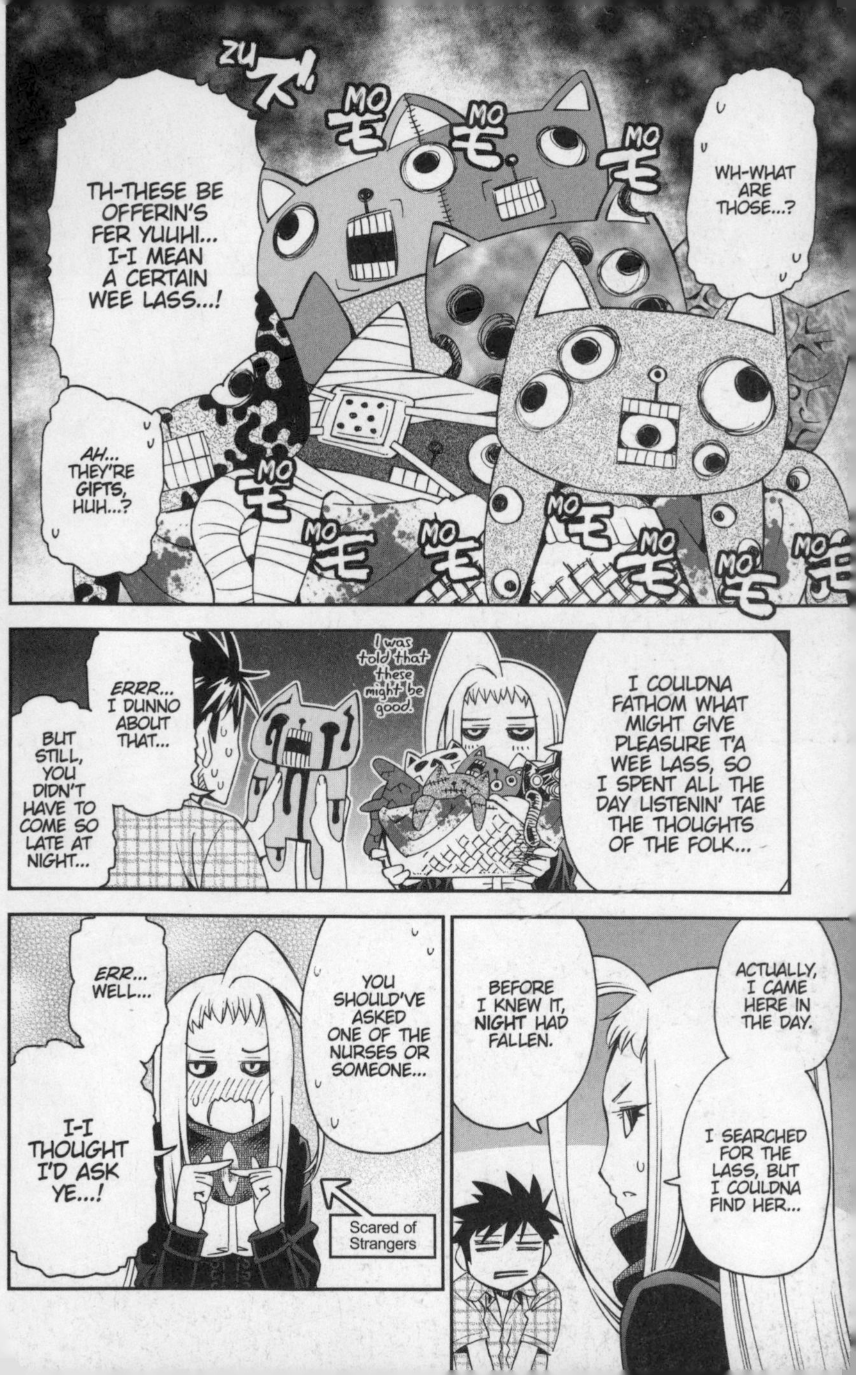
WH-WHAT ARE THOSE...?
ZU
MO MO MO
TH-THESE BE OFFERIN'S FER YUUHI... I-I MEAN A CERTAIN WEE LASS...!
AH... THEY'RE GIFTS, HUH...?
MO MO MO MO MO MO MO
I COULDNA FATHOM WHAT MIGHT GIVE PLEASURE T'A WEE LASS, SO I SPENT ALL THE DAY LISTENIN' TAE THE THOUGHTS OF THE FOLK...
I was told that these might be good.
ERRR... I DUNNO ABOUT THAT...
BUT STILL, YOU DIDN'T HAVE TO COME SO LATE AT NIGHT...
ACTUALLY, I CAME HERE IN THE DAY.
BEFORE I KNEW IT, NIGHT HAD FALLEN.
I SEARCHED FOR THE LASS, BUT I COULDNA FIND HER...
YOU SHOULD'VE ASKED ONE OF THE NURSES OR SOMEONE...
ERR... WELL...
I-I THOUGHT I'D ASK YE...!
Scared of Strangers

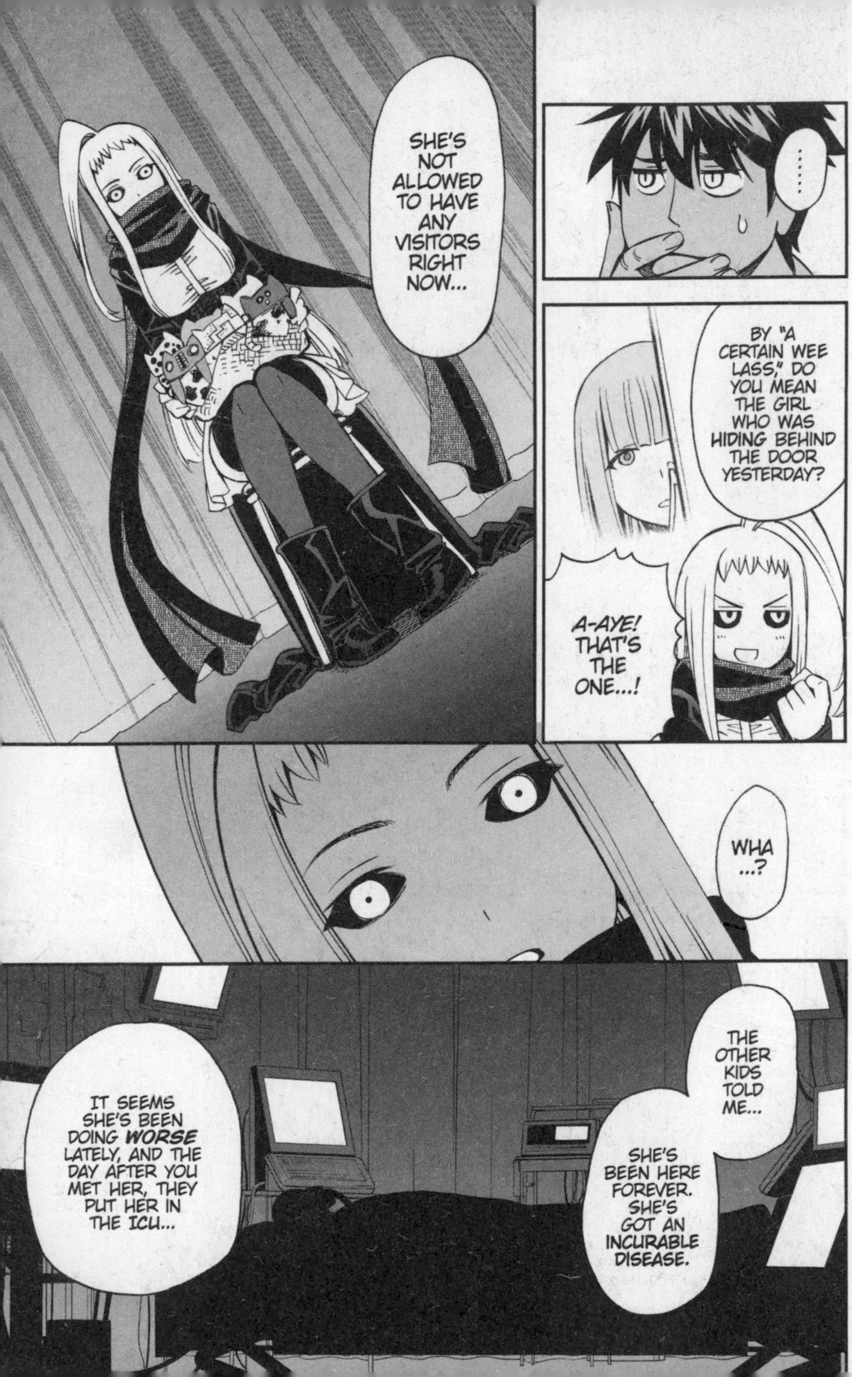
......
BY "A CERTAIN WEE LASS," DO YOU MEAN THE GIRL WHO WAS HIDING BEHIND THE DOOR YESTERDAY?
A-AYE! THAT'S THE ONE...!
SHE'S NOT ALLOWED TO HAVE ANY VISITORS RIGHT NOW...
WHA ...?
THE OTHER KIDS TOLD ME...
SHE'S BEEN HERE FOREVER. SHE'S GOT AN INCURABLE DISEASE.
IT SEEMS SHE'S BEEN DOING WORSE LATELY, AND THE DAY AFTER YOU MET HER, THEY PUT HER IN THE ICU...

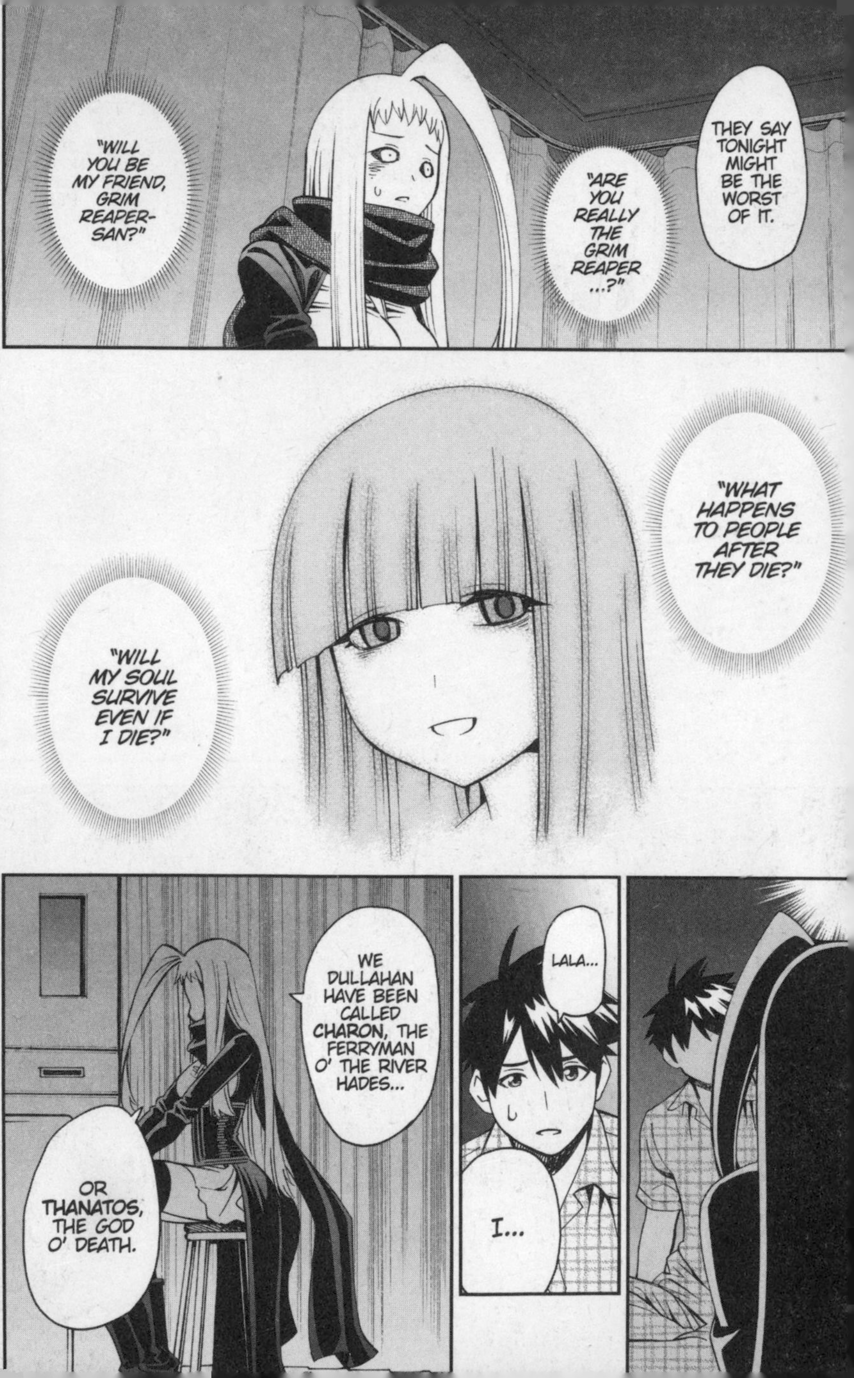
THEY SAY TONIGHT MIGHT BE THE WORST OF IT.
"ARE YOU REALLY THE GRIM REAPER ...?"
"WILL YOU BE MY FRIEND, GRIM REAPER-SAN?"
"WHAT HAPPENS TO PEOPLE AFTER THEY DIE?"
"WILL MY SOUL SURVIVE EVEN IF I DIE?"
LALA...
I...
WE DULLAHAN HAVE BEEN CALLED CHARON, THE FERRYMAN O' THE RIVER HADES...
OR THANATOS, THE GOD O' DEATH.

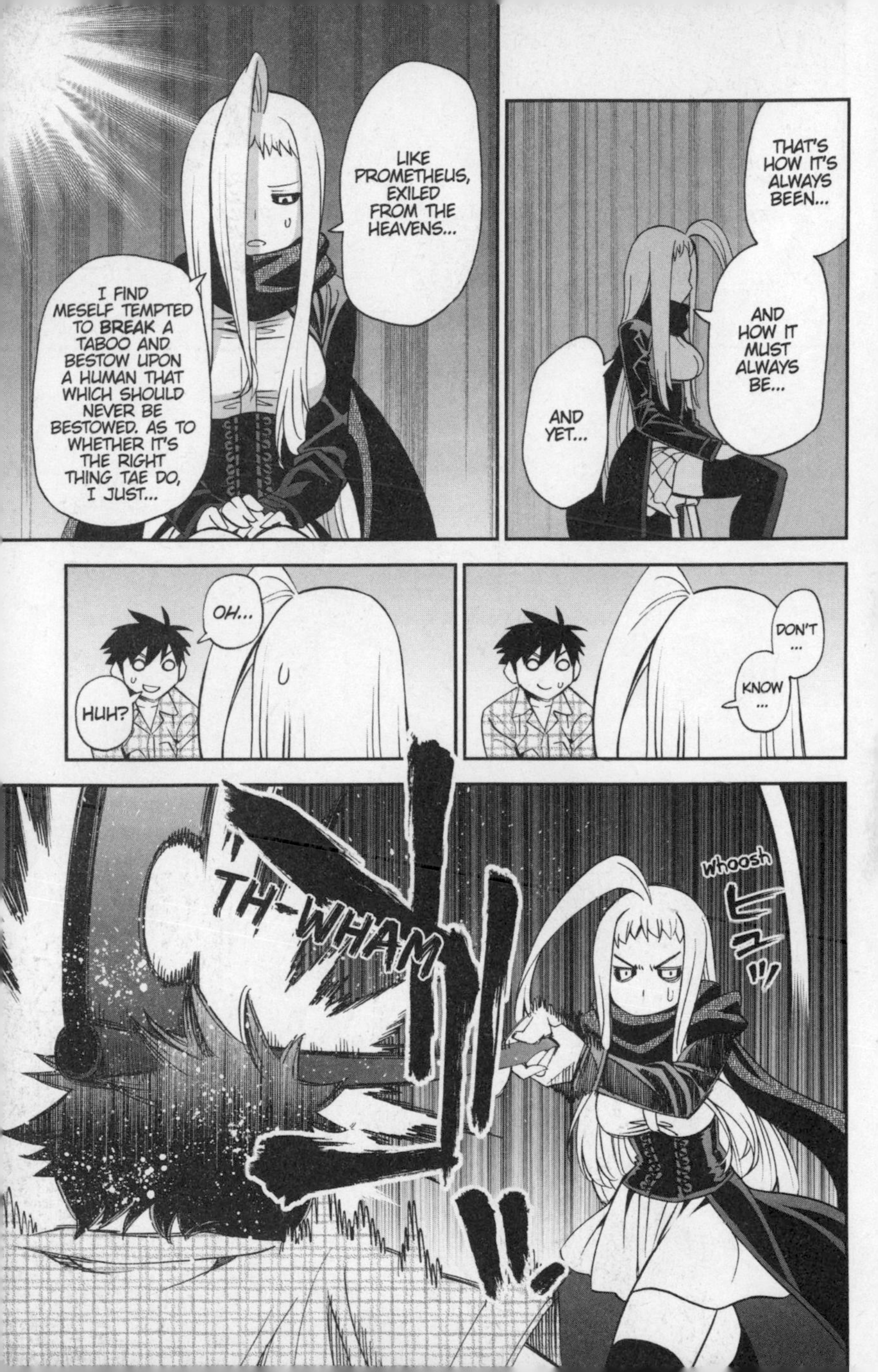
THAT'S HOW IT'S ALWAYS BEEN...
AND HOW IT MUST ALWAYS BE...
AND YET...
LIKE PROMETHEUS, EXILED FROM THE HEAVENS...
I FIND MESELF TEMPTED TO BREAK A TABOO AND BESTOW UPON A HUMAN THAT WHICH SHOULD NEVER BE BESTOWED. AS TO WHETHER IT'S THE RIGHT THING TAE DO, I JUST...
DON'T ...
KNOW ...
OH...
HUH?
Whoosh
ヒュッ
TH-WHAM

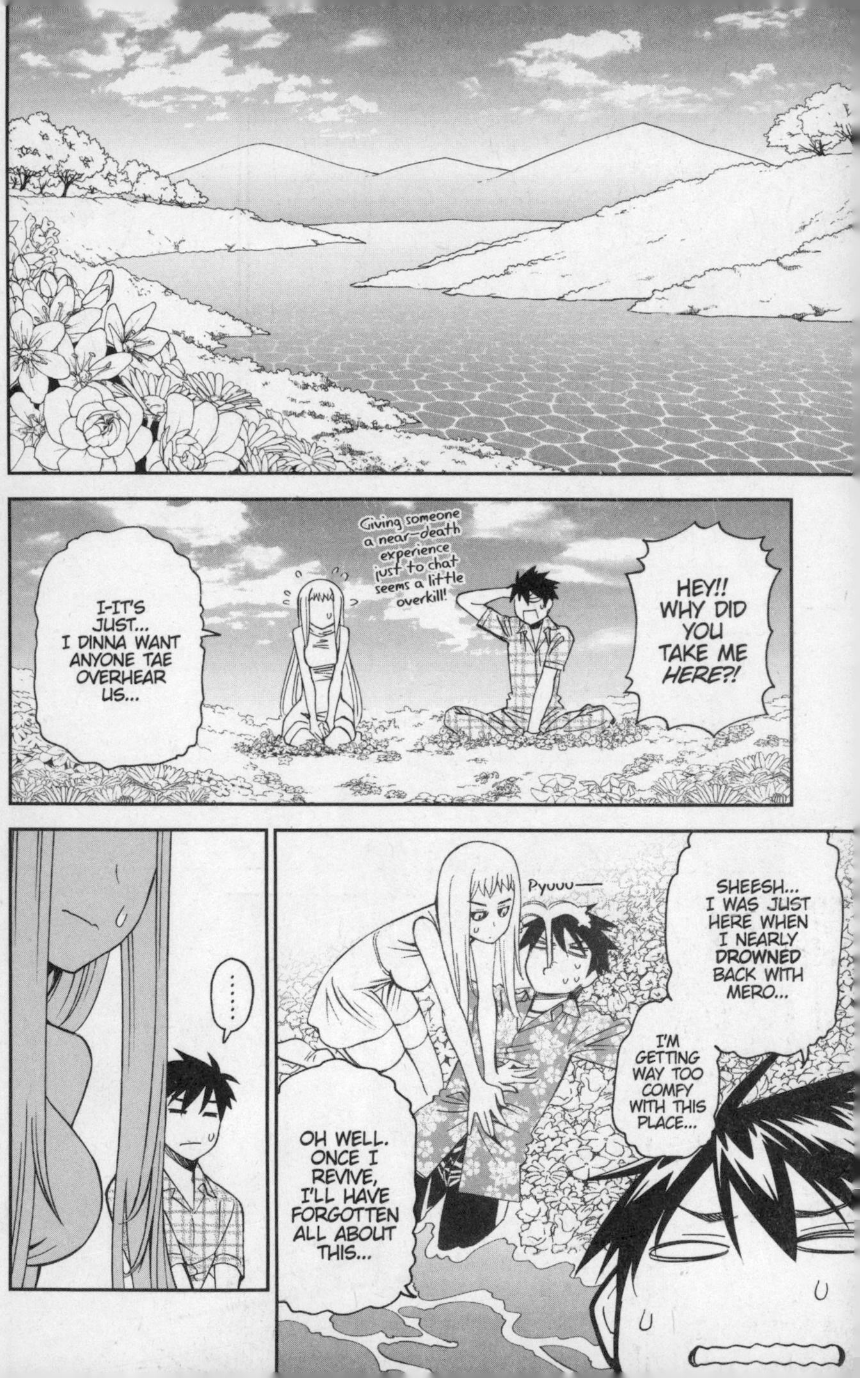
HEY!! WHY DID YOU TAKE ME HERE?!
Giving someone a near-death experience just to chat seems a little overkill!
I-IT'S JUST... I DINNA WANT ANYONE TAE OVERHEAR US...
SHEESH... I WAS JUST HERE WHEN I NEARLY DROWNED BACK WITH MERO...
Pyuuu—
I'M GETTING WAY TOO COMFY WITH THIS PLACE...
OH WELL. ONCE I REVIVE, I'LL HAVE FORGOTTEN ALL ABOUT THIS...
......

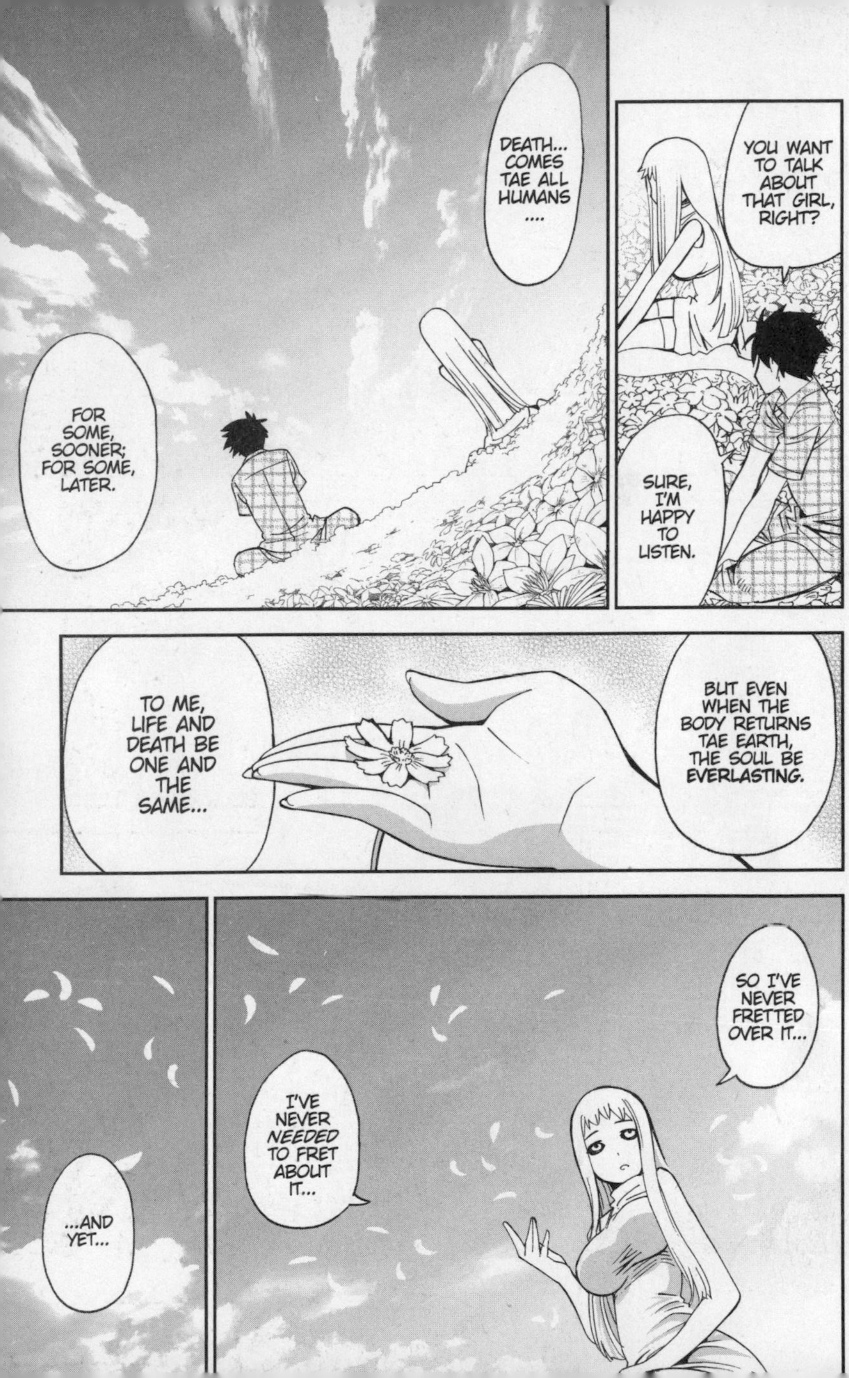
YOU WANT TO TALK ABOUT THAT GIRL, RIGHT?
SURE, I'M HAPPY TO LISTEN.
DEATH... COMES TAE ALL HUMANS ....
FOR SOME, SOONER; FOR SOME, LATER.
BUT EVEN WHEN THE BODY RETURNS TAE EARTH, THE SOUL BE EVERLASTING.
TO ME, LIFE AND DEATH BE ONE AND THE SAME...
SO I'VE NEVER FRETTED OVER IT...
I'VE NEVER *NEEDED* TO FRET ABOUT IT...
...AND YET...

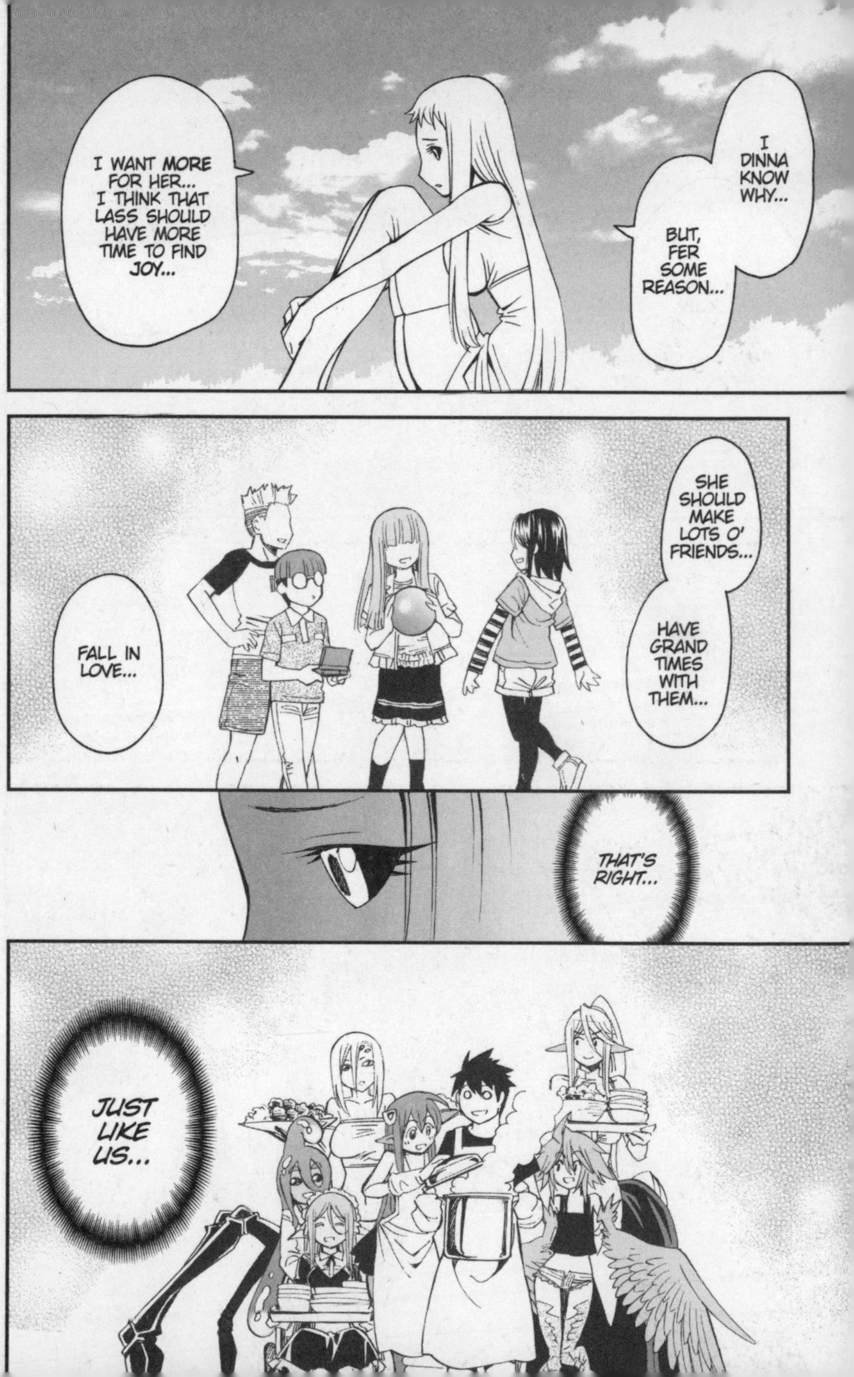
I DINNA KNOW WHY...
BUT, FER SOME REASON...
I WANT MORE FOR HER... I THINK THAT LASS SHOULD HAVE MORE TIME TO FIND JOY...
SHE SHOULD MAKE LOTS O' FRIENDS...
HAVE GRAND TIMES WITH THEM...
FALL IN LOVE...
THAT'S RIGHT...
JUST LIKE US...

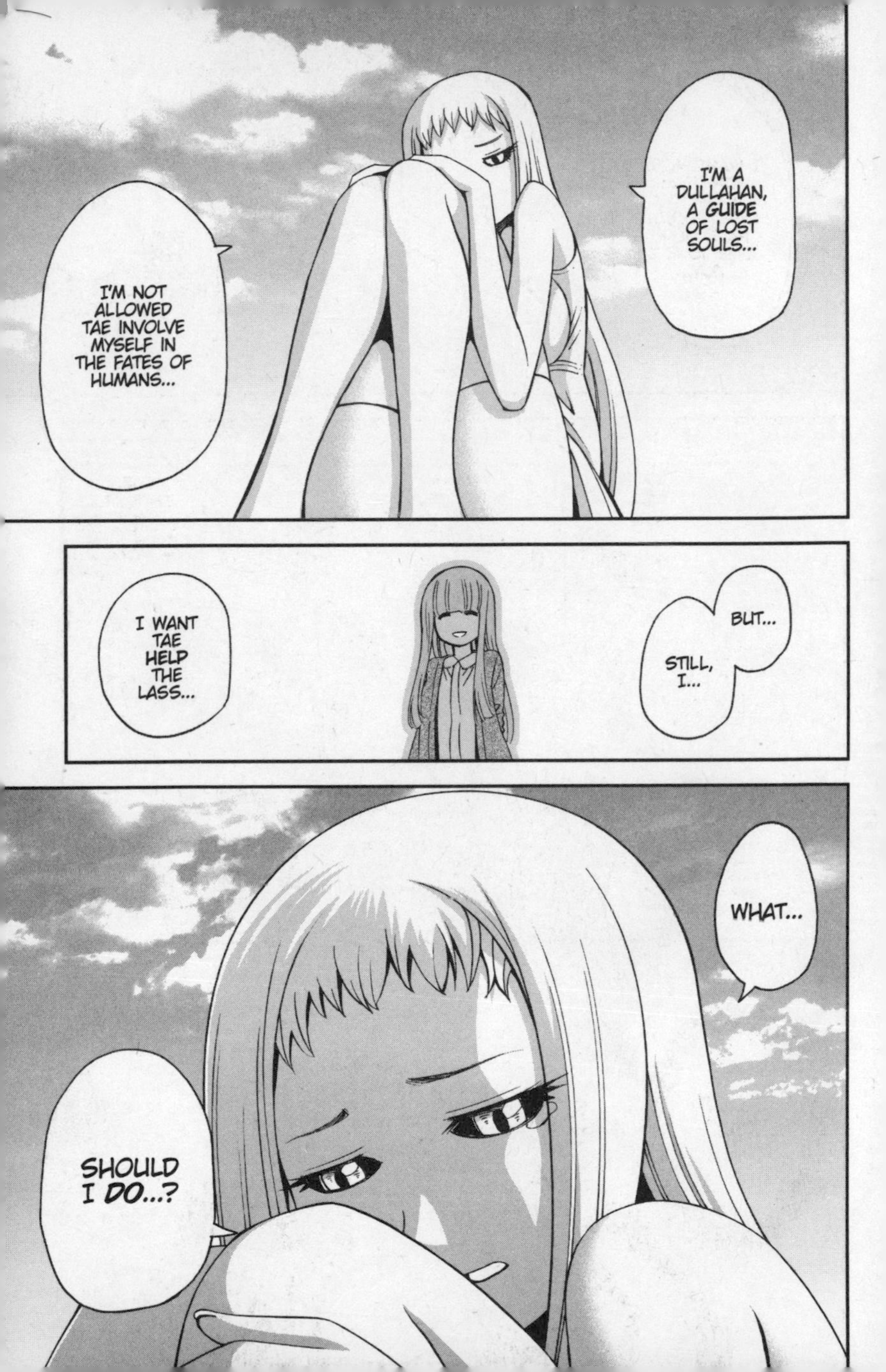
I'M A DULLAHAN, A GUIDE OF LOST SOULS...
I'M NOT ALLOWED TAE INVOLVE MYSELF IN THE FATES OF HUMANS...
BUT...
STILL, I...
I WANT TAE HELP THE LASS...
WHAT...
SHOULD I *DO*...?

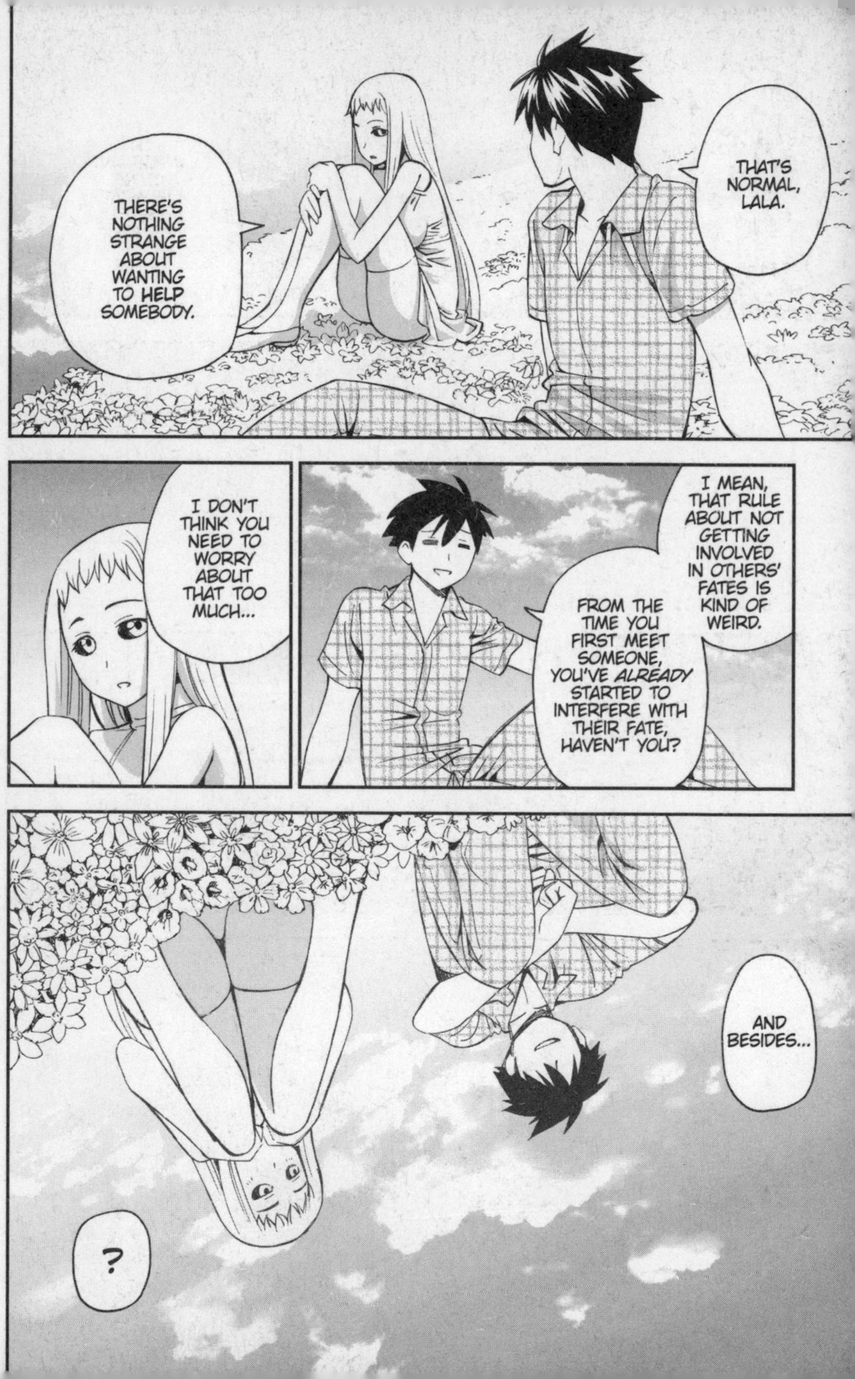
THAT'S NORMAL, LALA.
THERE'S NOTHING STRANGE ABOUT WANTING TO HELP SOMEBODY.
I MEAN, THAT RULE ABOUT NOT GETTING INVOLVED IN OTHERS' FATES IS KIND OF WEIRD.
FROM THE TIME YOU FIRST MEET SOMEONE, YOU'VE *ALREADY* STARTED TO INTERFERE WITH THEIR FATE, HAVEN'T YOU?
I DON'T THINK YOU NEED TO WORRY ABOUT THAT TOO MUCH...
AND BESIDES...
?

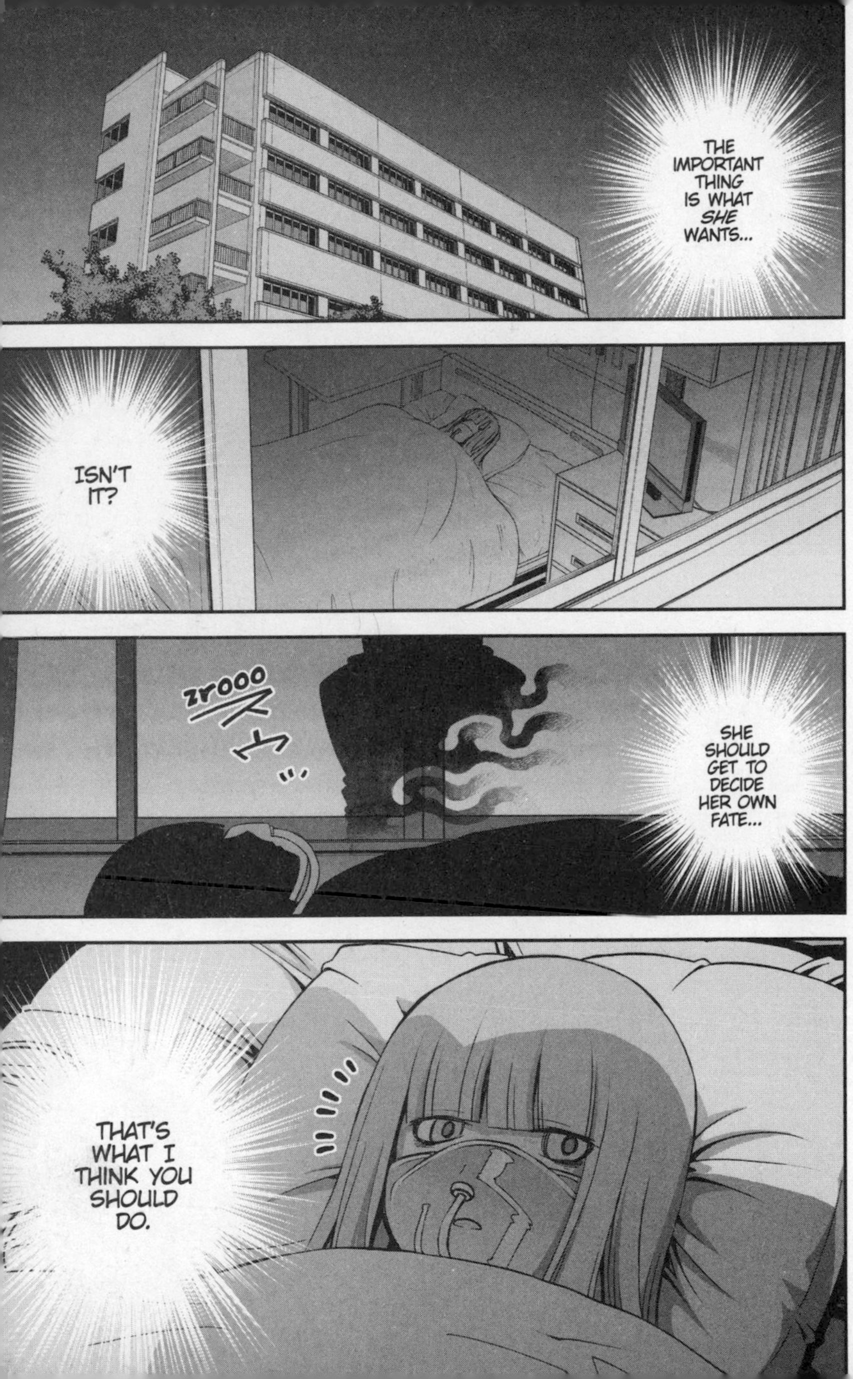
THE IMPORTANT THING IS WHAT *SHE* WANTS...
ISN'T IT?
SHE SHOULD GET TO DECIDE HER OWN FATE...
ZROOO
THAT'S WHAT I THINK YOU SHOULD DO.

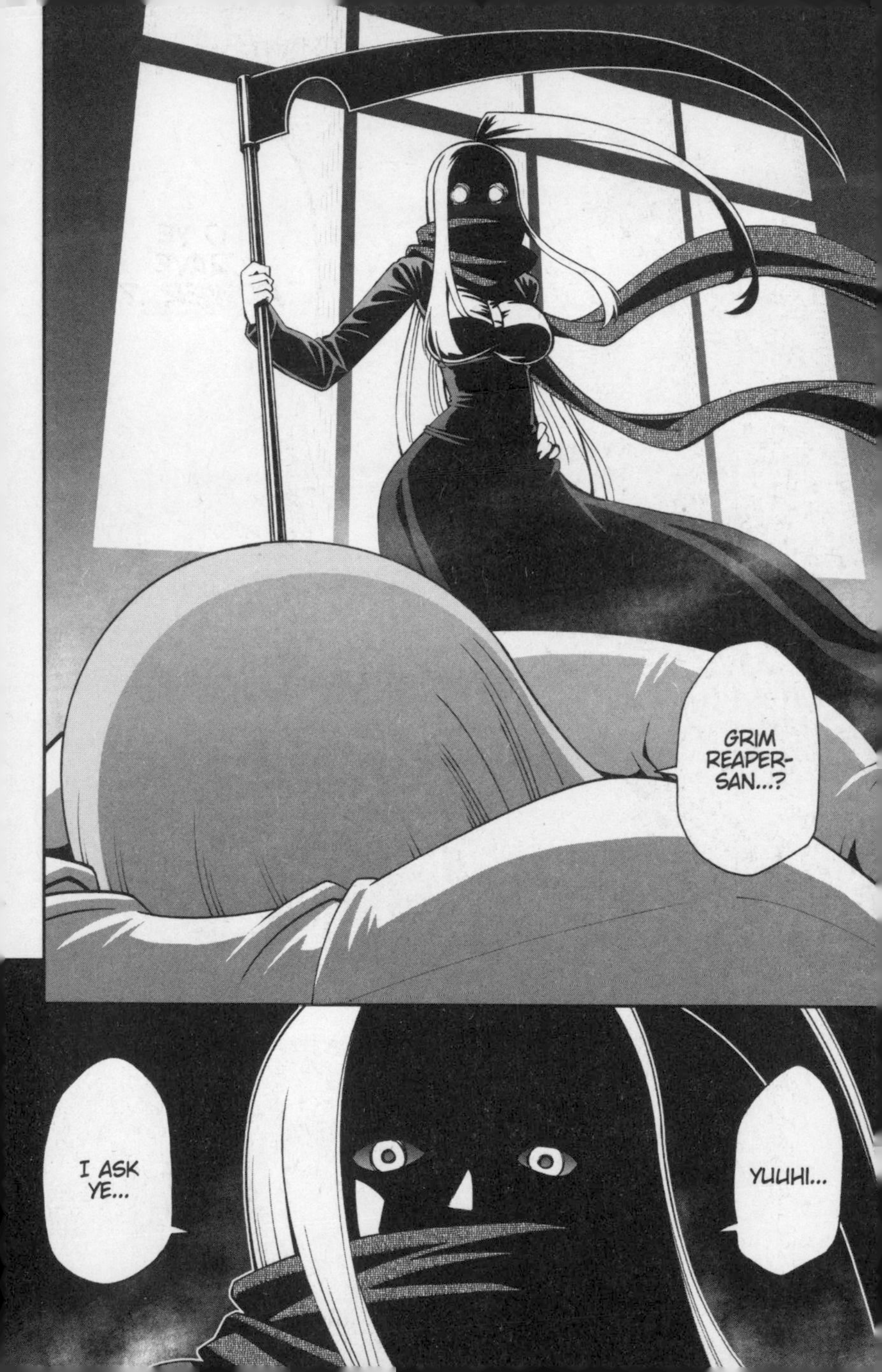
GRIM REAPER-SAN...?
YUUHI...
I ASK YE...

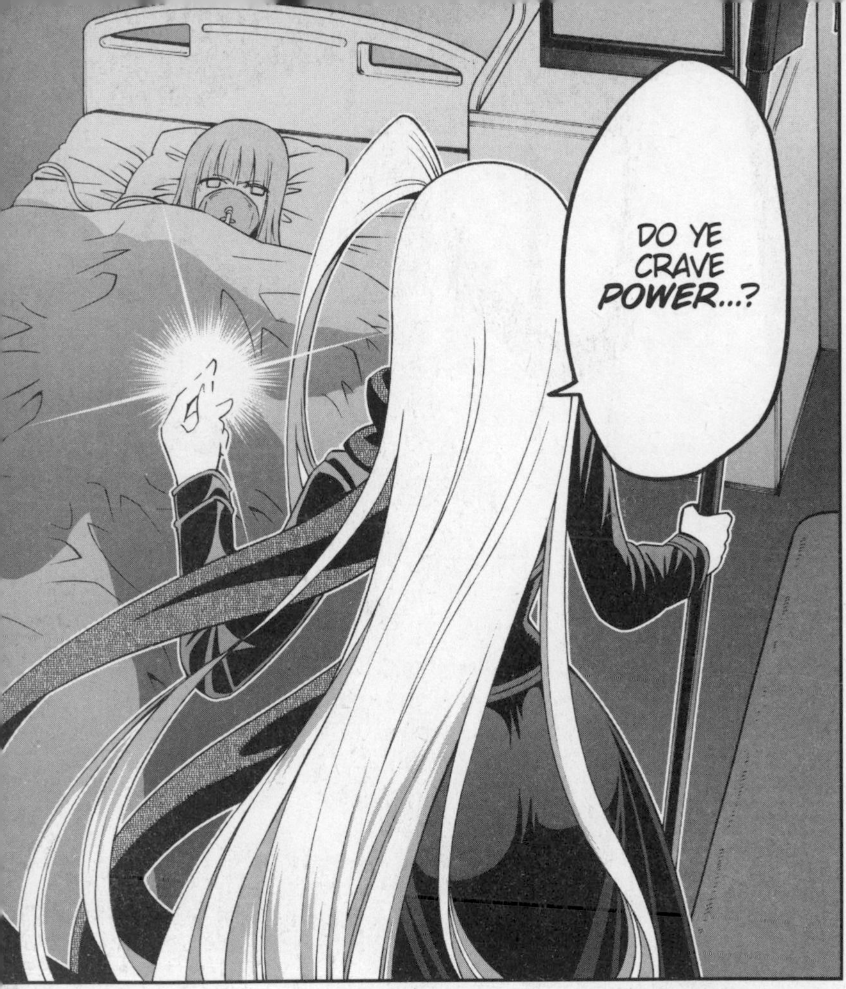
DO YE CRAVE POWER...?

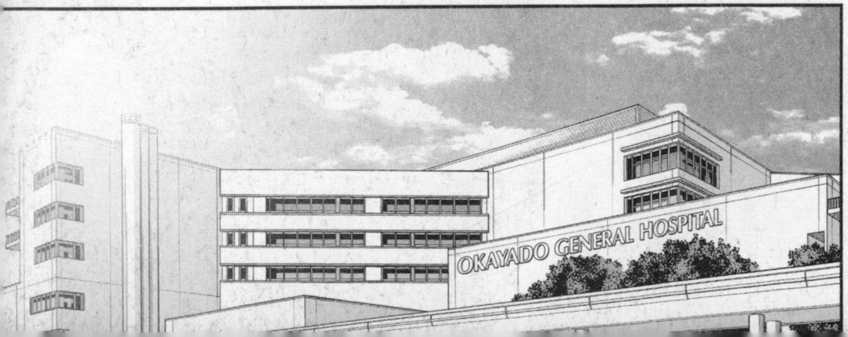
OKAYADO GENERAL HOSPITAL

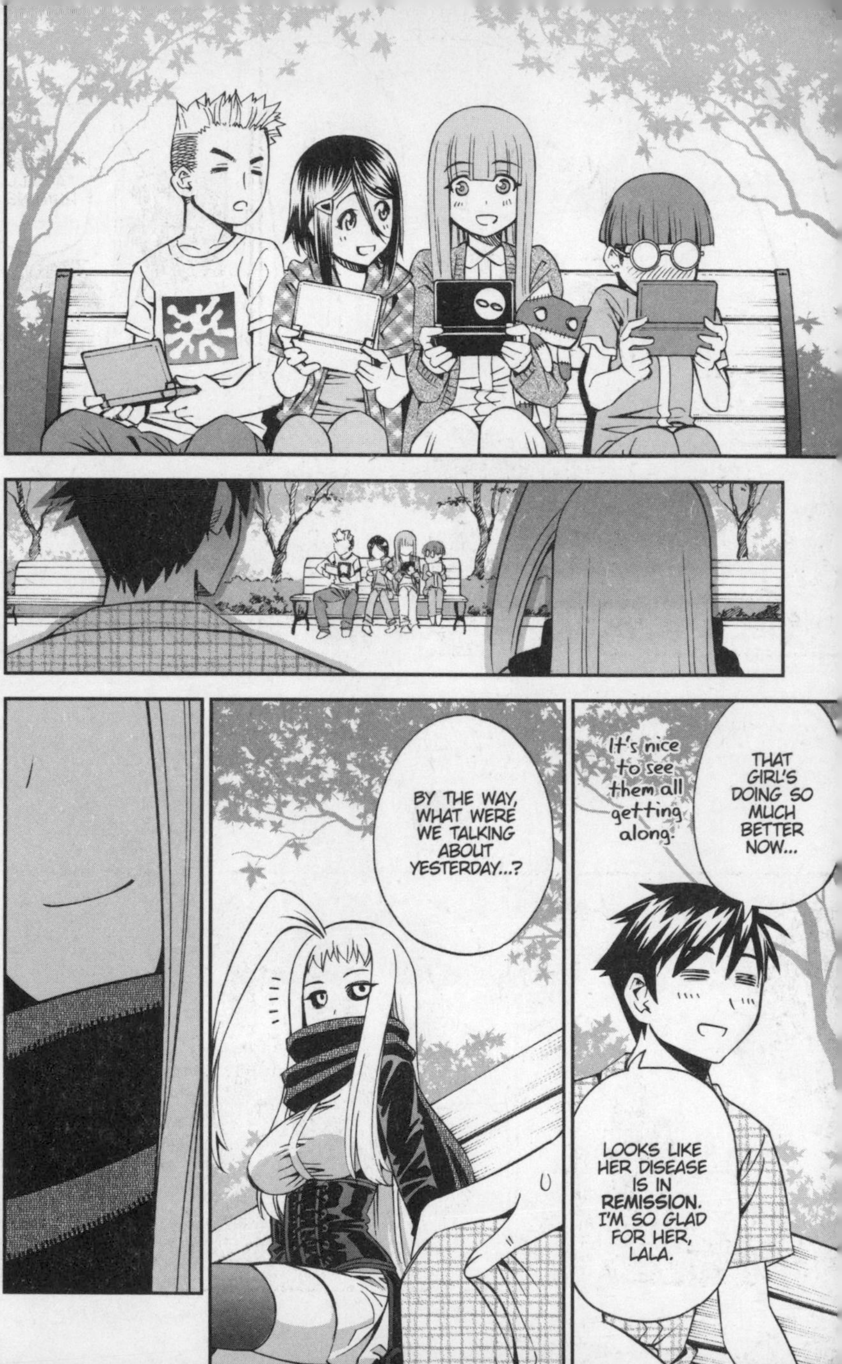
THAT GIRL'S DOING SO MUCH BETTER NOW...
It's nice to see them all getting along.
LOOKS LIKE HER DISEASE IS IN REMISSION. I'M SO GLAD FOR HER, LALA.
BY THE WAY, WHAT WERE WE TALKING ABOUT YESTERDAY...?

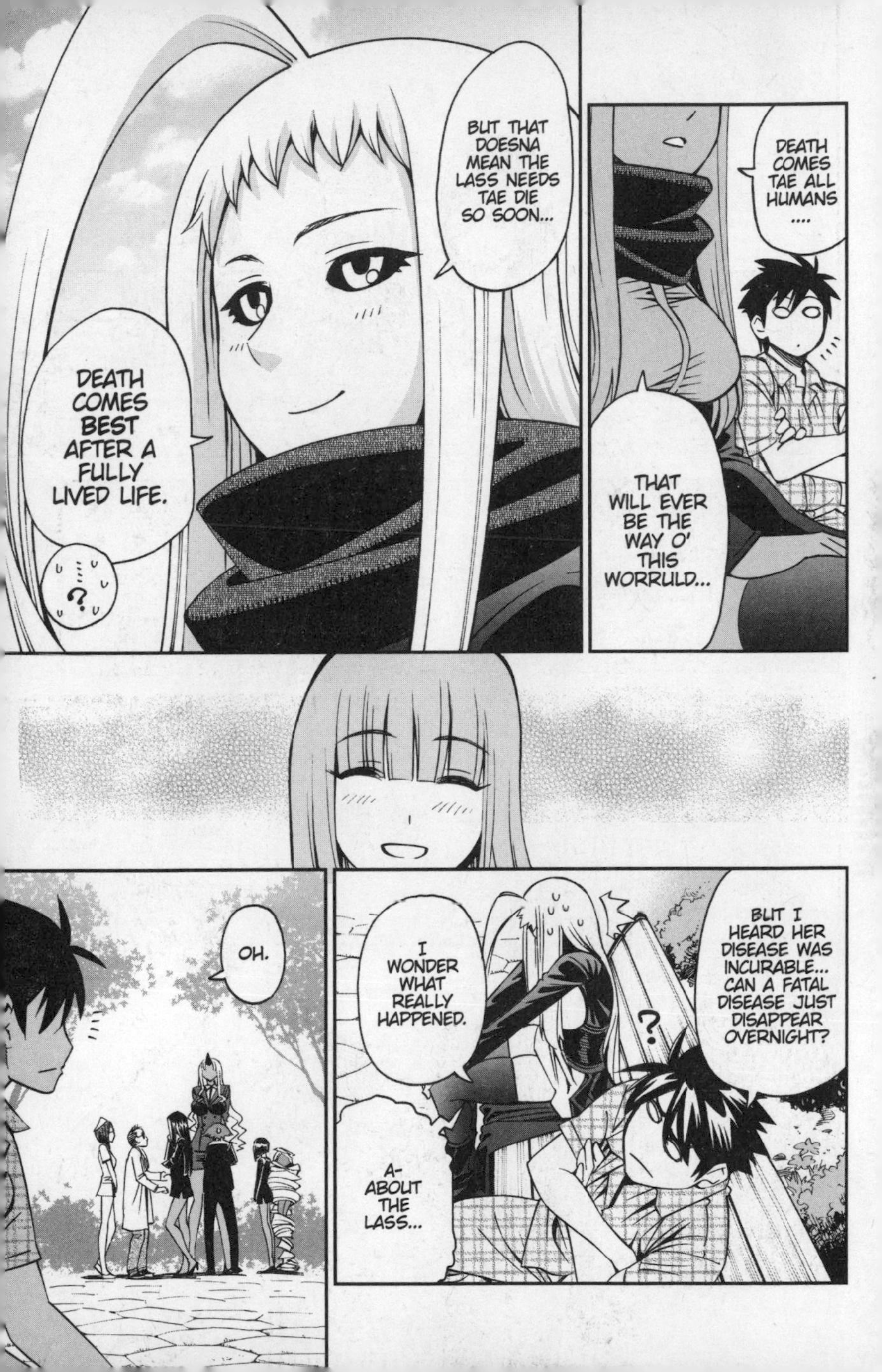
DEATH COMES TAE ALL HUMANS ....
THAT WILL EVER BE THE WAY O' THIS WORRULD...
BUT THAT DOESNA MEAN THE LASS NEEDS TAE DIE SO SOON...
DEATH COMES BEST AFTER A FULLY LIVED LIFE.
...?
BUT I HEARD HER DISEASE WAS INCURABLE... CAN A FATAL DISEASE JUST DISAPPEAR OVERNIGHT?
I WONDER WHAT REALLY HAPPENED.
A- ABOUT THE LASS...
?
OH.

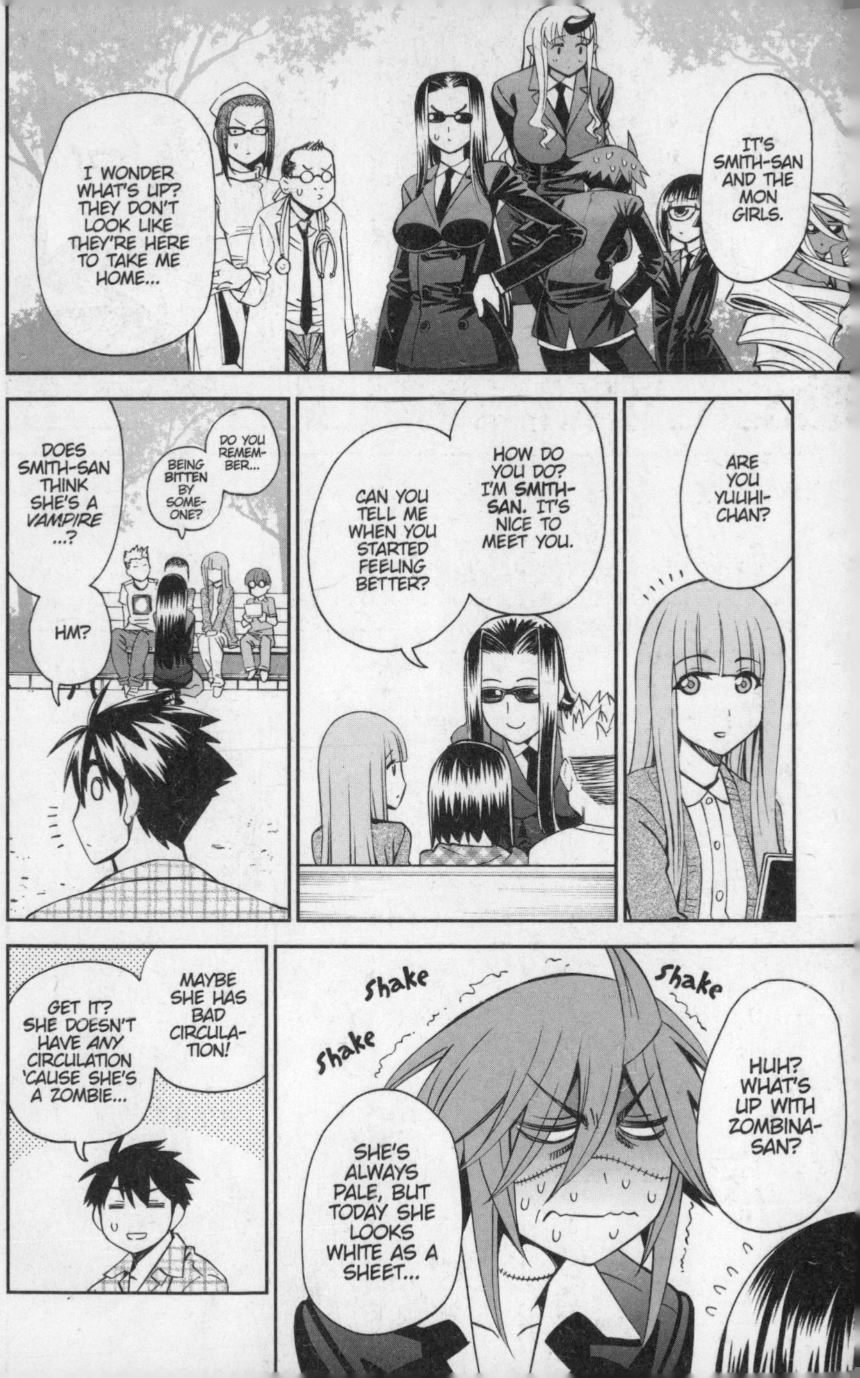

IT'S SMITH-SAN AND THE MON GIRLS.
I WONDER WHAT'S UP? THEY DON'T LOOK LIKE THEY'RE HERE TO TAKE ME HOME...
ARE YOU YUUHI-CHAN?
HOW DO YOU DO? I'M SMITH-SAN. IT'S NICE TO MEET YOU.
CAN YOU TELL ME WHEN YOU STARTED FEELING BETTER?
DO YOU REMEMBER...
BEING BITTEN BY SOMEONE?
DOES SMITH-SAN THINK SHE'S A *VAMPIRE*...?
HM?
Shake
Shake
Shake
HUH? WHAT'S UP WITH ZOMBINA-SAN?
SHE'S ALWAYS PALE, BUT TODAY SHE LOOKS WHITE AS A SHEET...
MAYBE SHE HAS BAD CIRCULATION!
GET IT? SHE DOESN'T HAVE ANY CIRCULATION 'CAUSE SHE'S A ZOMBIE...

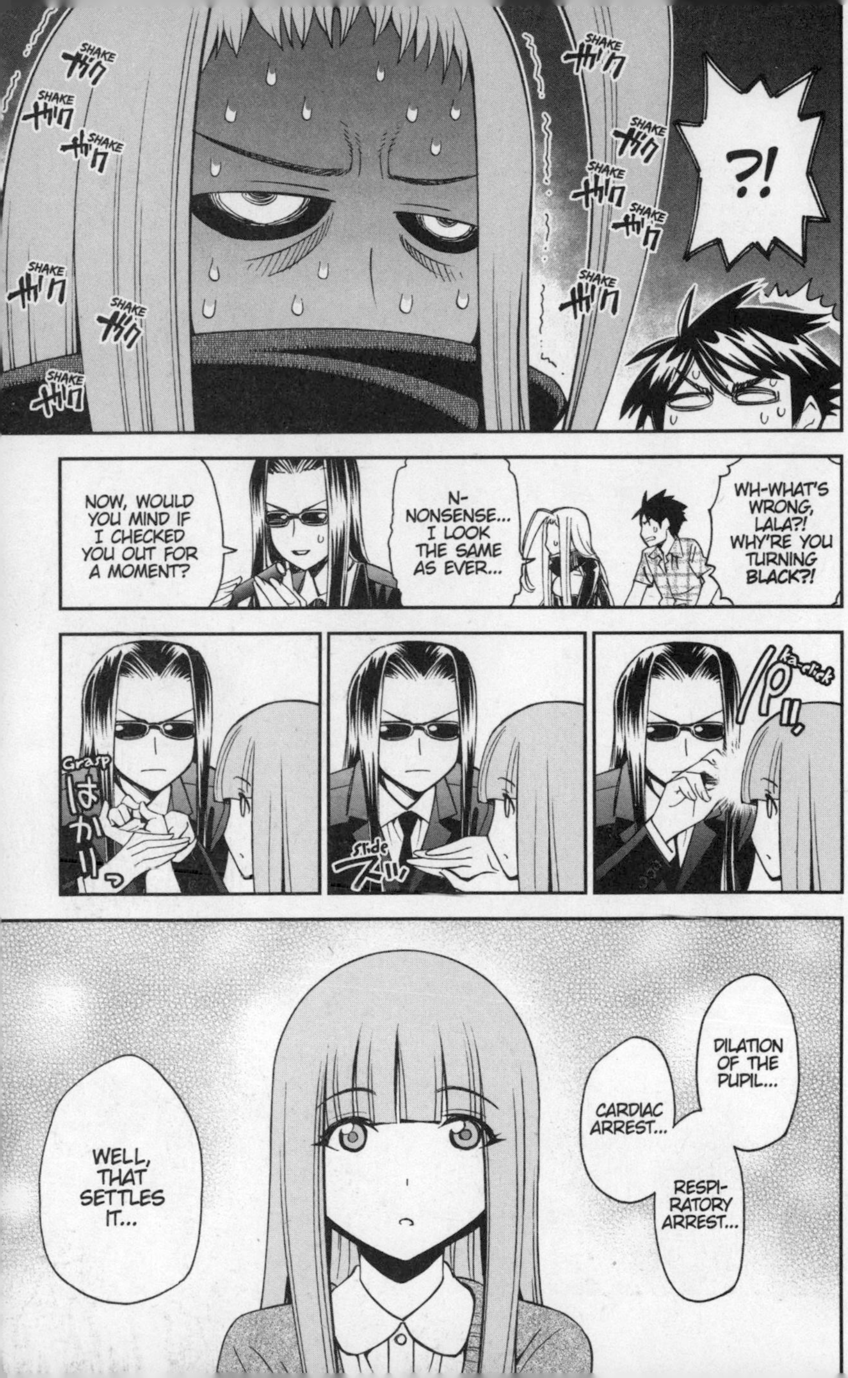
?!
SHAKE
SHAKE
SHAKE
SHAKE
SHAKE
SHAKE
SHAKE
SHAKE
SHAKE
SHAKE
WH-WHAT'S WRONG, LALA?! WHY'RE YOU TURNING BLACK?!
N-NONSENSE... I LOOK THE SAME AS EVER...
NOW, WOULD YOU MIND IF I CHECKED YOU OUT FOR A MOMENT?
ka-click
slide
Grasp
DILATION OF THE PUPIL...
CARDIAC ARREST...
RESPI-RATORY ARREST...
WELL, THAT SETTLES IT...

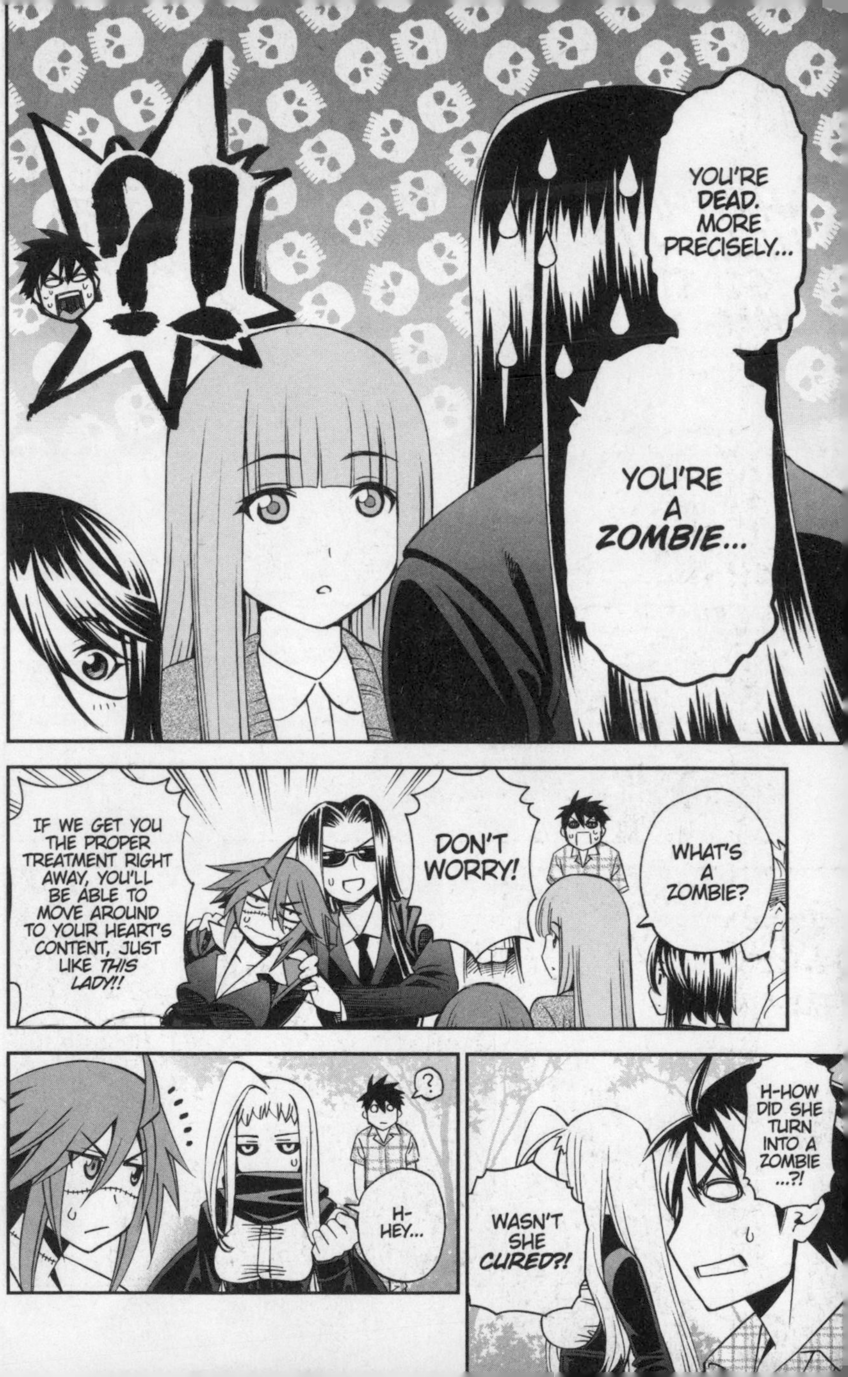
YOU'RE DEAD. MORE PRECISELY...
YOU'RE A ZOMBIE...
?!
WHAT'S A ZOMBIE?
DON'T WORRY!
IF WE GET YOU THE PROPER TREATMENT RIGHT AWAY, YOU'LL BE ABLE TO MOVE AROUND TO YOUR HEART'S CONTENT, JUST LIKE *THIS LADY*!!
H-HOW DID SHE TURN INTO A ZOMBIE ...?!
WASN'T SHE *CURED*?!
?
H- HEY...

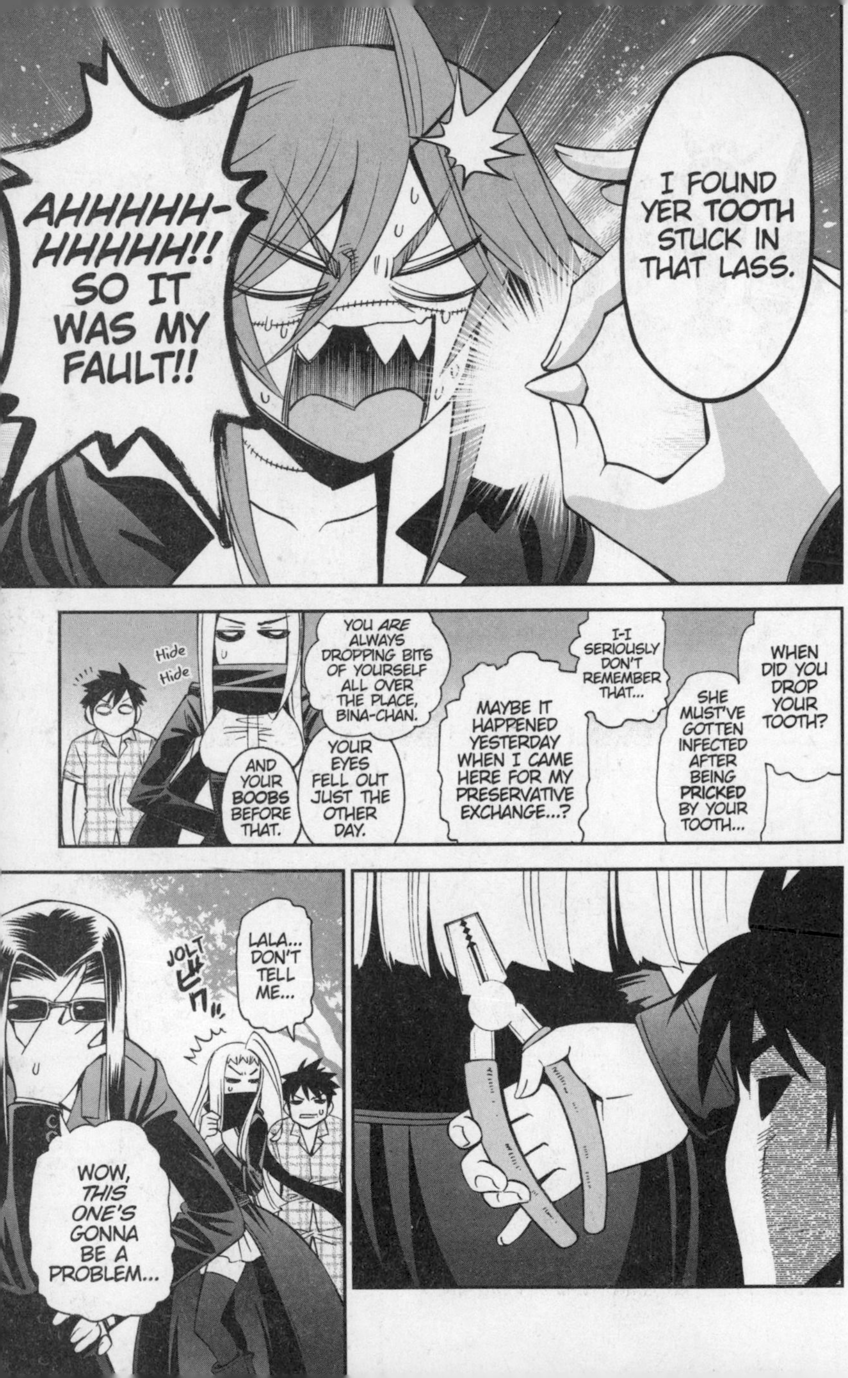
I FOUND YER TOOTH STUCK IN THAT LASS.
AHHHHHH-HHHHHH!! SO IT WAS MY FAULT!!
WHEN DID YOU DROP YOUR TOOTH?
SHE MUST'VE GOTTEN INFECTED AFTER BEING PRICKED BY YOUR TOOTH...
I-I SERIOUSLY DON'T REMEMBER THAT...
MAYBE IT HAPPENED YESTERDAY WHEN I CAME HERE FOR MY PRESERVATIVE EXCHANGE...?
YOU *ARE* ALWAYS DROPPING BITS OF YOURSELF ALL OVER THE PLACE, BINA-CHAN.
YOUR EYES FELL OUT JUST THE OTHER DAY.
AND YOUR BOOBS BEFORE THAT.
Hide Hide
LALA... DON'T TELL ME...
JOLT
WOW, THIS ONE'S GONNA BE A PROBLEM...

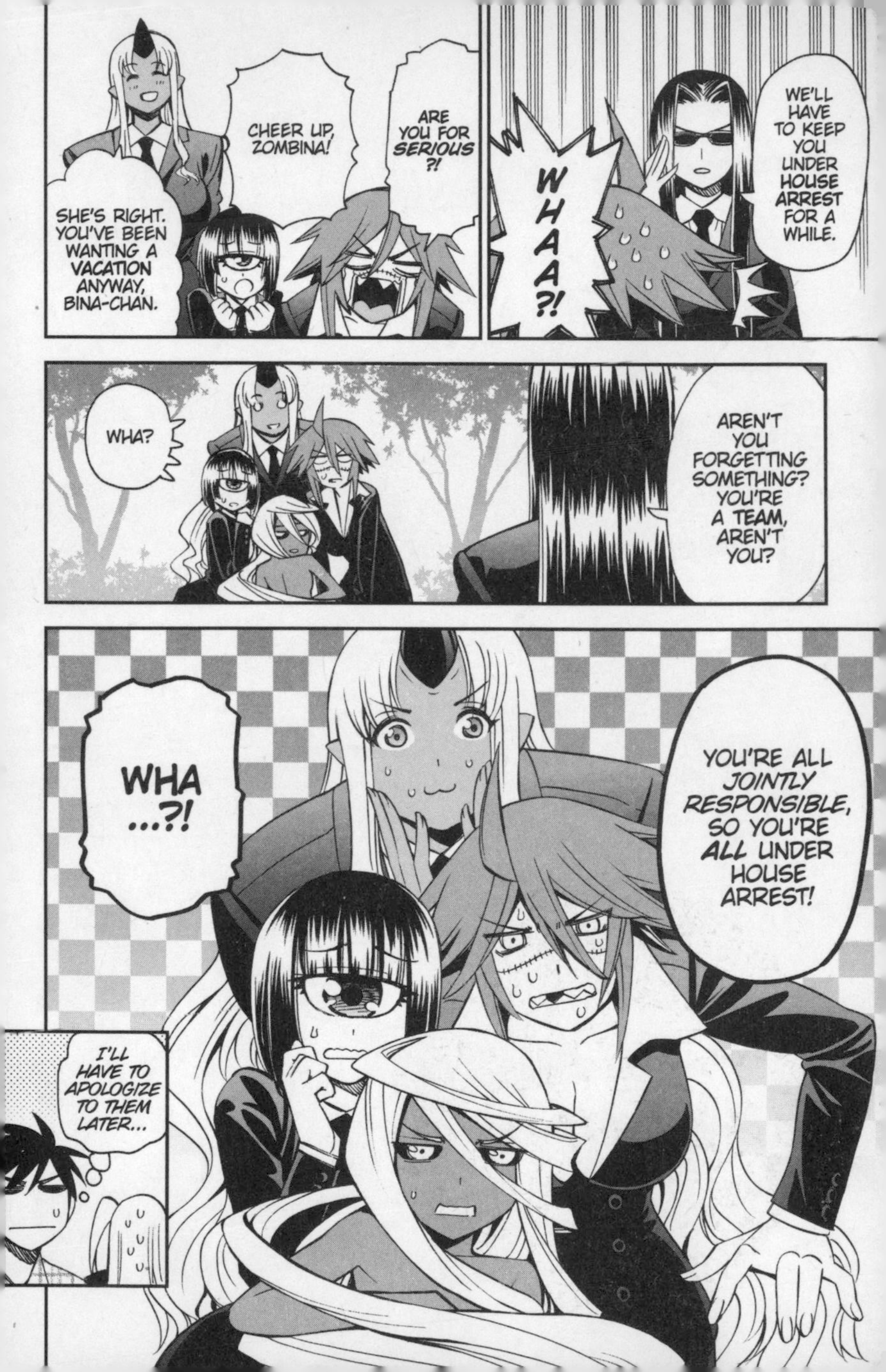
WE'LL HAVE TO KEEP YOU UNDER HOUSE ARREST FOR A WHILE.
WHAAA?!
ARE YOU FOR SERIOUS?!
CHEER UP, ZOMBINA!
SHE'S RIGHT. YOU'VE BEEN WANTING A VACATION ANYWAY, BINA-CHAN.
AREN'T YOU FORGETTING SOMETHING? YOU'RE A TEAM, AREN'T YOU?
WHA?
YOU'RE ALL JOINTLY RESPONSIBLE, SO YOU'RE ALL UNDER HOUSE ARREST!
WHA ...?!
I'LL HAVE TO APOLOGIZE TO THEM LATER...

Monster Musume

Everyday Life with Monster Girls

Octo's Advice Parlor

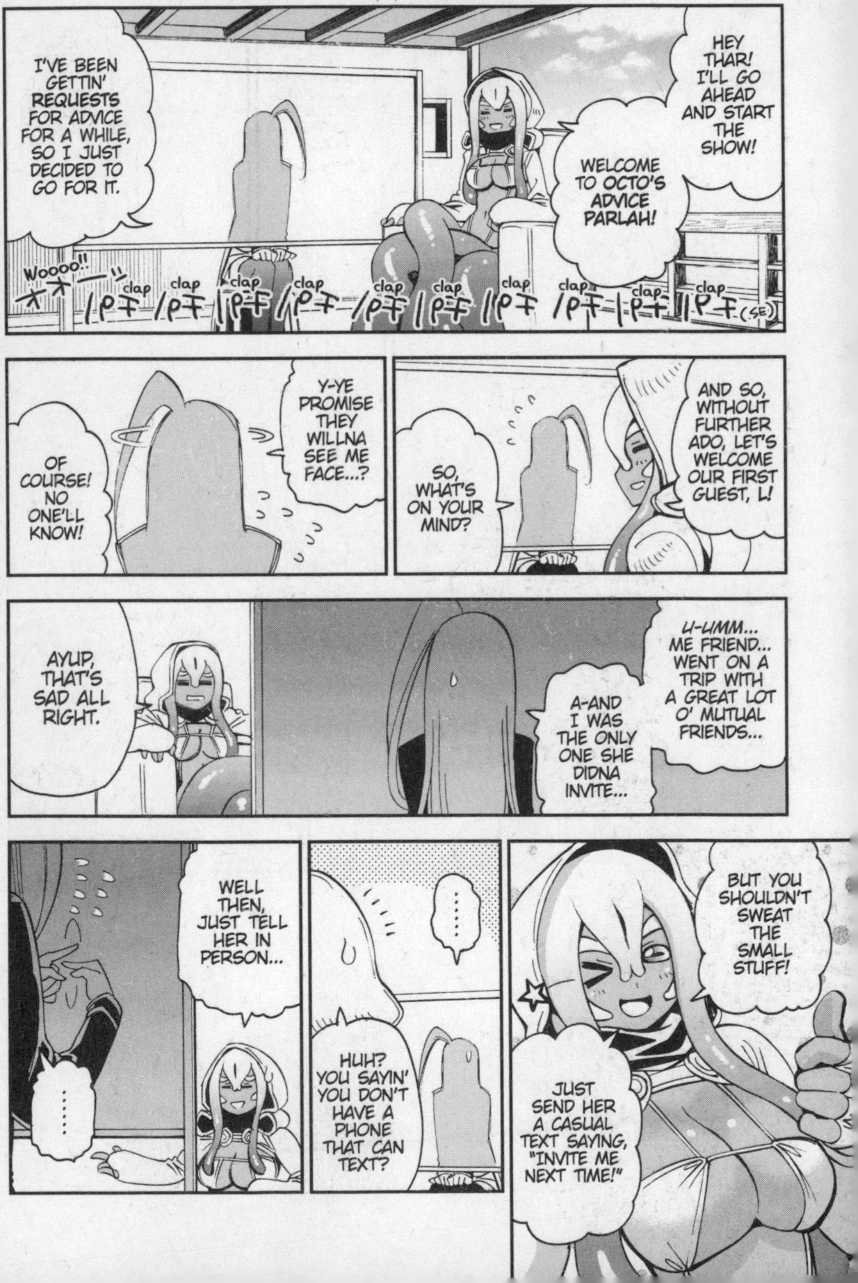

HEY THAR! I'LL GO AHEAD AND START THE SHOW!
WELCOME TO OCTO'S ADVICE PARLAH!
I'VE BEEN GETTIN' REQUESTS FOR ADVICE FOR A WHILE, SO I JUST DECIDED TO GO FOR IT.
Woooo!! オオーッ
clap パチ clap パチ clap パチ clap パチ clap パチ clap パチ clap パチ clap パチ clap パチ clap パチ (SE)
AND SO, WITHOUT FURTHER ADO, LET'S WELCOME OUR FIRST GUEST, L!
SO, WHAT'S ON YOUR MIND?
Y-YE PROMISE THEY WILLNA SEE ME FACE...?
OF COURSE! NO ONE'LL KNOW!
U-UMM... ME FRIEND... WENT ON A TRIP WITH A GREAT LOT O' MUTUAL FRIENDS...
A-AND I WAS THE ONLY ONE SHE DIDNA INVITE...
AYUP, THAT'S SAD ALL RIGHT.
BUT YOU SHOULDN'T SWEAT THE SMALL STUFF!
JUST SEND HER A CASUAL TEXT SAYING, "INVITE ME NEXT TIME!"
......
HUH? YOU SAYIN' YOU DON'T HAVE A PHONE THAT CAN TEXT?
WELL THEN, JUST TELL HER IN PERSON...
......

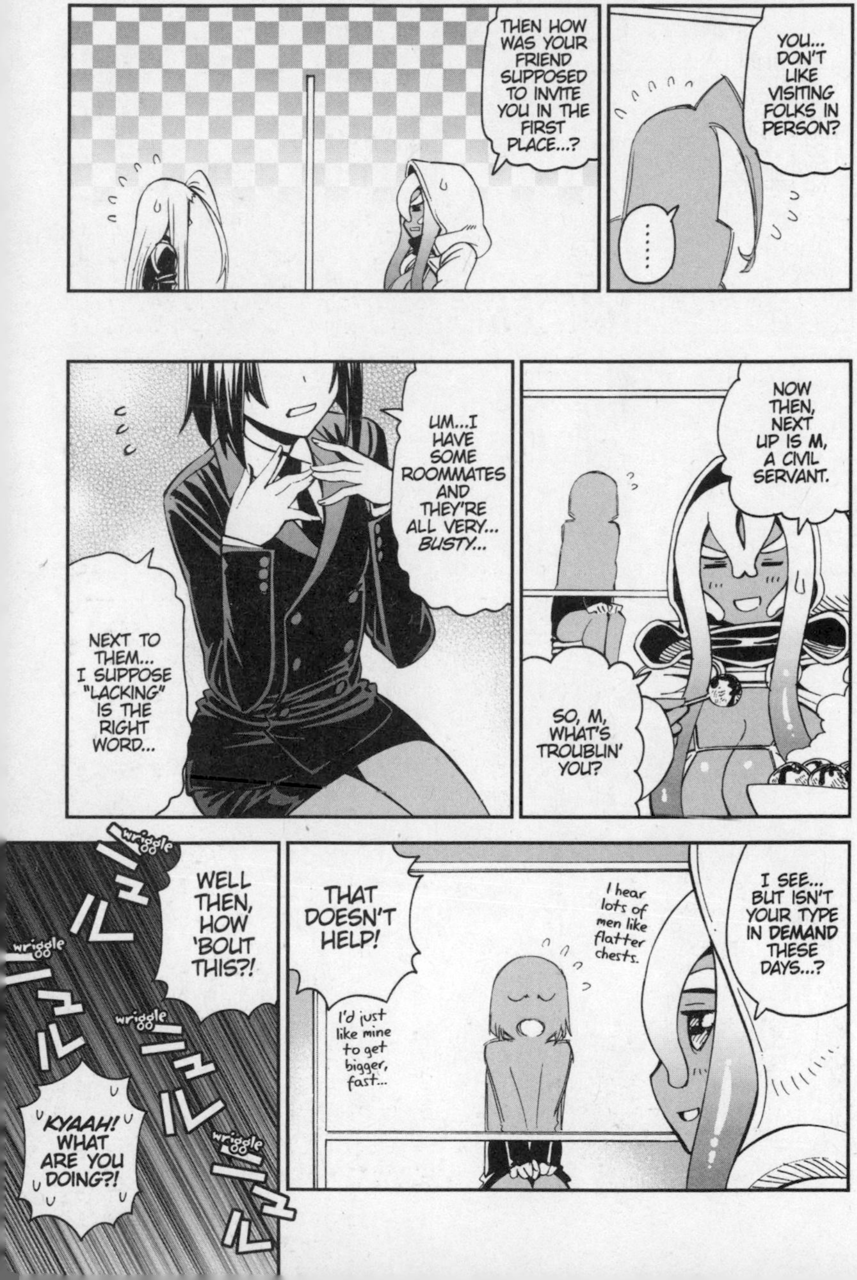
YOU... DON'T LIKE VISITING FOLKS IN PERSON?
......
THEN HOW WAS YOUR FRIEND SUPPOSED TO INVITE YOU IN THE FIRST PLACE...?
NOW THEN, NEXT UP IS M, A CIVIL SERVANT.
SO, M, WHAT'S TROUBLIN' YOU?
UM...I HAVE SOME ROOMMATES AND THEY'RE ALL VERY... *BUSTY*...
NEXT TO THEM... I SUPPOSE "LACKING" IS THE RIGHT WORD...
I SEE... BUT ISN'T YOUR TYPE IN DEMAND THESE DAYS...?
I hear lots of men like flatter chests.
THAT DOESN'T HELP!
I'd just like mine to get bigger, fast...
WELL THEN, HOW 'BOUT THIS?!
wriggle
wriggle
wriggle
wriggle
KYAAH! WHAT ARE YOU DOING?!

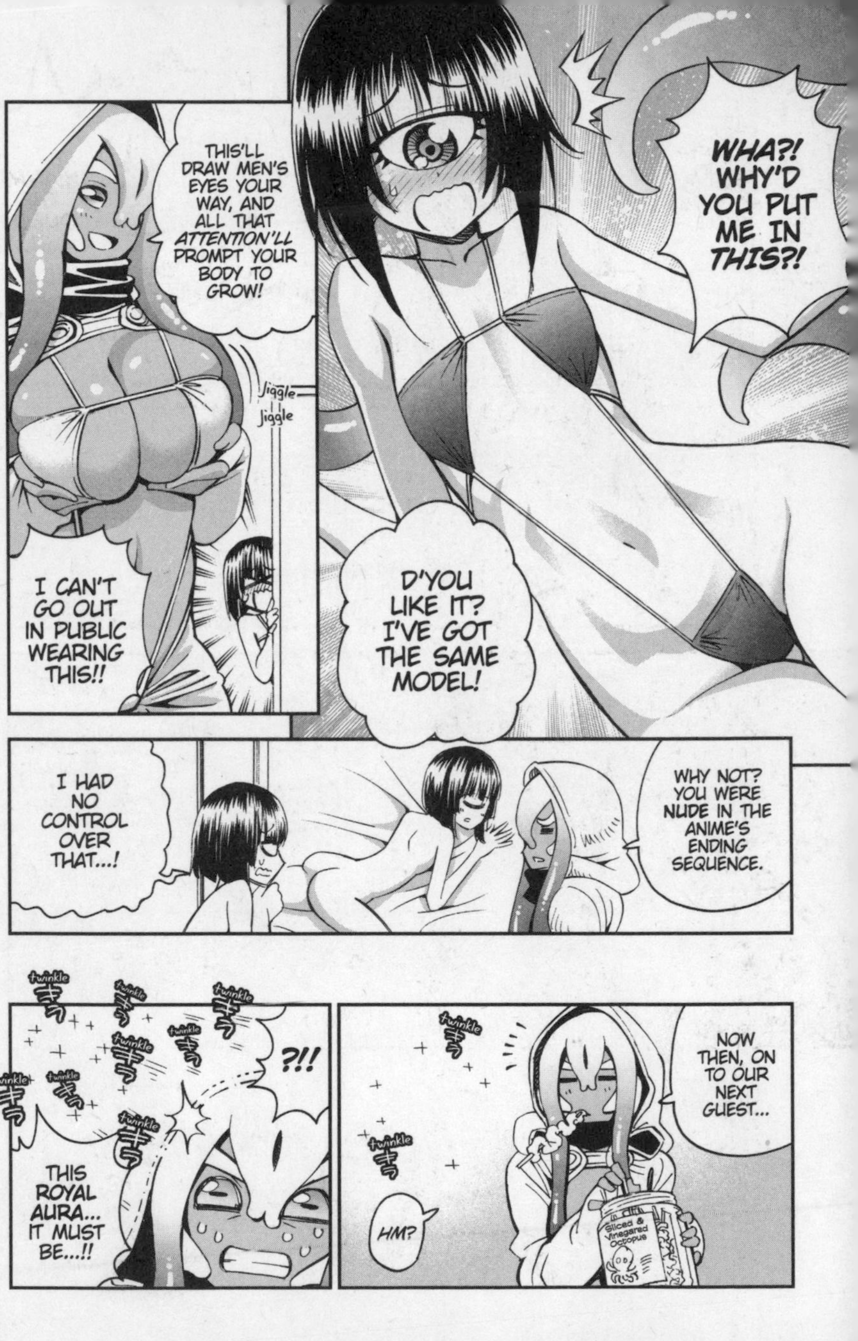
WHA?! WHY'D YOU PUT ME IN THIS?!
D'YOU LIKE IT? I'VE GOT THE SAME MODEL!
THIS'LL DRAW MEN'S EYES YOUR WAY, AND ALL THAT ATTENTION'LL PROMPT YOUR BODY TO GROW!
jiggle
jiggle
I CAN'T GO OUT IN PUBLIC WEARING THIS!!
WHY NOT? YOU WERE NUDE IN THE ANIME'S ENDING SEQUENCE.
I HAD NO CONTROL OVER THAT...!
NOW THEN, ON TO OUR NEXT GUEST...
twinkle
twinkle
HM?
Sliced & Vinegared Octopus
twinkle
twinkle
twinkle
twinkle
twinkle
twinkle
twinkle
?!!
THIS ROYAL AURA... IT MUST BE...!!

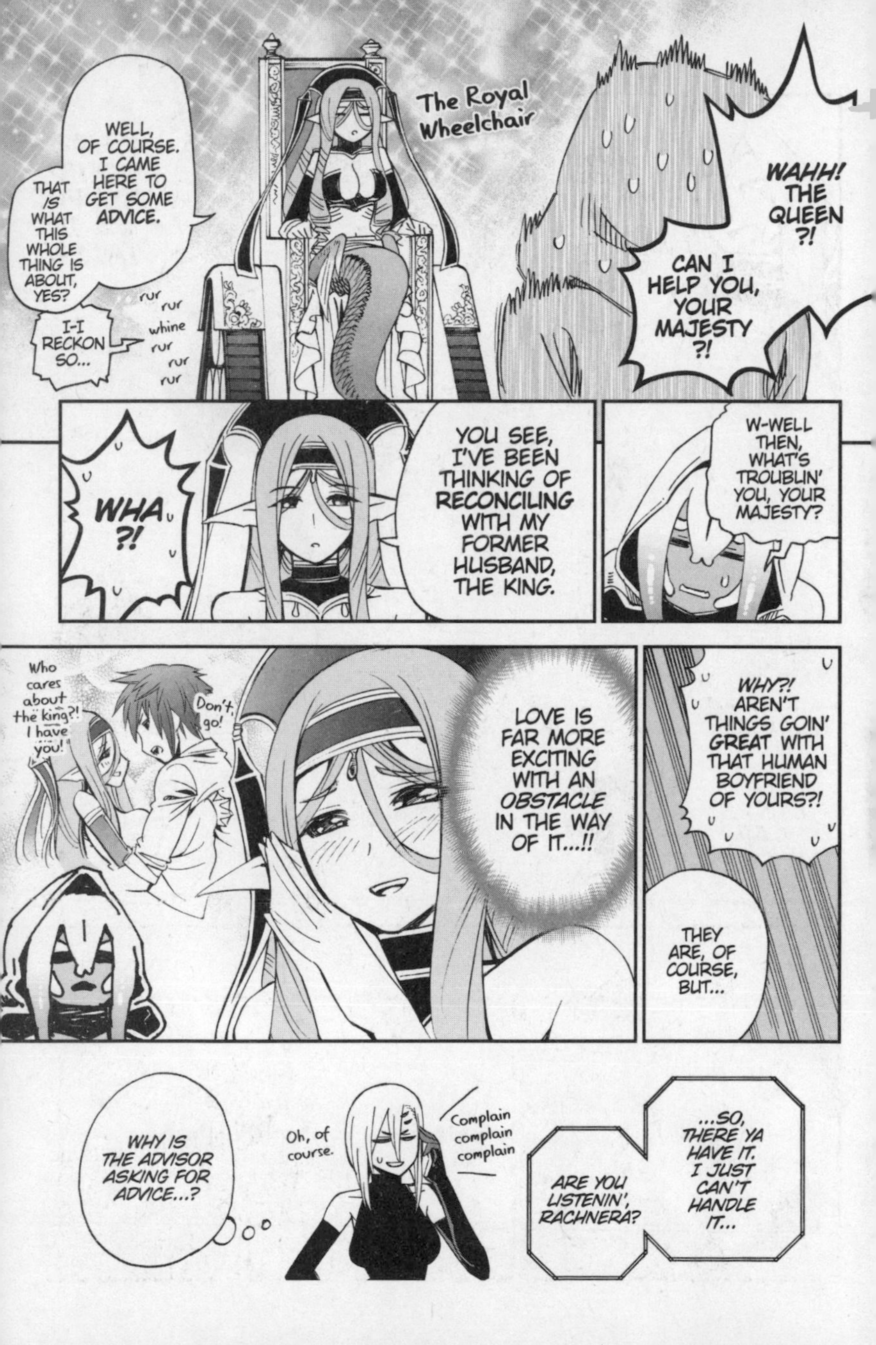
WAHH! THE QUEEN?!
CAN I HELP YOU, YOUR MAJESTY?!
The Royal Wheelchair
WELL, OF COURSE. I CAME HERE TO GET SOME ADVICE.
THAT IS WHAT THIS WHOLE THING IS ABOUT, YES?
rur rur whine rur rur rur
I-I RECKON SO...
W-WELL THEN, WHAT'S TROUBLIN' YOU, YOUR MAJESTY?
YOU SEE, I'VE BEEN THINKING OF RECONCILING WITH MY FORMER HUSBAND, THE KING.
WHA?!
WHY?! AREN'T THINGS GOIN' GREAT WITH THAT HUMAN BOYFRIEND OF YOURS?!
THEY ARE, OF COURSE, BUT...
LOVE IS FAR MORE EXCITING WITH AN OBSTACLE IN THE WAY OF IT...!!
Don't go!
Who cares about the king?! I have you!
...SO, THERE YA HAVE IT. I JUST CAN'T HANDLE IT...
ARE YOU LISTENIN', RACHNERA?
Complain complain complain
Oh, of course.
WHY IS THE ADVISOR ASKING FOR ADVICE...?

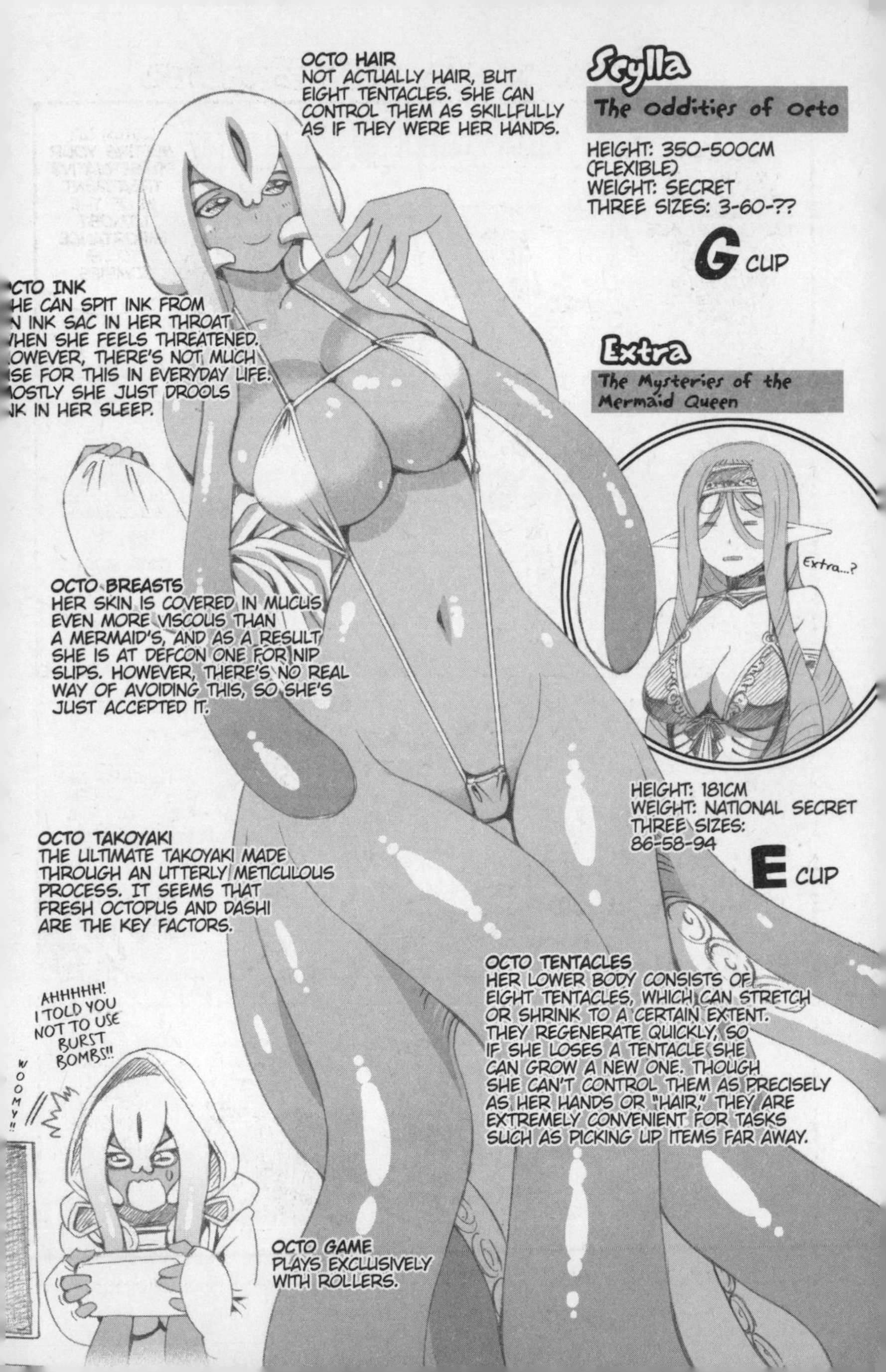
Scylla
The Oddities of Octo
HEIGHT: 350-500CM (FLEXIBLE)
WEIGHT: SECRET
THREE SIZES: 3-60-??
G CUP
OCTO HAIR
NOT ACTUALLY HAIR, BUT EIGHT TENTACLES. SHE CAN CONTROL THEM AS SKILLFULLY AS IF THEY WERE HER HANDS.
CTO INK
HE CAN SPIT INK FROM N INK SAC IN HER THROAT VHEN SHE FEELS THREATENED. OWEVER, THERE'S NOT MUCH SE FOR THIS IN EVERYDAY LIFE. OSTLY SHE JUST DROOLS NK IN HER SLEEP.
Extra
The Mysteries of the Mermaid Queen
Extra...?
HEIGHT: 181CM
WEIGHT: NATIONAL SECRET
THREE SIZES: 86-58-94
E CUP
OCTO BREASTS
HER SKIN IS COVERED IN MUCUS EVEN MORE VISCOUS THAN A MERMAID'S, AND AS A RESULT SHE IS AT DEFCON ONE FOR NIP SLIPS. HOWEVER, THERE'S NO REAL WAY OF AVOIDING THIS, SO SHE'S JUST ACCEPTED IT.
OCTO TAKOYAKI
THE ULTIMATE TAKOYAKI MADE THROUGH AN UTTERLY METICULOUS PROCESS. IT SEEMS THAT FRESH OCTOPUS AND DASHI ARE THE KEY FACTORS.
OCTO TENTACLES
HER LOWER BODY CONSISTS OF EIGHT TENTACLES, WHICH CAN STRETCH OR SHRINK TO A CERTAIN EXTENT. THEY REGENERATE QUICKLY, SO IF SHE LOSES A TENTACLE SHE CAN GROW A NEW ONE. THOUGH SHE CAN'T CONTROL THEM AS PRECISELY AS HER HANDS OR "HAIR," THEY ARE EXTREMELY CONVENIENT FOR TASKS SUCH AS PICKING UP ITEMS FAR AWAY.
AHHHHH! I TOLD YOU NOT TO USE BURST BOMBS!!
WOOMY!!
OCTO GAME
PLAYS EXCLUSIVELY WITH ROLLERS.

Zombies 101 with Zombina

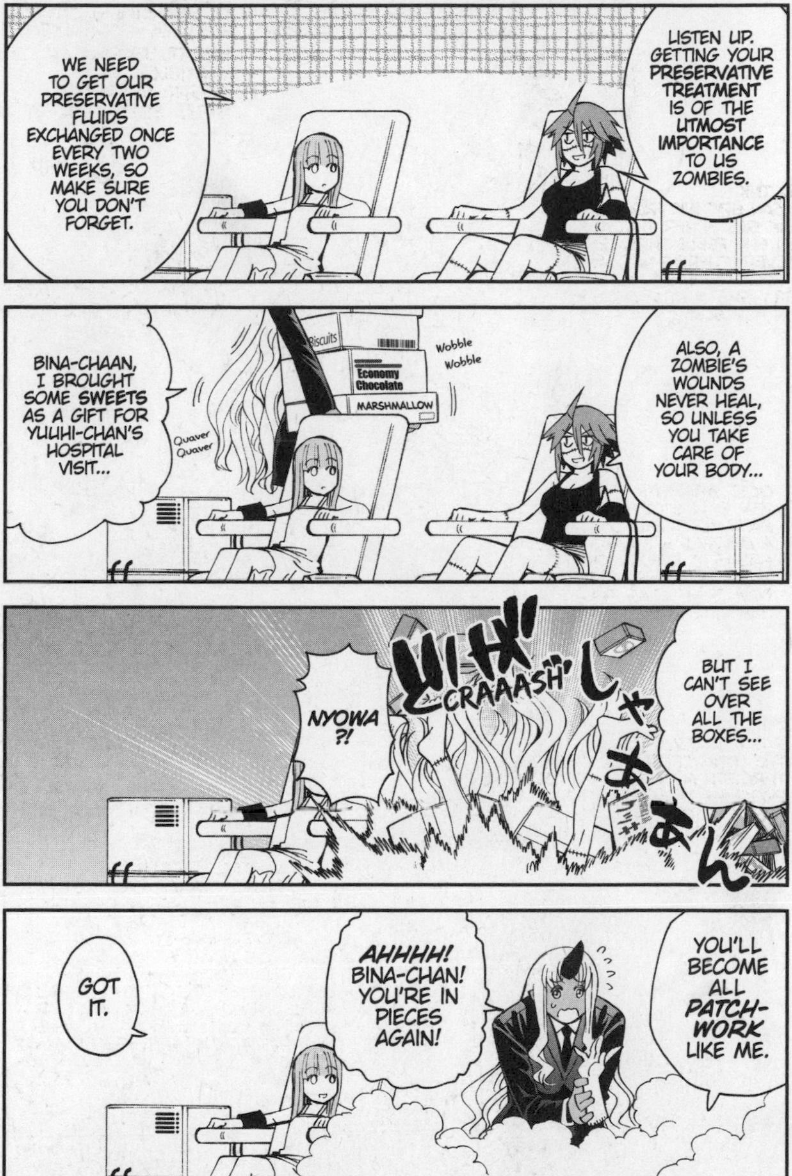

LISTEN UP. GETTING YOUR PRESERVATIVE TREATMENT IS OF THE UTMOST IMPORTANCE TO US ZOMBIES.
WE NEED TO GET OUR PRESERVATIVE FLUIDS EXCHANGED ONCE EVERY TWO WEEKS, SO MAKE SURE YOU DON'T FORGET.
ALSO, A ZOMBIE'S WOUNDS NEVER HEAL, SO UNLESS YOU TAKE CARE OF YOUR BODY...
Wobble Wobble
Biscuits
Economy Chocolate
MARSHMALLOW
BINA-CHAAN, I BROUGHT SOME SWEETS AS A GIFT FOR YUUHI-CHAN'S HOSPITAL VISIT...
Quaver Quaver
BUT I CAN'T SEE OVER ALL THE BOXES...
CRAAASH
NYOWA ?!
YOU'LL BECOME ALL PATCH-WORK LIKE ME.
AHHHH! BINA-CHAN! YOU'RE IN PIECES AGAIN!
GOT IT.

Masseuses vs. ...

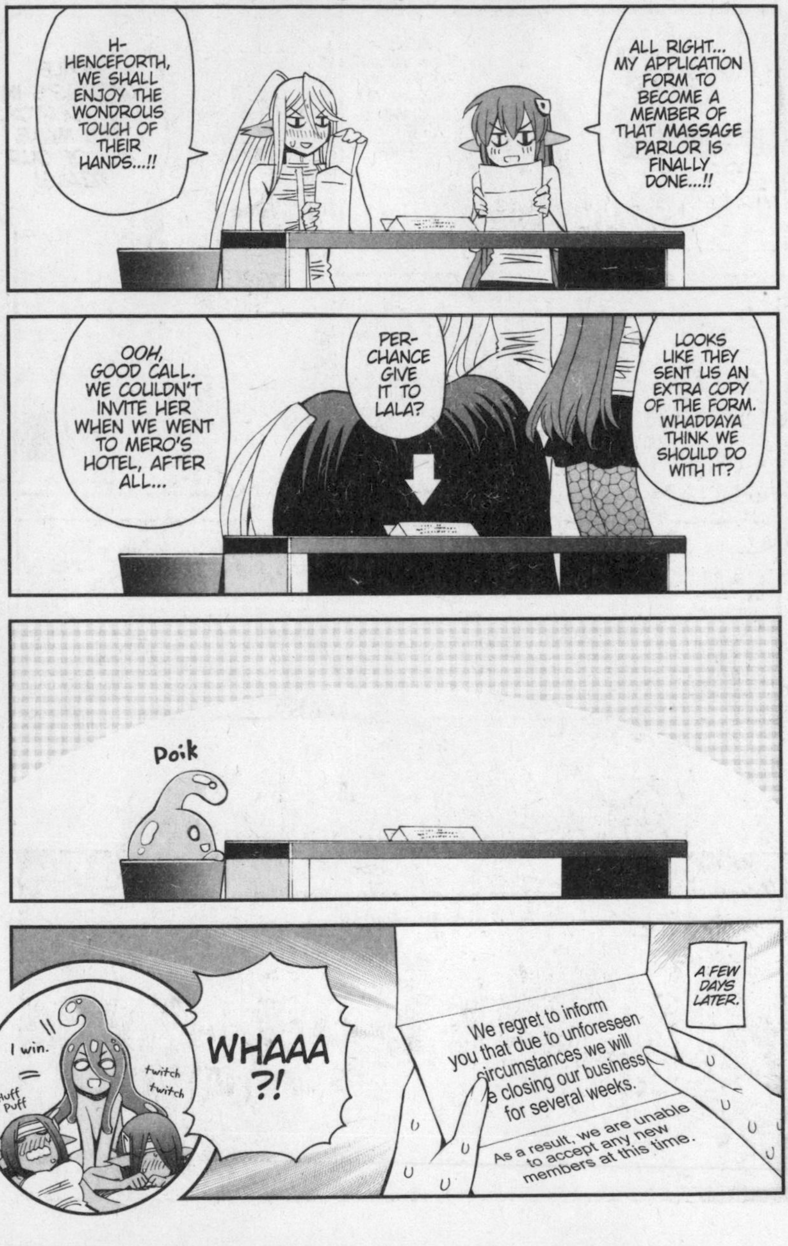
ALL RIGHT... MY APPLICATION FORM TO BECOME A MEMBER OF THAT MASSAGE PARLOR IS FINALLY DONE...!!
H- HENCEFORTH, WE SHALL ENJOY THE WONDROUS TOUCH OF THEIR HANDS...!!
LOOKS LIKE THEY SENT US AN EXTRA COPY OF THE FORM. WHADDAYA THINK WE SHOULD DO WITH IT?
PER-CHANCE GIVE IT TO LALA?
OOH, GOOD CALL. WE COULDN'T INVITE HER WHEN WE WENT TO MERO'S HOTEL, AFTER ALL...
Poik
A FEW DAYS LATER.
We regret to inform you that due to unforeseen circumstances we will e closing our business for several weeks.
As a result, we are unable to accept any new members at this time.
WHAAA ?!
I win.
twitch twitch
Huff Puff

The Absence of a Real Chef

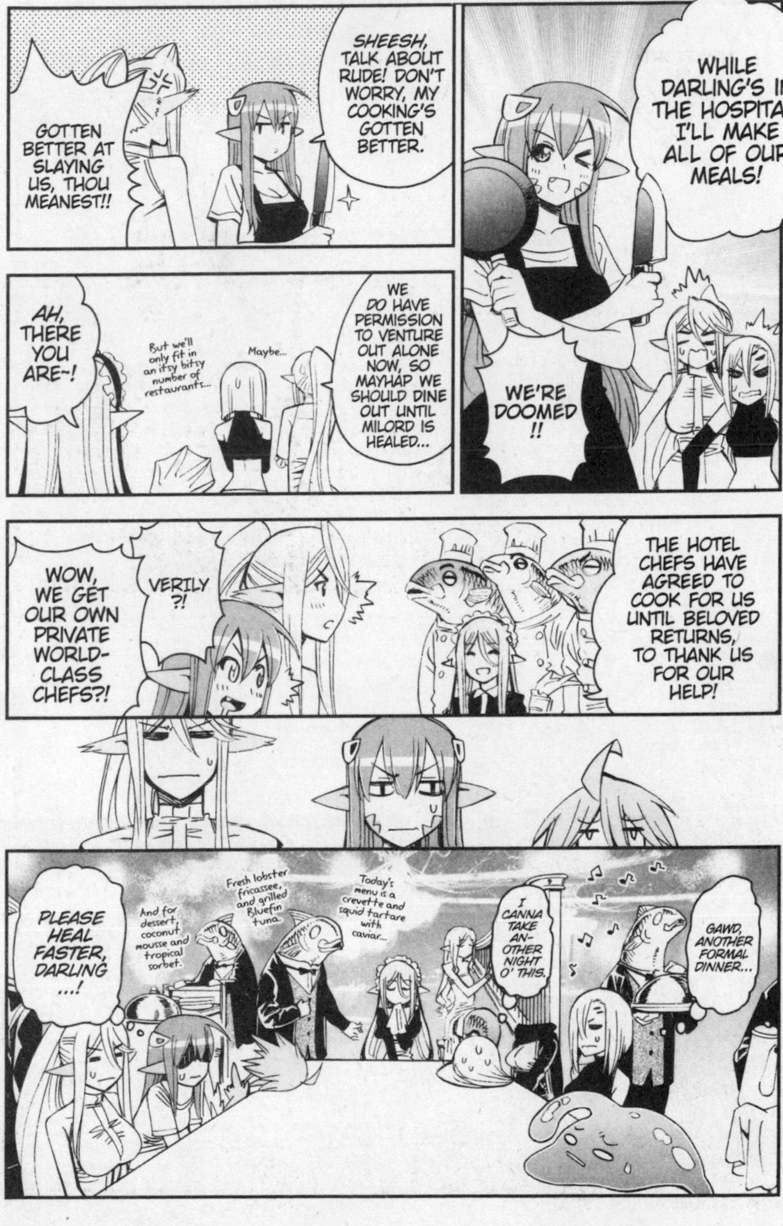
WHILE DARLING'S IN THE HOSPITAL, I'LL MAKE ALL OF OUR MEALS!
WE'RE DOOMED !!
SHEESH, TALK ABOUT RUDE! DON'T WORRY, MY COOKING'S GOTTEN BETTER.
GOTTEN BETTER AT SLAYING US, THOU MEANEST!!
WE DO HAVE PERMISSION TO VENTURE OUT ALONE NOW, SO MAYHAP WE SHOULD DINE OUT UNTIL MILORD IS HEALED...
Maybe...
But we'll only fit in an itsy bitsy number of restaurants...
AH, THERE YOU ARE~!
THE HOTEL CHEFS HAVE AGREED TO COOK FOR US UNTIL BELOVED RETURNS, TO THANK US FOR OUR HELP!
VERILY ?!
WOW, WE GET OUR OWN PRIVATE WORLD-CLASS CHEFS?!
GAWD, ANOTHER FORMAL DINNER...
I CANNA TAKE AN-OTHER NIGHT O' THIS.
Today's menu is a crevette and squid tartare with caviar...
Fresh lobster fricassee, and grilled Bluefin tuna.
And for dessert, coconut mousse and tropical sorbet.
PLEASE HEAL FASTER, DARLING ...!

SEVEN SEAS ENTERTAINMENT PRESENTS

Monster Musume

story and art by **OKAYADO**

VOLUME 9

TRANSLATION
Ryan Peterson

ADAPTATION
Shanti Whitesides

LETTERING AND LAYOUT
Ma. Victoria Robado
William Ringrose

LOGO DESIGN
Courtney Williams

COVER DESIGN
Nicky Lim

PROOFREADER
Janet Houck

PRODUCTION MANAGER
Lissa Pattillo

EDITOR-IN-CHIEF
Adam Arnold

PUBLISHER
Jason DeAngelis

MONSTER MUSUME NO IRU NICHIJO VOLUME 9
© OKAYADO 2016
Originally published in Japan in 2016 by TOKUMA SHOTEN PUBLISHING
CO., LTD., Tokyo. English translation rights arranged with TOKUMA SHOTEN
PUBLISHING CO., LTD., Tokyo, through TOHAN CORPORATION, Tokyo.

Seven Seas books may be purchased in bulk for educational, business, or
promotional use. For information on bulk purchases, please contact Macmillan
Corporate & Premium Sales Department at 1-800-221-7945 (ext 5442)
or write specialmarkets@macmillan.com.

Seven Seas and the Seven Seas logo are trademarks of
Seven Seas Entertainment, LLC. All rights reserved.

ISBN: 978-1-626922-78-5

Printed in Canada

First Printing: August 2016

10 9 8 7 6 5 4 3 2 1

FOLLOW US ONLINE: *www.gomanga.com*

READING DIRECTIONS

This book reads from *right to left*, Japanese style.
If this is your first time reading manga, you start
reading from the top right panel on each page and
take it from there. If you get lost, just follow the
numbered diagram here. It may seem backwards at
first, but you'll get the hang of it! Have fun!!

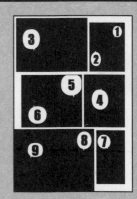